THE
SPORTS WRITING
HANDBOOK

Second Edition

THE SPORTS WRITING HANDBOOK

Second Edition

Thomas Fensch
Sam Houston State University

LEA LAWRENCE ERLBAUM ASSOCIATES, PUBLISHERS
1995   Hillsdale, New Jersey   Hove, UK

Lawrence Erlbaum Associates, Inc., Publishers
365 Broadway
Hillsdale, New Jersey 07642

Library of Congress Cataloging-in-Publication Data

Fensch, Thomas.
    The sports writing handbook / Thomas Fensch.
        p.   cm.
    Includes bibliographical references and index.
    ISBN 0-8058-1528-7. — ISBN 0-8058-1529-5 (pbk.)
    1. Sports journalism—Authorship. I. Title.
    PN4784.S6F46   1995
    808'.066796—dc20   94-23762
                                                        CIP

Books published by Lawrence Erlbaum Associates are printed on acid-free
paper, and their bindings are chosen for strength and durability.

Printed in the United States of America
10 9 8 7 6 5 4 3 2 1

These pages . . .
and all the pages of my life . . .
are for Sharon, with love.

Contents

Preface

Sports writing is not just scores and standings anymore. Consider these recent sports events:

- Magic Johnson retires from professional basketball with the admission that he has tested positive for HIV, the virus that causes AIDS. Others in professional basketball indicate an unwillingness to ever play with him for fear that a casual bump might lead to blood on the court and exposure to AIDS.

- Arthur Ashe is forced to "go public" with a news conference to announce that he, too, was infected with AIDS. Unlike Johnson, Ashe contracted the disease through a transfusion of tainted blood years earlier during open heart surgery. Ashe was forced to make his illness public when *USA Today* was ready to print a story that he had AIDS. Sports writers and media critics quickly pointed out that because Ashe contracted AIDS through no fault of his own (unlike Johnson), he should have been allowed to die with dignity without a public acknowledgment of the disease. Ashe did die of AIDS.

- Michael Jordan retires from professional basketball at the height of his game following the murder of his father, James Jordan. Some sports columnists quickly wrote that Jordan's father was murdered because Jordan had allegedly run up hundreds of thousands of dollars in gambling debts. When the murder was discovered to be a random act of violence by two teenagers, some columnists published apologies for the inferences that Jordan's father was murdered because of his son's alleged illegal gambling. (See pages 149–150 for an example of one of the columns written after the death of James Jordan.)

- Passage of the Brady bill causes a rush on handguns before the 5-day waiting period takes effect.

- Seven weeks before the 1994 Lillehammer Winter Olympics, figure skater Nancy Kerrigan is attacked during a practice and clubbed behind one knee. The attack was eventually traced to Jeff Gillooly, the husband (subsequently ex-husband) of skater Tonya Harding, another U.S. figure skater. Gillooly apparently hired others to carry out the attack on Kerrigan.

Did Harding know of the attack? She later acknowledged that she did know of the attack beforehand. Did she help plan it? She didn't admit that.

Week after week of Harding/Kerrigan, Kerrigan/Harding stories went by, making it a tawdry pre-Olympics soap opera. U.S. figure skating officials tried to bar Harding from Olympic competition. She countered with a $20 million lawsuit; the bar was lifted, and Harding skated to a dismal eighth place finish. Gillooly pleaded guilty to racketeering in the attack on Kerrigan.

Nancy Kerrigan skated to a second place finish in the Olympics, a fraction of one point behind gold medal winner Oksana Baiul, of Ukraine.

Kerrigan was signed to endorsement contracts worth millions, including a $20-million deal with the Disney Company. Shortly after the Olympic games, some thought she tarnished her image as ice queen when she appeared in a Disney parade sitting beside Mickey Mouse and was overheard saying (on an open mike) that "this is the corniest thing I have ever done." (She later said that referred to wearing her Olympic silver medal in public.)

- Darryl Strawberry was accused of cheating on his income taxes by failing to report over $300,000 in autographs and memorabilia sales. He was also dismissed from the Los Angeles Dodgers for alleged drug use.

- Federal prosecutors brought indictments against 19 individuals accused of brutally killing valuable show horses by electric shocks for millions in insurance money. The lead to Carol Marie Cropper's article "When Horses Are Worth More Dead Than Alive," detailing how horses were killed without leaving much trace of method, will sicken you.

The accused ranged from mafia members to lawyers to veterinarians to horse-showing socialites. Cropper, writing in *The New York Times* on September 18, 1994 called it "a nasty business" (p. F9). Cropper wrote that, for some, brutally killing horses for insurance payoffs was easier than taking income tax write-offs for non-winning horseflesh.

- In 1994, for the first time in 90 years, there was no World Series. Columnist Mike Lopresti wrote "For 89 years, the World Series has been a given. It has withstood the Great Depression and Prohibition, Hitler and Mussolini, the Black Sox and Korea and Vietnam and the Cold War and the Cuban missile crisis and an earthquake. Wind, sleet, hail and gloom of night" ("Baseball's date with infamy puts game into a deep abyss" *Houston Chronicle*, September 15, 1994, p. C 11). But, Lopresti said, baseball could not withstand the current owners, acting Commissioner Bud Selig, the current players, and player union attorney Donald Fehr.

The owners claimed they needed a salary cap on players' salaries. The players claimed that the owners used "creative accounting" to claim that most clubs lost money even though, the players charged, most clubs were profitable. The players also claimed that the legal monopoly major league baseball enjoyed was not only illegal but quaintly out of date, a question that the 1995 U.S. Congress may consider. (After the 1994 season was canceled in mid-September 1994, the Florida Supreme Court decided that most of the monopoly clauses that baseball enjoyed were, in fact, illegal. That may be the wedge that causes massive changes in the federal laws regarding baseball.)

In mid-October 1994, President Clinton appointed a veteran federal mediator, William Usery, to help resolve the stand-off between the baseball players union and the owners. He had little success.

• The National Hockey League delayed its 1994–1995 season, also because of an owner–player stand-off. Fans began turning from the National Hockey League to minor-league ice hockey when the major teams failed to begin their schedule.

This promoted late-night entertainer Conan O'Brien to quip: "The NHL players and owners aren't getting along, and it looks like the season could be in jeopardy. . . . I don't know about you, but I'm more of a baseball-strike fan than a hockey-strike fan" (first week of October, 1994).

• And finally, the O. J. Simpson story[1], the fall of the ultimate American sports hero.

The headline on the front of the Saturday, June 18, 1994 (national) issue of *The New York Times* told the entire story:

Simpson Is Charged, Chased, Arrested

Friday, June 17, 1994: Los Angeles. The Los Angeles Police charged O. J. Simpson in the death of his ex-wife Nicole Brown Simpson and a male friend, Ronald Goldman.

Simpson agreed to surrender to the police, escaped and then led police on a 50-mile chase on the Los Angeles Interstate highways. Simpson was driven by an old friend, Al Cowlings, who communicated to police via a car telephone. Simpson reportedly was in the back seat of Cowlings' car with a gun at his head.

The chase was telecast live on all major television networks and the Cable News Network (CNN).

Later it was reported that the police had been called to Simpson's home eight times in the past for incidents of spousal abuse.[2]

He eventually returned to his home and was arrested. He was jailed in a 9 × 7-foot cell with a suicide watch kept by the Los Angeles Sheriff's staff.

---

[1]This manuscript was completed in early November 1994, as the O. J. Simpson jury was being selected.

[2]For further examples of athletes such as baseball star Darryl Strawberry, golfer John Daly, basketball star Moses Malone, boxer Sugar Ray Leonard, and others who are confessed spousal abusers, and what the world of sport does to men's perception of women, see Nelson (1994).

The Simpson story quickly eclipsed all other national stories; it highlighted spousal abuse as a national issue and highlighted the question of how we revere athletes. (Earlier, the Hertz automobile rental firm continued his endorsement contract knowing he was involved in repeated incidents of spousal abuse.)

The Simpson case made the cover of *Time, Newsweek, People, Sports Illustrated,* and many of the tabloids, and it was a continuing story on CNN as well as the other television network news shows.

The article "Television, Meet Life. Life, Meet TV" by Walter Goodman in *The New York Times* (Sunday, June 19, 1994, Section 4, pp. 1, 6) was a particularly poignant summary of how television distorts our perceptions of athletes and reality.

Goodman discussed the 50-mile chase, television's docudramas, and Simpson's surrender. His article ended:

> For two hours Friday, our screens were filled with the real thing, and anesthetically unsatisfying as that might be, those silent ungiving images on a highway and in a driveway held the imagination prisoner in a public dream.

Few athletes have ever been accepted as an athlete, advertising pitchman (for Hertz and other firms), and movie star (the *Naked Gun* comedies and other films) as O. J. Simpson. And no U.S. athlete has ever fallen as far as Simpson.

These were national stories.

Were there regional stories that also made front page news, rather than the sports pages?

Consider these stories during the turbulent 1993 season of the Houston Oilers, the U.S. pro sports world in microcosm:

• David Williams, who plays offensive tackle for the Houston Oilers, refused to go to Buffalo early in the season for an away game at Buffalo (Houston won 28–14) because his wife Debi was having their baby, Scot Cooper Williams, in The Woodlands, a suburb north of Houston. He claimed that witnessing the birth of his son far outweighed playing in one game. Games could come and go, but the birth of this son, was a once-in-a-lifetime event, he claimed. The Oilers fined him one game check—$111,111. This mini-scandal was quickly called "Babygate," and even Vice President Al Gore called with support for Williams and his family and (shades of Dan Quayle) offered encouragement for "family values."

• Jeff Alm, who played defensive tackle for the Oilers, went out with a long-time friend, Sean P. Lynch, and had a late-night accident on a deserted Houston freeway early on Tuesday, December 14, 1993. Lynch was thrown from Alm's car and killed. In anguish, Alm called 911 and informed the operator that Lynch was dead along the highway. There was a pause. Gunshots could be heard on the 911 tape. Alm fired several test shots, then killed himself at the scene with a 12-gauge shotgun.

Experts expressed surprise at Alm's death: They indicated that suicides seldom occur immediately after a fatal accident.

• Offensive coordinator Kevin Gilbride and defensive coordinator Buddy Ryan sparred with each other throughout the season. Ryan called the Houston Oiler "run and shoot" offense the "chuck and duck," because it put quarterback Warren Moon at risk and was also an offense prone to interceptions.

In the middle of a late-season game with the Jets (Houston won 24–0), Ryan threw a punch at Gilbride, seen clearly on nationwide television. One headline read: "Ryan–Gilbride Spar On ESPN Undercard."

The ultimate result? Gilbride remained with the Oilers, and Ryan, who threw the punch, was rewarded: He moved to Phoenix, where he accepted a job as head coach and general manager of the Phoenix Cardinals.

• After the Oilers' season was over, former Oiler General Manager Ladd Herzeg, who reportedly once made $450,000 a year with the Oilers (Herzeg resigned in February 1989 and left Houston), sent a letter to the *Houston Chronicle*, denying he was a "deadbeat dad."

Herzeg was once featured on the NBC show "Prime Suspect" for failure to pay a court-ordered $100,000 in child support to his lover Joann Barbara DeNicola, for his daughter (unnamed in the *Chronicle* article). Herzeg is now reportedly living in hiding somewhere in Cleveland, Ohio, with his ex-wife.

Herzeg's letter was featured in the *Chronicle's* "City & State" section February 21, 1994, a top-of-the-page article under a banner head and subhead: "From Hiding, Herzeg denies he's deadbeat dad: Former GM writes letter to Chronicle"

The first seven paragraphs of the article, written by staff reporter Patti Muck read:

> Former Houston Oiler General Manager Ladd Herzeg—admired for his negotiating wizardry but reviled for his personal style—is a haunted and hunted man.
>
> The flamboyant former football executive, often credited with putting together a Super Bowl contender with his hard-nosed bargaining, is said to be on the run from a judge's $100,000-plus child support judgment won by his former lover.
>
> But while private investigators, reward offers, and at least one TV program have failed to turn up his whereabouts, Herzeg recently decided he could no longer remain mum about the deadbeat dad image of him that is being painted by his former lover and her attorney.
>
> In a five-page letter to the *Chronicle*—with some paragraphs highlighted in pink—Herzeg denies claims by Joann Barbara DeNicola that he slunk out of Houston to avoid his responsibilities to their child.
>
> Herzeg, 48, lashed out at DeNicola, accusing her of greed. But in his final paragraphs, he also shouldered the blame for "causing this maelstrom of chaos to the lives of four human beings."
>
> He once promised to marry DeNicola of Houston and have a "tribe of children" with her. But the couple has only the $6\frac{1}{2}$-year-old daughter Herzeg has not seen in five years.

Although the search for Herzeg has been fruitless thus far, DeNicola's Houston attorney, Robert Love, said tips are coming in since NBC-TV's *Prime Suspect* program featured a story seeking his whereabouts Feb. 12. Love launched a Christmas campaign to find Herzeg, mailing out more than 1,000 wanted posters offering a $500 reward. (p. A17)

- In mid-September 1994, The Riverview Country Club, near Cleburne, Texas allowed a private golf tournament to hire topless dancers as caddies. Although the main gates to the Riverview Country Club were locked for the occasion, TV news helicopters were able to get some long-distance shots of the tournament, including some of the caddies waving to the helicopters. Chris Carter, president of the men's golf association at Riverview, later admitted that some members resigned in protest.

These stories and more throughout the country mean that sports writers must compete more and more with radio and TV competitors for the best story of the day. To do that, reporters need to be armed with all the best skills and writing techniques possible.

This book does not attempt to examine the procedures and realities of being a sports beat reporter—this book concentrates on the techniques that make sports writing exceptional.

This revision follows the first edition of this book in format and takes writers through interviewing techniques, the art of observation, the inverted pyramid, the diamond structure for feature stories and other, modified structures. Then various types of feature leads and techniques for leads, style, covering a regional or national game, and other key elements needed for superior sports writing in the 1990s are covered.

Exceptional sports writing isn't just *scores* and *standings*. These days, sports is more *ethics* and *anguish*, more front page than back section.

Clichés won't work, and tired techniques won't help, especially when competition in the form of 30-second sound bites from ESPN and CNN are as immediate as the *on* knob on your TV. Exceptional sports writing is memorable. And contemporary sports offers unlimited possibilities for those who wish to invest the time and effort in mastering all the techniques that will bring sports writing alive.

In these days of ethics and anguish, just covering games—just producing scores and standings—is no longer enough.

ACKNOWLEDGMENTS

Grateful acknowledgment is made to the following for permission to reprint copyrighted material:

The Associated Press: material reprinted with permission of the Associated Press.

Chapter One
The Art of the Interview

Being an exceptional sports writer simply means being an exceptional interviewer—the writing pales if the interviewing skills are mediocre. You can't use in print what you don't get during an interview.

Some techniques are simply timeless. Consider the following three quotations, the first from William Zinsser's (1985) book, *On Writing Well, An Informal Guide to Writing Nonfiction*; the second is from John Brady's (1976) *The Craft of Interviewing*; and the last is from DeWitt Reddick's (1949) *Modern Feature Writing*.

These guidelines are as important today as when they were first published:

> Interviewing is one of those skills that you only get better at. You will never again feel so ill at ease as when you try for the first time, and probably you will never feel entirely comfortable prodding another person for answers that he or she may be too shy to reveal, or too inarticulate. But at least half of the skill is purely mechanical. The rest is instinct—knowing how to make the other person relax, when to push, when to listen, when to stop. And this can be learned with experience. (Zinsser, 1985, p. 79)

> Interviewing is the modest, immediate science of gaining trust, then gaining information. Both ends must be balanced if the interview is to be balanced and incisive. Yet they are often fumbled in the anxious heat of an interview. The interviewer will either yearn too desperately for his subject's trust and evoke flatulence, or he will restrain his sympathies, demand data—and get like in return. (Brady, 1976, p. 68)

> The writer should prepare in advance many of the questions he plans to ask. These questions should not be haphazard and unrelated, but should spring from the central idea of the story, as he sees it. Preferably he should visualize two or three possible lines of development for the story, and think out questions along each line; thus he

will be prepared to adjust himself to the line which seems most promising during the interview. The beginner will find it helpful to write out his leading questions; most experienced writers may prefer to think clearly through the story as it may develop along three or four angles, and to carry these lines of thought in mind. (Reddick, 1949, p. 94)

There are a variety of techniques and tricks of the trade regarding the *art* and *craft* of interviewing. Many can simply be summarized. Some rules and guidelines for interviewing may easily be recognized by novice writers—others, however, are matters of psychology and perception that may require some experience. Understanding these advanced principles and ideas may help the novice or intermediate interviewer obtain much more valuable interviews. (The techniques and guidelines in this chapter refer largely to the person-to-person interview. On occasion, however, the telephone interview or the mail response may be used.)

In this chapter, suggestions and guidelines are offered, generally in order from the basic to the most advanced and in the most logical order.

Read all you can about your subject before the interview. If you work for a newspaper, ask your newspaper librarian to dig up back files for you. Read everything in newspaper or magazine form that has been published about your subject. This will allow you to ...

Prepare in advance. Write down likely questions. Both DeWitt Reddick and John Brady refer to the Boy Scout motto: *Be prepared.* There is no substitute for preparation. If you prepare for two or three or four avenues of interview development, the more information you will obtain and the less likely you will be to be caught off guard mentally during an interview.

Time the interview to fit your subject's schedule. Change your own schedule first, if possible. Don't inconvenience the subject's time for your own schedule. If you have a *deadline* for the story, however, mention that. The subject will usually be willing to meet with you at a time that will allow you to complete the article prior to the deadline.

Be patient. If you are interviewing someone on the edges of the sports world, this might be the first time they have been interviewed. Many people are unacquainted with reporters or interviewers. In "The Interview or The Only Wheel in Town," the *Journalism Monographs'* Eugene J. Webb and Jerry Salancik (1966) suggested that there may be problems regarding your subject's answers:

1. The potential source may not know the information (the reporter seeks).
2. The source may be aware and want to tell but lacks the verbal skills to do so.
3. The source may be willing but not want to tell.
4. The source may be willing but unable to produce the information because it is buried beyond his conscious ability to recall it. (p. 21)

Ask questions in chronological order. If you are interviewing for a personality portrait or profile, proceeding through these five areas may give you comprehensive answers:

1. Birth—location and date—and youth;
2. Education;
3. Military service if any—dates, specialty, and location;
4. Marriage—including spouse's name and age of children, if any;
5. Career—to date.

Ask for dates. Ages, dates of marriage, beginning of career, career achievements—the subject's ages at those times. These dates supply readers with a ready reference to parallel their own life to the life of your subject.

Ask why *questions.* These demand the subject explain positions, career choices, and beliefs.

Why do you believe such-and-such?

If this is your best season as player, *why?*

Why is this team better than last year?

Why do you believe your coaching techniques are better than your opposition?

In addition to *why* questions, the *how* or *how did it happen* question may be equally important. Professional athletes may not be articulate enough to explain why something happened—why they have a particularly distinct golf swing or why they have a trademark style, or even why they chose a particular play at a particular time.

It might be more productive to ask: "Show me what you do—demonstrate your swing for me.... Show me what you did at that time.... *How* did you do that?"

In watching the *how's* of their technique, you may also be able to determine the *why's*—why they play the way they do.

Get a telephone number for any additional trivial details you may need to call back for. Don't drive across town for two or three additional questions if you can make a telephone call. If the subject has an unlisted telephone, promise you won't disclose it to others, and keep your promise.

Interview all possible sources. If you are interviewing Bonnie Blair or Picabo Street, two U.S. winners in the 1994 Olympics, for instance, ask them who else should be interviewed: parents, coaches, teammates, or others. The question often arises: How do I know when I have enough interviews for a major story? The cynical answer is: When is your deadline? How much time do you have, working backward from that time, to get interviews done and the story written?

The ideal answer is to interview until you come full circle. During every interview, you should ask, "Who else should I talk to?" If you are interviewing A for a major story, and A tells you to talk to B, C, and D, you work your way around the subject until persons X, Y, and Z tell you to see B, C, and D. When you have run out of interview subjects around A, it's time to start to write the story; or, when you begin to hear the same anecdotes from a variety of subjects, it's time to begin the writing process.

It is seldom good practice to arbitrarily limit yourself to five interviews or six or seven. How do you know that the eighth or ninth or tenth would not have given you the best material for your story?

Don't be a cheerleader. Asking a question like, "Sure was a good game, wasn't it coach?" leads to a laconic answer: "Yep." That is a very small crumb to use in your story. Even breaking the ice in a conversation with a comment like that is a lame beginning.

Be aware that many coaches and some players expect you to "be on their side." Indiana basketball coach Bobby Knight and many others adopt an "us against the media" attitude. As a sports writer, you have at least four choices when encountering these defensive (no pun intended) individuals:

1. Negotiate with them if they show an aggressive attitude toward you as an interviewer.
2. Interview assistant coaches—or "interview around the subject."
3. Trade notes with a reporter from a noncompeting publication. If you work for a newspaper that covers Bobby Knight's team, trade notes with a newspaper reporter in a noncompeting area.
4. Use the coach's belligerent attitude in the story—as accurately as possible. If he gets into trouble from the story, that's his problem, not your problem as a reporter.

Don't fail to ask the obvious.

Why did you, coach, go for that field goal instead of a pass? Why did you play for a tie instead of a win?

Why did you call for that particular play on the 37 with a minute and a half left in the game?

Games seldom explain themselves fully. Ask about the key play that won the game—or lost it—for a particular coach or team.

If you are a print reporter, learn as much as you can about tape recorders, modem connections, video cameras, and the like. Radio and TV reporters, for the most part, are adept at electronic equipment. Print reporters are less so. But there is little reason why, in these days, print reporters should not use quality tape recorders. And there are several good reasons why they *should*. If you are working on a controversial story about, for instance, ticket scalping, or illegal university football payoffs, interviews on tape are a sure source of proof of what exactly was said. This sort of taped proof is a good—although not complete—defense against a charge of libel, or a defense against a slightly less dangerous charge: "I was misquoted."

If you have the luxury to delay completing a story for a few days, or don't have an immediate deadline, the tape will stay fresh. It will be as easy to use several days, months, or years later, as it was the day it was made.

One key tip that many reporters do not use: If the first draft of a lengthy story "falls flat" or toneless and if the style is not exactly what the writer intended, or if the story has a lack of focus or is weak in transitions or style, reading the story onto tape and listening to it may help the reporter find dead spots that will have to be rewritten.

The reporter should go into an interview situation with the recorder ready for use. The reporter should proceed with the explanation (if an explanation is needed) that the tape will make the interview much more accurate and reliable. If the interview subject objects to a tape recording, then the reporter should go ahead with the interview without the tape—but should try first to negotiate with the subject that the tape is: (a) important, and (b) more accurate than handwritten notes. Few people these days object to tape recordings. (Hint: The reporter might offer to have a duplicate tape made for the subject—to reassure the subject that quotes used in the article were accurately taken from the tape. The cost is minimal and the good will earned is priceless.)

Avoid the moral problems of using "off the record" remarks. What if, during an interview, someone says to you "I'll tell you what you need to know, but don't quote me." What do you do?

First, don't agree to any conditions. Don't use the material you hear. If you use it without citing the source, what could be the result? Your interview subject may simply be lying to you and manipulating you (for his or her own purposes). If you didn't confirm the material and if you didn't use his or her name as the source, who is responsible for any potential libel suit? Whose name is on the byline?

As Leonard Koppett (1981) wrote, in *Sports Illusion, Sports Reality: A Reporter's View of Sports, Journalism and Society:*

> People have all sorts of ideas, opinions, judgments and intentions that they don't want to see attributed to them in print or on the air. As a reporter, you want to know as many of these things as you can, to increase your understanding of what goes on around you. So you must follow strictly two self-imposed limitations: Confidentiality and relevance.
>
> Some of the varieties of confidentiality are:
>
> 1. Off the record. Don't say I told you, but use the information if you can substantiate it some other way.
>
> 2. Know but don't use. Be aware that such-and-such is the situation, but don't make it public until I say O.K.

3. Not for attribution. Go ahead and use the information the way I'm giving it to you, but don't say it came from me.
4. Private. Here's what happened, but does it really have to be made public?
5. Top secret. If this gets out, I'm finished; let your conscience be your guide. (p. 149)

The reporter may have to determine which of these guidelines applies to the situation at hand, then work accordingly. Sometimes an agreement can be worked out with the interview subject in a nonverbal way; the reporter may say, "This is not for attribution to you?" The subject may agree with a wink and a grin.

Koppett (1981) also wrote:

In his relationship to news sources, the ideal journalist observes four "don'ts" along with stubborn devotion to the principles of confidentiality and relevance:
1. Don't take cheap shots.
2. Don't form close friendships.
3. Don't be afraid of arousing anger, but don't pick on people just to show you're not afraid.
4. Don't deny an error, or compound it by looking for justification. (p. 150)

Get your subject to confirm or deny previously published material. If there has been an article published recently that pertains to your story, ask your interview subject to comment on it. You may get powerful quotations to use, or a second breaking story. Asking your subject to confirm or deny previously published material also helps in other ways—it clarifies the record for you and eliminates any confusion you might have about the status of your subject in relation to the story in print. (Your subject may not have been able to tell his or her side of the story.)

Interview in tranquility. The best interviews are one on one. If you can, get the subject away from the locker room, or his favorite bar, or away from his cronies. The subject may use the locker room to be "on stage" for his friends. He may *play to them* instead of paying complete attention to you.

Ask for PR material, background material, or other material that the subject or press office may have. Many organizations are extremely helpful when it comes to furnishing an interviewer with background material, clippings, and other material. If you receive valuable or rare material of any kind, promise to make copies of it and return the original material as soon as possible. And keep your promise.

If you work with a PR office, be aware that on occasion, their job is to keep press *away* from an athlete or club owner, or to make sure that the writer receives only the "company line." PR staffers usually—but not always—work to aid the writer. If there is any doubt about their motives, ask yourself *who pays their salary?* You don't.

Be sure you use slang terms accurately. There is no easier way for a sports buff or interview subject to spot an error in an article than to see slang misused. If you have doubts about what a slang term means—especially in a sport you have never covered before—make sure you verify it; and not just the meaning—the spelling, too.

Court records, divorces, lawsuits, and the like are public property. You can and should look up this material if it is germane to your story. If you work for a newspaper and have any doubts about how court records can be obtained, consult with a police reporter, editor, or corporate attorney. If you are a freelancer, court clerks and staff members may be able to help you obtain court records.

Ask controversial questions at the end of an interview, not at the beginning. Don't begin an interview with a fired college football coach by asking about NCAA rules violations. Don't begin an interview with an athlete accused of steroid use by asking about the drug charges. In all probability, the interview will end just after it began.

If you ask these questions at the end of a 2-hour interview, the subject may relent and answer the question, because you have established a solid professional relationship. If, after 2 hours or x hours, the subject refuses to answer, you have your notes and material from the full interview and you can possibly use the anger or denial in the story itself:

"Even at the end of a 2-hour conversation, Coach A erupted in anger at a question about. . . ."

At the end of an interview, ask the subject if he or she has anything to add that hasn't been touched upon. Occasionally, a subject will withhold valuable information on the logical theory that if a writer didn't ask about it, it isn't important. The writer might not know about the valuable anecdote that the subject has on the tip of his tongue.

Don't be awed by your subject. In *The Craft of Interviewing*, John Brady (1976) quoted staff writer John Underwood of *Sports Illustrated*:

> Remember if you tend to be awed by athletes, you will never allow yourself to see a man's inner sanctum, and that will, in itself, distort the picture. The thing about sports heroes is that they are just a cut away from the friend you play golf with. There's a whole lot of difference between Einstein and the guy who makes A's in his college chemistry class, but the professional athlete and the kid who wins letters in college are only a shade apart. (p. 57)

Be skeptical—or wary—of any athlete, owner, or sports figure who has been interviewed frequently in the past. You may complete an interview that appeared to be completely spontaneous, only to discover later, from reading old files, that you got slight variations of the same interview that the subject has been giving for years. Without a fresh angle, your story is essentially worthless. Or, you may discover during an interview that your subject's mind is on "autopilot," rehashing old answers from months or years ago.

The *worst* situation as a reporter is having no story at all because you were asked to leave after your first question, a controversial one, which the subject refused to answer.

The *second worst* situation is ending an interview only to discover later, with a heavy sinking feeling, that you have the same material that your interview subject has given in interviews countless times before.

Be prepared for an occasional "confessional" or "guilt" interview. Although these are rare, some interviewees perceive an interview as the cheapest psychiatric hour possible, and will tell you stories you could not imagine. As a reporter, you should understand that some people will simply perceive you differently than you expect.

You will go into the interview simply as a reporter, but the interview subject may see you as an authority figure, a parent, almost a member of the clergy, a psychiatrist, a threat, a police figure, a temporary respite from their own world, a foil for their own jokes, or a vehicle to spread malicious rumors about others.[1] If they perceive you in the context of those personas, their answers will be "skewed," as researchers say.

Even if the interview subject doesn't specifically indicate that you, as a reporter, *are* a father figure, psychiatrist, priest, or cop, you may perceive that the thrust of the interview is going in that direction. When that happens, facts or data gathering become secondary in nature. Interview hours may become—for subject and interviewer—intense hours of personality analysis: background, motives, behaviors, and personal history.

Does this happen often? No, but when it does, the reporter must be observant enough to recognize what is taking place, how the interview is progressing, and the significance of how the interview subject is perceiving the reporter and the interview.

Personal interviews are often the keys to exceptional nonfiction writing. By remembering the two Ps: *preparation* and *professionalism*, sports writers should be able to turn significant and perceptive interviews into exceptional pieces of nonfiction.

---

[1]For a further explanation of the perceptions of interviewers by interviewees, see Webb & Salancik (1966).

Chapter Two
The Art of Observation

Careful observation is absolutely necessary for a nonfiction writer.

It is said that some writers have a "tin ear" for dialogue: Their conversation on the page simply doesn't sound real (because they don't really listen to how people talk). Other writers have a similar visual tin ear: They omit significant details or use inappropriate ones.

The use of observed details in nonfiction serves several important functions:

• *The use of substantial details draws the reader into the scene* and thus into the article. You can think of observed details as small brushstrokes that fill in a painting; without these details, the painting, the scene, lies lifeless on the page. Without details, you only half-convince readers of what is happening, where, and when. Without details, readers are left with static icons—cliché images in their imagination. Details add texture to the word painting you are crafting on the page.

As a sports writer, *you are the eyes of your reader*—you witness a scene when the reader can't. You must describe a scene or action the reader has not witnessed.

• *Observed details also prove the writer was there, witnessing the action.* In the following article, note the seventh paragraph from the beginning: "That would be his first time to ride Bodacious, and other riders had been razzing him about it all afternoon." How would the writer know that the "other riders had been razzing him about it all afternoon?" By being there; by watching and perhaps taking notes. Stated another way, observed details *validate* the writer's story.

• *Observed details reveal human behavior.* Writers should always look for significance in human behavior. Otherwise, the use of observation and dialogue are pointless.

The following article, "Tough Bucks," was written by *Houston Chronicle* staff writer Cheryl Laird. This article was published in the "Houston" section of the *Houston Chronicle*, Saturday, March 5, 1994, during the annual Houston Livestock Show and Rodeo, one of the biggest such events in the country.

Notice how physically close Laird gets to the chute where Bodacious, the bull, is ready. Note carefully how she describes the preride seconds, then Cody Custer's ride.

Later in the article, she describes Bodacious as an "arm-puller," and shows the reader "a star-shaped spot" (scar) on rider Cody Lambert's chin, the result of one ride on Bodacious.

Notice also how Laird's use of quotations supplement the observed details:

- "It's a strain," says Darrell Cholach, a bareback rider from Alberta, Canada. "If you're not riding him good with all parts of your body, you're on the ground. He's magnificent."

- "Bodacious is as rank as any there is in the world," says longtime bullfighter Miles Hare. "He'll turn sideways in the air, but he lands on his feet. He's like a cat."

- "He's electric," Hare says. "You react. He reacts. You jump. He jumps. He's on a natural high in life."

- "Bodacious, when he was a calf, you could tell he was an athlete. He could jump sideways and kick the side of a gate when walking through," says his owner, Sammy Andrews of Addielou in northeast Texas. "He's a Michael Jordan of animals."

Tough Bucks
Cowboys ride hard and earn every dollar

By Cheryl Laird

His eyes were those of a professional, calm and focused.

His ears were the only sign of what was to come. They flapped back and forth, pivoting at every noise.

Suddenly, with the speed and sound of a cannon shot, he slammed his forehead hard into the front of the bucking chute.

The cowboys pulling the straps around his white belly watched warily, with respect and, in some eyes, fear.

They were dealing with Skoal Is Bodacious—the baddest bucking bull in the Astrodome.

Cody Custer, an even-tempered world champion bull rider from Arizona, squatted in his chaps to stretch out his legs.

This would be his first time to ride Bodacious, and other riders had been razzing him about it all day.

He'd stared that afternoon at the oversize, off-white Charolais-Brahman crossbreed. "Hey, Bodacious," he'd called. The bull recognized his name and looked at him with placid eyes.

But Custer knew the bull wouldn't act the tame barnyard pet before 57,000 people in the Astrodome. Bodacious, in his mind and a lot of other opinions, was the rankest bull in the world.

"My heart's beating, and I'm a little bit butterfly-ish right now," Custer acknowledged before the ride. "This is probably the biggest challenge in my life."

The slim cowboy lowered himself carefully on the broad white back, held his hand high in the air, and nodded curtly. The gate flew open.

The bull jumped sideways once, then lunged forward in an elastic buck that sent his back legs flying above his rider's head. For a moment, it looked as if Custer could withstand the force.

Then his body flipped forward and to the side. A horn grazed his cheek as he hit the dirt. His attempt at Bodacious lasted two seconds.

"I don't know," Custer said afterward, as if he didn't quite believe what had just happened. "He does something to get your feet behind you."

* * *

In the rodeo world, tough bucking stock are admired almost as much as tough cowboys. Riders know bulls and broncs by their names, or at least their brands. They know their records.

Each year, they vote on the best bull, bareback bronc and saddle bronc in their rodeo circuits. Stock contractors whose animals are chosen receive cash awards and, more important, a major kind of parental ego boost.

Like baseball players who make it to the major leagues, the best animals end up on the Professional Rodeo Cowboys Association circuit. The best of those go on to the biggest rodeos, like Houston's.

Of all the bulls at the Astrodome this year, the unofficial consensus is that Bodacious is the rankest. Of the bareback horses, a big gray from Canada named High Chaparral Copenhagen wins top honors.

High Chaparral was voted PRCA bareback horse of the year in 1989 and 1992. Horses don't usually buck off top-ranked cowboys, but High Chaparral is an exception.

He's known as an "arm puller" because the force of his jump makes a rider feel as if his arm is being yanked out of its socket.

"He's kinda like standing by a railroad track and a train comes by and you grab onto it," says Marvin Garrett, a world champion bareback rider from South Dakota who has successfully ridden the bronc. "I don't know many guys who want to have him."

"It's a strain," says Darrell Cholach, a bareback rider from Alberta, Canada. "If you're not riding him good with all parts of your body, you're on the ground. He's magnificent."

Both Bodacious and High Chaparral are scheduled to be ridden, or at least attempted to be ridden, during Sunday's finals at the Houston Livestock Show and Rodeo. For rodeo fans, that lineup is about equal to a Hakeem Olajuwon-Shaquille O'Neal matchup.

Riders are randomly assigned to animals. Half of their possible 100-point score depends solely on how hard their mounts buck. For the most adventuresome and talented riders, drawing a Bodacious or a High Chaparral is a plus. If they stay on, they're guaranteed to do well.

But even the best riders don't usually stay on Bodacious. In 1993, he was voted the best bucking bull in Texas. Twenty-nine cowboys attempted to ride him for eight seconds last year. Only two did. The most recent was Tuff Hedeman in November. He scored a nearly perfect 95 points.

Behind the bucking chutes in the Astrodome earlier this week, world champion bull rider Cody Lambert leaned back his head and pointed to a star-shaped spot when asked about Bodacious.

"He put this scar under my chin at this here rodeo," Lambert said. "For six seconds, I thought I was going to be 90 (points). Then I was out. That's the only time I got on him, and that's the only time I want to ride him."

Despite his big size, Bodacious bucks with as much quick movement as a little bull. He doesn't have a set pattern. He jumps high in the air and twists. His front end drops to the ground, as Lambert says, "like an anvil."

"Bodacious is as rank as any there is in the world," says longtime bullfighter Miles Hare. "He'll turn sideways in the air, but he lands on his feet. This bull is like a cat."

Hare makes his living facing down bulls, trying to distract them as bruised riders hobble away. He has to be especially quick on his feet to stay ahead of Bodacious' curved horns.

"He's electric," Hare says. "You react. He reacts. You jump. He jumps. He's on a natural high in life."

Bodacious was born on a ranch in northwest Oklahoma. He was big, active and streamlined like a greyhound. Like about half of today's bucking stock, he was bred specifically for the rodeo circuit.

"Bodacious, when he was a calf, you could tell he was an athlete. He could jump sideways and kick the side of a gate when walking through," says his owner, Sammy Andrews of Addielou in northeast Texas. "He's a Michael Jordan of animals."

The first few times with a rider, Bodacious bucked only half-heartedly, Andrews says. But then a rookie caught his hand in the rigging, scaring both himself and the 3-year-old bull. Bodacious has rarely failed to put on fireworks since.

Stock contractors Sammy and Carolyn Andrews buy about 30 yearling bulls every year in hopes of getting a good bucker. They usually look for Brahman crossbreeds with broad faces and tiger-striped coats. According to rodeo lore, these usually buck the best.

They put the chosen animals in a wheat field for one year, and then send them to a dairy farm the next year in a sort of exchange program. The dairy farmer gets free mates for his heifers, and the Andrewses get free grain for their young bulls.

At 3 years, the bulls are big enough for riding. For the first time, the Andrewses usually strap a foam-rubber dummy wearing overalls onto the bull's back.

If the bulls don't buck at all, they are either retired as breeding stock or made into hamburger.

If they buck, they are matched with beginner bull riders. Usually the teen-age cowboys fall off, which is what the Andrewses want. There's no way to convince a bull to buck, they say. It has to enjoy seeing its rider hit the ground. Sometimes, if an older bull gets sour, Carolyn Andrews says she lets it "throw some kids off and build up his confidence again."

Rusty Bradberry, a wiry man with an easy grin, takes care of the Andrewses' bucking stock. Last year he drove Bodacious more than 40,000 miles around the country. He says the bull is starting to like him, but not so much that he allows petting.

"When we first got him, he didn't like anybody. He'd run away from you. Now when we go to feed him, he's the first one there. He kinda knows he gets special attention." Bradberry says. "Everybody thinks they're just dumb animals, and they're not."

When Bodacious is finished with his cowboy here Sunday, Bradberry will drive him home to his shaded 100-acre pasture for a week's rest before his next rodeo. The bull is almost 7 years old, and he'll probably travel for a few more years before being retired as a full-time daddy.

Cody Custer hopes he'll have another shot at him before then. After his ill-fated ride in the Astrodome, he glanced over at the big, white bull. Bodacious was standing passively in a metal corral with the other bulls.

The cowboy grinned and gingerly touched his swollen, raw cheek.

"I ain't ascared of him now," he said, almost convincingly. (pp. C1, C4)

In the following article, "KO'ed by His Demons" (Putnam, 1985), notice how much of the "detail" of the article is observed behavior. *Sports Illustrated* senior writer Pat Putnam not only captured Aaron Pryor's speech—slurred and incoherent as it was—but also his behavior, and added summary to buttress his observations, as in this passage: "Pryor, who had been on the verge of tears, now laughs, a tick of joy which passes swiftly. His moods alter from moment to moment, switching bewilderingly from dark storm clouds to bright sunlight." And: "Pryor's eyelids become heavy. His head nods forward. He seems asleep. Then his eyes pop open, blinking, and he rubs them furiously."

Putnam's observed details of Pryor's behavior and Pryor's statements are buttressed by police records and previous statements to the press (cited toward the end of the article).

It seems clear that "the visitor" mentioned early in the article and then again four paragraphs from the end of the article is Putnam the writer, a sophisticated method of "appearing" in the narrative without using the "I" form: "I asked him about such-and-such and he said _____."

Here is the complete article. What do *you* think of Aaron Pryor?

KO'ed By His Demons
Unbeaten and still a champion, Aaron Pryor is angry,
despondent and confused. And he's in no condition to fight,
either in or out of the ring.

By Pat Putnam

The spirit that helped make Aaron Pryor a great boxer seems burned out now. His eyes, half shut against Miami's summer sun, are dying embers in a face left gaunt by too many nights without sleep, too many parties, too many fears. He is surrounded by people with their hands in his pockets, but he drifts alone in a dark world of self-created demons, ever-changing suspicions that taunt and torment him.

He is the reigning and undefeated IBF junior welterweight champion, this gifted and exciting fighter, and each day he pledges that tomorrow he will go back into training. But for Pryor, a fatherless child of almost 30, such a tomorrow dances continually beyond his grasp. His life, always turbulent, has veered almost totally out of control.

He is suing to collect $300,000 that he claims promoter Richard Mangone refused to pay him for a June 22, 1984 decision over Gary Hinton in Atlantic City that left his professional record at 36–0. Pryor's second wife, Theresa, divorced him. A Cincinnati court awarded her more than $200,000 and Pryor's 1983 Cadillac. By June, rumors intensified that Pryor was wedded to another wife: cocaine. His mother, Sarah, signed papers in an attempt to have him committed to a Miami drug rehabilitation center. He refused to go. On June 30, Pryor told Miami police he had been abducted. The police, after investigating, discounted his story. He says that two of his cars—a 1985 Ford van and an '85 Saab turbo, distinguishable by bullet scars on their bodies, were stolen. He also claims someone made off with his M16 rifle.

Life has lain heavy on Pryor's psyche. He was born out of wedlock and left his home in Cincinnati at 14. "I was a kid nobody paid any attention to," he says. "Some nights I just said to hell with it and slept in a doorway. Wasn't anything at home for me anyway."

From such a beginning, it's not hard to understand why Pryor has always hungered for love and respect; why he has never quite been able to trust anyone. As a fighter, his strength and skills made him unbeatable. On the street, his suspicious nature and hidden rage left him vulnerable and winless. Still, despite his almost feral life-style, Pryor seemed in command of his actions.

Before the first of his two wins over Alexis Arguello, in November 1982, Pryor saw fit to change his image. He replaced his gold front tooth with a white porcelain cap. He abandoned his gaudy wardrobe for conservative suits, white shirts and striped ties. He even carried a briefcase. He was a time bomb in Brooks Brothers wrapping.

On this late summer day, Pryor is seated on a gray sofa in the screened-in pool area behind his well-kept home in southwest Miami. He has lived in the area since 1983. His upper body, once thick with muscle, is frail now, covered loosely by a Michael Jackson T shirt. He is holding Norra, whom he introduces as his 10-week-old daughter. "I can trust you," he tells the baby softly. He sighs and looks up. "And my dog, Clyde. I trust him. But nobody else."

Norra (her name is a variation of "Aaron" spelled backward) makes a small sound, and Pryor, who had been on the verge of tears, now laughs, a tick of joy which passes swiftly. His moods alter from moment to moment, switching bewilderingly from dark storm clouds to bright sunlight. Carefully, he sets the baby beside him on the sofa.

"Right now I am confused," Pryor says to a visitor. His voice, barely audible, is sad and wistful. "After my last fight, I felt nobody was concerned about injuries to myself. Nobody was really interested in me, only in what they can find to promote me or find out about me to hurt me. I was made to look the bad guy. Now as I look at you, as I talk to you, I find out even more of my problem. I swear. One of my eyes. I had an eye examination prior to my [last fight]." He switches thoughts without pause or reason. "Made me come across one way, yet at the same time meaning to come across another way to express myself."

Anger strengthens his voice. "Like my left eye here. They don't want me to tell nobody. I've got to tell somebody." Pausing, Pryor covers his right eye with his right hand. "You see that eye here?" he asks, meaning the uncovered left one. He looks down at a small table in front of him. "I can't see nothing on the table. But yet I can open it up," he says, uncovering the right eye, "and see things."

The baby begins to cry, and for a moment the sound washes away Pryor's anguish. "O.K., kid. Shut up," he says laughing. Through an open glass door he calls to his housekeeper. "Hey, Maggie, bring a bottle for the baby."

"Are you blind in the left eye?" the visitor asks Pryor.

"I believe I am," he says. "I don't have enough vision to see. But, yet, nobody wants to talk about the bad part of me, the things that are happening in my life. All they want to talk about is that Pryor has left boxing, he's out doing something else. I'm just doing something about trying to get my eyesight."

"When did you notice the eye?"

Pryor rubs his eyes. "Just after the last fight," he says.

"Was it bothering you before?"

He nods angrily. "It's been about three years now. But nobody was interested in me. Examined in Atlantic City. They told me not to come back there anymore until I can see. That was after my last fight. And, really, you know, my last fight I had a lot of problems."

Pryor's disjointed conversation settles randomly on moments in his career. After stopping Arguello for the second time on Sept. 9, 1983, he abdicated his WBA junior welterweight championship, saying that he was tired, that he didn't want to fight anymore. He was in his prime: just 28 years old and 34–0. Just before that fight, he had been served with divorce papers by Theresa, who once, before they were married, had shot him in the right forearm. But Pryor, who had retained his IBF title, came out of retirement and fought twice, the match against Furlano and the split decision over Hinton. He gave an uninspired imitation of the real Aaron Pryor in both fights.

"I didn't get paid the first fight, [with] Nicky Furlano," Pryor is saying. "I didn't get one dime. I quit boxing and gave up my title because [they] said I was . . . black bottle . . . and preached to me about it."

The black-bottle reference is to his first fight with Arguello, when it was suspected that Pryor had taken stimulants from a bottle wrapped with black tape. The late Artie Curley, who worked Pryor's corner that night, said the bottle contained peppermint schnapps.

"I said I'll fight Alexis again and there won't be no black bottle," Pryor says. "And then, after I beat him a second time, I thought I had cleared up the black-bottle thing, but I never got no credit for winning straight up. Then I didn't get one dime [for the Furlano fight]. I quit boxing and give up my title. . . . Then I laid off for a year and a half, and they don't pay me for my first comeback fight. Three hundred thousand. The promoter. Oh, man, why me?"

In fact, Pryor did receive some payment for the Furlano fight—$50,000 in front money and another $50,000 for training expenses. The dispute with Mangone is over whether any more money is due. In June, Pryor and his manager, Buddy LaRosa, were to fly from Miami to Boston to give depositions in their suit against Mangone. LaRosa says that after trying for four days to hook up with Pryor at the Miami airport, he returned home to Cincinnati. Pryor has earned some $4 million in his eight-year career, but friends say he is heading for financial ruin. LaRosa says that if Pryor doesn't get to Boston soon, the court may dismiss his claim against Mangone.

Now Pryor leans forward, his voice a conspirational whisper. "I don't want to elaborate too much because I do hope to fight again, and I don't want to [mess up] my career," he says. "I'm not supposed to mention it. But I'm tired of talking about everything else. Cataracts, cataracts. They told me not to come to Atlantic City or Vegas no more. Because I'm blind in one eye. I want to get my eye fixed and continue to fight."

If Pryor has been banned from fighting for medical reasons, officials in Nevada and New Jersey know nothing about it. "He's not under any suspension here," says Chuck Minker, a Nevada boxing inspector. Bob Lee, the acting commissioner of the New Jersey State Athletic Commission says Pryor is still in good standing in his state. An Atlantic City ophthalmologist, David Smith, did find a cataract in Pryor's left eye before the Hinton fight in March, and the commission warned Pryor to have the problem treated before it hampered his career. But, says Lee, "It wasn't bad enough to prevent him from fighting Hinton. And he's not barred here."

Pryor's eyelids become heavy. His head nods forward. He seems asleep. Then his eyes pop open, blinking, and he rubs them furiously. He calls for Maggie to bring coffee. "Cataracts, yeah," he says. "Then my mother. [I hadn't seen] her for at least a year. And she come up here. I didn't know she was coming, but one day she is here. She says what she's heard."

What she had heard were rumors of her son's drug problem. In July she told the Cincinnati *Post* that she had seen Aaron use cocaine.

"I got the baby and the van and just left home," Pryor says. "Hey, man! Are you giving me a charge or somethin'? You must be giving me a charge or something, in my eye."

"Something wrong?" the visitor asks.

"Need some coffee. Don't you ever get tired? Down in Florida, it's the air. Yeah, my problems. They started when my mother came here. She came to take over. She was handling my checkbook. I feel I'm back where I started because of my mother. She's got a nice house, a Cadillac, she's never worked. And she never introduced me to my father. About nine years ago I put my mother in an institution. I was only 21. She shot her husband. I was driving a school bus and I went home and they say my mama had shot my dad, my stepdad. I put her in a hospital because she had lost her nerves. I think. . . ." He pauses, shakes his head and sighs. "I think she don't like me because she done those things to me."

Mrs. Pryor would make no comment to SI about her involvement in any shooting. She was ordered into silence by William Hardy, her brother-in-law and Pryor's uncle, who is known to family and friends as Uncle Chocolate. "I'm his uncle and his trainer," he says of Pryor, "and this boy is gonna fight better than ever. You are getting that straight from the horse's mouth."

On the patio, Pryor's words continue to tumble forth. "My eye, shocks and everything," he says, casting suspicious glances in all directions. "I think somebody is looking in here and hearing every word we say. I'm a true person. I can feel it." He relaxes after Maggie shuts the patio door. "O.K., I feel better now. Anyway . . . here I am, 36 and oh with 32 knockouts. I went 15 rounds my last fight. I went four days before that fight without eating, I swear. I had to lay in the hallways to lose four extra pounds. I came home, and the only thing I worked on was not training, because when I train I build up a big appetite. I went on a diet, I lose weight, and people tell me I'm crazy." Pryor gives his weight this day as 138 pounds. He appears to weigh 120 at most.

He puts his face in his hands and gets around to talking about his "abduction." "Oh, it's kind of painful to talk," he says. "I don't have nobody to talk to; nobody comes here; nobody knows me. They all know me, and I don't know them. It hurts so bad. And then I picked a couple of guys up in Miami when I first got here, and we talk: 'Hey, what's going on. All right.' So Linda [Hill, his girlfriend] and the baby [Norra] was at her friend's house, so I go in the house with Linda, and when I come out they had stolen my van. I catch a cab and come home."

Throughout this part of the story there are long, painful pauses. He says that a friend took him to a house where he confronted the men who stole his van. "They said I owed them some money," he says. "Four hundred dollars. I say, 'I don't even know you, man. What do I owe you $400 for?' The guy who took me over, they let him go. So he called the police, and the police break in the place and they—these guys—run away, and now my van is gone."

The police released Pryor at 2 a.m. Another young man in the house was arrested for possession of cocaine. Detective Doreen Nash was one of the officers on the scene. "My part was to see if there was an abduction or not," says Nash. "The only means I had was speaking to the witnesses that were in the house with [Pryor]. They all said basically the same thing, that he went there on his own to try and get his van back. While in the house, witnesses say he did use cocaine and he wasn't abducted. I talked to Pryor but I couldn't get him to give me anything. He wasn't very coherent." Nash says that Pryor's friend, who gave a false name, told police that the fighter owed $1,000 to the people who took his Ford van.

In selecting friends, Pryor is always zero for whatever the number is at the moment. Not long ago a girl he knew named Candy accompanied Pryor's mother to a grocery store. When they returned, Candy helped carry in the bags, then got into Pryor's '85 Saab. Pryor hasn't seen the girl or the car since.

"Everybody robs me," he says. "I meet a girl and she robs me. I meet some guys and they rob me. People break into my house and steal things. They take my machine gun. I had an M16." The visitor asks about the gun. Pryor shrugs and says, very seriously, "I had planned one day to get on a boat and I don't have no license and I might go to Cuba. I wanted to shoot my way back home. I had plans, like if it is nighttime. They come on your boat and shoot you. I believe I'm getting tired. I'm getting hyper talking, and it's so hot. Oh, man, I feel just like getting into a car and running away."

"Why not go back into training?" he is asked.

Strength returns to his voice. "Oh, I'm ready to go tonight. I'm leaving tonight. I'm going back to Cincinnati. I'm going inside. Ain't you hot? I'm hot? The police come by and mess with me. I had a girl forge checks on me. This is my third checking account. People steal thousands of dollars out of my clothes. I don't even know where the money goes. Ransom. They threaten my kids [he has two besides Norra] that they will kill me if I don't give them money." He pauses, sighing. "Somebody breaks into my house . . . setting little things around, like drugs around my house and in my clothes. I can't take no more. You know, a lot of people lost a lot of money on the Alexis fight. They're a little angry. That's the only thing I can think of."

The champion rises and enters the house, taking his demons with him. He admits to the visitor that he has experimented with drugs. This alone is not necessarily a revelation, since newspaper stories have quoted Pryor as having acknowledged using marijuana. But he is vague, or evasive, about whether he has used any other drugs. On Nov. 23, 1983 he was arrested in Inglewood, Calif. for cocaine possession, a charge that was subsequently dismissed on the grounds that the arresting officers had illegally searched the automobile Pryor was driving. He continues to insist that he doesn't have a drug problem.

"Drugs is a big thing in Florida," he says. "Yes, it is. And I figure just one thing: If you can go to training and you can sacrifice sex and alcohol and go to bed early at night, you can sacrifice drugs. If you want to. There never was any drugs involved in me as far as winning a fight. Why does my eye hurt? You have an electricity charge or something? See my eye cross? That's automatic. I'm tired. I've got to get some sleep."

He starts out of the room, then turns and says, "I can buy anything I want: cars, a house, jewelry. I can buy anything but a friend."

Aaron Pryor didn't go to Cincinnati that night. He hasn't yet. He is still talking about going back into training. And he is still looking for a friend.

Chapter Three

Page One, Paragraph One—
Story Leads:
Types and Techniques

You write your stories like you eat ice cream cones—literally and figuratively, from the top down. Like that first delicious taste of ice cream, the reader savors your story from the top down. The lead is the key to any story.

The converse is also true—have you ever tried to read a story with a confusing or inappropriate lead, given up on the lead, and tried to read from the middle of the story to the end? I would assume you rarely do that. Most readers don't.

If you don't capture the reader at the top of the story, you lose that reader. The lead of any story—sports articles or any other beginning—attempts to accomplish at least six points:

- The lead draws the reader into the story.
- The lead educates the reader.
- The lead informs the reader about the story.
- The lead entertains the reader.
- The lead establishes the tone of the story.
- The lead establishes the expertise of the writer.

That's a lot to cram into the top of your stories, but it can be done.

How long should a lead be? In general, the lead of a news story is about three paragraphs. The lead of a feature story should be no longer than *about* one tenth of the complete story. If you have a 10-screen (10-page) story, then the lead could be up to about one page long. If you have a five-screen (five-page) story, then the lead could be about one-half page.

If the lead is too long, you risk having a reader ask, mentally, "What's this about and why am I reading this?"

No matter what type of lead you have, it should come to an obvious conclusion.

The more you know about types of leads, the better you will be as a writer, because you will have considerable choices of methods of beginnings.

Many sports writers who cover a game in progress—a university football game, for instance—will write the game as it progresses, on a laptop computer in the press box. When the game is over, they will scroll up through the story and "top" the story, by then adding the lead. The lead will usually come to them as the game progresses and "topping the story" is an easy method of adding the appropriate lead. *In all cases, the story dictates the lead, not vice versa.*

There are at least 25 recognizable types of leads appropriate for sports writing. They are discussed in the following sections of this chapter. When you are comfortable with all 25, don't forget they can be combined. In writing leads, you are limited only by your imagination.[1]

THE ANECDOTAL LEAD

An anecdote is a small, presumably true story about someone, showing character, behavior, or motivation. An anecdote placed "on top of" the complete story helps the reader understand the principal figure in the story.

All anecdotes should be meaningful—and should have an ending.

Here's a key to writing a story with an anecdote: When you are interviewing, ask Person A: "What is your favorite story?" That favorite story may well be a good anecdote to use to begin a feature.

Here Charles W. Hall of *The Washington Post* uses three anecdotes (high school lawsuit, college achievement, and a place on the Silver Bullets) to begin a feature about Julie Croteau, who always wanted to play baseball. (This also has elements of the timeline lead.) This article was run on *The Washington Post* wires in early April 1994.

> Since the age of 6, when she swung at baseballs perched on a tee, Julie Croteau has been a pioneer, a girl willing and able to play hardball with the boys.
>
> At her Prince William County, Va. high school, she sued for a chance to play on the varsity. As a freshman in college, she became the first woman to play on a men's NCAA baseball squad. And this week, Croteau won a place on the first women's professional baseball team in four decades.
>
> Croteau, who gained national attention when she played at St. Mary's College in Maryland, was named a first baseman with the Colorado Silver Bullets, a touring team that will play against men's minor-league and semiprofessional players.
>
> "I'm just elated," said Croteau, 23, who was one of 24 players chosen out of 1,300 women who tried out nationally. "I think this team will make a big difference for girls who are in the same shoes I grew up in."

---

[1] For leads in nonsports articles, see Fensch (1984, 1988).

Here is a perfect example of how a single anecdote is used to begin a story. Richie Whitt, writing for the *Fort Worth Star-Telegram*, shows quarterback Steve Beuerlein's personality with a brief glimpse at what he thinks of his championship ring, received when he was a member of the Dallas Cowboys. Beuerlein has since moved on to the Phoenix Cardinals. This article was run on the wires September 19, 1993:

PHOENIX—In a remote hallway of Steve Beuerlein's new, 4,000-square-foot home is a Super Bowl trophy replica from last year's championship season with the Dallas Cowboys. But the ring and the memories have been locked away.

"I showed the ring to the guys before the season started," Beuerlein said. "Then I put it in a safety deposit box. It's not my style to go flashing it around. Besides, I've got a new life now."

The Cowboys' backup quarterback last year, Beuerlein is the Phoenix Cardinals' handsomely paid savior.

In return for a three-year, $7.5 million contract (the most lucrative in team history) he signed as a free agent April 21, Beuerlein is expected to give a passing game, experienced leadership and a play-off berth to a franchise that is 42-86-1 the past nine seasons. The Cardinals last finished with a winning record in 1984 and last qualified for a non-strike postseason in 1975.

Tim Layden, writing for *Newsday*, uses an anecdote lead about Florida State University football star Charlie Ward's basketball techniques in an article run on the wires December 10, 1993:

When football season is finished at Florida State, players often congregate in the belly of the Moore Athletic Center, on the concrete-walled basketball court adjacent to the weight room. They play pickup games, fierce and serious, without form, only with bravado.

"Every man for himself," said defensive back Clifton Abraham. "Bring your best."

In the spring and summer, when his basketball season is finished, after the NCAA Tournament, Charlie Ward joins them. And wouldn't you know it?

"He's out there trying to set people up, use his basketball technique, playing team ball," Abraham said. "Everybody else is just firing it up. Charlie, he's not much for street ball."

Alan Page, once a key player with the Minnesota Vikings, is now a respected jurist in Minnesota. Here Jeremy Schaap uses an anecdotal lead to show Page as a member of the Minnesota Supreme Court. Schaap's article, headlined, "NOW HE TACKLES INJUSTICE," appeared in *Parade* magazine, the Sunday supplement, May 15, 1994 (p. 12).

The article was subtitled "Alan Page, once a mainstay of the Minnesota Vikings' defense, now fights for equality as a state Supreme Court justice."

"Would you please all rise for the honorable justices of the Supreme Court of Minnesota?" says the court clerk. One by one, four women and three men enter

Courtroom 300 of the Minnesota Judicial Center. The junior justice, Alan Page, bespectacled and bow-tied, leads the procession. He is wearing a black robe. He used to wear purple and white—the uniform of the Minnesota Vikings.

When he was elected to a six-year term in November 1992, Page moved from the state attorney general's office to the Minnesota Judicial Center, only a few miles from where he once anchored the Purple People Eaters, the Vikings' fearsome defensive line of the '70s.

"I love what I'm doing," says Page, Minnesota's first African-American Supreme Court justice, who looks distinctly judicial with his white beard and dark suit. "What you do on the playing field is great—for a moment—but what one does in a courtroom can have some real meaning, some lasting effect."

THE "BIG PLAY" LEAD

The home run that won a World Series game; a last-second touchdown that won a major college bowl game; a sprinter who lunged to break the tape and win by a millisecond. . . .

They often furnish sports writers ideal leads but the sports writer must watch and recognize the "big play" when it occurs. As a football game, an Olympic event, or a baseball game is in progress, sports writers must make mental notes regarding the lead to the story. A big play lead may present itself; the sports writer needs to recognize it when it takes place.

John Ferro of the Gannett News Service uses a key play—a missed field goal—to begin his story of the 1993 Army–Navy game.

(Note: In any game story, the names of the teams, where the game was played, and the score should all be somewhere in the top three paragraphs. Other items, such as a key play or the weather, if it was a factor, should also be in the lead.)

This article was run early in December 1993.

EAST RUTHERFORD, N.J.—The Navy football team could not have gotten much closer. Just one yard from the goal line, the Midshipmen were achingly close to a come-from-behind victory over Army, the Commander In Chief's trophy and a chance to honor a fallen teammate.

But the weightiest of moments fell on the shoulders of a freshman kicker with just two attempts in his career.

And so it was that Ryan Bucchianeri's 18-yard field goal try with six seconds remaining sailed wide right and gave Army a 16–14 victory before 67,852 at Giants Stadium Saturday.

The key to a game may not necessarily be a play on the field. Here Leonard Laye, writing for *The Charlotte Observer*, uses a key halftime event as the lead to a story about a Louisville–University of Minnesota baseball game, from late March 1994:

SACRAMENTO, Calif.—At half-time, his team trailing Minnesota by a dozen points, Louisville coach Denny Crum zipped into the locker room and headed straight for Clifford Rozier.

"Coach just asked me to do one thing. He begged me to do it," said Rozier, an All-America center. "He said, 'Son, we can't win if you keep forcing things.' "

Rozier got the message, albeit along with some very un-All-America stats. And the Cardinals got a 60–55 victory Sunday in Arco Arena, earning a spot in the NCAA Midwest Regional semifinals Thursday in Los Angeles.

THE CLASSIFIED AD LEAD

If you are stuck for a lead and nothing fits—no good quotations, no good descriptions, no question lead is apparent—and nothing works for your lead, turn to the nearest Sunday newspaper. How many categories of classified ads are there?

Dozens? Hundreds? You may be able to use a variation of a classified ad as the lead to a sports article.

In the following article, Neil Hohlfeld (1994) of the *Houston Chronicle* uses a help wanted ad to begin a story about baseball managers. (Notice also the interesting simile in his fifth paragraph: "Like building a fire or running a hotel, everyone in America believes he can do a better job managing a baseball team. . . ." That also, it seems to me, is an exceptional lead.)

Use of a variation of a classified ad for a story lead is limited only by your imagination, but bear in mind, this is a bit of a novelty lead—used once every hundred articles is about the right average. Otherwise, the uniqueness of this lead quickly fades.

Help Wanted

Brilliant tactician, media darling, ticket salesman, matinee idol. Must be able to think on feet 162 times a summer. Knowledge of baseball essential. Communication skills a must. Compensation: Low to mid-six figures—but be advised you will earn one-tenth the salary of some of your employees.

By Neil Hohlfeld
Houston Chronicle

So, you want to be a baseball manager? It looks easy, right? Make out the lineup card, bunt when you should bunt, pull the pitcher when you should pull the pitcher. Go on the talk shows, sit in first class, drive a big car, and let everyone hail your genius.

Explain, then, why every manager—in the language of baseball-ese—is on a day-to-day basis. Why every manager is an interim manager. Why the managerial carousel never stops, but merely slows to toss one victim off and take on another.

Just five managers in the 14-team National League have held their jobs longer than 18 months.

Since 1984, seven of the 12 NL teams (not counting the two 1993 expansion franchises) have had five or more managers. Chicago and Cincinnati have had seven apiece, an average job life span of less than 1½ years.

Like building a fire or running a hotel, everyone in America believes he can do a better job managing a baseball team than the 27 men who currently hold the coveted major-league jobs.

THE COMPARISON–CONTRAST LEAD

Compare two athletes, two coaches with different coaching philosophies, or two teams with different training styles and you pull your reader into your story:

- Which athlete is better?
- Which coach has the better technique?
- Which team should win and why?

Here John Jeansonne of *Newsday* uses this technique lead to compare two ice skating teams in the Lillehammer Olympics: Gordeeva and Grinkov and Mishkutenok and Dmitriev. This article was run on the wires February 15, 1994, during the Lillehammer Olympics.

HAMAR, Norway—Gordeeva and Grinkov were formal, Mishkutenok and Dmitriev industrial. The first couple seemed to be at a royal ball, the second in some Russian factory.

Actually, they all were in the middle of the best Olympic pairs figure-skating final anyone could remember.

Gordeeva and Grinkov were precision, taking traditional pairs skating—with him as the quiet straight man and her as the smiling, graceful butterfly—shining it up and putting it on display the way it rarely can be seen.

Mishkutenok and Dmitriev were passion, beginning with their costumes already slashed open at the thighs and arms, working as equal partners in an effort of creativity bordering on anger.

Mark Woods of the Gannett News Service uses a comparison of Shaquille O'Neal and David Robinson to begin a story about an April 30, 1993 game between the Orlando Magic and the San Antonio Spurs. Note that Woods uses the key word *contrasts* in the first paragraph.

ORLANDO, Fla.—The first meeting of the All-Star centers turned into a study of contrasts.

Shaquille O'Neal was youth, relying on muscle and anxious energy. David Robinson was experience, turning to patience and the flick of a sore wrist.

And, at least this time, the flick won.

Robinson, still hampered by a sprained thumb on his shooting hand, scored 23 points and grabbed 16 rebounds Sunday to lead the San Antonio Spurs out of a slump and to a 94–90 victory over the Orlando Magic.

"With my hand the way it was," Robinson said, "I didn't want to try and get it slapped a lot. So I really tried to isolate (O'Neal) on the floor. I think the key was that I made him work."

Rich Hoffman, writing for the *Philadelphia Daily News*, compares Duke's Grant Hill and Purdue's Glenn Robinson in the southeast regional NCAA basketball tournament, late in March 1994:

KNOXVILLE, Tenn.—Two dunks. We will begin there.

Duke's Grant Hill takes the ball somewhere near Nashville and begins his drive. He leaps; he flies. The poor fellow between him and the basket is Marquette's Jim McIlvaine, all 7–1 of him. Hill ends up dunking the ball, fiercely. McIlvaine ends up in a heap. Hill stands over him, then ends up woofing—at his teammates.

"I was excited," he said. "I just wanted to share the emotion."

Next game in the NCAA Southeast Regional. Purdue's Glenn Robinson is down at the same end of the Arena. His victim is Greg Ostertag, a 7–2 guy from Kansas. Robinson annihilated him. After the dunk, Robinson just stood over the body. He stared Ostertag down, until Ostertag reacted in the perfect way. He shook Robinson's hand.

Congratulations.

Hill and Robinson. Make that Robinson and Hill. They are the two best players left in this NCAA Tournament. Jalen Rose and Juwan Howard of a Michigan will make a lot of money in the NBA, as will Connecticut's Donyell Marshall. But Robinson is best and Hill is next. After today, only [one] will be left.

The life of two University of Michigan basketball players is compared in a story by *Detroit Free Press* writer Greg Stoda. He clearly uses a comparison–contrast lead in his article about Bobby Crawford and Dugan Fife. This article was run in early December 1993.

ANN ARBOR, Mich.—One sat on the bench, and sometimes played. The other sat in the living room, and sometimes dreamed.

A year ago, the distances from the bright lights of Michigan basketball were vastly different, but in another way much the same for Bobby Crawford and Dugan Fife.

Life on the fringe.

Fife was then a Michigan freshman. He arrived in Ann Arbor with a reputation as a big scorer after averaging 27.7 points as a senior at Clarkston (Mich.) High, where he threw in a 49-point outing along the way.

And promptly made not a single field goal in his first season as a Wolverine.

"That was the hardest thing—not shooting," said Fife, who took only nine shots last season. "That was an adjustment."

So Crawford, then a high-scoring senior at Houston Eisenhower who had signed with Michigan, saw little of Fife when he tuned in Michigan games on the family television.

After five games as a freshman this season, Crawford hasn't experienced the scoring frustrations Fife did, but there have been troubling moments.

"It was tougher than I thought it would be coming in," Crawford said. "An open shot is an open shot, but you have to do so much more to get one."

Alan Truex, sports writer for the *Houston Chronicle*, clearly uses a comparison lead in a story about Art Howe, fired manager of the Houston Astros and his replacement, Terry Collins. This article was run under a headline "On Top and Nonstop," and subhead "Collins' revved-up style will give Astros a new look" and was published in the *Chronicle* on December 24, 1993.

There are obvious contrasts between Terry Collins, the Astros' new manager, and his predecessor, Art Howe.

Howe is tall—6–1. Collins is short—5–8.

Howe is bald. Collins can be hair-raising.

Howe seemed incapable of anger. Even when he stalked an umpire, it seemed he was operating out of a sense of obligation rather than conviction.

Howe was stoic, imperturbable, laid-back. Collins is animated, intense, involved.

Pausing for an interview after a recent whirlwind day at the Astrodome, Collins said: "I'm not like Art. I have a temper. I won't kick any water coolers, but I might swear on the bench."

And in the clubhouse. (p. C1)

THE DELAYED CLIMAX LEAD

Occasionally, a writer may delay the point of a lead; the reader has to read down through the lead to discover the point. Thus the name *delayed climax.*

Here Charlie Meyers of *The Denver Post* uses a delayed climax lead for his story of the Italy–Norway cross-country ski race during the Lillehammer Olympics. This was run on the wires February 22, 1994.

His key line (the fourth paragraph): "In the Super Bowl of Nordic skiing, Buffalo won."

LILLEHAMMER, Norway—To the shock and chagrin of 105,000 Norwegians, interlopers from Italy stole the grandest cross-country ski prize of these Olympic Games, the men's 4x10-kilometer relay.

The Italians did it when their youngest racer outkicked Norway's great champion, Bjorn Dahlie, on the final leg. And they did it by selecting a 43-year-old in his final season to start the race.

When Silvio Fauner, a 25-year-old with a modest portfolio, beat Dahlie to the finish line by four-hundredths of a second following a dramatic side-by-side sprint, a roaring throng fell deathly silent as if someone had flipped a switch.

In the Super Bowl of Nordic skiing, Buffalo won.

Here is a perfect example of a delayed climax lead. Michael Murphy, writing for the *Houston Chronicle*, profiles a Houston-area pitcher, Ronny Carroll, who had decided to attend Southwest Texas State University in San Marcos. After a key telephone call, he changed his mind and decided to attend Texas Christian University in Fort Worth. This article was published in the *Houston Chronicle* May 11, 1994. The headline is shown under the lead.

> Ronny Carroll still smiles when he talks about "the phone call."
>
> A senior pitcher for Langham Creek High School, Carroll was home icing his arm last month after a District 20-5A victory over Cy-Fair when the phone rang.
>
> Carroll picked up the phone and heard an oddly familiar voice.
>
> "Hi, Ronny," the voice started. "This is . . ."
>
> Before the caller could finish, Carroll knew. He was talking with Nolan Ryan.
>
> "I knew right away (who it was)," he said. "I recognized the voice from somewhere. I just said, 'Whoa.' It was wild."
>
> It would get wilder.
>
> "I was wondering why he was calling me," Carroll said. "I figured there was no way he was calling to congratulate me on the game I just pitched. Then, he told me about TCU."
>
> Ryan, a restricted-earnings coach at Texas Christian, was calling in an official capacity. He had seen a pitcher he wanted on the Horned Frogs' staff. In other words, he wanted Carroll.
>
> "I just liked him," Ryan said. "He had good command of his breaking ball, and he throws the ball with good velocity. I think his velocity will improve, too."
>
> Ryan should know. So it was goodbye, Southwest Texas—where Carroll was originally planning to go—and hello, TCU.
>
> "When Nolan Ryan calls, you go," said Carroll's father, Ronny Sr. "What a huge recruiting tool. He wanted Ronny, so that's where he's going."
>
> It didn't matter one bit that Carroll, who has compiled an 8–3 record with a 0.79 ERA for the Lobos, has only one arm, his left. (p. C1)

The *Houston Chronicle's* headline for this story was: "What handicap?"

THE DESCRIPTIVE LEAD

Descriptions can often mean exceptional leads for sports features. The keys to writing description are:

• If you are writing about a location so well known that readers may have *icons*—mental pictures of it in their minds—like the Kentucky Derby or a typical major university football stadium, go behind the scenes to show the reader some aspect of the location they could not imagine or have not seen on ESPN.

• If you are writing about a remote location, fill in all the details so readers can see that location in their own imagination.

- If you are in a remote location, don't naturally assume your readers know what to look for.

- If you are on location to witness an event, "talk the details" of the scene into a tape recorder. Listening to the tape later will help you reconstruct the picture you need to show in your lead.

In this descriptive lead Sandra Blakeslee shows a remote and captivating location for kayaking—the Sea of Cortés—to begin her article "Kayaking In Splendor for Cardiac Fitness." Her article appeared in *The New York Times Magazine*, April 24, 1994.

> Dawn is breaking over the Sea of Cortés. The horizon, an inky blue, is crowned with an iridescent, salmon light that paints the underside of meandering clouds with the rays of a sun that has not yet climbed up to the edge of the earth. In utter stillness, the little sea kayak moves easily out toward the Mercenaries—a jagged outcrop of volcanic and sedimentary spires two miles from the coastline of Baja California Sur in Mexico. Bestrewn with osprey nests, the rocks also shelter flocks of cormorants, blue-footed boobies, peregrine falcons, ravens, hawks and score of pelicans preening before breakfast. Near the kayak, six porpoises leap from the water, their backs glistening in the rising light.
>
> Halfway to the rocks, a pair of fins stick out of the water.
>
> Actually, they turn out to be flippers, and they belong to a sea lion, asleep on its back. It seems to be snoring, but opens one eye, sees the kayak and, with a comical, shocked look, dives below. (p. 60)

THE "EPIC GAME" LEAD

How often can you call a game an epic? One game in a season? Perhaps not even one in a season for many college and university football teams. One game in a hundred? One game in a decade?

Bob Ryan, writing for *The Boston Globe* called the October 2, 1993 Boston College–Syracuse University football game an epic. Boston College won 33–29 at Syracuse. Notice Ryan calls the game an epic without the use of overblown style. Nothing wrecks a true epic story as quickly as excessive gushing on the part of a sports writer.

> SYRACUSE, N.Y.—There are 106 Division I-A teams playing college football, and they are going to play a whole mess o' games this season. Not many will be better than Boston College–Syracuse.
>
> This will be remembered as the Great Carrier Dome Shootout. This is one game which will surely be recalled when the Boston College team members get together in their future reunion guises as insurance agents, high school coaches, Commonwealth of Massachusetts political appointees and perhaps even NFL players.
>
> As the years roll by, they're going to be telling taller and taller tales about who did what in the Carrier Dome, making even more of Saturday's epic 33–29 conquest

of Syracuse than they were doing in the immediate aftermath of a victory which might very well send them on the way to a highly satisfying season.

Dennis Georgatos, writing for the Associated Press, called the October 2, 1993, California–Oregon game "one of the greatest comebacks in college football history." California came back from a 30–0 deficit to beat Oregon 42–41. His lead read:

> BERKELEY, Calif.—California staged one of the greatest comebacks in college football history Saturday.
>
> Dave Barr threw three second-half scoring passes, the last a 26-yarder to Iheanyi Uwaezuoke with 1:17 left as the Golden Bears overcame a 30–0 deficit to beat Oregon 42–41.
>
> "People were going crazy," Barr said. "I don't know if I'll ever have a feeling like this again. We were down, beaten. We were hurting. We weren't feeling good about ourselves, and we came back. We wouldn't accept no for an answer."
>
> The return from 30 points down to win was second only to two 31-point comebacks, by Maryland in a 42–40 victory over Miami on Nov. 10, 1984, and Ohio State's 41–37 win over Minnesota on Oct. 28, 1989.
>
> It was the biggest comeback ever by Cal, surpassing a 29–28 win against Arizona on Nov. 4, 1989, in which the Bears overcame a 21–0 deficit.

THE "FALSE" LEAD

Writers don't lie to their readers. But occasionally, an ingenious writer *can leave out* one element of a lead—to suggest a different place, time, idea, or possibility.

Here is the title: "I'm not just a jock." It appeared in *The Houston Post* on September 14, 1993.

Here is writer Bonnie Gangelhoff's first two paragraphs:

> First the pale pink nail polish. Then the gold stud earrings and the monogrammed purse.
> Is this any way for a football player to dress?

Well, you think, some players wear ear studs. Joe Namath used to wear pantyhose under his Jet uniform. Pale pink nail polish? Could be. Monogrammed purse? Errrr, maybe.

Here is Gangelhoff's third paragraph:

> It is if she's a girl. (p. D1)

Gangelhoff omitted Erin Shilk's sex momentarily, in an attempt to convince the reader that she was talking about someone else; someone male.

Here are Gangelhoff's next few paragraphs:

Meet Erin Shilk, 5-foot-3 and 108 pounds: lover of the Aggies, boys, soccer, country & western music, cooking and chemistry. She's a girl blazing a trail for the '90s.

Two weeks ago, amid a media blitz, Shilk, 15, kicked her way into the history books of the Cypress Falls sophomore football team. The barefoot place-kicker made two extra points and became the only area girl to play high school football. Then, last Thursday, Shilk kicked another two extra points against Sharpstown High School. Her team won, 14–6.

Shilk is one of five girls in Texas taking advantage of a University Interscholastic League rule passed last year, which for the first time allows girls to participate in the sport.

She's grabbed headlines for her football abilities, but happily consented to an interview off the playing field because she wants people to know, "I'm not *just* a jock." (p. D1)

This is a variation of the delayed climax lead, discussed earlier. How can the false lead be used?

Like Gangelhoff's article, the sex of a subject can be omitted. The writer could omit the age of an athlete, to convince the reader that a golfer, for instance, is a national tournament-caliber player. The actual player could be a teenager (or younger) or the player could be a senior citizen, shooting well under his or her age.

As in the Michael Murphy story about Texas Christian University pitcher Ronny Carroll (see p. 27), the writer can let the reader assume the pitcher has both arms. Murphy tells the reader at the end of the lead that Carroll has only his left arm.

The writer could omit the time (date) when the action occurs to convince the reader that the sports event took place years ago, or the writer could omit the time to convince the readers that a decades-old boxing match took place this year, for instance.

The writer could omit the time and details to convince readers that a gladiator was dressing for the Roman arena. In fact, the story could be about a pro football player today (although a football players as gladiators or football as war is something of a cliché).

There is a great deal of current interest in re-enactments of Civil War battles, with 1990s "summer soldiers and sunshine patriots" (p. 41) in blue and grey, to quote Kuklick's (1989) *The Crisis Papers (Thomas Paine: Political Writings)*.

Clearly, this is an ideal story assignment for use of a false lead. Should your readers be thinking of the original Battle of Gettysburg, or a re-enactment of that battle? Leave out the date and let them believe, momentarily, that the re-enactment is the original battle.

THE FUTURE LEAD

Can you use an educated guess about the future to begin a feature article? Of course. The guess should be based on logic and plausibility. A future lead should trigger all sorts of possibilities about the sport you are discussing.

A future lead could begin something like this:

By the year 2010, Japanese teams will have won the Super Bowl three times and be aiming for a fourth win.

That string of consecutive Super Bowl wins was triggered when Jimmy Johnson was fired as coach of the Dallas Cowboys after the 1993–1994 season.

The actual chain of events that culminated in the Japanese victories began when Johnson was hired by a group of Japanese officials three years after he left the Cowboys.

That management group, headed by officials from Sony with virtually unlimited financing, allowed the Japanese to buy an available NFL franchise and move it to Tokyo.

And never again would a Super Bowl victory be guaranteed for USA teams.

Do you recall a sci-fi film called *Rollerball*, about futuristic gladiators in massive "pinball" roller-derby events? That film, starring James Caan, was originally a short story in *Esquire* magazine.

THE "I" LEAD

The first-person "I" is the writer talking to the reader. This technique is often used in a personal column, but can be used in a participant article ("This is what I did when I ran the Boston Marathon. . . .").

Here Steve Wilstein of the Associated Press uses the "I" form in a piece about how many players in the 1994 college basketball Final Four Tournament had tattoos. In addition to Corliss Williamson, who is mentioned in the lead, Lee Wilson, Corey Beck, and Darnell Robinson of Arkansas all had tattoos. Marty Clark of Duke and four members of the Purdue women's team had tattoos.

This article was run on the wire services on April 4, 1994.

CHARLOTTE, N.C.—I'm at the Final Four and I have to get a tattoo. It's the thing to do.

I'm wondering how an ornery Arkansas Razorback, tusks and all, would look side by side with a Duke Blue Devil.

Or maybe the Corliss Williamson look: Tasmanian devil near his heart, his initials on the right side of his chest, and his nickname, "Nasty."

I asked him why he did it and he said:

"It's just one of the wild things you do when you first get into college."

Raoul Estlinbaum of *The Houston Post* went fishing for redfish in the Gulf of Mexico near Houston and not only came back with a big one ("maybe 35 pounds") but also an "I" lead for a story, run September 23, 1993, under the headline "With redfish, it's a fight to the end."

Estlinbaum omitted the "I" form after the first six paragraphs of the story.

The strike caught me off-guard, almost yanking the rod out of my hand. The line ripped sideways as a big redfish surfaced briefly, then executed a power dive, taking out 30 yards of line.

For the next 15 minutes, the bronze brute and I engaged in a game of tug-of-war, a seesaw battle that went back and forth with neither side gaining much ground. Slowly, the battle started to swing my way, but not without considerable effort.

Finally, an exhausted red, maybe 35 pounds, came belly up, no longer able to resist. Mike Williams lifted the hardy fish out of the water, removed the hook and revived the weary warrior, sliding it gently back and forth to get water moving through its gills.

"These reds are big-time fighters," Williams said, watching the fish swim away. "Like tarpon, they give it everything they've got." (p. C-10)

Steve Howland, of *The Houston Post*, uses an appropriate "I" beginning in an article about deer hunting in east Texas. He also uses the "I" form throughout the article. His article was published December 2, 1993, under the headline "Patience pays off big time for hunter."

BRUSHY CREEK EXPERIMENTAL FOREST—This place is definitely a successful experiment.

I'm sitting here in a ground blind, being eaten alive by a large family of mosquitoes, and not feeling a thing because I'm looking at the biggest deer *I've* ever seen in the flesh.

I haven't been to Champion International's 25,000-acre game and timber reserve since 1988, when Houston Post carpentry supervisor and master deer hunter Henry Duran and I made a visit to gather venison for his booth at The Post's annual Chili Cookoff.

That was my first visit here and I got a nice nine-point, my best buck in seven years of deer hunting, on the first night out. (p. B-12)

Howland's end paragraph refers to his colleague Henry Duran and Duran's promise that Howland would get his deer.

The ending was:

Henry and I meet up in camp. He has harvested an antlerless for the chili pot. He will get the venison from my deer, and I'll settle for the horns and a backstrap or two. Henry casually looks at the deer, congratulates me and sums it all up:

"I told you," he says, shaking his finger my way, "I told you he'd be there."

Fred King of *The Houston Post* uses an "I" lead to begin a story about how *not* to begin hunting season. *The Houston Post* ran this article under a headline "Abundance of game makes Hill Country hunt a snap" on November 18, 1993. (The Hill Country is a huge swatch of woodlands beginning west of Austin. Fredericksburg and Kerrville, Texas, are in the middle of the Hill Country.)

I breathe and exhale, and the crosshairs settle exactly where I want them. Baalowww! . . . Damn!

I've drawn blood with my first shot. But the season's not open yet. And it's my blood.

I'm at Bayou Rifles checking my zero two days before the whitetail season starts in most of Texas. Since I got a hard case for my rifles, the zero has changed little. However, things happen. In my book, it is unethical to go hunting unless you have checked your zero.

And, this year, for the first time in many years, I'm not using my favorite handload in the .264 Winchester Mag. I just ran out of time to reload and was lucky to find both my license and a box of 140-grain factory ammo in the same place.

I'm going with new ammo to a new place, Bill Carter's Apache Springs Ranch at Hunt, in the Hill Country.

What was eagerness a moment ago feels like dumbness. The spots on my finger confirm it's my blood, from just above my right eyebrow. Settling in on the bench, wearing the field jacket I'll wear if it's really cold at Carter's, I've held the rifle too loosely and edged too close to the scope.

THE INTERIOR MONOLOGUE LEAD

Try to think about how other people think. It's almost impossible, and there is seldom a perfect method in print to show how people think, brainstorm, and scheme.

The novelist James Joyce used interior monologues, or *thought processes*, in his book *Ulysses*. (The voice-over in some films is often the thought processes of the hero, especially a detective tracking a case: *I thought he was a crook because of his shifty eyes* . . . , or words to that effect, so viewers can better follow the film.)

It's possible, however, to sometimes use thoughts of others in articles. You first have to know—by interviewing—what they were thinking, what they were planning, and what they were trying to do. Then you can attempt to get this on the page, usually by fragmented sentences, often set apart typographically with italic type or boldface.

In this article by Jim Reeves of the *Fort Worth Star-Telegram*, from March 1994, the thought processes of Jose Canseco are shown in the fourth paragraph, beginning: "The trade to Texas? No big deal. . . ."

Later in the article, Reeves quotes Canseco explaining what he was thinking, which is always a good idea to backstop the thought processes.

PORT CHARLOTTE, Fla.—The thought came to him in his darkest hours over the last year, when he could see no way to slow the careening, runaway horror that his life had become.

"Suicide."

On the outside, Jose Canseco laughed.

The trade to Texas? No big deal. The divorce? Shrug. Lots of women out there. Blow an elbow trying to pitch? Just another of life's little speed bumps.

On the inside, Canseco twisted and writhed in the stew of his own despair. He seriously considered, on more than one occasion, taking his own life.

"You have all this money, all these material things, and you're still not happy," Canseco says. "What's the sense of going on with it all? That (suicide) is the next stop."

THE "LETTER TO" LEAD

Every newspaper publishes a letters-to-the-editor column or page. Sports writers might occasionally use a "letter to" or "memo to" technique, either as the lead to a feature article or, usually, as a column or opinion piece.

Here Mike Cochran, staff writer for the Dallas–Fort Worth bureau of the Associated Press, uses a "letter to" format in an article about the Dallas Cowboys. He uses this technique throughout the article. This was moved on the AP wires January 29, 1994.

Last year, AP correspondent Mike Cochran followed the Dallas Cowboys to Super Bowl XXVII to report on the offbeat activities of the Boys in La La Land. This year, with no sand, sea, surf or starlets in Atlanta, he is sending a letter.

By Mike Cochran
Associated Press

DALLAS—Hey, there, Big Guys, how's it going in the land of grits and gravy?

I know you plan to kick some serious Buffalo tail today, but some folks felt a letter from home might be in order. Frankly, we're a bit worried about Super Bowl XXVIII.

A rematch with the Bills doesn't exactly light a roaring fire.

And after La La Land, and that Southern California sun, it's gotta be tough. No stars and starlets. No Sunset Strips and Beverly Hills. No beaches and bikinis. No sushi and champagne.

Mark Purdy, of the *San Jose Mercury News*, writes a letter to Joe Montana, late of the San Francisco 49ers, traded to the Kansas City Chiefs. This article, under the headline "Dear Joe: Steve gives thumb up to Week 1" was run in the *Houston Chronicle* on September 7, 1993 with the subhead "Commentary." The entire article, some 29 paragraphs long, was written as a letter. Purdy signed the letter: "Yours truly, The scarlet Heroes of Yore."

PITTSBURGH—Dear Joe:

Howdy. It's us. Your old pals, the San Francisco 49ers. Hey, congratulations on the victory. We had a great opener, too. Wish you could've been here.

It was a swell weekend for us, except for Ricky Watters' interesting career decision to become a pro wrestling promoter and provoke the entire Steelers roster into a Three Rivers death match.

Anyway, since you weren't able to see the game—which we the Niners won, of course—let us give you a summation in the form of a riddle.

Question: How many Pittsburgh Steelers does it take to screw in a light bulb?
Answer: Only one. But if you are linebacker Kevin Greene and no light bulbs are handy, you try and screw Steve Young into the ground instead.

THE "LIST" HEAD

We use the term *menu* daily regarding computers and computer usage; sports writers may also use a menu or "list of ingredients"—usually highlighted with black bullets, asterisks, or boxes. Highlighting this list material on the page helps readers comprehend it visually.

Here John Hillyer of the *San Francisco Examiner* uses such a list to highlight the competition between the Golden State Warriors and the Portland Trail Blazers. (This is also an example of a comparison–contrast lead). This article was moved on the wires March 8, 1994.

SEATTLE—The Warriors meet the Trail Blazers again Thursday night in Oakland. After Monday night's precedent-setting 137–108 loss in Portland, what might the world expect in the rematch?

"We got 'em right where we want 'em," Don Nelson said.

Golden State's coach must be counting on the Blazers showing up overconfident. After what happened Monday, it would be a remarkable example of mental discipline if they didn't.

Just count the new season highs—or lows, depending on your perspective—to emerge Monday night:

- Biggest margin of defeat by the Warriors.
- Biggest margin of victory by the Blazers.
- Most points allowed by the Warriors.
- Most points scored by the Blazers.
- Most first-quarter points (38) scored by the Blazers, and a tie for the most allowed by the Warriors.
- Most fourth-quarter points (44) scored by the Blazers.
- Most baskets (59) made by the Blazers.
- Most baskets allowed by the Warriors.
- Most assists (38) by the Blazers, and a tie for the most allowed by the Warriors.

THE LITERARY REFERENCE LEAD

One of the never-to-be-violated commandments of sports writing should be: *Never use a cliché*. It is, however, occasionally clever to turn a phrase sideways or upside down and come up with a fresh lead to captivate your readers.

Here Mike Conklin of the *Chicago Tribune* recasts the old phrase "No greater love . . ." for a clever lead, run February 15, 1994.

GJOVIC, Norway—Greater love hath no U.S. hockey player than to donate two front teeth to the Olympic cause.

In the case of left winger Craig Johnson, the gap he displayed after getting introduced to the stick of a Slovakian player late in Tuesday's 3–3 tie meant everyone in the U.S. contingent could keep smiling.

But, as you might suspect, it wasn't pretty.

This was the second tie in as many games for the Americans, who must finish no worse than fourth in its six-nation pool to advance to the quarterfinals. The United States is deadlocked with Slovakia, which tied Sweden in their opener, in the third spot with three games remaining.

It is also possible to use song lyrics, lines of a poem, or a quotation from a novel or play, either in the lead or above the byline. The more sophisticated the quotation, the more sophisticated your lead.

On December 26, 1993, the *Houston Chronicle* used the first page of the Sports 2 section (p. B19), their section of sports features, and ran a banner headline: "HELLO, GOODBYE." It was in 1¼-inch high type, blue with black shadows. On the right was a major story about the year in sport, nationally. In the middle of the page was a six-column-wide color photo of Michael Jordan during his last press conference. Down the left-side column was a highlight story of key sports events of 1993 in Houston.

Jayne Custred wrote the national wrap-up story and because sports and country music are king in Texas, she began with a Garth Brooks lyric, for her story, subheaded:

Dance Ends Far Too Soon for Big Stars

And I'm glad I didn't know
The way it all would end
The way it all would go
Our lives are better left to chance
We could have missed the pain
But we'd of had to miss the dance.
—Garth Brooks

By Jayne Custred
Houston Chronicle

Davey Allison danced through life, living it to the fullest, embracing its wonders along with its dangers.

Heather Farr never missed a beat, never lost a step despite her battle with cancer. And Reggie Lewis was dancing at the end, doing what he loved best despite the risks.

The music stopped for many in 1993, long before the dance was supposed to end. Yet the melodies of their lives remain with us, reminding us that tragedy comes to everyone, whether superstar, hero or idol.

It was an amazing year in sports. The Chicago Bulls captured a third straight NBA title—then saw their hopes for a fourth virtually disappear when megastar Michael Jordan shockingly retired; the USA hung on to the coveted Ryder Cup trophy; Joe Carter ripped a dramatic homer that handed the Blue Jays a second straight World Series; and Don Shula broke George Halas' NFL record for career wins.

But the triumphs and victories were so overshadowed by the tragedies and the losses that 1993 will best be remembered as the year of goodbyes.

Neil Best of *Newsday* uses a Thoreau quotation to begin an article about runner Keith Brantly who found the heart of Africa in, as Best writes, "of all places, Concord, Mass." Best's article ran in November 1993.

> *"The mass of men lead lives of quiet desperation."*
> —Henry David Thoreau

> By Neil Best
> Newsday

NEW YORK—Not Keith Brantly. He rejected the notion American men can't win the New York City Marathon anymore and boldly struck out in search of the figurative heart of Africa, home to many of the world's best long-distance runners.

He's found it in, of all places, Concord, Mass., site of an early battle in the Revolutionary War and hometown of Henry David Thoreau—about as American a place as you'll find.

Brantly, a 31-year-old Floridian, spent most of August there. He trained with elite Kenyan athletes, living their Spartan lifestyle, sleeping in a dorm at Concord Academy (where Thoreau studied in the late 1820s) and running the perimeter of Thoreau's beloved Walden Pond.

It was an anthropological adventure in his own land.

"You can't be successful unless you emulate success," Brantly said of his decision to accept an invitation to join the Kenyans.

Shannon Tompkins, outdoors writer for the *Houston Chronicle*, uses an old song lyric from the Lovin' Spoonful to begin a nice piece about the simple magic of fishin'. This article, under the headline "Childhood bass-fishing memories live," appeared in the *Chronicle* on August 1, 1993.

> *"Do you believe in magic? . . . It'll free your soul."*
> —The Lovin' Spoonful, circa 1967

Magic is everywhere when you're a kid.

Whitey Ford and Mickey Mantle were magic. So was a grove of trees where the shadows and bushes became Yankee soldiers that you vanquished with a saber made of cane. Every day was a new adventure and no seam separated the physical from the metaphysical.

But then you grow up, read *Ball Four*, see the unspeakable horrors of war, learn other brutal truths of life . . . and the magic evaporates. Childhood's magic becomes like a cup of coffee left out too long, eventually, all you're left with is the ugly crust of what once was something enjoyable.

If you're lucky, a few faint embers of that early magic hide somewhere deep in the synapses, waiting for just the right breeze to fan them back to life.

It wasn't much of a breeze—more a breath of humid fog than wind—but it was enough. Standing on the banks of a little lake an hour before sunrise a week ago, that feeling of magic surged out of the past. It was the magic of a topwater plug and summer bass. (p. B21)

In this lead, Neal Farmer, sports writer for the *Houston Chronicle*, uses a quotation from Tennyson to begin an article about Rice University's long losing streak in football against the University of Texas. (This lead also contains elements of a timeline lead.) This lead, in a story headlined "Rice looking to snap skid against Texas," was run in the *Chronicle* on September 28, 1993 (PS: Rice lost again to Texas, 55–38).

> *"Forward the Light Brigade!*
> *Charge for the guns," he said:*
> *Into the valley of Death*
> *Rode the 600.*
> —from Alfred, Lord Tennyson's
> *The Charge of the Light Brigade*

By Neal Farmer
Houston Chronicle

Twenty-seven times the Rice Owls have ridden into battle against the University of Texas, and 27 times they have lost. Twenty-two starters over 27 years means 594 Rice starters—nearly 600—have lost to the Longhorns.

It is the second-longest such current streak in NCAA football, behind only the 29 consecutive decisions Notre Dame has over Navy.

Fifth-year Rice coach Fred Goldsmith said his troops have not lost 27 games, just four since he has been here. And the burden is not as big as one might think. (p. B1)

Larry Dierker, TV–radio analyst for the Houston Astros, uses a quotation from Jim Bouton above paragraph one to begin an article about Black National League President Len Coleman. Dierker's article appeared in the *Houston Chronicle* on March 21, 1994.

> *"You spend a good piece of life gripping a baseball, and in the end it turns out that it was the other way around all the time."*
> —Jim Bouton

KISSIMMEE, Fla.—Last week, when Len Coleman addressed the media at Osceola Stadium, it became evident that you do not have to actually play in the major leagues to feel the grip of the game.

Coleman grew up in New York. His mother, who taught him about baseball, was a Dodgers fan. His father liked the Giants. And directly upstairs lived a neighbor who rooted for the Yankees all the way.

That was how it started for the new president of the National League. "I was a Dodgers fan like my mother," Coleman said. "But as you can imagine, things got pretty lively around the house when the topic turned to baseball."

Like his predecessor, Bill White, Coleman is a black man who grew up in the era of Jackie Robinson. Now as an adult, he looks back on the game of his youth and sees something uniquely American. And as he embarks on his own baseball odyssey, Coleman knows he is treading on hallowed ground. (p. C2)

Houston Chronicle writer and columnist Ed Fowler used a quotation from Shakespeare above the first paragraph to begin a story about the 1993 Ryder Cup matches. This piece appeared in the *Houston Chronicle* on September 24, 1993.

Young Cassius has a lean and hungry look. He thinks too much. Such men are dangerous.

—Julius Caesar,
from William Shakespeare's *Julius Caesar*

SUTTON COLDFIELD, England—Tom Watson, freckled-faced and gap-toothed, has been compared to his fellow Middle American Tom Sawyer often enough, but never to a scheming Roman. Perhaps he has been transformed here in Warwickshire, which as the road signs remind us is "Shakespeare's country."

This weekend it's the land of high tea and sniper fire as that serialized international incident known as the Ryder Cup returns to the Belfry. We recently have seen that there is room enough on this mortal coil for Israelis and Palestinians, but can it accommodate American and British golf pros?

At a black-tie dinner Wednesday night, Watson, the U.S. captain, instructed his players not to sign autographs and himself twice refused to sign for Sam Torrance, a member of the European team. Man the ramparts, boys. The battle is joined. (p. B1)

A quotation from Pat Riley's book was used above the lead paragraph to begin an article about the Knicks and the Bulls. This article, by Rich Hofmann of the *Philadelphia Daily News*, was run in May 1994.

Knicks overcome loss of Harper to take control

"In every contest, there comes a moment that defines winning from losing. The true warrior understands and seizes that moment by giving an effort so intense and so intuitive that it could only be called one from the heart."

—from Pat Riley's *The Winner Within*

By Rich Hofmann
Philadelphia Daily News

NEW YORK—Gifts from the sky. Free throws from the heart. The Knicks have survived a Game 5 against the Chicago Bulls. And there is a pattern developing here. They came from behind early. They came from behind late. Three times out of

four in this series, they have won the end game when the end game was in doubt—
including Wednesday night at Madison Square Garden 87–86.

The Knicks have seized the moment, as Riley wrote. But this night, they seized it
after it was dropped into their laps.

Terry Blount of the *Houston Chronicle* uses a memorable Dickens line to begin
a story about Jerry Glanville's tenure as head coach of the Houston Oilers. This
article was run in December 1993 when Glanville was fired as head coach of the
Atlanta Falcons. The headline was "Oilers recall Glanville era with mixed emotions."

To hear the Oilers players describe the Jerry Glanville era, it sounds like the start
of a Charles Dickens novel:

It was the best of times. It was the worst of times.

"Jerry is a complex individual," quarterback Cody Carlson said. "I think down
deep, he's a good man. But I could see what was coming here. It was a circus and
we should have put a tent around the facility.

"A lot of people had gotten tired of him because they really didn't understand him.
And I don't know that he wants to be understood."

Glanville was the head coach for four full seasons in Houston (1986–89) and led
the team to the playoffs in his last three years. The players who were here at the time
have mixed feelings about his tenure, which sometimes seemed like a roller-coaster
ride in the dark.

Shannon Tompkins uses another literary reference, to the novel *The River Why?*,
to begin an article about duck hunting.

His article, headlined "Of dawn, ducks and memories," was published in the
Houston Chronicle on November 25, 1993.

In his transcendental novel, *The River Why?*, author David James Duncan's lead
character is a young adult man consumed by fishing and trying to come to grips with
it.

The character, Gus, comes to understand that some people don't share his
commitment, but can live happy lives nonetheless. But Gus also understands that *his*
life is and almost certainly always will be defined by fishing, both in the physical and
metaphysical sense.

That epiphany hits him when he realizes he can remember every one of the hundreds
of fishing experiences he's had. And that, he sees, is not so much a sign of his cognitive
ability as it is a manifestation of fishing's hold on his soul.

"It's not an ability to remember," Gus says to himself. "It's an inability to forget."

A couple of hours before dawn Saturday morning, with the stars of Orion the
Hunter hanging in the cold sky overhead, I stood in the coastal marsh I've hunted for
almost 25 years and felt a lot like Gus. (p. B16)

Kevin Kernan, writing for the Copley News Service, uses a reference to Norman
Rockwell's nostalgic paintings to begin an article about Lenny Dykstra. This article
was run the first week in October 1993. Kernan uses an apt reference, but with any

such dated references the question should be asked: Because many baseball fans are, say, under 25, how many of them will know who Norman Rockwell was?

> PHILADELPHIA—Picture a Norman Rockwell painting of a baseball player surrounded by young fans. Phils center fielder Lenny Dykstra wouldn't be the ballplayer, he'd be the dirty-faced kid trying to sneak onto the field.
>
> If there's one player who epitomizes the hard-nosed style of the Phillies, it is Dykstra. While the Braves may be America's Team, the Phils are painted as America's Bad Boys.
>
> As reliever Mitch Williams said of the National League Championship Series battle that begins tonight at Veterans Stadium, "(The Braves) were expected to win. We were expected to be in prison."

Kevin Blackistone, writer for *The Dallas Morning News*, refers to the Addams Family (and Clyde the Glide and Earl the Pearl and Magic Johnson) in the lead of his article about Arkansas basketball player Dwight Stewart. This article was run late in March 1994.

> DALLAS—Dwight Stewart stands 6–8. He weighs at least 260 pounds. Much of his bulk looks to be in his shoulders, which are hunched and rounded like Morticia and Gomez's butler.
>
> But Stewart is no Lurch. He's Nimble B. Quick on, of all places, the basketball court.
>
> In the second half of an NCAA Tournament game last weekend against Georgetown, Stewart dribbled into the paint like Clyde the Glide, made an Earl the Pearl twirl and passed with Magic precision to a cutter on the baseline for a slam.
>
> And Stewart's real specialty is 3-point shooting. On the tip of his toes he stroked four against the Hoyas without a miss.
>
> "He . . . can pat it. He can dance with it," Stewart's coach, Nolan Richardson, said of him. "I'm not going to take the gift the good Lord gave to him. I told him in practice one day. 'Hey, Big Dog, you're a guard, son. Go on and shoot your shot.' "
>
> The NCAA Tournament is supposed to be a fair contest. But with guys like Stewart, it isn't.

Mike Lopresti, of the Gannett News Service uses a variation of an Elizabeth Barrett Browning poem: "How do I love thee? Let me count the ways. . . ." in an article lead about the Nebraska Cornhuskers. His article was run on the wires Christmas, 1993, prior to the Orange Bowl.

> LINCOLN, Neb.—How does the nation disrespect Nebraska? Let us count the ways:
>
> • Ranked No. 1 in the CNN/USA Today poll, Nebraska nevertheless is a 17-point underdog against Florida State in the Orange Bowl, an unprecedented position for a top-ranked team.
>
> • When the Cornhuskers left the field in Lawrence, Kan., having slipped by the Jayhawks 21–20, the Kansas crowd stood and shouted at them, "Overrated! Overrated! Overrated!"

- Nebraska hasn't been out of the Associated Press rankings any week in 12 years, and hasn't had fewer than nine victories in a season in a quarter century. The AP media poll ranks the Cornhuskers No. 2 behind Florida State. All that, and if Notre Dame hadn't lost to Boston College, the Cornhuskers may never have even had a chance to play for the national championship with an 11–0 record.

- One oddsmaker in Las Vegas said there were 10 teams in the country better than the Cornhuskers.

"We can't please anybody, it seems like," linebacker Mike Anderson said.

Here Mike Kern of the *Philadelphia Daily News* uses a turn of phrase on the old sports quote "Win one for the Gipper." This article appeared in the *Anchorage Daily News* on December 31, 1993, under the headline "Bowden's had it with poll racket."

MIAMI—Win one for the quipper.

That's what some coaches, most notably West Virginia's Don Nehlen, have said the media are trying to do.

It's become a political thing, they contend. Bobby Bowden is a decent guy, always there with a catchy quote, win or lose, and the writers who vote in the Associated Press poll want to see him rewarded with his first national championship. Or so the theory goes. (p. B7)

Here Steve Aschburner of the *Minneapolis-St. Paul Star Tribune* uses a variation of the "inmates running the asylum" cliché to profile the San Antonio Spurs. His article was published the first week of March 1994.

When inmates start running the asylum—and the asylum starts running better than it did before—people take notice.

No NBA team has been hotter over the past six weeks than the San Antonio Spurs. Since a 108–98 loss to the Timberwolves at Target Center on Jan. 11, the Spurs are 14–2 and have wiped out the Rockets' seemingly insurmountable lead in the Midwest Division. Spurs center David Robinson has emerged as a leading candidate for the league's MVP award, rainbow-haired Dennis Rodman brought a pot o' rebounds with him from Detroit, and John Lucas could wind up as coach of the year.

One key to San Antonio's success, most of its players agree, is Lucas' willingness to let them take a significant role in running the team. His "board of directors"—made up of Robinson, Terry Cummings, Willie Anderson and Dale Ellis—is consulted on many decisions. From what plays to call during a timeout to the team's practice schedule to trade proposals and disciplinary action, the Spurs have a say.

A NEWS LEAD

Some sports articles are simply news articles. Here Linda Leavell of the Associated Press writes a news article, with a summary news lead, about a fire in Texas Stadium on Wednesday, October 13, 1993.

IRVING—A three-alarm fire that raged Wednesday evening at Texas Stadium severely damaged a dozen luxury suites and set about 10 rows of general admission seats ablaze. No one was injured.

Irving Fire Battalion Chief Jimmy Sims said the fire damaged seven suites on the lower level and five on the upper level. Three more received extensive water damage. The boxes' contents, including television sets, furniture, mini-bars and other amenities, also were destroyed, he said.

No events were taking place Wednesday, a Dallas Cowboys' spokesman said.

Associated Press writer Nasha Starevic covered the trial of German Guenter Parche, who stabbed Monica Seles while she was on the tennis court in April 1993. This article ran on the AP wires on October 13, 1993. Starevic's lead was:

HAMBURG, Germany—A tennis fan who stabbed Monica Seles out of an obsessive love for her rival, Steffi Graf, walked away free Wednesday when the court that convicted him gave him a suspended two-year sentence.

Guenter Parche, 39, an unemployed East German lathe operator who had been detained since the April 30 attack at a Hamburg tournament, could have received a three-year, nine-month jail term.

But Hamburg District Judge Elke Bosse said she took into account a psychiatrist's testimony that Parche had a "highly abnormal personality" that could have diminished his ability to reason.

NEWS REFERENCE LEAD

In early November 1993, Cleveland Browns coach Bill Belichick cut quarterback Bernie Kosar, who was the most beloved athlete in Cleveland in many, many years. Belichick thus became the most hated man in Cleveland. The Browns went nowhere the rest of the season, and Kosar went to Dallas, where he played backup to Troy Aikman and earned himself a Super Bowl ring.

Terry Blount of the *Houston Chronicle* referred to a cut of an entirely different kind in the lead of an article headlined: "Angry fans cutting Belichik no slack." The *Chronicle* ran this article on November 22, 1993.

CLEVELAND—The most painful banner of all was unfurled with a few seconds left in the game:

"Hey Bill: Lorena Bobbitt wants to make your next cut."

Browns coach Bill Belichick continues to be the most hated man in northeast Ohio after Sunday's 27–20 loss to the Oilers. Never has so much animosity been directed at anyone involved in the Browns organization, although team owner Art Modell is running a close second.

Most of the 71,668 fans at Cleveland Stadium weren't about to let Belichick and Modell off the hook for their decision two weeks ago to waive beloved quarterback

Bernie Kosar. Sunday was the team's first home game since the decision was made. (p. C8)

THE PROMINENT NAME LEAD

The use of a key name is often a valid method to begin a story—as the name prompts reader recognition—whether the name is a local, regional, or nationally known figure. In Texas, Troy Aikman, quarterback of the Dallas Cowboys, would qualify as a "name" player.

Denne Freeman of the Associated Press Dallas bureau uses Aikman's name to begin a story about a then-upcoming Cowboys–49ers game. This story was run on the AP wires on October 16, 1993.

> IRVING—Troy Aikman puts Sunday's showdown with the San Francisco 49ers in this perspective: "It's as important as an NFL game can get in October."
>
> The Dallas Cowboys want to know how far they've progressed since a stumbling 0–2 start, and they figure the 49ers will let them know in the Texas Stadium rematch of NFC title opponents. The Cowboys are 6½-point favorites.
>
> The Super Bowl champion Cowboys and the 49ers, who lost 30–20 in the NFC championship game at Candlestick Park, have had their problems as they've each posted 3–2 records.
>
> The Cowboys have bounced back since Emmitt Smith ended his holdout to defeat Phoenix, Green Bay and Indianapolis after losses to Washington and Buffalo.
>
> The 49ers, one of the NFL's best road teams in recent year, have lost at Cleveland and New Orleans.

Here Indiana's Bobby Knight is used as the key name in the lead of a story by an unnamed Associated Press writer. This event took place in December 1993.

> BLOOMINGTON, Ind.—Bob Knight swung his foot. Whether his son was the intended victim or just happened to be in the way, the reaction from Indiana fans was enough to send the General into another tirade.
>
> It's nothing new, of course. Just the first time this season. But considering the No. 12-ranked Hoosiers' campaign is only three games old, their coach already appears in midseason form.
>
> His outburst in Tuesday night's 101–82 victory over Notre Dame was triggered by some sloppy play in the closing minutes by the Hoosiers' mop-up crew, which included his son Pat, a 6-foot-6 junior.
>
> Indiana was up by 28 points when the younger Knight made a bad pass that Notre Dame's Ryan Hoover intercepted and took in for a fast-break layup. That was too much for the old man, who already was in a bad mood after scolding some fans for displaying a sarcastic sign directed at the Irish.
>
> During a time out, Knight went face-to-face with his son, screaming at him as the players went to the bench and sat down. Knight apparently kicked at something, and

some fans thought it was his son's leg and started booing. That's when Knight turned from his seat and glared at the anonymous offenders behind him, his face as red as his trademark sweater.

You didn't need to be a lip-reader to make out his four-letter response.

The crowd of players surrounding the bench prevented most people from seeing the apparent assault. Knight refused to speak to the news media after the game and did not return a phone call to his office on Wednesday.

Athletes with unusual names or nicknames can also offer sports writers interesting ways to begin articles. One of the most interesting U.S. athletes to emerge from the Lillehammer Winter Olympics was women's skiing champion Picabo Street.

This Associated Press article, sent on the wires the third week in February 1994, during the Olympics, stressed the pronunciation of her unique name:

RINGEBU, Norway—Pronounce it Peek-a-boo, then keep an eye on her.

"Watch for her tomorrow and the rest of the season, and next year, and in four more years," said Picabo Street's mother, Dee.

Street won a silver medal in the women's downhill at the Olympics on Saturday. And America now has four Alpine skiing medals—one shy of its all-time best in 1984, courtesy of this 22-year-old daughter of former flower children Dee and Stubby Street of Sun Valley, Idaho.

"There's a little tiger in me that comes out of the middle of nowhere that I really don't have control of sometimes," Street said. "I'm just glad I didn't freak out."

Robes Patton of the *Fort Lauderdale Sun-Sentinel* uses a litany of names to begin an article about the big, *big* men in basketball. This article was run in October 1993.

LAKE WORTH, Fla.—Even in a league brimming with tall men, there remain some who stand above the rest.

Manute Bol, Mark Eaton, Chuck Nevitt, Shawn Bradley, Gheorghe Muresan.

At 7–4 and up, they are the tallest of the tall.

As such, they occupy a rarefied niche reserved for those who lack the package of skills required of others.

When the Miami Heat signed Bol on Tuesday, it landed one of those rare players whose mere presence makes others—even near 7-footers such as Rony Seikaly and John Salley—appear small.

THE QUESTION LEAD

Can you begin a story with a question?

I just did.

Features can begin with questions because they involve the reader in the story, but they should be clear, understandable, and answerable. Give the reader an answer in the article, but not too soon. If you ask a question in paragraph one, and answer it in paragraph two, your reader may not be compelled to read paragraph three.

Hal Bock of the Associated Press uses such a question lead in an article about former athletes who turned to coaching. This article was run on the AP wires approximately in April 1994. (This article also has a solid quotation used as paragraph four.)

> If Magic can coach, why not Kareem?
>
> On the 10th anniversary of becoming the NBA's all-time leading scorer, Kareem Abdul-Jabbar thinks about teaching basic skills to a new generation of basketball players.
>
> "If you had asked me three years ago, I'd have said, 'Forget it. Are you out of your mind?' " Abdul-Jabbar said.
>
> "Now, it's not quite like that. There's a great need for people to teach the game. I don't think a lot of the young players, especially the front-line players, are learning the fundamentals.... That's something I know very well and could teach very well. So it's something that I would entertain, given the right offer in the right circumstances."

Bob Glauber of *Newsday* uses a question lead to begin an article about recent changes in the NFL. This article was sent on the wires the end of February 1993. After his lead, he uses a question-and-answer format to explain the changes. His lead and his first Q & A were:

> Confused by the NFL's complex new free-agency system? Join the crowd.
>
> Even league executives have been working long hours to make sure they understand the fine points. So cumbersome are the details that the NFL has published a booklet explaining the rules.
>
> With the signing period for restricted and unrestricted free agents set to begin today, here is a guide to the rules:
>
> **Q:** Which players are unrestricted free agents?
>
> **A:** Any player with at least five years' experience whose contract has expired is a free agent and can negotiate a new contract with any team. If a salary cap kicks in next year or thereafter, players who have at least four years' experience and whose contracts have expired will become unrestricted free agents.

John Jackson of the Gannett News Service asks a key question in the lead of an article about the Detroit Pistons. This article was run on the wires November 20, 1993.

> AUBURN HILLS, Mich.—Mark Macon and Marcus Liberty, acquired from the Denver Nuggets for Alvin Robertson, arrived in town Friday night and took part in their first practice Saturday. Now just one question remains:
>
> What are the Detroit Pistons going to do with these guys?

Macon, a shooting guard, and Liberty, a small forward, play positions where the Pistons are deepest, so playing time figures to be a problem.

Ray Buck, writer and columnist for the *Houston Post* uses a question lead in an article about the midseason success of the 1993 Houston Oilers. His column was run under the headline "Pardee's steadying hand pulls Oilers through" and was published December 5, 1993.

CAN YOU REMEMBER how the Oilers looked when they were 1–4? And how they look now after a six-pack of victories without a loss?

All together now: *Can this be the same team?*

Now think back to how Jack Pardee looked and sounded and acted at 1–4? During 6–0? Notice anything different?

Bzzzzz. Time's up. There is no discernible difference.

"The only thing I noticed," said Phyllis Pardee, Jack's bride of nearly 36 years, "is that instead of calling me once a day like he always does, he'd call me a couple of times a day when we were losing. Isn't that cute? I don't even think Jack realized it." (p. B17)

Steve Hershey of the Gannett News Service uses questions in his lead about who will win the next Masters Tournament in Augusta. This article was run in April 1994.

AUGUSTA, Ga.—Let's see, who's next? How about Colin Montgomerie or Peter Baker? And it's only a matter of time before young stars South Africa's Ernie Els or Sweden's Joakim Haeggman do it.

We're talking about winning The Masters, of course. You remember that folksy, Southern tournament Arnold Palmer and Jack Nicklaus used to dominate. It was a fun affair in the '70s when Tom Watson, Ray Floyd and Fuzzy Zoeller used to win.

That was before the foreigners invaded. It started innocently enough, with Spain's Seve Ballesteros winning in 1980 and again in '83. But we should have known. After missing the cut in '84, he finished 2-4-2 the next three years and in between told all his pals on the European Tour to come on over, it's easy pickings.

Chris Sheridan of the Associated Press uses a key question to begin an article about a fight during a Miami Heat–Atlanta Hawks game. This article was run on the AP wires May 1, 1994.

Was it the punch felt 'round the NBA?

Players and coaches seemed to think so Sunday.

The punch in question happened Saturday night in the Miami–Atlanta game. It was a windmill right, and it landed squarely on the jaw of Keith Askins of the Miami Heat. It was thrown by Douglas Edwards of the Atlanta Hawks in the most violent incident in a weekend of flagrant fouls, hip checks, chokes, finger-pointing, trash talk that cast a cloud over the first few days of the postseason.

Askins, Edwards and Grant Long (the choker) were ejected in Saturday night's three-minute free-for-all that brought players from both benches, coaches and even police officers onto the court at the Omni. Miami assistant coach Alvin Gentry broke his hand and finger trying to restrain Long.

A "pretty good fight," said John Salley of the Heat.

Pretty ugly was more like it.

THE QUOTATION LEAD

A quotation that is meaningful, interesting, challenging, fascinating, hypnotic, or curious may well be a solid type of lead for a sports story.

The quotation should not be a cliché (unless you use it to indicate a shallowness of thought by someone) and it should not be a phrase used to death, or a misleading one. The quotation should show the character or personality of the speaker.

Denne Freeman, sports editor of the Dallas–Fort Worth bureau of the Associated Press, uses a solid quotation in the lead of an article about Michael Irvin. This article was run on the AP wires on January 27, 1994.

(The quotation can be used to start a feature story or can be used, as this quotation is used, beginning in the third paragraph.)

ATLANTA—Michael Irvin was talking lucky. About life. About being a millionaire. About playing in the Super Bowl.

And whenever he hears about some of his former buddies around Fort Lauderdale, Fla., he realizes just how lucky he has been.

"A buddy of mine calls and somebody has either died, or been put in jail," Irvin said. "There's always some problem. I was lucky."

John Roe, writer for the *Minneapolis-St. Paul Star Tribune*, uses an enchanting quotation beginning in the third paragraph in an article about golfer Vinny Giles.

Giles was playing in the Walker Cup matches, the Super Bowl of amateur golf. Roe's article ran in August 1993.

EDINA, Minn.—Of all the shots Vinny Giles has struck during his long and illustrious amateur golf career, two remain indelibly etched in his memory.

One was his first shot in his first Masters. The other came on the first hole at the Milwaukee Country Club. He was about to be the first U.S. golfer to tee off in the 1969 Walker Cup match against Great Britain.

"As I got ready to hit my tee shot, I looked down at my feet and I noticed that the cuffs of my pants were blowing around like they were in a hurricane," Giles recalled. "That didn't make any sense since it was a dead calm day. But I quickly realized my knees and legs were shaking like crazy. I mean I've had butterflies before, but you want to talk about chill bumps and the shakes, well, I really had 'em that time."

That's what playing in the Walker Cup can do to a golfer. The chance to be part of the biennial international matches against a team of amateurs from England,

Scotland, Ireland and Wales is the ultimate for a U.S. male amateur golfer.

It will happen to 10 men today and Thursday at Interlachen Country Club when the 34th Walker Cup Match is played.

David Williams of *The Memphis Commercial Appeal* uses a quotation from former coach Pepper Rodgers to begin a story about NFL expansion plans. This article ran the first week in October 1993. After his lead, Williams devotes a section to each of the five cities considered on the NFL short list. His five cities: Baltimore, Charlotte, NC, Jacksonville, Memphis, and St. Louis.

Pepper Rodgers, spokesman for Memphis' NFL drive, said of the expansion process, "This is like a jury trial."

Meaning, Memphis and the four other finalist cities are awaiting the verdict, which won't come from 12 angry men, but rather from 28 wealthy owners. But while they wait, the expansion hopefuls will keep busy, fine-tuning, fixing what's broken and even some of what isn't.

Here, then, is a reader's guide to the final weeks before the NFL's planned awarding of two franchises Oct. 26.

A writer for the *Fort Lauderdale Sun-Sentinel* used a quotation lead in this article about Miami Dolphins linebacker Bryan Cox. This article was published in December 1993.

DAVIE, Fla.—After talking to his wife and watching his daughter nearly break into tears, Miami Dolphins linebacker Bryan Cox on Monday issued an apology for his antics at the end of Sunday's game against the New York Giants.

"I was an embarrassment to the team, this organization and to my family," said Cox, who was critical of the officiating and challenged a fan to a fight at the end of the 19–14 loss.

Monday, Cox said he had a heart-to-heart discussion with his wife, LaTonia. "I've got to sit back and think about what I do a little more because it's starting to have an impact on my family."

Cox said his 9-year-old daughter, Lavonda, had to endure the questions of friends that nearly forced her to tears.

"They kept asking her, 'Why does your daddy always get into fights?' " a rather humble Cox said.

Johnny Paul of the *Fort Worth Star-Telegram* uses a simple quotation to highlight his lead in a January 1994 story about Texas Christian University basketball.

DALLAS—Heavy chalk marks underlined the only four words written upon the blackboard.

"Will you rebound today?"

TCU basketball coach Moe Iba may never receive bonus points for his chalkmanship. Those four words tended to float aimlessly across the blackboard. Yet he gladly settled for the simple fact his Horned Frogs—particularly Byron Waits—received his message.

For only the third time in the past 12 games, the Frogs outrebounded an opponent. In the process, they snapped a two-game losing streak with an 89–75 victory against SMU before 3,003 Saturday at Moody Coliseum.

Tom Wieberg of *USA Today* uses three paragraphs of quotations by Barry Switzer in his lead about how Switzer took the job as Dallas Cowboys head coach following the resignation of Jimmy Johnson. This article was run on the wires in April 1994.

VALLEY RANCH—One month ago Friday night, Barry Switzer was steering his white BMW along Interstate 35, crossing the Red River from Oklahoma into Texas, his doubts about what he was doing multiplying by the mile.

"I was getting depressed," he said, "thinking about living in Norman (Okla.) for 27 years, my personal commitments, my financial commitments, the people, relationships and friendships I had.

"I thought, 'I'm giving that up at this point in my life, when those things mean more to me than anything? What do I have to prove?' I got to wondering, and I got to vacillating.

"Everybody likes to dream. But when you're faced with reality, and you've got to say yes or no, you do think about it. How does it affect your life, impact your life? And I got to really thinking about, 'How do I get out of this?' "

Ultimately, Switzer thought otherwise. He arrived in Dallas and sealed the deal making him the Dallas Cowboys coach.

The quotation can be used *above* the story instead of in the lead. Here Sheldon Spencer of the *Seattle Post-Intelligencer* uses a quotation from Dennis Rodman of the San Antonio Spurs above the story.

"If I get thrown out because of a head butt, then this league has a problem. It's getting to where you can't touch anybody. You've got to stand up for what you believe in."

—Dennis Rodman, San Antonio Spurs, after a recent ejection

By Sheldon Spencer
Seattle Post-Intelligencer

Now that you mention it, Dennis, the NBA does seem ticky-tacky with its rules regarding forbidden physical contact.

Besides the head butt, there are the eye gouge, the Adam's apple chop, and assorted other staples of professional wrestling that will earn the offending player an unsportsmanlike conduct penalty. Even wedgies are *verboten*.

Whatever his troubles with playing within the rules, the electric Rodman, like an assortment of other ill-tempered but talented types, will always have a place in the NBA. Pro basketball is driven by personalities, good and bad, more than any sport.

No other game provides its fans with such an intimate view of its competitors' raw emotions. The fan can almost reach out and touch the NBA's heroes and villains.

Here Dale Robertson, sports writer and columnist for the *Houston Chronicle*, uses a key quotation from a previous Michael Jordan interview in *Playboy* to begin a story about Jordan's retirement. This article was run under the headline "He's Michael to the bitter end" and appeared in the *Chronicle* on October 7, 1993.

> *"People say they wish they were Michael Jordan. OK, do it for a year. Do it for five years. On one road trip, we got into Denver at 3 in the morning and there were people sitting around the hotel lobby. I was tired. I said, 'I'm sorry, please. I'm tired.' Then I heard, 'I guess that's the Jordan rules.'*
>
> *"I just kept on walking. One of these days I'm going to say, 'Go screw yourself.' Maybe when I'm walking out of the league."*
>
> —Michael Jordan in Playboy

Michael Jeffrey Jordan walked out of the NBA on Wednesday morning, and if you listened to his farewell news conference—Jordan is so big, the networks carried it live—you would have heard him say essentially that.

Not in so many words, of course, but the greatest basketball player who ever drew a breath is leaving the game he loves—a game he practically reinvented and one that made him unfathomably wealthy—a bitter man. The painted-on smile, the upbeat rhetoric and the happy prospects of spending quality time with his family couldn't hide this.

It came through loud and clear. (p. B1)

Jim Litke of the Associated Press uses a quotation by Mickey Lolich to begin an article about pitcher Dave Stewart. Litke's article ran on the AP wires on October 23, 1993.

> *"I have a name now. They'll be looking for new heroes next season. But I will be remembered by someone some day."*—Detroit's Mickey Lolich, after beating Bob Gibson and the St. Louis Cardinals in Game 7 of the 1968 World Series.

By Jim Litke
Associated Press

TORONTO—The World Series is like a beacon. By October, the light diffused over an entire season has tapered to become a single beam. It lengthens the shadows behind a very select few hitters and pitchers. It exposes the weaknesses of most of the rest.

"You get nervous when you don't really want to be in a situation," Dave Stewart said before taking the ball to the mound for the Toronto Blue Jays in Game 6 on Saturday night. "But I'm really looking forward to this."

Those were brave words, but perhaps only Stewart really knew how much he risked this particular night.

Already acknowledged as one of the greatest playoff performers ever—he is 8–0 in league championship play, an even more incredible 4–0 in pennant-clinching games—Stewart had yet to be similarly recognized in the best-of-seven sets that followed. And that task never seemed more daunting Saturday night.

Bob Kravitz of the *Rocky Mountain News* uses two quotations above the first paragraph of an article about Denver Nuggets' player Mark Macon. This article was published in November 1993.

"He's the next Oscar Robertson."

—Dick Vitale on Mark Macon

"He'll be much better as a pro. He has some very good point guard skills. He has skills people don't even know about."

—NBA scout Marty Blake

DENVER—It is the strangest thing. How did Mark Macon become such a certifiable bust? How did it all go so wrong, so haywire that in only the third year of his career the Denver Nuggets had to admit his selection as the eighth pick in the draft was a mistake?

The real story of Friday's deal to Detroit is not Denver's acquisition of Alvin Robertson but the unfortunate demise of Mark Macon, a young man his former coach at Temple University, John Chaney, calls "one of the most extraordinary human beings I've ever known."

Steve Wulf, staff writer for *Sports Illustrated*, uses a quotation from the late Branch Rickey to begin an article about the new alignments in baseball. His article appeared under the headline "Scouting Reports" in *SI* on April 4, 1994.

Baseball people—and that includes myself—are slow to change and accept new ideas. I remember that it took years to persuade them to put numbers on uniforms.

—Branch Rickey, 1954

Forty years after the Mahatma said that, baseball people are again wringing their hands over a fundamental change in the game. For the first time the World Series can conceivably be won by a team that finishes … painful as it is to write it … second.

Yes, there are now three divisions (East, Central, West) in each league and a new best-of-five round in postseason play. In that new format, the division winner with the best record meets the second-place finisher with the best record while the other two division winners play one another, with the victors moving on to the time-honored best-of-seven league championship series, which determines who's in the best-of-seven World Series, which could possibly produce—if delayed by weather a day or two— baseball's first Mr. November. (p. 93)

Can you use a single word as a quotation lead?
Yes.
Here Christopher Clarey of *The New York Times* uses such a one-word quotation in a story about the 1993 Ryder Cup golf matches in England. This article was run

in *The New York Times* on September 24, 1993, under the headline "When Continents Collide, In New Blazers and All."

> SUTTON COLDFIELD, England—"Apprehensive" was the word Tom Watson chose to describe his mood just before lunch.
>
> He would feel considerably better as he headed off to dinner.
>
> Trailing by three points after losing three of four Ryder Cup matches in the morning, Watson's United States team roared back Saturday afternoon. With two notable exceptions, the U.S. team lived up to its considerable potential, winning three matches to narrow the European edge to 8½–7½.
>
> The biennial match-play event between American and European teams concludes today with 12 individual matches that will start with two former Masters champions, Ian Woosnam and Fred Couples, teeing off first, and end with sizzling Nick Faldo playing Paul Azinger.

THE SIMILE (OR METAPHOR) LEAD

A simile compares Item A to Item B. Strictly speaking, the usage is *A is like B*. The more unusual the match, the more interesting the simile.

Ken Rodriquez of *The Miami Herald* uses a simile lead in his story about the January 1994 Fiesta Bowl game in Tempe, where Arizona beat Miami 29–0.

> TEMPE, Ariz.—Under a shadow of mountains, cactus and blood-red Arizona fans chanting, "U of A! U of A!," the University of Miami went down like a wounded gunslinger Saturday, ambushed in the desert.
>
> A dynasty lay sprawled. A rising challenger stood tall, strutting into the sunset after a shocking Fiesta Bowl massacre: Arizona 29, Miami 0.
>
> "They just kicked the living heck out of us," said Miami coach Dennis Erickson, whose No. 10 Hurricanes (9–3) completed their worst season since an 8–5 record under Jimmy Johnson in 1984. "We never could get anything going."

Mike Lopresti of the Gannett News Service uses a nice simile ("College basketball looks like . . .") to begin an analysis piece about college basketball. This was run in January 1994.

> Here at the season's halfway post, college basketball looks like a messy closet, where No. 1 is a revolving door and the biggest story has been a walkout that didn't happen, but still might.
>
> There is no place to turn for neatness. Parity is cluttering up the college game. Not to mention energizing it.
>
> We could start by talking about the top-ranked team, but that's assuming there is one, which may be stretching things. Four teams have been there—Kansas, North Carolina, Duke and Arkansas—and four teams have lost, two of them at home.

Larry Dierker, TV–radio analyst for the Houston Astros, uses a simile lead in an analysis article about the Phillies. His article appeared in the *Houston Chronicle* on August 23, 1993 under the headline "Primordial Phils reflect Fregosi."

> In this age of artificial intelligence, the Phillies are like cavemen. They're way behind the times.
>
> The Phillies don't have a nutritionist on staff.
>
> "Our nutrition is a hot dog and a beer," says manager Jim Fregosi, sitting with his legs crossed in the visitors' dugout at the Astrodome, grinning as he watches his warrior clan stretch lazily on the turf.
>
> The Phillies don't employ a psychologist, either. They like to hang around in the training room after the hunt, in an area where outsiders are forbidden. It's a let-your-hair-down, let-your-feelings-out sort of place. It's an ice house, an infirmary. A healing place. A cave. (p. C5)

You can also use a metaphor instead of a simile.
The simile is *A is like B*; the metaphor is *A is B*.
In the cases of the similes shown here, the metaphor versions would be:

- The University of Miami was a wounded gunslinger Saturday. . . .
- College basketball is a messy closet. . . .
- The Phillies are cavemen. . . .

When should you use a simile and when should you use a metaphor? There is no rule; the choice simply depends on how you want the sentence to sound.

THE STATISTICS LEAD

Occasionally, a sports writer can use statistics to show winners and losers. After all, many sports fans are numbers junkies. Statistics must be clean and clear; you don't want to sink a good story in an unfathomable sea of numbers.

Controversies about Black student athletes and Black coaches erupted in 1994. Liz Clarke of the Knight-Ridder Tribune News service uses statistics in the lead of an article about this issue. This article was run on the Knight-Ridder Tribune News wires in January 1994.

> Behind the war of words that nearly triggered a college basketball boycott earlier this month is an issue larger than scholarships:
>
> It's the lack of black voices in debates that produce NCAA rules—such as the one limiting men's basketball to 13 scholarships per team.
>
> Blacks account for just 3.2 percent of 312 key NCAA delegates—composed of college presidents, athletic directors, top women's administrators and faculty members—from schools in the nation's eight biggest athletic conferences.

In the nine-member Atlantic Coast Conference, none of 36 campus delegates to the NCAA is black.

It's the same in the 12-member Southeastern Conference, where none of 48 campus NCAA delegates is black.

It's that lack of representation—mirrored to a less dramatic but consistent extent throughout the NCAA—that spurred the Black Coaches Association to call for a basketball boycott on Jan. 15, the Rev. Martin Luther King Jr.'s birthday. The boycott has been postponed while the Congressional Black Caucus and the Justice Department mediate the dispute.

THE STATEMENT LEAD

Simplicity is often best.

Short declarative sentences have impact.

You have just read two, short, single-sentence paragraphs.

The statement lead is not as elegant as some other types of leads, but is workable in many cases.

Here Bill Knight of the *Seattle Post-Intelligencer* uses this type of lead in a story about the NBA. This article was written in January 1994.

Success breeds hostility. At least that's the way it seems in the combative relationship of professional basketball fans with rival players and referees.

Fans who follow winners take the outcome of every game more seriously and are more abusive in the stands, according to an informal survey of NBA teams.

"Fans seem to get a lot more hostile when it's a big game that means something," said Dale Ratermann of the Indiana Pacers. "One or two plays can incite a crowd in a hurry. When all games mean something it does make a difference in how people behave."

Elizabeth Leland of *The Charlotte Observer* uses a simple statement of fact to begin an article about the death of Michael Jordan's father. This article was published in August 1993.

CHARLOTTE, N.C.—There's a lot of James Jordan in his superstar son.

Father passed on his looks to Michael Jordan—broad nose, prominent cheekbones, a smile that curves at the corners into dimples—his high spirits and sense of mischief.

And now, after James Jordan's slaying, a world of Michael Jordan worshipers struggles to understand why anyone would kill the hero's father.

Bill Sullivan of the *Houston Chronicle* uses a simple statement lead to begin an article about Jimmy Johnson and Cowboy "problem players." The article was run under the headline "Cowboys try Roper experiment" in the *Chronicle* on August 20, 1993.

AUSTIN—Jimmy Johnson has been down this road.

Tony Casillas, you might recall, came to the Cowboys from Atlanta with the reputation of being a bad actor. Charles Haley, whose behavior in San Francisco could be considered "colorful" only on the best of days, was a virtual giveaway when the 49ers decided enough was enough.

But in Dallas, each found a place in Jimmy's Home for Wayward Boys. Each contributed greatly to a Super Bowl win. Each, by the way, is still around.

Small wonder, then, that Johnson is willing to roll the dice again.

"John Roper won't make or break our football team," the Cowboys' coach said after picking up the former Yates and Texas A&M star in Tuesday's trade with the Bears. "But if he fits in, and the chemistry is right, then we've got a bonus because he's a talented player."

On the other hand.... (p. C2)

Malcolm Moran used a simple statement of fact to begin an article about former University of Washington Husky head coach Don James. This article appeared in *The New York Times* on September 3, 1993, under the title "Don James Finds That Roses Outnumber The Thorns."

SEATTLE—The former coach will arrive by yacht.

As the players, coaches and fans at the University of Washington continue to cope with emotions usually reserved for a death in the family, Don James will begin his season outside football the way he has always wanted—relaxing on Lake Washington as he approaches Husky Stadium Saturday.

Less than two weeks after his sudden, emotionally charged resignation, touched off by a two-year bowl ban imposed on Washington by the Pacific-10 Conference, James has begun to grow apart from the program he led for 18 seasons.

Cynthia Thomas of the *Houston Chronicle* uses a statement lead to begin an article about Karen Voight, workout expert. This article, published on September 9, 1993 was run under a headline "Woman of Steel," with an accompanying color picture of Voight in front of a workout class.

The woman with "the perfect body" leads a boring life.

Glamour magazine dubbed her "the Empress of Abs." The London tabloid Today called hers "the $3 million body." She's one of the most sought-after instructors in the fitness industry, commanding five-digit fees to teach at conferences.

Still, given the hours she and husband Henry Siegel put into their business, her lifestyle can sound more akin to that of a worker in a family-run grocery than a fitness guru flitting from the aerobics studio to the television studio. (Granted, the grocer doesn't get to tutor Tina Turner on her "abs.")

When the couple opened their studio in Los Angeles in 1981 they did everything themselves. She taught. He ran the business. Between classes they cleaned the mirrors and swept the floors. They started early in the morning and worked into the night seven days a week.

Now the Voight Fitness and Dance Center teaches 3,500 students a week in classes such as Step 'N' Pump; Bodysculpt; and Abs, Thighs and Buns. Voight's six videos are well-reviewed and have sold hundreds of thousands of copies. (p. C1)

Robes Patton of the *Fort Lauderdale Sun-Sentinel* uses a statement lead in an article about the 1993 Sugar Bowl, in which Florida beat West Virginia, 41–7. This game was played New Year's Day, 1994.

> NEW ORLEANS—This is why they play the games.
> After a month of whining and bemoaning a perceived lack of respect and poll unfairness, West Virginia was muzzled by Florida 41–7 Saturday night in the Sugar Bowl.
> It was a Florida performance that was dazzling in its completeness.
> "Overall, I think this is one of our best games of the season," said Florida senior running back Errict Rhett. "I wanted to go out just like this right here. It'll be the game I'll always remember as a Gator, so it felt really good."

A simple statement can often be used effectively to underplay a dramatic event. Mike Monroe of *The Denver Post* uses such a lead in a copyrighted story (often stated incorrectly as a "copyright story" in the press) announcing the retirement of Michael Jordan. This article was moved on the wires late on October 5, 1993 in advance of Jordan's announcement, and was run in the October 6, 1993 *Houston Post* under the headline "Jordan to announce basketball retirement today."

> By Mike Monroe
> The Denver Post
> ©1993, The Denver Post Corp.

> The Michael Jordan era in professional basketball has ended.
> Jordan, the Chicago Bulls superstar who is one of the most popular personalities in the world, today will announce his retirement from the game after nine amazing seasons that brought him three Most Valuable Player awards, seven NBA scoring titles and the highest career scoring average (32.3) points in NBA history.
> A source close to Jordan told The Denver Post of Jordan's plan to announce the end of his career, and Bulls coach Phil Jackson confirmed it Tuesday night. (p. B1)

THE SUMMARY LEAD

Who played, where and when, the score, and a key play or key statistics: These are the key elements of a summary lead.

Here is a perfect example, in an article about a Bulls–Knicks game in December 1993.

> CHICAGO—B.J. Armstrong scored 20 points, 11 in the final 6:06 Friday night, boosting the Chicago Bulls to a 98–86 victory over New York that snapped the Knicks' five-game winning streak.

Charles Oakley's 18-foot jumper from the corner with 8:16 left gave the Knicks their first lead of the game at 76–75. After an exchange of baskets, the Bulls scored the next eight points, four by Armstrong, for an 85–78 advantage with 5:39 left.

John Starks, who had 19 points, responded with a 3-pointer at 5:13 and another basket at 4:14, closing the Knicks to 85–83. But Chicago coasted to its eighth victory in nine games after Scottie Pippen, who had 18 points, scored on a layup with 1:54 left and Armstrong hit a 3-pointer 25 seconds later for a 90–83 lead.

In some cases, the most natural lead for a sports story is the summary lead, in which the writer summarizes or capsulizes the achievements of a player, team, or coach.

Associated Press writer Dave Carpenter used a summary lead to begin an article about the triumph of U.S. speed skater Dan Jansen. This article was run on the AP wires on February 18, 1994 after Jansen's dramatic victory in the Lillehammer Olympics:

LILLEHAMMER, Norway—Skating for redemption and a gold medal, Dan Jansen got both emphatically Friday with a world record in his final Olympic race after seven failures over a decade of heartbreak.

"I guess good guys do win," said Jansen's coach, Peter Mueller.

The world's fastest skater thrust his arms up triumphantly after crossing the finish line in the 1,000-meter race and put his hands to his head, no doubt as much in relief as in ecstasy. The crowd erupted as the record time flashed on the Viking Ship Hall scoreboard: 1 minute, 12.43 seconds, .11 faster than Canadian Kevin Scott's 2-month-old world record.

After 10 years of agony, Jansen still had to wait for another 1½ hours before his long-awaited gold was made official, with three dozen competitors skating behind him.

THE "THEME" LEAD

Writers can sometimes use a continuing *lyric* or *theme line* to emphasize a lead throughout a story. In this story, Claudia Feldman of the *Houston Chronicle* uses "Pow!" to show how golfer Teri Lee not only swings her golf clubs, but also how she visualizes conquering cancer cells. This article, under the headline "Hard Hitter" and the subhead "Cancer scare teaches CPA to fight, relax," was published in the *Chronicle* on October 4, 1993.

A lyric word or theme line should be short or concise to emphasize the writer's point.

Teri Lee was practicing her golf swing in preparation for today's First Annual CAnCare of Houston Golf Classic.

Pow!

She had a radical mastectomy in the spring, three years ago.

Pow!

She's a CPA. It was tax season. She still got her work done.

Pow!

It was her right breast, and she's right-handed. Her teacher said it might help her swing.

Pow!

She didn't play much golf before her surgery. She didn't have time. But if she learned anything during her cancer scare, it was to slow down, spend more time with her family and enjoy herself.

Pow! Whoa! Ouch! She almost brained a man crouched 10 yards away who was trying to take her picture.

Pow!

Every time she swings that club, she sees herself pulverizing cancer cells.

Pow! She's a hard hitter. She has golf gloves, golf clubs, golf shoes and a golf bag with her name inscribed on it. But no, she doesn't take her golf score that seriously. Life's too short. (p. D1)

Houston Chronicle columnist Fran Blinebury uses the same technique in an article headlined "Cowboys smart but get wiser." This article ran in the *Houston Chronicle* on November 22, 1993.

ATLANTA—It was the game when the silver and blue became black and blue. An afternoon when the sides of their helmets weren't the only place they saw stars.

The Cowboys expected a nice day at the beach and wound up washed away by a tidal wave. They probably thought the worst thing that could happen was a little fender bender on the road back to the Super Bowl and nearly found themselves smack in the middle of the Hindenburg disaster.

Boom!

Kenneth Gant had to leave the game with a dislocated left shoulder.

Boom!

Nate Newton hobbled out with a bruised right knee.

Boom!

Kevin Gogan limps off with a twisted left knee.

Boom!

Bernie Kosar stayed on the field, but had visions of Quasimodo running around inside his skull after having his bell rung in a big way by the Falcons' Jessie Tuggle.

Boom!

Emmitt Smith had to be taken to the locker room on a cart after going down to the artificial turf in a heap late in the second quarter.

The next explosion you heard figured to be the Cowboys' dynasty collapsing upon itself like one of those old buildings that has been rigged with so many sticks of dynamite. (p. C6)

THE TIMELINE LEAD

Sports writers can use a chronology to show the progress of an athlete, a team, or a sport. This can be used with the earlier date first, or today's date, then a flashback to previous months, years or conditions.

Here Christine Brennan of *The Washington Post* used such a lead to show how long the British team of Jayne Torvill and Christopher Dean have been champions of the sport of ice dancing. This article was published in February 1994, during the Winter Olympics in Lillehammer, Norway.

> HAMAR, Norway—Ten years later, the perfect 6.0s still popped onto the scoreboard and the Union Jacks still waved in the stands.
>
> Torvill and Dean are back, and they are precisely where they are expected to be, leading the ice dancing competition at the Winter Olympics.
>
> With tonight's free dance portion remaining, Jayne Torvill and Christopher Dean hold a slight edge over two Russian dance pairs after 50 percent of the competition. The 1984 Olympic gold medalists took the lead with an elegant original dance Sunday night at the Olympic Amphitheatre after falling behind two nights ago in the compulsory dance.

Here is another version of the timeline lead. Dave Goldberg, writer for the Associated Press, uses it well in a 1993 article about Miami Dolphins coach Don Shula.

> MIAMI—Oct. 5, 1963. Don Shula is standing on the sidelines at Wrigley Field in Chicago, watching George Halas coach the Bears to a 10–3 victory over his Baltimore Colts.
>
> "I was just in awe of him," Shula says. "Here I was this 33-year-old rookie and I was standing there trying to coach against this legend."
>
> Oct. 30, 1993. Scott Mitchell, who the next day will quarterback the Miami Dolphins to the win that ties Shula with Halas for the most ever by an NFL coach, is recalling when he first met Shula in 1990.
>
> "I was standing there when he came up to me, stuck out his hand and said 'I'm coach Shula,' " Mitchell recalls. "Of course I knew him. I'd seen him a million times on television. I was born in 1968 and he was already a legend by then."

Cathy Harasta uses a timeline lead in a story about UCLA–Houston basketball, 1968 style and the same teams, playing each other in 1993 for the first time since that 1968 game. Her article appeared in *The Dallas Morning News* on December 20, 1993, under the headline "Hayes played large role in biggest game."

> Abdul-Jabbar still was Alcindor.
>
> The Astrodome still was an anomaly.
>
> At the time, Elvin Hayes wondered if anyone would be there for the Jan. 20, 1968, UCLA–Houston game. "Anyone" was a relative term, because some fans certainly would show for a No. 1 versus No. 2 matchup of undefeated teams.
>
> But this game was an unusual test, not just of the Cougars, then 16–0 and ranked second, and the top-ranked Bruins (13–0). This game would chart the future of the sport. It would become a touchstone for basketball, for Hayes, for sports television, for arena management and for millions of fans.

Hayes and his Houston teammates were to be part of a new-fangled notion. Basketball never had been played in a domed stadium. Regular-season college basketball had yet to enjoy national television exposure. Nobody knew the sport's potential, what it could be worth, or if anybody cared.

The game, in a novel building in a football state, would be known as The Game of the Century. But nobody knew it, going in.

Hayes did not feel like a frontiersman.

"The players were conscious of a building of that size and magnitude," said Hayes, whose No. 44 will be retired during a ceremony at halftime of UCLA's game at Houston Monday night. "We wondered if there would be any people in the stands. Was anybody going to come?"

Crowded house

What came out of that game was a national awareness of college basketball and its potential. The game drew 52,693—a record paid crowd for basketball at the time.

Hayes, a 6–9 senior, led the Cougars to a 71–69 victory. Fouled with 28 seconds left, he made the decisive free throws against the Lew Alcindor-led Bruins. Hayes played all 40 minutes, scored 39 points and had 15 rebounds.

On Monday night, UCLA will play the Cougars in Houston for the first time since that 1968 landmark game. This time, the Bruins will meet UH in Hofheinz Pavilion. Many of Hayes' teammates plan to be there. (p. B1)

Here, sports writer Melanie Hauser of *The Houston Post* uses a timeline lead to show how long Billie Jean King has been a tennis star. Hauser's article appeared under the headline: "King part of gala to combat AIDS." The article appeared in *The Houston Post* on February 15, 1994.

Twenty-five years ago, a visit to Houston changed Billie Jean King's life and the face of women's tennis. Still another King visit here in 1973 helped change the perception toward females and female athletes.

Two decades later, King is out in front once again, this time teaming some legendary Virginia Slims players with headline entertainers Liza Minnelli and Angela Lansbury for a nostalgic weekend benefiting the American Foundation for AIDS Research.

As a lead-in to this year's Virginia Slims of Houston, the 50-year-old King has helped put together Virginia Slims Legends weekend—a two-day affair March 19–20 that includes a pro-am, a concert by Minnelli and a round-robin exhibition featuring King, Martina Navratilova, Virginia Wade and Tracy Austin. (p. C9)

Here Owen Davis, writer for the *Detroit Free Press*, uses a timeline lead to show the progress of a U.S. luge sledder, run on the wire services February 18, 1994.

LILLEHAMMER, Norway—Mark Grimmette grew up sledding down hills in Muskegon, Mich., in the wintertime.

"One day I heard some noise on my favorite sledding hill," Grimmette said Friday. "All these bulldozers were carving out a luge track. I helped them."

An Olympian was born.

Ten years later, Grimmette and Jonathan Edwards finished fourth in Olympic luge doubles, the best performance ever by American lugers—singles or doubles. Chris Thorpe of Marquette, Mich., and Gordon Sheer were fifth.

Alan Solomon, writing for the *Chicago Tribune*, uses a timeline lead to show how much difference a year makes. This article, about Michael Jordan, was run on the wires March 21, 1994.

> SARASOTA, Fla.—A year ago, Michael Jordan was a member of the NBA champion Chicago Bulls, cheered by thousands.
>
> Monday, he was a member of the Prince William Cannons, cheered by 32.
>
> As the national anthem was being sung by a sellout crowd in full throat at Ed Smith Stadium, a few hundred feet away the greatest basketball player who ever played the game trotted out to right field on a place with a decidedly unmagical name: Field 4.
>
> He is a minor-leaguer now. He will play, for the next week or so, on whatever White Sox farm team has room.
>
> "Today, it's (Class A) Prince William," said general manager Ron Schueler. "Wednesday, it might be (Class AAA) Nashville. It's where we can get him in games or where we can get him the most at-bats."

Writer Joe Gergen of *Newsday* uses a timeline lead to begin a story about Louisville basketball coach Denny Crum's induction into the Basketball Hall of Fame, late in March 1994. With the lengthy association of Crum and John Wooden of UCLA, such a timeline lead is a natural.

> LOS ANGELES—Denny Crum doesn't get nostalgic about buildings. He didn't shed a tear when he walked inside the Sports Arena on Wednesday although it might have been appropriate.
>
> It was here in 1968 that he sat on the UCLA bench alongside John Wooden as a celebrated center named Lew Alcindor led the Bruins to a second consecutive NCAA championship.
>
> It was here, four years later, that he first opposed the man he still calls Coach (with a capital C) in the semifinals of another Final Four.
>
> The center on that UCLA team was Bill Walton so don't bother asking if he won.
>
> Still, it was a great moment for Crum in his first season as head coach of the Louisville Cardinals.
>
> "That was a long time ago," Crum said.

Were you alive when Franklin Roosevelt was president?

Ken Grissom, Outdoors Editor of *The Houston Post*, uses a timeline lead to begin a story about a gulf fishing tournament, held annually in Port Aransas, Texas. His article was published on March 20, 1994.

(My pocket calculator tells me that the tournament began in 1935. If you use numbers, dates, and years in a story—make sure they add up correctly. Grissom's numbers did add up: Roosevelt's first term began in 1933.)

Franklin Delano Roosevelt was in his first term when the first Deep Sea Roundup was held in Port Aransas. They're doing it again—the 59th annual—July 1–3 with separate competitions in the Offshore, Bay & Surf, Junior and Piggy Perch divisions. More than 500 anglers are expected in Texas' premier saltwater tournament.

If one of them happens to break the present state record for kingfish, 71⅕ pounds, the prize is $50,000. For winning catches in the regular categories, trophies, plaques and other prizes will be awarded. Entry is $60 per angler before June 15, $70 afterward.

Categories are:

Offshore—Amberjack, barracuda, bonito, ling, ... (p. B20)

If you ask "whatever happened to . . . ?" you may be able to develop a fascinating sports story of an individual, a team, or an era. Curt Brown, of the *Minneapolis-St. Paul Star Tribune*, uses a timeline lead to write about the NFL "Class of '83." His article was published in November 1993.

Most classes hold their 10-year reunions at some posh hotel, toasting plastic champagne glasses while comparing hair lost and weight gained. The NFL's rookie class of '83 was never like most classes, though.

"We were a class of our own, the cream of the crop, we were amazing," said Vikings running back Roger Craig, one of five members from the Class of '83 who played in Sunday's Vikings-Broncos game. "Our class made a serious, serious impact. I mean, man, we kind of made the league at the time by giving fans a whole new corps of guys."

The bulbs behind the marquee names of Terry Bradshaw, Bob Griese, Mean Joe Greene, O.J. Simpson, Roger Staubach, Frank Tarkenton, Alan Page and Franco Harris had burned out by the early 1980s, leaving the NFL in a black hole. When the '83 draft rolled around, the stars were instantly realigned with the likes of John Elway, Jim Kelly, Dan Marino, Eric Dickerson, Curt Warner, Richard Dent, Joey Browner, Darrell Green, Karl Mecklenburg and Charles Mann.

THE "YOU" LEAD

Every article "talks" to the reader. Style is a matter of how your material "sounds" to your reader's inner ear. The use of the second-person "you" lead speaks directly to your readers. This technique makes it seem as if you are speaking to a good friend, telling them exactly what will happen to them if. . . .

Here Ken Grissom of *The Houston Post* tells you what will happen to you when you first take a snorkeling trip to the Florida Keys. Notice the use of the key word *you*. The complete article is published so you (there's that word again) can count the *you*'s if you like.

This article was published under the headline "Snorkeling off the Keys opens eyes to new world" and was published March 27, 1994.

LOOE KEY, Fla.—You won't know the half of it until you step off the *Emerald See* into the invisible water over this fabulous, accessible coral reef.

As you swing around and make your approach from the south, the world is a slightly rumpled sheet of azure Atlantic, with the Lower Keys just a smudge on the horizon. In the immediate foreground is an orderly line of boats, some passenger-carrying 40-foot catamarans like the *See* and some smaller private craft. What makes the anchorage so orderly is the line of anchor buoys you're required to use to avoid dragging your hook over the precious creation below.

Capt. Alex Creedon has gotten you here. Now divemaster Margi Austin takes over, showing you how to apply anti-fog lotion to your diving mask, outfitting you with a flotation vest should you get tired of kicking. Maybe you don't need such attention, but some of those on the half-day tour have yet to clamp their teeth on a snorkel.

It doesn't matter. You can float on the surface right by the boat and see a big barracuda lazing 20 feet below. The coral bank becomes shallower, more profuse, vastly more colorful as you swim southward toward its crest within a foot or so of the surface. By comparison, the world above the surface is monochromatic, blue on blue.

The sea life is abundant, too. One of the youngsters in your group babbles excitedly through his snorkel at the sight of a dazzling parrotfish. The fish is used to human sightseers and allows the boy to follow it on its rounds of the reef.

All of this comes without having to hold your breath. If you do want to swim beneath the surface, there are sand-bottom channels through the reef which give the snorkeler a taste of what scuba divers call "wall diving."

Snorkeling is something that can be done by people with a wide variety of skill levels and physical conditions, from relaxing on the surface with your personal window on the underwater world to the very taxing "free-diving" done by those who spearfish without the aid of scuba in the same spirit that some deer hunters like to use archery equipment or muzzleloaders.

Equipment is fairly inexpensive, too.

Of course, dive boats like the *Emerald See* have all the equipment available.

The *See* is operated by Strike Zone Charters out of a marina on Big Pine Key (mile 29½).

For more information, call 800-654-9560. (p. B21)

Cary Estes (1993) writing for the *Birmingham Post-Herald*, talks to the reader most dramatically in this article about Alabama's George Wilkerson. Note the nice touch after the lead: "He is 'The Club' in human form."

BIRMINGHAM, Ala.—He is in your face. Right there. A living shadow, relentlessly following your every step.

You move right, he stays with you.

You juke left. No good. He sticks to you like gum on a shoe. You cannot simply shake him off.

His breath hits your face. His taunts pierce your ears. You feel his sweat. He senses your fear.

He is in constant motion, even while standing still. His hands flicker. His eyes dart. He is tightly coiled and ready to strike.

Finally, out of frustration, you shoot the ball. You know you are off balance and too far from the basket. You know he will extend his arms and make you put too much arc on the ball.

Still, you have to do something. So you shoot.

Clang.

And so ends the first possession. In less than a minute, you have to do it all over again.

This is the nightmare faced every game by the player who is guarded by Alabama Birmingham's George Wilkerson.

Wilkerson's statistics seldom make much of an impression. He is averaging five points and four rebounds per game. He will make a few steals, dish out a couple of assists. Nothing special overall.

But Wilkerson's contribution to the Blazers goes far beyond mere stats. He is "The Club" in human form. He clamps down on the opposing team's top perimeter scorer and never lets go.

Gannett writer and columnist Mike Lopresti uses a "you" lead on the new NFL rule that will allow a 2-point conversion. This column was moved by Gannett late in March 1994. (This lead is especially appealing for all the fans of the NFL who believe—Monday morning—that they could do better than that sorry fellow who was coaching their team Sunday afternoon.)

Imagine you're an NFL coach (headphones are optional). Your team has just scored a touchdown late in the fourth quarter to go ahead by seven points, and now you walk the sideline and face the PAT dilemma.

You can take the easy kick for one. Go by the book.

But your heart is whispering something else into your ear. The wind is against you. Your defense is hurt and tired. Go for two. Get a nine-point lead, put this game away, slip a shiv into the back of that team across the way. The fans will cheer your bold move. The players soon will be pouring Gatorade upon your head.

Or. You'll blow the game. You'll fail on the two-point PAT and the other team will come back to win, and the fans will be dialing up radio talk shows to call you names, you dummy.

You pace, you wonder. What would Lombardi have done? Or Noll? What would Don Shula be deciding right now?

Well, that's the point. Or, to be more precise, the two points. Lombardi and Noll and Shula and the rest never have had to ask themselves that question. Not on the pro level, anyway. The PAT was a pat hand. You scored a touchdown, you sent out the kicker. One point was the only item on the menu.

COMBINATION LEADS

Previously we have cited several leads that are a combination of techniques. Lead techniques can often be combined for a solid article beginning.

Here Brian Ettkin of the Scripps-Howard News Service uses a statement and then a comparison of Kevin Johnson of the Phoenix Suns and Mark Price of the

Cleveland Cavaliers in an article about the sports marketing attractions of various players. This article was run on the Scripps-Howard wires in March 1994.

Combinations of various types of leads are limited only by your imagination, and your knowledge and use of various leads.

> There's such a fine line in sports between marketable and dull.
> Phoenix all-star point guard Kevin Johnson is flashy, exciting and plays for the Western Conference champion Suns. Advertisers find him marketable.
> Cleveland all-star point guard Mark Price is plain, equally talented and plays for the Cavaliers. He is dull—advertisers often lose his phone number.
> As the market for athletes who endorse everything from shoes to frozen pizzas has become saturated, companies aren't shelling out their money as freely.

Here's an unusual combination lead and story.

Ken Grissom of *The Houston Post* begins with a "you" lead, that leads to a "test" style. He had four questions in the article. One is reprinted here.

This article, under a headline "Patience key in trophy hunting," ran in *The Houston Post* on December 9, 1993.

> Take this quick test:
> You are on a big South Texas ranch, sitting in a tripod stand on a narrow sendero, hunting for a big deer known to be in the area.
> The buck—and it *is* a monster, heavy and wide with 10 points—suddenly appears in the sendero about 250 yards away. It turns and weaves down the edge of the sendero, coming toward you—now in the open, now in the brush. Continually moving.
> What do you do?
> 1) Shoot.
> 2) Don't shoot.
> The correct answer is don't shoot. Why risk a moving shot at 200-plus yards when the animal is still coming toward you? (p. B12)

Using the "you" of the reader and the "I" of the writer *can* be done. Here Vin T. Sparano of the Gannett News Service uses both in an article about hunting and fishing trips. This was run early in December 1993.

> Sportsmen can spend months, even years, planning that great hunting or fishing trip, but everything still can go wrong and destroy a journey.
> Unless you are an experienced traveler, you may not be aware of the problems that can ruin your trip. If you're a hunter or fisherman, there are some precautions to consider.
> Several years ago, I decided that I would no longer travel with sporting arms. It was just too much trouble at most airports. I would carefully pack my shotgun or rifle and tape all hinges and latches of the case with duct tape to protect them from the usual battering inflicted by baggage handlers.

To repeat, combinations of lead types are limited solely by the writer's imagination:

- A *quotation* from an athlete, player or coach might be followed by a *description* of that person.
- An *anecdote* about a person might be followed by a *rhetorical question* at the end of the lead: "Do you think he did the right thing in that circumstance?"
- A *statement*: "It was the highest scoring football game ever played (in the state of . . .)" might easily be followed by *contrasting quotations* from, *or contrasting anecdotes* about, the winning and losing coaches.
- A *false lead* (perhaps about a Civil War battle re-enactment) might be followed by a *quotation* from a participant in that battle re-enactment.

A reminder: All leads must come to an obvious conclusion, before the writer (and eventually the reader) begins the body of the article.

In *Modern Sportswriting* (1969), Louis I. Gelfand and Harry E. Heath Jr. wrote:

Regardless of the type of story being written, however, the sportswriter should examine his notes carefully, select his lead elements, and make a mental outline of the story before proceeding. The beginner will find it helpful to number the facts in his notes in the order of their importance. *The veteran automatically turns over lead possibilities in his mind as the game is played. In many cases he has mentally concocted a half-dozen leads before the contest has ended. This procedure is second nature with him; indeed, he may be entirely unaware of it. The beginner will develop it only through practice.* (p. 38; italics added)

Chapter Four

Quick 'n' Dirty Guide to Sports Leads

On occasion, even the best writer "runs dry" at the beginning of a story. The writer has no lead; no beginning. The blinking cursor just seems to say: "No lead. . . . No lead. . . . No lead. . . . No lead. . . ."

There is nothing like that cold, empty feeling when there is no lead in sight for a story that has to be written—especially if the writer is on deadline and can hear the ticking clock as the deadline grows nearer.

Fortunately, there are some keys to help the writer find that ideal lead for the story in progress. Answering these questions may help the writer find the best type of lead for the article in progress.

- What is the best anecdote I have in my notes?
- What is the best quotation?
- What is the best description?
- What did I see when I was covering the story?
- Was there anything important behind the scenes?
- What would the reader expect to know?

It may help the writer discover the right lead by considering the category of the story. In the following, a list of leads is offered after each type of story. These are leads that, in general, may be the most appropriate for these types of articles. Although this is not a completely fail-safe method, these charts may help the writer select the lead based on the type of article in progress. (You can consider this a rudimentary computer-check program in type form.)

Are you writing *about yourself* as observer or participant in a sports event? Consider:

- A first-person lead
- The anecdotal lead
- A big play lead
- A descriptive lead
- An interior monologue lead
- Combinations of two or more of these types
- Other type of lead or leads

Are you writing a profile or biographical article *about an active or retired player or someone else in sports*? Consider:

- An anecdotal lead
- A descriptive lead
- A quotation lead
- A timeline lead
- Combinations of two or more of these leads
- Other types of leads

Are you writing about *any active sports event* (baseball game, football game, tennis match, etc.)? Consider:

- A summary lead
- A prominent name lead
- A big play lead
- A descriptive lead
- A quotation lead
- A comparison–contrast lead
- Combinations of two or more of these types of leads
- Other types of leads

Are you writing about a *trend in sports or a problem in sports and society*? Consider:

- A question lead
- A summary lead
- A statement lead

- A timeline lead
- Combinations of two or more of these lead types
- Another type of lead, or leads

Are you writing an *essay, editorial, or personal philosophy*? Consider:

- A first-person "I" lead
- A statement lead
- A question lead
- An anecdotal lead
- A summary lead
- Combinations of two of these leads
- Other type of lead or leads

Are you writing about *a specific scene or location*? Consider:

- A descriptive lead
- A second-person "you" lead
- A summary lead
- Combinations of two or more of these leads
- Other types of leads

Are you writing about *an accident or other incident that includes a fatality, injury, or property damage (or potential for such)*? Consider:

- A summary lead
- Prominent name lead
- A descriptive lead
- A statement lead
- A quotation lead
- Combinations of these types of leads
- Other types of leads

Are you writing *how-to-do-it material*? Consider:

- A descriptive lead
- A statement lead
- A second-person "you" lead
- A summary lead

- Combinations of two or more of these types of leads
- Another type of lead or leads

Are you writing *inspirational or motivational material*? Consider:

- A first-person "I" lead
- A second-person "you" lead
- An anecdotal lead
- A question lead
- A statement lead
- Combinations of these types of leads
- Other types of leads

Are you writing *publicity material, press releases, or formal documents*? Consider:

- A prominent name lead
- A summary lead
- A statement lead
- Combinations of these types of leads
- Other types of leads

Are you writing about *sports and government, sports in the courts, sports and the law, or sports and politics*? Consider:

- A summary lead
- A prominent name lead
- A statement lead
- A timeline lead
- A quotation lead
- A question lead
- Combinations of these types of leads
- Other types of leads

Are you writing about *sports and medicine or sports and science*? Consider:

- A descriptive lead
- A summary lead
- A question lead

- A statement lead
- An anecdotal lead
- A quotation lead
- Combinations of these types of leads
- Other leads

Are you writing for *radio or TV*? Consider:

- A comparison–contrast lead
- A summary lead
- A prominent name lead
- A descriptive lead
- A big play lead
- An anecdotal lead
- A quotation lead
- A question lead
- A first-person "I" lead
- A second-person "you" lead
- A statement lead
- Combinations of these types of leads
- Other types of leads

Are you writing an *advance* story? Consider:

- A comparison–contrast lead
- A summary lead
- A statement lead
- A prominent name lead
- A quotation lead
- Combinations of two or more of these types of leads
- Other types of leads

Are you writing a *follow-up* story? Consider:

- A summary lead
- An anecdote lead
- A big play lead
- A comparison–contrast lead
- A quotation lead

- A prominent name lead
- A statement lead
- Combinations of these types of leads
- Other types of leads

LEADS CHARTED BY GENERAL DEGREE
OF DIFFICULTY OF USE

The following list indicates how hard these types of leads are, or how often they can be seen in general sports usage. Although this is *not* a fail-safe guarantee either, the numbers indicate the degree of simplicity or complexity of use for the writer.

1–3 indicates generally easy to use and often seen;

4–7 moderately harder to use, takes more planning or is more complex;

8–10 difficult to use in most situations.

An asterisk after the number indicates that this type of lead is seldom seen in most sports articles.

- The anecdotal lead: 2–3
- The big play lead: 3–5
- The classified ad lead: 4–6
- The comparison–contrast lead: 4–6
- The delayed climax lead: 4–6
- The descriptive lead: 3–5
- The epic game lead: 3–5
- The false lead: 8–10*
- The future lead: 7–9
- The "I" lead: 1–3
- The interior monologue lead: 9–10*
- The "letter to" lead: 2–3
- The list lead: 2–4
- The literary reference lead: 6–9
- The news lead: 1–3
- The news reference lead: 2–5
- The prominent name lead: 2–3
- The question lead: 2–4
- The quotation lead: 2–4
- The simile (or metaphor) lead: 8–9
- The statement lead: 1–3

- The statistics lead: 3–5
- The summary lead: 1–3
- The "theme" lead: 3–5*
- The timeline lead: 4–5
- The "you" lead: 2–4
- Combination leads: ?

QUICK 'n' DIRTY GUIDE TO GAME STORIES

In general, the complete game story, no matter what sport, should contain these elements or items:

- The final score, usually in the top three paragraphs, often in the first paragraph
- Names of the teams
- When the game took place and where (the where is often in the dateline)
- Key players or outstanding plays or both
- Coaching strategies
- Crowd
- Quotations from players or coaches
- Injuries
- Records set during the game
- Effect of game on league standings
- Any oddities, length of game, number of penalties, etc.
- Weather—if a factor in outcome

Chapter Five
Outlining and Transitions

How important is the outline? Extremely important. In *Modern Feature Writing* (1949), DeWitt Reddick offered five rules why outlining the article is important:

1. *A good outline insures logical development of thought.* The outline permits the writer to view the structure of the whole before he begins writing. By looking at this skeleton he can make sure that each major idea has a proper relationship to the central theme.

2. *A good outline helps to secure unity.* For every article the writer should gather more information than he uses. It is important that he see clearly what to leave out as well as what to include. The outline aids in proper selection of material.

3. *A good outline aids in securing proper emphasis on the various elements.* After the author has selected his material, he still faces the task of deciding the emphasis to be placed on each of the items or groups of facts. An outline clarifies the main points to be introduced as topic sentences and indicates the material to be subordinated.

4. *Careful preparation of an outline permits the writer to consider in advance the style to be used in developing each important section.* One idea in the article, perhaps, can be presented most clearly by a narrative incident; another is complex and needs clarification by means of a hypothetical situation; a direct quotation from an authority will give greatest force to another important thought. As he prepares his outline, the writer can decide upon the literary devices for the effective presentation of each idea.

5. *An outline aids spontaneity in writing.* The preparation of an outline exercises the mind of the writer, steeps it in the material, and creates the mood of the article. Thus, when he begins to write, he will have less trouble overcoming initial inertia and will be able to move along more swiftly because he knows in advance how he will approach each section. (pp. 78–79)

SIX NO-FAIL TRANSITIONS INSIDE AN ARTICLE

In long, complicated articles, such as those written in the diamond structure, the writer may encounter three or four or as many as nine or ten subsections. Certainly, in the diamond format, there will be at least three separate sections: the lead, the body of the story, and the end; or four: the lead, the theme segment, the body, and the end. Many articles will have subtopics or subsections inside the body of the story, anecdotes from various personalities, short profiles inside the article, summary material, and other necessary material.

Trying to tie all these subsections together involves the use of transitional devices. Most writers don't have trouble with transitions *inside* the subsection that may be one or two or three pages (screens) long: The problem lies in bridging the gap between one major section and another. Following are seven types of transitions that the writer may use to bridge this gap. (They appear in order from the easiest to use to the most complex.)

1. The Concluding Statement

In a personality section of an article, in which the writer is profiling subject "X", the writer may effectively draw the section to a close by using a quotation from "X" that is very clearly a definitive statement by the speaker: For example: "He squinted into the sun and shuffled his feet in the dust. 'I've had a good life. I wouldn't have changed it for anything. Not for anything at all.' "

This type of concluding statement is often followed by three ellipsis points (. . .).

2. The Spacebreak

This is a physical separation of text on the page (or on the screen, when you are using a word processor). If you are typing double-spaced copy, when you need a spacebreak transition, jump six lines. The "air" or white on the page will indicate to the reader that a different topic is upcoming. Many writers use one or more *bullets*—large, heavy dots (or the asterisk key on the keyboard)—in the middle of the spacebreak to indicate to editors and readers that this jump is deliberate. (On a word processor, a jump of a few lines is very easy to do accidentally.)

The English call this *line white* because it is literally a line of white space on the copy. It is also literally a line of white added by word processors.

The spacebreak should not be overused. In a 10-page article, for instance, the spacebreak should only be used perhaps three times; otherwise the writer has copy that reads "too choppy," as if the reader is watching a freight train moving across a highway intersection. The white between the article sections is like the space between individual freight cars. If the writer uses too many spacebreaks, the article may read like many brief freight cars, passing the reader.

On the page, the spacebreak looks like this:

"XXXXXXXXXXX. XXXXXXXX. XXXXXXXXXXXX."
* * *
"XXXXXXXXXXX. XXXXXXXXXXXXXXX. XXXXXXXXXXXXXXXXX."

3. The Spacebreak-With-Filler Material

This is the spacebreak on the page, with additional material inserted, such as a headline or subhead, song lyrics, poetry selections, an excerpt from a short story, or perhaps a quotation picked up from later in the article. Use this material with discretion. If you are citing the work of a poet or writer, or lyricist, be sure to get formal permission to quote material that may be copyrighted. Use small amounts of filler so as not to confuse or sidetrack the reader. The filler material should read like a headline, for it is exactly that, a subhead inside the article.

4. The Dateline or Diary Transition

This is a simple time technique: "By late 1992, Joe Smith had gone to Canada and had become involved in. . . ."

This offers a quick and clean transition into an anecdote or other subtopic within your article. It may be used with a spacebreak or without.

5. The Argumentative

Let one personality (A) in your article make a statement: Let another personality (B) answer pro or con as a way to transition into a subtopic about (B). For example:

"I think such-and-such is true," "A" said finally, resting his arms on the table and looking out the window. "I've always believed that."
* * *
"I just don't believe in such-and-such at all," "B" said later. "That's never been true as far as I am concerned."

"B"'s life, from the early 1940s, indicates that . . . .

6. The Metaphor Transition

Here the writer uses a fanciful style to move smoothly from one subtopic to another. The metaphor is a connection between two items—a sports writer can use it to transition from one of the items to another, like this:

Joe Jock paused during a practice climb up western Massachusetts's Mount Greylock. He carefully re-coiled his climbing rope and slowly re-tied his bootlaces.

"The thing about climbing, he said, gazing at the top of Greylock, shrouded in haze, "is, the closer you are to the top, the faster you think you can get there."

In fact, during the last six years of his career, the closer he got to the top, the faster he got there. When he isn't climbing, his career as a sports equipment developer and innovator has moved him from rock bottom to the pinnacle of success faster than he or anyone else could have guessed.

His business, ...

Here, of course, the comparison is mountain climbing to career ladder.

The metaphor transition is a very difficult one to use because it is rare that such a combination of literal and figurative combinations would occur (or probably occur to the writer to use). Other transitions are much easier to use.

Chapter Six

Two Types of Article Structures: The Inverted Pyramid and the Diamond Structure

When newspaper or magazine readers read sports articles, they are seldom concerned—or perhaps never notice—the structure of an article: the *internal order* or organization of that article. There is, in fact, no reason for a reader to be concerned about structure. Readers read articles for entertainment, information, education, and amusement.

But there is every reason for writers to be concerned about how they structure articles. There are two key structures writers need to be familiar with.

The *inverted pyramid* is an old, old structure that can be seen in every newspaper in the United States every day. The *diamond* structure is a more complex form, originally a magazine-oriented form. Writers can usually write inverted pyramid articles by instinct after some practice, whereas the diamond form is more complicated and usually requires an outline (and often requires more time to complete).

To use a simile, the inverted pyramid is like a plain pine box: You can carry things in it (in this case articles—information) but the box is not elegant. The diamond structure is like a toolbox lined with velvet. One is plain, the other is fancier, but both boxes could carry the same tools.

Both the inverted pyramid and the diamond structure carry information to the reader, but you can fit a lot of different tools inside the diamond format—and carry them better (and even impress the reader more).

Sports writers should know when each is appropriate to use and particularly *why* it is appropriate in some cases and inappropriate in other cases.

THE INVERTED PYRAMID

This is an article structure that has existed since about the Civil War. With the advent of the telegraph as a means of distributing news stories (the "wire story"), wire editors looked for a story structure that would be universally acceptable to editors of different newspapers with differing news styles and differing design and editing formulas. They looked for a story structure that editors would need and readers would accept. The inverted pyramid met everyone's expectations.

The inverted pyramid style is a news article or sports article that is written like an upside down triangle, with the base at the top and the point at the bottom. The top contains (usually) a summary lead, with the key elements of *who, what, where* and *when* in the top three paragraphs or so. Other elements, *why* and *how*, may be left until later in the story. This summary form using *who, what, where*, and *when* is universally appropriate for news articles, at the national, regional, and local level.

For example, a hypothetical news story might begin like this:

> WASHINGTON—President Clinton announced a "complete package" of reform measures for the National Park System Wednesday.
>
> The package, labeled "Parks for the Next Century," will cost $250 billion and will involve upgrades for user services in Yellowstone, Yosemite, and many of the other major parks in the National Park system.
>
> The $250 billion package will be paid for in a special proposal which will be presented to Congress soon. It is expected that user fees for all national parks will increase, although administration officials did not estimate the increase for individual park users.

Here is the *who* (President Clinton); the *what* (announced the National Park package); the *where* (the Washington dateline) and the *when* (Wednesday).

On national wire stories, the *where* is usually a dateline before the first sentence and then *when* (Wednesday) often "fits best" at the end of a sentence or paragraph. Generally, a summary of the most important key facts, financial costs, key facts, key details, and key quotations are used in the top three paragraphs.

If the news article in the inverted pyramid form is nine paragraphs long, a general rule would be this: The first one to three paragraphs would be a summary lead of the key elements of the story. The middle three paragraphs would be major facts, major details, and major quotations in the order of importance, most important at the top, least important details toward the bottom. The bottom of the article, written in this inverted pyramid, should contain the least important material in the story. The inverted pyramid should be written in such a manner that if the article was 9 inches in column form, and there was only 7 inches of space for the article, the last 2 inches of copy could literally be cut off the story *without crippling* the meaning of the story.

The inverted pyramid is "top heavy" with *key facts*, details and quotations. This type of article structure is perfect for international, national, regional, and local news

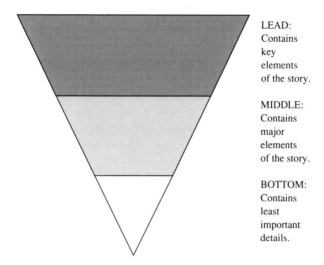

LEAD:
Contains
key
elements
of the story.

MIDDLE:
Contains
major
elements
of the story.

BOTTOM:
Contains
least
important
details.

TIME: All inverted pyramid articles are assumed to have happened in the *immediate past*. Friday traffic accidents are in Saturday's newspapers. Saturday football games are in the Sunday sports pages. There is usually no "historical" segment of an inverted pyramid article. There is no significant end section. The article just "dribbles off the bottom of the page."

FIG. 6.1. Structure of an inverted pyramid article.

and is mandatory for front-page articles that involve fatalities, whether they are airplane crashes, automobile crashes, shootings, accidents, or weather stories, such as hurricanes and other storms (see Fig. 6.1).

In general, everything in an inverted pyramid story is immediate. In the newspaper business, yesterday's news is on today's front page. In the Clinton parks story, earlier, the Wednesday announcement of the parks package would (presumably) be on the front page of Thursday newspapers.

In general, *everything* in the inverted pyramid story is "yesterday": yesterday's announcement by the president, yesterday's air crash, yesterday's areawide tornado, or yesterday's local town elections, but the day is used to avoid confusion.

The focus of the inverted pyramid is *immediate news*. Details, facts, and information become less important as the writer works through the middle of the story. Minor details are used toward and at the bottom of the article. This becomes an instinctive form for daily newspaper news writers. It is just as appropriate in sports writing, especially for sports news articles. The sports writer often answers *who's involved, what's happening, where,* and *when* at the top of the article, then works through the key facets or key topics of the story, to the minor details at the bottom.

Here is a similar example of an inverted pyramid sports story. This article, by Gary Long of *The Miami Herald,* was published in the *Houston Chronicle* on February 12, 1994 under a four-column headline and subhead:

Bonnett dies pursuing his dream

Driver suffers fatal head injuries as car crashes in Daytona 500 practice

By Gary Long
Miami Herald

The lead of this article runs four paragraphs, down through the paragraph about the time of his death.

DAYTONA BEACH, Fla.—Neil Bonnett, a popular stock car driver who had raced only twice since an April 1990 crash that caused severe head injuries and temporary amnesia, died Friday afternoon trying to keep alive a high-risk career that he wouldn't give up.

Bonnett, 47, from Bessemer, Ala., suffered massive head injuries when his Chevrolet slammed the fourth-turn wall nose-first. He was practicing for the 36th annual Daytona 500 a week from Sunday.

Bonnett would have tried to qualify for his 16th Daytona 500 this afternoon. Instead, he became the 25th fatality in all forms of racing at Daytona International Speedway since its 1959 opening.

He was pronounced dead at nearby Halifax Medical Center at 1:17 p.m., less than an hour after the accident.

How the accident happened is described here, toward the middle of the article.

Bonnett, who ran fifth in his first Daytona 500 in 1976, lost control of his Chevrolet as he exited the 31-degree banking in Turn 4. The car skidded down on the flat apron and then veered straight back into the outside wall brutally hard.

Bonnett had to be cut from the wreckage, and NASCAR officials promptly ordered that a tarp be placed over the Chevrolet, a grim signal.

Initially, there were rumors that he might have hit an oil slick. Briefly into the practice, a red flag had been waved so that oil-dry powder could be spread between Turns 1 and 2.

But NASCAR official Chip Williams said there was no sign of oil in the fourth turn and that other drivers reported no problems there. Williams said indications were that Bonnett lost control.

Bonnett's car hit just a few feet from where ARCA rookie Andy Farr knocked a hole into the concrete in a crash in practice Thursday. Track officials worked overnight replacing a section of the wall and catch fencing that had been torn out.

Farr remained hospitalized in good condition Friday.

Summary of his career begins here.

Bonnett, survived by wife, Susan, and two children, interspersed 18 victories through a successful NASCAR Winston Cup career that appeared at an end after a serious accident in the 1990 TranSouth 500 at Darlington, S.C.

Bonnett had been most visible since as a television analyst for CBS, WTBS and The Nashville Network on race telecasts.

But he began subbing for close friend Dale Earnhardt during off-season testing before the 1993 Winston Cup campaign.

Then, at the invitation of Earnhardt's car owner Richard Childress, Bonnett qualified an Earnhardt backup car for the midsummer DieHard 500 at Talladega, Ala.

He was running in midpack in his first race in more than three years when he got caught up in a multicar tangle in which his car became airborne and ripped apart fencing that kept it from sailing into packed grandstands. Not only did Bonnett escape injury, but his appetite was whetted.

Minor details, quotations, and facts are used toward the end of the article.

"You can't walk away from the sport you've spent your entire life around," he said after signing a limited six-race 1994 contract to drive the Country Time Chevrolet for James Finch of Panama City, Fla.

"Television was a good avenue for me to get involved in racing again," he said. "It opened the door for me to come back and be around all of my friends. But it also stirred up that interest to get back inside of a race car."

A year ago, Bonnett worked in the CBS booth with Ken Squier and two-time NASCAR champion Ned Jarrett as Jarrett's son Dale raced past Earnhardt on the final lap to win the Daytona 500.

"I'm sure a lot of people wonder why Neil Bonnett ever got back into a race car again after what he had gone through in 1990 and then the things he had seen happen to his very close friends, the Allison family," Jarrett said Friday afternoon.

A protege of Bobby Allison, Bonnett provided support through Allison's recovery from near-fatal injuries in a June 1988 crash and also after the deaths of Allison's racing sons Davey and Clifford 11 months apart.

"But having been a former racer myself," Jarrett said, "I can understand. Neil wanted to drive a race car. That's what he wanted.

"He knew the risks that could be involved, but he was willing to accept those risks." (pp. B1, B11)

There is one obvious problem with the inverted pyramid form. As Brooks, Kennedy, Moen, and Ranly wrote in *News Reporting and Writing* (1985), "For all its strengths, the inverted pyramid has a telling weakness. It cannot maintain, let alone build, reader interest as the story progresses. After the first three paragraphs, *it's not going to get any better*" (p. 260, italics added). The diamond structure, or the newsmagazine diamond described in the following section solves that problem—the diamond format article becomes richer, more detailed, and more interesting paragraph by paragraph as the article continues. That's why the diamond structure form is preferred for sports features, profiles, trend articles, and all types of sports articles other than the "game" or "score" article.

THE DIAMOND STRUCTURE

Although few textbooks identify this form, it is an obvious structure for many general articles and many sports articles. It differs from the inverted pyramid, but is just as easy to learn.

The key difference between the inverted pyramid and the diamond structure is this: *The diamond allows room for historical perspective in the article.*

Everything in the inverted pyramid is the immediate past. Saturday's football games are in Sunday's newspapers; Sunday's games are in Monday's newspapers.

A summary of the growth of baseball, ever since Abner Doubleday "invented" the game, however, would likely be written in the diamond structure, allowing the writer room in the article for the early days of the game.

A profile of any athlete would likely be written in the diamond format, which allows the writer space in the article for the player's youth, education, and early playing days—in short, a biography of the player.

In general, the structure of a diamond format article looks like Fig. 6.2.

Lead: in the Present

(or in the Immediate Past)

the article jumps to:

The Distant Past

The writer then uses a general straight-line chronology to . . .

The Recent Past

and back to:

The Present

The inverted pyramid article is usually one "block" of material. The diamond article consists of at least three separate elements: the lead, the body of the story, which begins with "the historical past," and the end segment.

Unlike the inverted pyramid article, which can be cut from the end toward the middle of the article, the diamond article *cannot* be cut from the end. The diamond format article has a specific and important end segment. If the diamond article must be cut anywhere, it must be cut carefully somewhere in the middle.

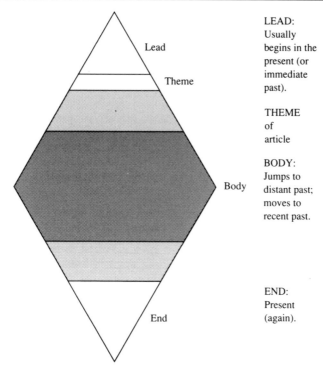

LEAD:
Usually
begins in the
present (or
immediate
past).

THEME
of
article

BODY:
Jumps to
distant past;
moves to
recent past.

END:
Present
(again).

Keys to the diamond structure: Article begins in *present* (or immediate past, as in the case of a football game or boxing match); the article jumps to the *distant past*, then to the *present* again at the end of the article. This article cannot be cut at the end—there is a definite end segment for emphasis. The article will consist of at least three segments: lead, body, end, or, more likely, the lead, theme section, various subtopics in the body, and the end segment. The end segment may "echo" the lead; the end may be about the same person, or may be about the same theme, or may be about the same local as the beginning, giving the reader a sense that the subject is complete because the writer is "back where the article began."

FIG. 6.2. Structure of a diamond article.

Long profile articles and trend articles and articles that have a rich historical middle may have three or four or as many as eight or nine subtopics in the middle of the article. Writers using the diamond format should make it a practice to outline their articles as carefully and as completely as possible to make sure they have included all key facts, anecdotes, and quotations.

Although many sports feature writers know that the diamond format involves at least three divisions of the article—lead–body–end—freelancer William B. Hartley believes that article writers should consider *four* elements in the article. In "Building the Magazine Article" (*The Writer*, March 1972), he suggested: "In general . . . the usual magazine article has four basic sections. Generalizations are notably dangerous, but I would suggest that most successful articles are built with a *lead, a statement of theme or intent*, the *body* of the article which supports and advances the theme, and a *conclusion*."

Hartley suggested that "an old nursery rhyme provides a simple illustration of four-element construction":

Jack and Jill went up the hill
(Anecdote lead)

To fetch a pail of water:
(Statement of theme)

Jack fell down and broke his crown
(Body: the story itself)

And Jill came tumbling after.
(Conclusion) (pp. 12–14)

The theme section need only be a concise paragraph that summarizes the article. It certainly need not be a major section. It acts simply as a reminder to the reader of what the article is about.

Additionally, if the article begins with a person "A," then it ends with "A": if the article begins in the present, it should end in the present; if it begins with a description of scene "X," it should end with "X" again. *Returning to the same individual, theme, time, or location gives the reader an instinctive sense that the article has come full circle and the writer has completed the story.* In some cases, the end segment will offer the reader a *glimpse of the future* or an educated guess of the future.

Here is an example of a diamond structure article. This profile, of Kansas City-area student athlete Lisa Davies, was published in *The Kansas City Star* on May 15, 1994, under a two-column headline and subhead:

15 varsity letters,
but she still ranks
No. 2 in her class

Top girl scholar-athlete
has been chosen All-Metro
five times, in four sports

By Terrance Harris
Staff Writer

The *Kansas City Star* reporter uses an anecdote lead—how hard she studies for an upcoming exam.

Her eyelids grew heavier and the temptation to allow them to simply shut grew stronger as night turned into Wednesday morning for Lisa Davies.

"I just have to do well on this psychology test," she repeated, often in concert with yawns.

Davies was forced to study past midnight after a whirlwind Tuesday, which began with morning classes in Oak

Grove, continued in Boonville at 1:30 for the Missouri River Valley Conference track and field championships and finished at Adair Park in Independence for an early-evening game in the Greater Kansas City Softball Tournament.

We're talking mileage.

In the process, Davies gathered conference titles in the triple jump, high jump and long jump in helping the Panthers bring back the league championship with three points to spare. She later blasted a bases-empty homer in the bottom of the seventh inning, but it didn't prevent a 5–2 loss to Truman.

"It was definitely a very stressful day," she said. "I didn't feel right leaving the track team because I could have possibly given them more points had I run the 400. But I also would not have felt right not showing up for the softball game because I have a commitment to them.

"I've always been taught that you honor a commitment no matter the personal sacrifice."

This paragraph and the next summarize the theme of this article.

That strong sense of dedication and devotion has propelled Davies to the highest levels in all her endeavors at Oak Grove, whether in the classroom, on the basketball court, in front of a volleyball net, on a softball diamond or floating through the air in track and field competition.

Davies' selfless commitment and never-tiring work ethic have not gone unnoticed. She was selected *The Kansas City Star's* top girl scholar-athlete for 1994.

Statistics help prove how exceptional she is.

In addition to winning 15 varsity letters in four sports since her freshman year, Davies holds three academic letters for her 3.95 grade-point average on a 4-point scale. She will graduate this year as salutatorian in her class of 109.

Davies also serves as the National Honor Society president and vice president of Interact Club, and she is a member of student council.

Quotations from others begin to appear in the article.

"Lisa is just very self-disciplined, goal-oriented and motivated," said Leland Loux, Davies' counselor. "To be able to juggle as many things as she does also says a lot about Lisa's organizational skills. She budgets her time and uses it wisely. Lisa doesn't waste time.

"She realizes that she has so much time for academics, athletics and extracurricular activities. And she balances it out real well. Better than most."

Through this all, Davies manages to be a popular person outside of sports. The consensus at Oak Grove is that Davies is as caring and genuine away from sports as she is fierce and competitive as an athlete.

"Lisa has always been a person I could come and talk about anything and no matter what is going on in her life, she will make you feel that your problem or situation is the only one that matters," said Sarah Munson, a close friend since fifth grade. "And one of the things I've always really enjoyed about Lisa is that she is really modest about her accomplishments in sports and in academics. She's never been like 'Hey, look what I did.' "

"You often have to drag things out of her. Lisa doesn't ever make other people feel less than her. Come to think of it, she's actually quite humble about all of her accomplishments."

Jim Borland, her math teacher and a longtime friend of the Davies family, said: "Lisa doesn't flaunt anything, which is another one of her many admirable traits. She's just like everyone."

Strong background

The historical background part of the article begins at this subhead.

To know Ron Davies and Beverly Davies and their backgrounds leaves little to wonder about the foundation of their youngest of four children.

Both Ron and Beverly competed in athletics in college, and both are now educators. Beverly played basketball for Kansas during 1964–68 and now is a teacher in Blue Springs. Ron played football and baseball for Central Missouri State during the 1960s and now is superintendent of East Lynne School, kindergarten–eighth grade, near Harrisonville.

"If young people get anything from their parents, I'm sure Lisa gets a lot from them," Borland said. "I guess you could say she's a chip off the old blocks."

But Davies and her parents, who are divorced, said Lisa carved her way independent of their influence.

"My parents didn't really value one thing over the other," Davies said. "Their outlook was 'As long as you work hard and try your hardest, then we'll be happy with whatever you do.' They made it clear right from the beginning that if I didn't want to play any sports, then great, or if I got all C's, then great also.

"Their only concern was that I worked my hardest."

Beverly confirms her daughter's appraisal, but she added that Lisa displayed an uncommon inner drive at an early age that made it easier to let her daughter define her own level of achievement.

"Lisa is a very self-motivated person who has never needed to be pushed at all," Beverly said. "We never had to push her to study or participate in athletics. Her self-motivation has always pushed her to go above what's required, which is why she has achieved so highly in so many different areas."

Beverly, however, also a recalls a brief period in her daughter's life when achievement did not come easily. She was placed in a low reading group during first grade in Colorado and second grade in Alabama.

Beverly Davies attributes it to the family moving around, but by the time she was in the fifth grade and had returned to Oak Grove, Lisa had climbed to the top of her class.

"She just kept gaining momentum by the time she reached fourth and fifth grade, and we just kept being surprised at how well she did," Beverly said. "Watching her grow up and develop into the person she is today has been a lot of fun and enjoyable. Lisa just never ceases to amaze us with the things she can do."

Four years of excellence

Oak Grove basketball coach Brad Gaines recalls a tall and scrawny seventh-grader who used to come around during his varsity practices, shooting at one of the vacant baskets.

Shot after shot, seldom making as much as a peep.

"When she'd come over we never really said much to each other," Gaines said. "I'd just give her a ball and let her shoot. I'd be on one end of the court doing my thing, and she'd be at the other end just shooting.

"You could tell back then, and even in elementary school, that she was going to be a gifted athlete someday.

"I remember one day Dr. Roger Nelson (Oak Grove principal) and I were watching her shoot from upstairs, and I told him then that he was looking at the next Oak Grove stud. This is Lisa Davies."

Call Gaines a prophet or a vulture, but Davies roared onto the high school set as a freshman starter in varsity volleyball, basketball and track. She added softball to her list as a sophomore.

But her basketball draws the most attention, and it is basketball that will pay for her education beginning next fall at Southwest Missouri State in Springfield. She passed on offers from Notre Dame, Alabama, Louisiana State, Northwestern, Illinois and Colorado.

Additional details prove what an exceptional athlete she is.

During her four years of basketball at Oak Grove the Panthers were 105–15 overall and 32–0 in the MRVC, including an undefeated Missouri 3A state championship season in 1992. Davies averaged 21.1 points and 11 rebounds, receiving All-Metro and all-state honors last season.

Davies, who is 5 feet 11, leaves Oak Grove No. 2 on the school's career rebounding (979) and steals (462) lists. And her 1,657 career points rank third.

The volleyball team also went undefeated in the conference since 1990, and it won district titles in 1991 and 1993. For her efforts, Davies received All-Metro accolades as a junior and senior.

Finally, in her three-year dual spring seasons, Davies has contributed equally in softball and track. Last season she was All-Metro in softball after hitting .413 with 15 RBIs, 16 stolen bases and three home runs. All-Metro teams have not been selected this spring, but she is batting .508, with 27 RBIs and 12 stolen bases. Her six home runs

A box with a feature story helps the reader quickly understand her achievements.

Winner's profile

OAK GROVE

Lisa Davies

3.95 on 4.0 scale . . . four letters basketball, three times all-conference, all-state, All-Metro as senior . . . four letters volleyball, twice All-Metro . . . three letters softball, All-Metro as junior . . . four letters track, all-metro, state high-jump champ as junior . . . homecoming queen . . . student council . . . National Honor Society . . . second in class of 109.

Also nominated: Ryan Fry, Brandon Reinbold.

---

this season set a school record.

In track Davies was an All-Metro selection after winning the 3A state championship with a jump of 5 feet, 6 inches. She also finished second at state in the long jump (18-4½) and third in the 400 meters (57.15) and triple jump (38-11¾). Davies holds the No. 2 spot on *The Star's* honor roll in all three jump categories this season, including 5-6 in the high jump.

In her last two years of competition Davies has been All-Metro five times in four different sports, and she has been recognized twice as an all-state athlete.

"Lisa has no idea of the impact she has had here at Oak Grove, because we push the team concept first—putting others before yourself," Oak Grove Athletic Director Randy McClain said. "But Lisa has been instrumental and monumental in the success of every team she has been a part of."

Gaines said he would like to take credit for Davies' success, but he cannot. He said all of her achievements have grown out of hard work, discipline, dedication and determination. Also throw in a heap of innate ability. Or as Gaines put it, "Nobody can ever make mashed potatoes from rice."

Epilogue

The end of the article is tied to the beginning. The end segment is often shorter than the lead.

By the way, Davies received an A on that psychology exam Wednesday. (p. C-13)

Gerri Hirshey's article, "Arc of a Diver," a profile of diver Greg Louganis, is also a classic example of how the diamond structure should be used. This article appeared in the September 22, 1988 issue of *Rolling Stone* magazine.

Arc of a Diver

To stay at the top of his sport for ten years,
Greg Louganis has had to face down a lot of fears

The article begins with a spectator's view of high diving.

"SHEL, IT'S FOUR FLIGHTS UP, WILL YOU *LOOK*, SHEL?"

Shel, a straw-hatted retiree, squints into the Florida sun, up to the ten-meter diving platform at the Mission Bay Aquatic Training Center.

"Like jumping off a brownstone, huh? *Meshugah*. Nuts," Shel says, shaking his head. "But beeyootiful, I gotta say."

Shel and his wife, retirement-condo shoppers, have wandered out to the pool grandstand from the real-estate office also located in the Mission Bay center. In matching shorts sets, with floor plans in hand, they stand watching some of the nation's best divers arc and plunge. It was the condo developer's idea to put an Olympic-quality diving and swimming facility in his Boca Raton Utopia, hire one of the best diving coaches in America and make a Family Attraction that would elevate his tracts of stucco duplexes above the others gouged into the sandy scrubland north of Miami.

He's planted young gods amid the pensioners, and it's working. Mission Bay hosts worldclass diving and swimming meets, collects fat media fees for photographing and videotaping and runs clinics and camps that draw hopefuls from all over the United States and Canada. This is the business end of Olympic dreams, with a sweet real-estate tie-in. And bunking in the heart of it, in a rent-free model unit, is the most beeyootiful dreamer of all.

The two paragraphs beginning "high up" are summary paragraphs proving his international expertise.

High up on the tower, preparing to jump from brownstone height, is Greg Louganis, who swept the platform and springboard gold meals in the '84 Olympics and hopes to repeat in Seoul. He has been called the best ever; he's the only man in history to earn over 700 points in a single Olympic diving event, the only human—ever—to score seven perfect 10s for one dive in national and world competition. He is the gold standard for the sport. Single-handedly, Greg Louganis raised the degree of difficulty in world competition. The diving competition was not diluted by the Eastern-bloc boycott in '84; this year, as it was then, the chief rivalry will be between the Americans and the Chinese.

Most of his competitors, but especially the Eastern-bloc teams, are known to study tapes of Greg Louganis, who has dominated the sport for the last ten years. He was just sixteen when he won a silver medal in Montreal in 1976 and became the One to Watch. Since then, he has been the One to Beat, and to that end, they fret over the tapes, freeze-frame his dives and analyze the parts. But they cannot come up with the impossible sums that judges award Greg Louganis.

"The Soviets and the Chinese seem to have developed programs that teach Louganis techniques to every one of their divers," says Louganis's coach, Ron O'Brien. "[The communist countries] have developed an acrobatic, a mechanical copy of Greg. They haven't been successful at teaching a rhythmic, dancelike quality."

They've called him a Nureyev, a Baryshnikov. No one is better at aquatic, serial, kamikaze ballet. He walks like a dancer, back straight, shoulders square and high, legs turned out slightly. Louganis has been pacing along the platform, unrolling a chamois that he squeaks over a diver's hard torso and a dancer's outsize thighs. He has been dancing since he was eighteen months old, diving since he was eight, and the resulting sculpture draws stares even while he's performing this high-rise toilette. Poolside, and in the grandstand, they gawk as water sluices down a pair of Rodin-quality calves. In sacks of letters, in poetics and porn, men and women inflict their reactions, say they cannot help themselves, he is so . . . so . . . beeyootiful.

Even Shel, who doesn't know an inverted triple from a club sandwich, is spellbound as Louganis readies himself for liftoff.

One, two, three. He always eyes the water, then, counts it down in his head. Arms out, head straight, Louganis pushes off the concrete, rises straight up, high, higher, with a vertical leap that has been measured at thirty-three inches, blocking the noon-day sun in a gleaming brown flash. Now he is tucked, spinning, falling at 40 mph, counting the revolutions, looking for his spots, the visual reference points essential to spinning ballet divas. And trapeze artists. And fancy divers.

Top of platform, *kick*.

Bottom of platform, *kick*.

Bottom, water, open and *stretch*.

The astonishing silhouette is torn from the blue sky, slipped beneath the water with a mere surface dimple and a sound they call the rip.

It sounds like taut silk tearing. Blazered, stat-fed guys like Jim McKay wax lyrical about the rip on TV, but you cannot hear it on any network satellite feed. The rip is the diver's sonic boom, the aquatic Mach III. It's the screech of water molecules giving it up to a force greater than their pissant specific gravity.

Louganis's rip is followed by an instant of reverent silence and a cacophony of claps, whistles and the crack of wet chamois slapped against the concrete deck.

"Way to rip it, Lugo!"

"Nine point five," rasps O'Brien, who is scoring practice dives over the poolside P.A. "Real soft, Grego."

In a hard, competitive sport, a soft entry is highly prized. Despite the intricate acrobatics of the three-second performance, the entry, or bottom, is the last thing the judges see. And if Louganis has any chronic weakness, it is the bottom of his dives. He says he wishes he could rip consistently, like the Chinese; he wishes he could concentrate on the end better.

"The problem I have," Louganis says, "is getting in the water."

The problem he *had*, says O'Brien, was getting out of himself. Ask O'Brien about the greatest reward of coaching the world's best for over a decade, and there is no talk about pikes, triples and perfect scores.

"To see him grow as a person," O'Brien replies. "He used to be very introverted. He was in a lot of turmoil. I've seen him grow to being a very relaxed, confident, comfortable person who can deal with media, speak in front of crowds and just be happy. When I first started coaching him, he wasn't a real happy kid." He was always a brave, strong diver, O'Brien says. "But he was a scared kid. Scared of so darn many things."

LOUGANIS IS SMALLER AT EYE LEVEL, JUST FIVE FEET NINE, a god turned garbage man. He has put himself on trash

---

Good feature articles should offer the reader material they cannot get from television. There should be a "gee whiz—I didn't know that" quality to good nonfiction. In this case, the explanation of "the rip."

detail, his tough feet scudding on the griddle-hot concrete, picking up empty Gatorade cups discarded during the last session of Mission Bay's summer diving camp. In a second, the children are on him, shy but insistent, a knot of brown, peely-nosed kids in wet Speedos and BODY AND SEOUL T-shirts. Some just stare; some are nudged by parents aiming Canon Sure Shots. Louganis poses with tiny springboard fliers, signs T-shirts. The bolder ones ask the questions he hears over and over: "What if you get scared?" "What if you wipe out?" "What if you get all the way up there and you *just can't do it*?"

He talks to them gently, patiently, about fear. Sometimes Greg Louganis thinks there are more kinds of fear than Baskin-Robbins flavors. He's tasted quite a few, has rolled them around in his mouth, taken their measure, given them their quarter of respect. He admits he's been scared of a lot of things. Dangerous dives. New dives. People. Failure. Success.

"And snakes," he is saying as he stuffs towels and a wet Speedo into his battered Gap tote bag. "I really had a thing about snakes as a kid. But the thing about fear is that sooner or later you have to face it down or you'll be, like, nuts."

So he faced down some snakes?

"I saved up and bought one," he says. "A boa constrictor. Not too big. But a *serious* snake."

He made himself feed it live mice and sacks of squirming worms, and he came to see it as a thing of beauty and strength. "It was kind of gross at first," he says. But he got past it.

"The other thing about fear?" he says, posing his own question. "Is that there's always another one to take its place. It doesn't have to be a bad thing if you *deal* with it."

Eat the boa before it eats you?

"Nah," he says. "Just remember to buy the mice."

HERE'S THE BIG BOA NOW: LETTING ONE OBSESSION GO AND committing to another. He wants very much to act; he has studied the craft for nine years, since he majored in drama at college. He signed with William Morris right after the '84 Olympics, has kept studying, auditioning, chatting up casting directors. He is looking forward to what he calls an emotional rather than a physical obsession, but he wants to go out of diving just right. Can he rip it, leave the sport with a clean, golden finish? And when should he leave it? In October? Or in '92? Divers are said to peak in their mid-twenties, and he is twenty-eight.

Margin notes:

Here is the underlying theme of the article: overcoming fears. Notice the author's nice phrase "Louganis thinks there are more kinds of fear than Baskin-Robbins flavors."

The author uses the spacebreak technique to separate sections of the article.

"I am totally consumed by the limitations of age," he says. "The young kids on the team say, 'Show us how to do it, Grandpa.' I keep reminding myself that Dr. Sammy Lee was thirty-two when he won his last Olympic gold medal. And I'll be thirty-two at the '92 Olympics."

Once before, after the '84 games, he announced his retirement, then ignored it. Leaving is scary in itself. It means the end of an obsession that's fueled half his life. Diving cleaves the years, neatly, into a progression he can understand. "I went through so many stages," he says, and proceeds to tick them off:

Grammar school through junior high: "When I first started out, this [diving] was the one area of success. So it was almost like my survival."

High school and college: "It became something I was good at but I wasn't really enjoying. And then it was something that I wanted to do well at."

From eight to twenty-four, he lived his life hungry, troubled, pressured by great expectations and deferred payoffs. Like so many American athletes, he endured an eight-year wait for his gold because of the '80 U.S. boycott of the Moscow games, and it nearly unnerved him. Before '84, says Ron O'Brien, "he was not a happy camper." And then, after the Los Angeles Olympics?

"I was doing it because I enjoyed it," says the camper, happy as a clam. "I was having fun, so really, these last four years have been for the enjoyment."

He stops and smiles, then he shakes his head. "I never thought I could get to this point."

He has described the common pathology of obsession. It was keenest when he was hungry. But he has been losing some over the last year, which is to say placing fourth or fifth in Olympic tuneup meets that he used to win by 50 or 100 points. Right now he has to control his appetite for other things—quit reading the scripts, auditioning, forget about the appearances and endorsements. Since December 1st, he has been training hard at Mission Bay, two workouts a day, six days a week. Right now he has to summon up the hunger that used to come unbidden.

"I AM AFRAID OF GETTING FAT. SOMETHING HAPPENED TO my metabolism when I hit twenty-five."

Louganis is fretting over the menu at a Boca fern bar, which is pushing pastas, pizzas and other enticing carbs. He does not wish to go an ounce over his 160 pounds, and he normally lunches on liquids—soup and water—and a salad of some sort. He endures two workouts a day,

more exercises, weight workouts, a nibble of chicken for
dinner, more vegetables. Milk. Sleep. Do it again.

"Ohhhhhhhh, oh, look."

Lasagna floats by on a tray, steaming, oozing cheese.
Spotting the well-muscled ascetic in tank top and shorts,
the waitress cannot BAHLEEEEEVE she is waiting on
Greg LOOGAAAAAAYNIS.

"Well, um, yea. Hi."

Louganis orders up some Spartan gazpacho and green
salad but cannot resist a small side order of fried calamari.
He is an enthusiastic foodie, conversant with Korean barbecue, Szechwan lobster, Greek *dolmades*, but he fears
his fat-burning capacities are sliding toward the levels of
the silver-haired seniors tearing into early-bird specials at
surrounding tables.

"Stop me," he says. "Don't let me eat that garlic bread.
I mean, when the time comes, feel free to say, 'Meal's
over, Greg.' "

HE'S ALWAYS HAD TROUBLE WITH ENDINGS, BE IT A SINGLE
dive, a diving career, a lite lunch. The first time Greg
Louganis had trouble finishing his act was in his first
dance recital, in El Cajon, Southern California. He'd been
at it since eighteen months, when he begged to join his
older sister's class. At three and a half, he was good enough
to have a solo song-and-dance number in tiny top hat and
tux.

Owing to the lights, he couldn't see to find his exit. So
he sat down on the edge of the stage, where he could
watch the show and see his mom in the audience. Fran-
tically, the teacher waved him off, but he sat there grinning.

"I was having a great time," he says.

Twenty-one years later, when the stage was global, he
stood on the ten-meter platform at the Los Angels Olympics—at the very end of his performance; perhaps, he
thought then, the end of his Olympic career—and it was
no fun, no way. His mom was there, along with 13,497
people holding their collective breath at the USC pool and
about 35 million people nationwide on TV. You couldn't
have staged a better, a more dramatic Olympic Moment.

It was down to one dive. Oh, he had won before he
was finished; the nearest competitor was over fifteen points
away; even if he missed the dive entirely, the gold was
his. The only competition was with himself. Louganis's
score stood within reach of the 700 mark, which no man
or woman had ever achieved. He stood above the silent
crowd and prepared for the last dive on his list, number

307C, a reverse three-and-a-half somersault. Degree of difficulty, 3.4, then the highest that had been done. A year earlier, in another meet, Louganis had been about to climb the platform when 307C fatally injured Soviet diver Sergei Shilbashvili. And as the ambulance bore him away, Louganis performed 307C flawlessly. He was not afraid of the dive; his trajectory is always too high and far and fast to send his skull crashing into the platform like the doomed Russian.

Nonetheless, as he prepared to do 307C at the end of his program in the '84 Olympics, he says, "I *was* scared. The fear was a number of things. The fear was a fear of failure. Coming so close and not achieving that [breaking 700], especially at the Olympic games. Another fear was fear of success. If I achieved breaking 700, then *what else can I do*? So it was fear—of many different fears that were just kind of hitting me."

He knew they were there, but he would not let them in: "I just didn't *acknowledge* it."

Louganis stood on the edge of the platform and said this to himself: "No matter what happens, my mother still loves me."

Final score: 710.91

His early history appears well into the middle of the article, well after the lead.

ALWAYS, THROUGH SOME VERY BAD TIMES, FRANCES LOUganis has loved her adopted son. His birth parents were both fifteen when he was born: his father wanted to raise him as a brother but was persuaded to give him up. Peter Louganis, a hard-drinking tuna fisherman, brought the nine-month-old boy home to his tall, fair Texan wife and vowed to raise him strong and strict. No nonsense, no coddling. He would study and work on the tough docks near San Diego and obey, and if it was a matter of honor, he would fight. He would be a man—in the old way.

There were plenty of chances to get in a fight, but the boy never did. Instead, he got beat up, day after day. He would fib about the bruises and fret about the reason.

"Nigger!" they called him at school. His birth father was Samoan, and as a child, Gregory Efthimios Louganis turned very, very brown in the California sun.

"Stupid!" they taunted before dyslexia was a commonly diagnosed reading problem. He inverted sentences, flip-flopped letters. Mistakenly, teachers had him tested for mental impairment.

"Reeeetard!" He was too shy to answer back, too scared. And he stuttered—badly enough to require speech therapy. When he sought haven from it all, it was in Frances Louganis's kitchen.

"My mother is Scotch-Irish, and my father is Greek, so my mother had to learn how to cook Greek," he says. "We learned—I always helped my mom in the kitchen, because this is where I felt most comfortable."

It was a safe place for a dark-skinned, stammering, dyslexic loner. They made spinach-filled *spanikopita*. He drizzled honey over the transparent pastry dough for world-beating *baklava*. "To me, it's relaxing," says Louganis. "I had companionship, you know, from my mother. It gave me a good sense of self-esteem."

He hated when his father dragged him to a club for boys and made him wrestle, loathed the combative contact. But he loved to dance.

"Sissy!" they called him then, and that bothered him more than the other stuff, but not enough to make him stop.

No one understood him better than his dance partner, Eleanor Smith. They were a team from age three to twelve. Almost every day, they went to the dance studio; when one changed teachers, the other followed. They moved alike, thought alike, were best of friends. Eventually, Eleanor headed off toward gymnastics, and Greg followed, but there was no men's gymnastics team in San Diego. Knee injuries were aggravated by gymnastics and dance.

"So," he says, "I learned to dive."

Early on, he was exceptional. Ron O'Brien has watched thousands of grade-school hopefuls with Olympic dreams and chlorine-pink eyes. But he can still remember his first look at Greg Louganis at a Florida meet: "I saw him when he was ten and I was coach at Ohio State University. He had a different quality to his diving than I had seen with anyone else. He was stronger. His body lines were sharper. For a ten-year-old, he was extremely strong. And he had a presence about him."

On the springboard, still his strongest event, there was no hesitancy. No fear.

"As long as I had water under me," Louganis says, "I wasn't afraid."

When he calls diving his "survival" during that early period, he means that it raised him above other, darker things—the torments of school and the increasing difficulties at home. Peter Louganis proved a hard man who could not understand his more vulnerable son: the sweet, strong boy could not bear the drinking, the yelling, the strain on his mother. Once, when he was thirteen, they came to blows, and Greg was hauled to juvenile hall. Despite the turmoil, his diving got stronger, and as it did, each year took him farther outside of El Cajon.

"I went to Europe when I was thirteen for a world competition," he says. "When I was fourteen, I lived in Arizona for the summer with a diving family so I could get coaching. When I was fifteen, I spent the summer in Decatur, Alabama, in Ron O'Brien's camp."

He also worked. Diving, coaching and travel was expensive. Peter Louganis helped his son get coaching, and he also made sure Greg had work at the tuna dock in which Peter owned an interest. Greg started at fifteen, mending the heavy tuna nets, putting his well-developed shoulders to the work of cutting the nets away from the buoys and loading the gunlike needle with the marine-grade twine that repaired the nets. Later, in high school and college, he worked three part-time jobs at once, in two clothing stores and a recreation center. He paid his expenses, and he put some money away. Since he was fifteen, he's had a special savings account.

"For a house," he says. "I always wanted a house. It was like something that was out there that I was never going to get."

Other fifteen-year-olds were saving for surfboards and Pink Floyd tapes. But a house?

"See, I needed a place to go. I wanted out of the house, but I needed a sense of security, a sense of roots. I think that's what I was most obsessed with. It is something that's mine . . . my roots."

But there were more immediate goals. In January of '76 when he was sixteen and about to begin training for that year's Olympics, he left home entirely and moved in with the family of his coach, Dr. Sammy Lee, himself a 1948 and 1952 gold medalist. A busy ear, nose and throat specialist, Lee took as much time off as he could to coach the boy he felt could be the very best diver in history. Once again, Louganis felt himself adopted and found himself headed for the warmest room in the house.

"Dr. Lee is Korean; Mrs. Lee is Chinese," Louganis says. "I always helped her out in the kitchen, too, so I learned how to cook Chinese and Korean stuff."

His new high school was more of a culture shock. "I went from an upper-middle class high school to a school that was seventy to eighty percent Chicano. They had seven security guards. The week before I got there, one of the security guards was put in the hospital by some students. So I was a little nervous. But I kind of fit in because I was dark haired and dark complected."

He says he kept his mouth shut and focused on diving. When he came home from Montreal with a silver medal in springboard and some headlines, he went back home to El Cajon and Valhalla High, which, despite its name, was not necessarily a hall of hero worship.

The nigger-dummy-sissy was a hero, but a lonely one—even though more people said hello in the halls.

He kept saving for his house, training, going on college-recruiting trips.

He chose the University of Miami, largely because "it was far away" from California. He says he really "grew up" in south Florida, majoring in theater and hanging with drama students who knew virtually nothing about his diving. He stayed there from 1978 to 1980, when he transferred to the University of California at Irvine. By then he was swimming under Ron O'Brien at the Mission Viejo Club, a worldclass tank near San Diego. And he was not a happy camper. He was withdrawn, uncommunicative. He began a quiet assault on the body and the image that had so far ensured his survival. Aware that it could have gotten him booted from the team, he smoked. A lot.

"My smoking was out of rebellion," he says. "I didn't want to fit the mold of this 'goody-goody-two-shoes jock.' "

So he swaggered around with the burning cylinders hanging off his lip. He thought they said, "I'm bad."

He drank, too, mostly beer and fruity swill wine. And he worried, convinced that owing to his home environment, he was destined for alcoholism. He says he was desperately unhappy, he was spinning. He was in danger of losing the water—the thing a diver fears most of all.

Like "the rip," the author explains an insider's knowledge of diving—the fear of "losing the water."

LOSING THE WATER—GETTING DISORIENTED AND LANDING badly—happens to everyone at least once, even the best. But fear of it can cripple a diver's nerve the way a bad entry can bend his body.

Ron O'Brien can only recall one time when his student seized up with serious angst on the platform, when he was trying to teach him the inward three-and-a-half tuck. It involves three and a half tight, dizzying revolutions in the direction of the platform, and when O'Brien came at Louganis with it, the dive had just been entered into the official book. It was so new, so difficult that no one else was doing it. They worked on it in stages, and Louganis had done it on dry land, in a spotting belt. Finally, says O'Brien, "it was time for him to do the dive. He went up to do it, and he wouldn't go. He'd stand on the end of the platform and stand and stand and step back."

They got to the end of the practice, and he still hadn't done it. He was trying to sneak off when O'Brien caught him.

"I told him he just had to learn that dive. That if he wanted to bring his lunch and dinner the next day, to do so, because he was going to stay up there till he did do it. Do it or else."

Ask Louganis about it, and he grins. "Yeah, that was probably the most difficult dive I had to learn. Because I spin pretty fast. And I was afraid that I wasn't going to know where I was in the air."

It is easy to lose the water in a tight spin, and there is nothing worse, tumbling upside down, falling at 40 mph. It's a thirty-three-foot drop to the surface, another seventeen feet to the pool bottom. Hit on your side, and you can puncture an eardrum; land on your back, and you can do worse.

The day after he had balked on the inward triple, Louganis thought about losing the water, and he thought about losing his nerve and his place on the team, and he climbed up to the platform and nailed the dive on the first try.

Good anecdotes help the reader understand the subject.

That was in 1982. He was diving well then. But on dry land, he still didn't know where he was at. He was sneaking the smokes, chugging beers he had no taste for. He thought about cleaning up, but he had no motivation until one day, at a meet, he ran into a subteen diver, a kid puffing absurdly at a cigarette.

"Why are you doing that?" Louganis asked him.

"I want to be just like Greg Louganis."

Stupid, too stupid. He decided to cut the crap. He cut it all out in '83, the year before the Olympics. He did it himself, no counseling, but with the help of friends.

"I don't think anybody can do it all by themselves," he says. "I had a support group . . . Ron O'Brien and his wife, Mary Kay. And Jim [Babbitt, a UC-Irvine friend who is now his manager]. And Megan Neyer, another diver.

"I found I even had to stay away from my dad," he says. He realized this one evening when Peter Louganis took him out to dinner.

"Every time he'd order a drink for himself, he'd order one for me. By the end of the meal, I had five untouched beers lined up in front of me, and I said, 'Dad, I won't be coming around for a while.' "

He says that people have told him that he overreacted, that he probably wasn't a real alcoholic, and he says yes, maybe it wasn't so bad, but he wasn't going to keep drinking and find out for sure. Besides, the worst part was why he did it.

"I was scared," he says. "And I guess I wasn't real happy with who I am."

He was just twenty-three, a year from the Big Test in Los Angeles, but he felt he was being tested all the time, especially the day he Lost the Water for real.

Earlier the author explained the idea of "losing the water." Here is what it means when that really happens to a diver.

LOUGANIS HAS HAD INJURIES, A DISLOCATED SHOULDER, chronic wrist problems aggravated by a ganglion cyst, one horrible crackup where he knocked the base of his skull on the platform and was unconscious for fifteen minutes. But he says the worst was a wipeout at a meet in New Zealand in early '84, because it bruised him body and soul. He can remember it all too well:

He is standing on the platform during practice, looking down at this strange pool with stripes across the walls and ceiling, long narrow stripes that ripple if you look at them too long. He is preparing himself for an inward three and a half. He counts, springs up, out, spinning, seeing the stripes fly by, and then he loses the water. Is it up, down, where? No time to decide. He sees the windows at the far end, stretches for them and lands, hard, flat on his back with a sickening slap.

Around the pool, there was silence.

"Because everybody on the team was just like 'Oh my God, Greg Louganis just *wiped out.*'"

He's not sure how, but he got out of the water laughing. The next day, he couldn't get out of bed.

"I just ached so much, I felt like I had the flu," he says. "I had trouble walking, because I had hit my calves on impact, too. I broke a lot of blood vessels in my back and the back of my legs. It had welted up."

He was in serious pain for four days and decided not to compete in the meet. He didn't want to screw himself up in a lousy striped tank of water.

"I was afraid," he says. "I was afraid if I had wiped out again, then I would have to go back to easier dives. I didn't feel that I could afford to do that during the Olympic year."

His coach agreed, but, Louganis says, "I got a lot of flak from other divers. Had it been anybody else, they probably would have been consoling, saying, 'It's okay.' But I caught so much flak."

"Chicken!" they were calling him behind his back.

The flap was such that a team meeting was called, and while he was still sore and welted from losing the water, Greg Louganis finally stood up for himself. He talked back. He did it in front of a group of people. And it felt okay.

Now Louganis talks to many groups: organizations for

the dyslexic, youth clubs, drug- and alcohol-rehab places, diving clinics. He talks easily, about what it was like to be dyslexic, dependent on alcohol, and dozens, scores of times he has had to reassure young divers about chickening out or losing the water. He's comfortable with people who admit to their fears. He thinks he helps a little.

There are a lot of stories about healing and forgiveness in Louganis's narrative. His parents divorced four years ago, "and they're dating again," he says with a smile and a shake of his head. On his left hand, he wears a diamond ring that once belonged to his grandfather Louganis and was given to him by his father.

"He was supposed to leave it to me. But he said that he wanted to see me enjoy it."

His parents come to see him compete; recently, he sent his mother and an aunt to Europe on his frequent-flier miles. He often has his parents to a barbecue at his home in Malibu—the one he finally got to buy, the only thing he owns. It has a panoramic view of the Pacific from a bluff above the beach, a redwood deck, a custom-built swimming pool with a one-meter platform. He looked for the right house for two years, searched from Santa Barbara to San Diego, and he works hard at appearances and endorsements to make the mortgage. When he is home, he spends a lot of time in the kitchen. For Christmas, for Thanksgiving, friends, neighbors and relatives come to him, and he loves feeding them.

"At times, you know, I feel guilty," he says of his home, "because it's nicer than anything I grew up in."

Like "the rip" and "losing the water," the idea of the social acceptance of perfection is an interesting concept to show readers.

THERE ARE CERTAIN INEFFABLE, YET IN-YOUR-FACE QUALIties that elevate an American Olympian to seven-figure, network, cereal-box, Battle of the Endorsement Stars status; there is Pluck 'n Perk, as in a Dorothy Hamill or Mary Lou Retton; there is the outright Yankee Yahoo factor of Bruce "Tropicana Pure Premium" Jenner, the man single-handedly responsible for the insertion of "Go for it" into sitcoms, stump speeches and bumper stickers. But there is no direct commercial tie-in for Perfection itself; especially in what remains a relatively esoteric sport. Diving is not a widely appreciated art form. And at bottom, Americans don't quite know what to do with undiluted male grace.

There is a man trying to help them figure it out. His name is Jim Babbitt, Louganis's friend since their days at UC-Irvine, a rower, psychology major and, since 1985, Louganis's manager.

Working out of Louganis's Malibu home, which they

Louganis "says he is comfortable with who he is, at peace, even enjoying himself" (see below right). That was when writer Gerri Hershey interviewed him for this 1988 article. But during the last week of February 1995, Louganis admitted publicly that he has AIDS. He also admitted that he knew he had AIDS before the 1988 Olympic Games in Seoul, Korea. It was during the preliminaries of the springboard events in Seoul that Louganis cracked his head on a reverse dive and became "paralyzed with fear" when he started bleeding in the pool.

He did not tell the doctor who stitched the wound that he had AIDS. The doctor stitched it without gloves or other precautions.

Louganis was taking the AIDS drug AZT around the clock during the Seoul Olympics. He said he was encouraged by his coach and a few others not to indicate he had AIDS.

In 1989, Olympic officials set strict guidelines regarding prevention of contact with athletes' blood. Reports indicated that because the pool was chlorinated, there was an almost zero chance that other athletes could have gotten AIDS from his blood in the pool.

share, Babbitt negotiates poster deals, interviews, personal-appearance contracts with car dealerships. Despite the beauty, talent and affability of his client, the deal roster is split between name brands and also-rans: American Express and Banana Boat skin-care products. TV is the same: *Hollywood Squares* and *Double Dare*. Via William Morris, scripts arrive to be read, with some queries from casting directors. Feeling that his client needed a sample of his acting abilities on film, Babbitt urged him to take a bit part in a movie, *Dirty Laundry*, which proved so execrable it went straight to video rental, without theatrical release in the U.S.

It is difficult to assess the dramatic future of Greg Louganis from his appearance as beach bum Larry, a happenin' dude wearing surf baggies and a bimbo on each arm. Larry's few lines could torpedo Olivier: "Hey, Corinne really digs your sound system. I think she wants to check out your tweeters."

"I felt good about it," Louganis says of his performance. Asked about the movie, he laughs. "I heard it's terrible."

He got the part when a casting director saw him in an L.A. workshop. Unlike Bruce "Can't Stop the Music" Jenner, Louganis has taken years of classes, has gone to cattle calls, readings. He says he's come close—he read for the spacey Prince Valium in Mel Brooks's *Spaceballs*, for the part of a cadet in the miniseries *Dress Gray*. *Dirty Laundry* may not be much, he says, but he came by it honestly.

"I got the part based on the showcase," he says. "A lot of people think that the reason I got the part is because they used Carl Lewis and myself—two Olympians—in the same film. They kind of figured I didn't have to audition."

Carl Lewis is a beautiful, talented athlete who won virtually no endorsements, owing to what has been termed an "attitude problem"—and unsubstantiated rumors of homosexuality that created an adversarial relationship with the press. Since sports establishments—organizational and media—are notoriously homophobic, the Wheaties box was more than a world-record long jump away. Lewis is talking now, about the bitterness, the pain, the sportswriters in his face bawling, "Are you on drugs?" "Are you homosexual?" It has taken him four years to be able to speak about the whispering campaigns.

Greg Louganis has heard all kinds of sighs and whispers, but he is facing them with good humor and no fear. He says he is comfortable with who he is, at peace, even enjoying himself. His sexual preference is nobody's business; his business arrangements are just fine, thank you, despite a recent article that hung Jim Babbitt out to dry.

"I usually don't read any of my press," he says. And while Babbitt was upset with the portrayal of him as a grasping *arriviste*, his client just giggled when a fellow diver read the article out loud.

"It was just so funny," says Louganis. "And it was totally off base."

The theme of conquering fears continues throughout the article.

What the writer didn't seem to understand, he says, is that the "demons he lives with"—the fears, the past hurts—have largely been banished, and he's not about to let others take their place. Louganis is not afraid of Hollywood, not of studio neurotics and agency piranhas, not even of Rumor. He treats it just the way he did the swarm of fears on the Olympic platform four years ago. He just doesn't acknowledge it.

"I'm oblivious," he says. He listens, and usually he laughs. He's heard that he's been seen chasing women in bars—teammates no less. "I've heard I'm having an affair with [diver] Tracy Scoggin. And then every four years I am having an affair with Megan Neyer."

Beautiful men must suffer this, and more. He says he's also heard a popular rumor that he has been living with a powerful, older Hollywood studio head. He laughs. "Yeah. Right. I'm *sure*."

And Greg Louganis wants you to know this, all you enquiring minds. If it's true, if he's being grandly kept by this mogul, *how come he has to run around pumping hands for car dealerships*? What's he doing *living in a free development condo*, driving a sober little compact *on loan from a car-rental company*?

"I mean," he says. "I'd be living much more comfortably than I am."

While rumor places him in Tinsel Town love nests, he says he is really in Dr. Sammy Lee's back yard, playing Pictionary and wolfing down Korean barbecue with the Lee family, Aunt Mary, her son Herb. He's cleaning dishes and playing Trivial Pursuit.

And so, to most of the rumors, he and Babbitt laugh and say yeah, right, they're *sure*.

The author wraps up the idea of conquering fears in this effective concluding section.

WHAT IT COMES DOWN TO IS THIS: YOU HAVE TO PICK YOUR fights with fear. You have to know which ones matter and which ones aren't worth the energy. Some fear is good and honest and can teach you buckets, and some of it is flat evil. Louganis has watched a special friend fight that kind of fear for five years now. He explains:

"I was following this story about Ryan White—he's the boy who contracted AIDS through the clotting agent.

And he was going through the court system to fight his way back into school."

It was a real spook show, the six-o'clock news awash with screeching adult fear masks, hate masks. The Whites lived in Kokomo, Indiana, which is close to Indianapolis, where the national diving championships were being held. Louganis called Ryan White and invited him to the pool.

"In a way, I was hoping that if some people saw that I don't have anything to fear, and if I can be accepting . . ."

Here was a kid in the fatal embrace of the biggest, fiercest boa, facing death and going further still—to Congress, to TV stations and to school-board meetings—a frail kid letting a tidal wave of dread and prejudice break over him.

Ryan and his family came to the meet, and since then, he and Louganis have become friends, with frequent phone chats and visits to Mission Bay and to Louganis's home, in California. Ryan is doing well, Louganis says, just got his driver's license and has friends now that the family left the hate in Kokomo for Cicero, Illinois, and a more accepting environment.

"What's sad about the situation is that Jeanne, his mother, she's probably going to have to let the banks foreclose on her house in Kokomo, because nobody will buy the AIDS house," Louganis says. "I mean, the Realtors want Jeanne to get some sort of written statement that nobody can get AIDS from a house. It is pathetic. It is sick."

For the first time, there is an edge to Louganis's soft voice. "A lot of the fear is out of ignorance," he says.

Stupid people, calling a young boy names. So Ryan is going around talking to anyone who will listen, trying to hold the fears up to the light, and when it comes to valor and insight and calm, Greg Louganis thinks this boy is a perfect master. No matter what happens, Ryan White will rip it in the end.

Notice what a nice twist this ending has, compared to the "high dive" lead.

"Fear makes a big splash, you know, in the headlines and all," says Louganis. But when everything settles, "it's just a little puddle." (pp. 87–91)

CHOOSING A STRUCTURE

When to use the inverted pyramid structure:

- If the writer is working for a daily newspaper.

- If the article is about a game played in the previous 24 hours.
- If space is short and the writer must be concise.
- If there is no historical nature to the article.
- If it is a news-oriented article.

When to use the diamond structure:

- If the writer is working for a magazine.
- If the article is not specifically a "score" or "game" story.
- If it is a profile story or a trend story or "think" article.
- If the article contains a specific historical section or segment.
- If space is not a significant factor and the writer can "write long."
- If it is clearly a feature article.

Chapter Seven
Other Structures

There may be cases in which the writer needs to write a story chronologically or nearly chronologically. The inverted pyramid would not be appropriate and the diamond format not necessary. The chronological structure is perfect for showing a trend in sports or for clearly showing the progress of a personality in the sports world.

David Ramsey, staff reporter for the *Syracuse Herald American* has used the chronological structure well. He shows the public fall and the unpublicized aftermath of Cleveland State University basketball coach Kevin Mackey. Notice how this article is structured differently from the *Kansas City Star* article about athlete Lisa Davies.

The article was run in the *Herald American* on January 10, 1993 under the title and subtitle:

Mackey reaches again for basketball's glory
In CBA, former Cleveland State coach tries to escape past

ALBANY—Even on the best night of his basketball life, a night he should have rejoiced, Kevin Mackey couldn't shake his fury.

He tried to bask in his triumph. Everyone wanted to be near him, to drink Miller Lites with him in his room at Syracuse's downtown Holiday Inn. He and his no-name Cleveland State Vikings had just defeated Bobby Knight's Indiana Hoosiers in the 1986 NCAA sub-regional.

From his room, Mackey seethed as he watched cars whiz by on Interstate 81. He saw the Carrier Dome, site of his triumph.

Boosters and university officials slapped him on the back. Unbelievable upset, they kept saying.

108

Mackey didn't see it that way.

Couldn't they see the endless hours of labor he had put into this team? Couldn't they see his team's 28–3 record, see his team's ruthless hunger for victory?

Couldn't they see?

Mackey eventually was left alone with his rage.

He reached for another beer. And another. And another.

He pushed himself and his players with an endless fire, but the acclaim never seemed enough. Always, he sought more. Mostly, he sought more beer. Mackey says now he was an alcoholic, had been since he was 16.

A couple of years after his triumph in Syracuse, he was offered cocaine. He said yes. Alcohol, he says, had ceased to entice him.

He soon found he couldn't say no. For Mackey, the toast of Cleveland, cocaine was easy to find.

"I really didn't have to spend much money," he says. "It was given to me. All kinds of people wanted to give me cocaine."

He believed he could master cocaine. He believed he could continue to win games. He believed he could hide his addiction the same way he had hidden his voracious thirst for alcohol.

On July 13, 1990—Friday the 13th—someone called Cleveland police. Mackey's long time of hiding was about to end.

Mackey, the caller said, could be found in a crack house on Edmonton Avenue. The same tip was made to Cleveland's Channel 8.

Mackey had made a dangerous choice of destinations. He had much to lose by being there.

He had signed a $175,000-per-season contract with Cleveland State two days earlier.

In seven seasons he had compiled a 144–67 record. He took his 1986 team to the NCAA's Sweet 16 and came within a last-second shot by David Robinson of carrying the Vikes past Navy and into the final eight.

He owned a 13-room home in Shaker Heights, a swank Cleveland suburb.

He had a wife, his college sweetheart, and three children.

He did commercials for McDonald's. It was perfect; Mackey talking up the Big Mac.

"I was the king," Mackey says, closing his eyes as he gazed back at the old days. "The King of Cleveland, that's what they called me."

Mackey is now the coach of the Capital Region Pontiacs, a Continental Basketball Association team based in Albany. Nobody calls him the king.

He talks, with the thick New England accent of his native Somerville, Mass., as he eats a salsa-smothered burrito in an Albany restaurant. He wears blue coaching sweats and a CBS-Sports hat. He is 46 years old with a deeply lined face.

He winces as he thinks back to the crack house on Edmonton.

Mackey stumbled out of the crack house, accompanied by Alma Massey, his mistress of several years. He climbed into his Lincoln Town Car. With the police and a television camera crew following, he drove a couple of blocks. The police pulled him over.

Out of the car stepped a rich college coach high on crack. With TV cameras rolling, he was frisked, arrested, charged with drunk driving and, later, drug abuse. He was tossed in jail.

"I had no idea," says Shawn Hood, who played for Cleveland State's 1986 team and worked as Mackey's assistant coach when the arrest was made.

"The only thing I was aware of was that he was a great coach. He had two lives, basically. He was very intelligent with his madness."

Cleveland State fired him six days later.

His wife kicked him out of the house in Shaker Heights.

McDonald's no longer wanted to pay him to talk up their Big Macs.

After being sentenced to 90 days treatment in lieu of conviction, Mackey underwent drug rehabilitation in Cleveland and Houston, where he attended the John Lucas clinic. Lucas was the first pick in the 1976 NBA draft, a brilliant point guard with an appetite for cocaine. He now coaches the San Antonio Spurs.

Mackey says he has, with the aid of Lucas, shackled his thirst for alcohol and his itch for cocaine. He has not, he says, taken a drink or a hit since his Friday the 13th visit to Edmonton Avenue. He is randomly tested, as are all CBA players and coaches, for drug use.

He is beginning what he hopes is his climb back.

The Pontiacs are 10–11, but on a tear. Mackey acquired Chuck Nevitt, a 7-foot-5 center and NBA journeyman, to anchor the middle of his defense. The big man's arrival started a five-game winning streak.

Mackey has long envisioned a giant on his team. While at Cleveland State, he recklessly pursued a 7-foot-7 African named Manute Bol, a pursuit that left the Vikings with two years of NCAA sanctions.

Now, Mackey watches Nevitt during practices at Albany's Knickerbocker Arena. He strolls the sidelines yelling, "Repetition is the mother of learning." He tells players he is offering defensive techniques "no other coach" is teaching.

His players seem to be listening.

"I don't care a thing about his past," says Pontiacs' starting point guard Sean Gay, who has read and heard all about Mackey's tumble in Cleveland.

"Everyone, you know, has a past they would like to forget. He's a good person now. That's what I care about."

The Capital Region CBA team has been a step to the NBA in the past. Phil Jackson, coach of the World Champion Chicago Bulls, once directed the team. So did George Karl, coach of the Seattle Sonics.

Mackey wants to follow that legacy.

He lives in a small apartment in Troy. He earns $40,000 a season. He coaches in front of only a few hundred fans on most nights.

He wants more. He wants what he had in Cleveland—the big house, the big crowds, the big money.

That might not be easy. The lurid facts of the past, Mackey says, are still fresh in the minds of many basketball fans.

Mackey often hears the volume go down when he enters a room. Those who know the Kevin Mackey Story, those who know about the booze and the coke and the mistress, begin to whisper. They whisper and they stare.

"I see those people," Mackey says. "I see those people looking at me everywhere I go. I figure they're wondering if I have a crack pipe in my back pocket or a bottle of Jack Daniel's in my gym bag. I wonder that."

He is driven by those doubters, though he admits a continued vulnerability to alcohol and cocaine. He is quick to affirm cocaine's lure, its power.

He had been a heavy drinker for years, he says, and always managed to prosper. Drinking didn't stop him from winning four state titles in his nine seasons as a high school coach.

When he was an assistant coach at Boston College from 1977–82, he cruised the interstates of the East Coast with a cooler full of Miller Lite in the passenger's seat.

He cranked the radio up loud, drank his beers and drove, always, in the inside lane as he searched from town to town for recruits.

He found players who helped BC win Big East titles in 1981 and 1983, a feat the school hasn't managed since Mackey's departure. He found John Bagley, a fat kid from Bridgeport now in his 11th NBA season. He found Michael Adams, a short kid from Hartford now playing for the Washington Bullets. He found the players others missed.

Somehow, the highway patrol missed him.

"Hey, the troopers don't stop you in the inside lane," he says of those hazy rides. "It's a fact of life, you know."

His driving luck ran out on Friday the 13th.

Talking about cocaine with Mackey is a vivid experience. His eyes get this dreamy look. His voice grows soft. The tone is wistful as if he is recalling an intense but failed romance.

"Cocaine—it takes you to another world," he says. "Cocaine, you get that hit and, ah"—he's smiling now, looking out the window—"you know, it's 'Beam me up, Scottie.' The thing for me, I didn't like it. I, oh, I loved it."

Some days, he says, he still misses it.

Last spring Mackey coached the Fayetteville (N.C.) Flyers to the best record (41–23) in the Global Basketball Association, another minor-league. After the season ended, he felt a degree of vindication.

He also felt the old hunger for acclaim, and he wanted—desperately wanted—to drink and snort.

"I told myself, 'You done a good job. You deserve something,' " Mackey remembers. "I thought about going off by myself and, you know, rewarding myself. I thought about checking into a hotel."

His word choice in the next sentence is chilling.

"I wanted to lay in some alcohol and cocaine."

He picked out the hotel. He pictured the entire scenario. He was all ready to jump off the sobriety wagon.

But he didn't "lay" in alcohol and cocaine.

"I'm not sure why," he says. "I don't know if it was because of good reasons. I don't really think so. But I didn't go to the hotel."

He won that day, but not every past scar has been mended.

Mackey shakes his finger when asked about his family. He will not say a word about his wife, his children or about Alma Massey.

"Nothing about that," he says.

Kathleen Mackey, Kevin's wife of 27 years, works as a nursing supervisor at the Cuyahoga County Jail in Cleveland. She answers the phone minutes after returning from her lunch break.

"It was a great, great thing," she says, her voice bright as she remembers the victory night in Syracuse. "It was a natural high, so to speak."

The voice continues to hop as she talks about the fast-talking Irish man she met at St. Anselm's College. She is still married to Mackey.

"Kevin, he was a lot of fun," she says. "He was very good-looking. He played ball. We had a very nice relationship. You know, I've known him more than half my life. I met him when I was 19."

Her tone changes as the subject moves closer to the present.

She says she had no idea her husband had a serious drinking problem, no idea he abused cocaine, no idea he had a mistress.

No idea.

"The whole thing was quite a shock," she says. "The depth and the breadth of it was quite a shock. I knew maybe he was drinking a little bit too much, but I wasn't looking for anything like what happened. It was shattering."

Kathleen still waits for her husband to say he's sorry. He never apologized, she says.

She waits for him to say anything. She hasn't spoken to him in months. He knows the number, she says, but he chooses not to call.

"Silence," she says, "is not always golden."

Mackey is quiet after declining to talk about Kathleen and his children. He gazes out the window. The sun's rays bathe his face. The former King of Cleveland, today an unknown at a restaurant in Albany, smiles.

"I don't feel guilty," he says. "I take full responsibility for what happened, but I don't feel guilty. I've put the guilt down.

"Yesterday is a canceled check."

He has so much to do, so far to climb.

"I'm not satisfied," he says. "I want it back."

His wife is confident he will succeed—on the basketball court.

"He really is an excellent coach," she says, her voice cracking at the Cuyahoga County Jail. (p. D7)

The writer could even highlight the straight-line time chronology by using a *diary format*, by beginning key sections or paragraphs with a time:

12:52 p.m.—xxxxxxxxxxxxxxxxxxxxxxxx
xxxxxxxxxxxxxxxxxxxxxxxx.
2:13 p.m.—xxxxxxxxxxxxxxxxxx
xxxxxxxxxxxxxxxxxxxx.
5:05 p.m.—xxxxxxxxxxxxxxxxxx
xxxxxxxxxxxxxxxxxxxxxx.

The use of a diary or time format article would be particularly appropriate in an article such as "24 Hours Behind the Scenes at the Indianapolis 500" or other similar articles.

This type of article pulls the reader through the story because the reader is constantly wondering what will happen next.

Staff writers and editors for *The Wall Street Journal* have devised their own structure, which bears examination.

In *News Reporting and Writing* (1985), the Missouri Group, Brooks, Kennedy, Moen, and Ranly, wrote:

> For centuries, writers have used the literary device of telling a story through the eyes of one person or by examining part of the whole. The device makes large institutions, complex issues and seven-digit numbers meaningful. Few of us can comprehend the size of the U.S. budget, but we can understand the numbers on our own paycheck. Not many of us can explain the marketing system for wheat, but we could if we followed a bushel of wheat from the time it was planted until a consumer picked up a loaf of bread in the supermarket.
>
> Even though Joseph Stalin was hardly talking about literary approaches, he summed the impact of focusing on a part of the whole when he said, "Ten million deaths are a statistic; one death is a tragedy."
>
> Individual newspaper journalists have used the technique often, but no newspaper has seized upon it like *The Wall Street Journal*. In its daily one-column feature examining national and international issues, *The Journal* routinely and expertly puts a literary magnifying glass on the individual involved in an issue or institution. (pp. 261–262)

The Wall Street Journal article has four distinct parts:

1. The lead begins with *a focus on an individual* and his or her problems or concerns about an industry or a work environment.
2. There is a *transition* to a larger level—the same issue across an industry or at the national level.
3. There is a *lengthy report* on the larger scope—the issue at the industry or national level.
4. There is a return to *end the article with the focus again at the local level*—the article usually ends with an anecdote or quotation from the same person cited in the lead, or with a similar person.

The key to *The Wall Street Journal* structure is:

Individual → Industry → Individual

Another way of viewing this structure or method would be:

Simple → Complex → Simple

The first four paragraphs of a typical *Wall Street Journal* article begin with the individual, then there is a subhead. The subhead acts as the transition to the body of the article, which examines the problem across an industry. At the end of the article body, there is another subhead, which again acts as a transition, and the end of the article is the last four paragraphs, to exactly match the lead.

A typical article in this format for *The Wall Street Journal* would be how one auto worker, Joe, has been replaced on a Ford assembly line by a robot welding arm. Then the body of the article is devoted to how many workers throughout the auto industry are being replaced by robot welders and how the human workers are being retrained for other jobs. The end of the article might be a look at how auto worker Joe was successfully retrained for another position at Ford.

This is a variation of the diamond format. Sports writers might use this technique to show how one pro football player's career was ended by a crippling injury, then show how all injured football players are rehabilitated, then return to show how the single player successfully overcame his injuries. The article may not need to use exactly four paragraphs in the lead, then the body, and then exactly four paragraphs at the end of the article, as *The Wall Street Journal* does.

CHOOSING A STRUCTURE

Use the chronology structure if the writer is writing a trend or profile story, or if there is no real historical nature to the story.

Use the diary structure if the writer is covering an event like the Indianapolis 500 or the Kentucky Derby, or if the writer is planning a first-person article about "How I Went Over Niagara Falls in a Barrel" or something similar.

Use *The Wall Street Journal* structure if the writer needs to clarify a problem in terms of one person or one small unit, such as a family. It is also useful when there are clearly smaller and larger components to the story or when the writer would normally use the diamond structure.

Chapter Eight
Techniques for Effective Endings

Most writers labor over their beginnings, because the beginning—the lead—must be perfect to lure the reader into the story. The same writers, however, are often far less careful with their endings. But the endings shouldn't be just a relief ("Thank goodness that's over!") for the writer *or* the reader. Rather, the ending should fit the story as well as the beginning.

Most articles should have effective, emphatic, obvious endings. Most articles (and *all* feature articles) shouldn't just trail down the last column of the last page and fall off the bottom of the page.

It should be of little surprise to know that techniques for effective beginnings can be used for effective endings. There are, however, not quite as many techniques for effective endings as there are techniques for effective beginnings. Some techniques for effective beginnings simply don't work as endings.

The anthology *The Best American Sports Writing, 1993* (Deford, 1994) comprises 25 articles that are, indeed, the best writing about sport in America in 1993. How do the writers represented in this collection use effective endings? Let's see.

There are several key techniques for effective endings.

THE ANECDOTAL ENDING

An anecdote can be a short but significant story about an individual that shows that person's character. The anecdote can also show the character of a team or institution.

One of the exceptional articles in *The Best American Sports Writing, 1993* was a *Sports Illustrated* article by Rick Reilly about athletic abuses (including severe hazing), human rights abuses, and racism at the Citadel. Reilly's piece, "What Is the Citadel?" appeared in *Sports Illustrated* on September 14, 1992. Reilly ended his article with a quotation ending, but then, as the article went to press, added a one-paragraph anecdote, as a postscript:

> "I can tell you one thing," said the wrestler, Reaves. "I'm going to be *hell* when I'm a sophomore. I took a lot of crap. I've gotta get *somebody* back." Here's hoping they beat Wofford.
>
> Postscript: Just before this story went to print, a black Citadel freshman told authorities he woke up on August 20 to find a string noose hanging from the bunk above him. Some say the noose was there because the freshman refused an upperclassman's demand that he sing *Dixie* in the barracks shower. The Citadel says it has completed its investigation and has asked the South Carolina Law Enforcement Division to take over. (Reilly, 1994, p. 350)

THE EDITORIAL ENDING

If you write about two boxers, two football coaches, two runners, or two teams, you could begin the article with a comparison of the two. You can end the article with an editorial (or judgment) ending.

Humor columnist and author Dave Barry traveled from Miami (when Floridians were anticipating the first season of the Florida Marlins) to Erie, Pennsylvania, the home of the Erie Sailors, a Marlins farm team.

He found the Sailors' stadium quaint, the operation a nickel-and-dime affair, and the players more human and certainly more approachable than in the big leagues.

Barry's article, "The Old Ball Game," appeared in *Tropic* magazine and also in *The Best American Sports Stories, 1993*. His ending:

> The 1992 Sailors season ended September 1. As I write this, the Marlins haven't decided whether to remain affiliated with the Sailors for the 1993 season. And if Erie doesn't solve its stadium problem by 1994, the Sailors won't be affiliated with any big-league team.
>
> Of course, by next year, South Florida won't care about Erie: the Marlins will be playing here. We'll have a big-league team to follow, with big-league stars making big-league money, playing in a big-league stadium in front of big-league crowds. Everything will be bigger.
>
> Although not necessarily better. (Barry, 1994, p. 321)

THE "I" ENDING

If you are writing a first-person article, "There I Was, Running the Boston Marathon," and if you begin with the "I" of the author as participant, then the "I" of the author is certainly appropriate at the end of the article. If the "I" of the author does not appear anywhere else in the article, it is usually inappropriate—and jarring to the reader—for the "I" viewpoint of the author to appear *for the first time* at the end of the article.

Ray Blount Jr.'s article, "Blunder Road," from *Men's Journal*, is in the tradition of George Plimpton's inept-amateur-as-athlete books. In "Blunder Road," Blount attends the Skip Barber Racing School to learn to drive a formula race car.

Of course he does everything wrong, including never learning quite well enough how to anticipate a high-speed turn.

His end:

> But I want them to know this: The next time I drove my Jetta on the highway, I found that if I concentrated I could look further up the road than usual and plot my course smoothly through a series of turns. Well, two turns. A turn and a half. At one point, as I swung all the way to the far edge of the right lane and unwound smoothly back to the far edge of the left, I felt something. A fleeting connection with some Platonic vector matrix stretching from Detroit to heaven.
>
> I like to think it was my apex. (Blount, 1994, p. 30)

THE QUESTION ENDING

Can you end an article with a question? Certainly, but you must give the reader enough evidence—pro or con, yes or no—in the article for the reader to be able to answer the question. Asking a question at the end of a feature requires that the reader *continue to consider* the article.

In his article "A Tragedy Too Easy to Ignore," *Detroit Free Press* writer Mitch Albom chronicled the Damon Bailes story. Bailes, a Detroit native, was shot in the back of the head during a pick-up basketball game, apparently because an opposing player thought Bailes wanted his red basketball shorts.

The bullet, Albom wrote:

> had hit the lobe that controls vision and left Bailes with only partial sight, paralyzed on the right side. In the months that followed, he would regain a slurred speech, partial vision and some feeling in his otherwise dead right leg and arm. The vision bothered him most. He would cry for hours over his near-blindness. (Albom, 1994, p. 412)

Albom's end:

> What are we supposed to do? The future of our city is being taken down, gangland style, one ambulance after another. We have to do something. Tonight is Christmas Eve, they are talking flurries, and that should make our suburbs pretty and white. But try to remember, while you open your presents, that somewhere, not far away, Damon Bailes is struggling to see the drawings on the wall, the ones teaching him how to walk again. For what, you keep asking yourself? For what? For what? For what?
>
> For nothing.
>
> And the snow falls. (Albom, 1994, p. 415)

If you ask a rhetorical question, as Albom does, the ending also carries an implication of the editorial ending.

Car and Driver tested the new Dodge Neon and reported the test in the April 1994 issue, in an article under a headline and subhead:

Dodge Neon
A little car with a big motor and a big grin

Writer Patrick Bedard's ending was:

> Can we live with an $11,552 Neon? Yes, very well, thank you. The lesson of the Neon is that common sense makes a real nifty car. Which is bad news for Saturn and other small cars that have relied on low prices. They simply can't measure up for roominess and performance.
>
> Would we prefer a plusher version? Well, yes, and we'll have a test of such a Neon within a few months. (p. 57)

THE QUOTATION ENDING

This is an almost no-fail ending, especially for personality portraits. A quotation from the principal subject of a profile leaves the "voice" of the personality in the reader's inner ear and should, additionally, reinforce the character of the speaker that has been established throughout the article.

Writer Pat Jordan (1994) profiled baseball manager Whitey Herzog for the *Los Angeles Times Magazine*, in an article titled "The Wit and Wisdom of the White Rat" (Herzog's nickname).

Jordan's last three paragraphs were:

> Herzog today seems less passionate about the game he loves, though still intellectually involved. He seems more determined to enjoy his life outside of baseball, too. So he accepted a no-lose situation. The Angels can only get better, not worse, and the credit will go to Herzog. So what if he was overruled about Joyner and Abbott, if he must listen to Jackie Autry say she had no money to throw around, and to Richard Brown warn that all Herzog's suggestions must be filtered through a committee.
>
> A younger Herzog might have raged, or even quit, over such things, insisting on the last word. The loss of such power doesn't seem to bother him now, because the game has changed and so has his place in it. The power has shifted to the players, and that rankles him.
>
> Suddenly he lurches forward, his elbows planted on the table. "You know what I don't understand," he says. "One year I made six thousand dollars as a player and I had to buy my own tickets to the game for my family. Today, you got players making two million a year and they want five hundred free tickets." He shakes his head in despair. "I just don't understand it," he says. "I never saw so many unhappy millionaires in my life." (Jordan, 1994, p. 266)

THE SUMMARY ENDING

Using this technique, the writer completes the article by summarizing the story. Charles P. Pierce uses such an ending in a profile about Shaquille O'Neal. Pierce's article, "The Next Superstar," appeared in *The New York Times Magazine*. His last two paragraphs were:

> O'Neal plays with consummate ease and confidence. He blocks shots by catching them. He whips down the lane for a dunk off an inbounds play, and he winks at Leonard Armato's four-year-old son while he does it. He tosses the veteran Pistons center Olden Polynice this way and that, once bouncing the ball off the backboard, retrieving it with a lightning first step, and then slamming it through as the women from En Vogue rock and Arsenio grabs his head. He ends up with 36 points and 19 rebounds. "Shaquille, the best part about him is that he's mean," Magic Johnson says later. "He's going to be one of those guys that, after you play him, you sleep real good. He's gonna put guys to sleep."
>
> He does not look mean. He does not look like a product here. He looks like a twenty-year-old discovering himself all over again. There is a purity that extends from north Orlando to this gathering of gaudy dilettantes. He will be comfortable in both places. He will be a kid and a corporation. He will be for sale and he will be free. He will be a Goliath for everyone to love. (Pierce, 1994, p. 335)

THE "YOU" ENDING

If you are giving advice to the reader, or suggesting products or services, using the "you" ending is often appropriate. In the April 1994 issue of *Car and Driver*, in addition to the Neon test report article, the editors tested five brands of automobile radar detectors. The article, headlined "Lidar Enters the Radar Wars," written by Don Schroeder, ended:

> For skinflints torn between these last two detectors in the test, try this advice. If you despise false alarms and are willing to sacrifice laser protection, go with the Cobra. If your car is so loud that you can't hear a falsing detector anyway, go with the Uniden. Make sure you're buying the LRD 9000W-1, not the LRD 9000W, which covers only wideband KA. (Schroeder, 1994, p. 95)

COMBINATION ENDINGS

These categories are part of the vast panorama of endings that writers can use. There are as many variations of endings as there are articles and writers. Can you use a description of an empty racetrack, then a quotation from a driver who won (or lost) a major motorsports race? Surely.

Can you end an article with the "you" ending—talking to your reader—then end with a rhetorical question? Of course.

Can you use an anecdote about a personality, then a description of them? Yes.

Can you contrast two principal subjects at the end of an article?

Can you match a technique used at the end of a feature to the same type of beginning used in the lead?

You are limited only by your imagination—and your knowledge of leads, structures, transitions, and endings. The more you know about writing techniques, the better your material becomes. Count on it.

Chapter Nine
Guidelines for Writing About Women

In writing about women, writers should not use prefixes indicating marital status. First reference should include a person's title (if any) and given name; later references should include last name only. Use of Mr. and Mrs. is limited to discussions that include a married couple, where the last-name-only rule might cause confusion. Miss and Ms. are not to be used at all. First names alone are also not appropriate for adults.

Females over the age of 18, should be referred to as *women*. They are not *girls, gals, ladies, chicks, broads, lovelies,* or *honeys*. Words like *homemaker* and *housewife* are also not synonyms for woman; check carefully for accuracy before they are used. *Coed* does not mean woman any more than *ed* means man; persons who attend school are *students*.

Gratuitous physical description, uncommon almost to the point of absence in news stories about men, should also be eliminated from such stories about women. If you would not say, "The gray-haired grandfather of three was elected senator," then do not say, "The gray-haired grandmother of three was elected senator." This rule does not apply with equal force to feature writing, especially profiles, in which physical description is often an essential aspect. However, care should be taken to avoid stereotypical descriptions in favor of describing an individual's unique characteristics.

Similar considerations apply to the mention of an individual's spouse and family. In a news story about a man, his wife and family are typically mentioned only in passing and only when relevant; the same practice should apply to news stories about women. See the previous examples. Again, the practice is slightly different for feature stories and profiles, but the test of relevance should always be applied.

Most achievements do not need sexual identification; those that do should be so identified for both men and women. If you would not say, "Dan Rather is a male reporter," do not say "Helen Thomas is a female reporter." Instead of "Arthur Ashe is

121

one of the best American tennis players and Billie Jean King is one of the best American women tennis players," say, "Arthur Ashe and Billie Jean King are two of the best American tennis players," or "Arthur Ashe is one of the best American male tennis players and Billie Jean King is one of the best American female tennis players."

Avoid sins of omission as well as those of commission. If, for example, an expert is sought in a given field, or if an example is needed to make a point, women should be used in these cases as a matter of course—not simply as "oddities" or representatives of "a woman's viewpoint."

Man, used alone and in words like *chairman,* is a sexually exclusive term and should be avoided when possible. "Man-on-the-street," for instance, can easily be changed to "person-on-the-street" or "ordinary person"; "chairman" to "chairperson." The federal government has begun to change its job titles to reflect this problem; persons formerly called "mailmen" are now "mail carriers."

Women's professional qualifications or working experience should always be acknowledged, to forestall the common (and incorrect) expectation that most women are full-time housewives.

Feminist is the correct term to describe a woman committed to equal rights for women. "Women's libber" is an unacceptable pejorative.

Headlines seem to be particularly susceptible to the use of stereotypical, simplistic language. As in other areas, play on these stereotypes is to be avoided.

When you have completed a story about a woman, go through it and ask yourself whether you would have written about a man in the same style. If not, something may be wrong with the tone or even the conception of your article. Think it through again.

Do major publications discriminate against women, consciously or unconsciously? *Houston Post* columnist Bonnie Gangelhoff raised this issue in her February 23, 1994 column headlined:

Magazine cheats women athletes

Stabbed. Widowed. Abused. Clubbed. Who are they?

The women on TV miniseries during sweeps week?

Guess again. They are the women in jeopardy on Sports Illustrated magazine covers for the past 12 months. While plowing through Sunday newspapers, an article by Boston broadcaster Lynda Truman Ryan touched a nerve. It seems Ryan's daughter plays baseball and the girl, 10, eagerly awaits Sports Illustrated each week. She likes to read about baseball or anything about girls' sports.

A year ago, Lynda Truman Ryan began to tally how many women attained SI cover status from swimsuit issue to swimsuit issue. What Ryan discovered is surprising. Six Sports Illustrated covers out of 52 featured women. Four of the six women were victims of some sort. The other two SI covers featured female models in bikinis.

Weak moments

What really disappoints is that the only women athletes to grace SI's cover are ones who have been rendered helpless in some way. Usually tough competitors and fighters, they are caught in a rare moment of victimhood. The four covers:

- Monica Seles, a tough tennis player, wears tennis whites with a knife stuck in her back.
- A picture of the widows of Indian pitchers Steve Olin and Tim Crews, two players killed in a boating accident.
- Tennis player Mary Pierce looking as if she is going to cry. The headline: "Why Mary Pierce Fears For Her Life." The story is about her dad who beats her.
- The most recent cover woman is Nancy Kerrigan. By now we know she's a natural for an SI cover. She's been clubbed. "Why me?" rang out the headline.

But we should ask Sports Illustrated "Why them?" Why put women athletes on the cover only at their low points. The magazine sends out a message. This is the way we like our women—beat up (or in a bikini).

That some of the best and brightest talents in women's sports get cover play only when they suffer is ridiculous.

To wit: Will we see four-time gold medal winner Bonnie Blair on an SI cover? Not unless someone sabotages her skates today as she goes for her fifth gold medal.

But Roger Jackson, SI spokesman, says the magazine regularly writes about women's sports. He defends cover choices, saying it's not accurate to call them victims. They are newsmakers, he says: "Sports Illustrated is a news magazine that publishes the top news story or newsmaker in the world of sports each week."

So, not one other woman athlete was deemed top newsmaker status for the entire year?

Wrong message

Sports Illustrated is a magazine read by thousands of kids. Ryan's daughter and others like her who love sports should see some women triumph and honored when they are up, not just down. Somehow the message emerging from such one-note cover choices is bad things happen to women who try to excel. And what about all the boys who read SI? Their opinions are shaped by such images of top women athletes honored only when helpless.

Get a grip, Sports Illustrated. Abuse is no excuse for a cover.

- P.S.: Check out the Feb. 21 issue of SI. Sure, we like to read about Tommy Moe and Dan Jansen but there's not one story about a woman athlete on the U.S. Olympic team. The one feature story about a female focuses on a basketball player from Canada. She had a leg amputated. There's a full-page photo of her. It's shot to display her right leg cut off below the knee and posed next to her artificial limb. (p. D1)

Gangelhoff printed letters a few weeks later from readers in response to that column. The readers wrote:

- Dear Bonnie,

You whine and bray that only six SI covers featured women. My complaint is, why were there any at all except for the swimsuit issue of course? Ten percent of the covers of SI featured a gender that is basically a non-factor in revenue producing sports. Get it? People who care about women sports are also probably 10 percent of the sports market. Live with it! The only way women will ever be on a par in popularity with men in sports is when they start playing their sport topless!

Sincerely, Cowboy

Dear Cowboy,

I'm really impressed with your enlightened attitudes. By the way, what about the millions of women who watched the Olympics, and made it a windfall for CBS?

• Dear Bonnie Gangelhoff,

How many men have graced the cover of Women's Sports and Fitness over the last year? Or Woman's Day? Or any of the other 2 million publications devoted exclusively to females? Of course, the title of the magazine in question must be Sports Illustrated and not Men's Sports Illustrated despite the fact that male sports account for 99.99999 of all sport-generated revenues and garner a like proportion of all sports readers interest.

From R.B.A.

Dear R.B.A.,

If the magazine is for men only, why not call it Sports Illustrated for Men Who Love Women in Bikinis in Exotic Locations? The fact is, boys and girls read this magazine, as do women. SI is missing out on revenue. They might have even more readers if they carried a few more covers and stories about girls and women.

• Dear Bonnie,

Thank you for your reaction to the covers of Sports Illustrated . . . If you want to have another reaction, I urge you to look at the Sports TV page at the front of The Post's TV Week. Please note the number of men's basketball games scheduled for televiewing, and the number of women's games likewise.

Sincerely yours, Betty Rudnick

Dear Betty,

I checked it out. Lean. (p. D1)

Can more publications devote more space for more articles about women's sports? Surely. Can we all be more careful in writing about women? Of course.

Chapter Ten
Writing Advance Stories

The advance is an article written prior to a major football game, bowl game, national or international tennis match, championship boxing match, baseball playoffs, World Series, or any other major sporting event.

If you are a staff writer on a newspaper, keeping your readers involved with your newspaper (and remember, newspapers are losing readers by the thousands these days) means anticipating coming events and writing about them.

There are many guidelines about advances, most based on tradition and common sense.

In *Modern Sportswriting*, authors Louis I. Gelfand and Harry Heath Jr. (1969) suggested 13 key guidelines for writing a substantial advance story. They are:

- Significance of the game.
- The tradition and history of the teams, how their rivalry began, the most exciting games of the past, how they stand in won–lost figures in the series, and the last game.
- Records of the teams or individual competitors during the current season, and comments on the records of the two teams. Perhaps one has played a tougher schedule than the other, or one team may have scheduled a "weak sister," between tough games, and so on.
- Analysis of comparative scoring records against mutual opponents.
- Squads' condition, both physical and mental.
- Starting lineups and comments on changes in lineups.
- Weather: how possible changes may affect the outcome, records of teams in different climates (e.g., northern athletes in the South, track and field athletes in high altitudes, football team on muddy field).

- System of play: Compare them and the advantage one may have over the other; e.g., in tennis, a player's volley attack compared against his opponent's backcourt game.
- Individual angle: In team sport, the importance of one player.
- Local situation: Atmosphere in the city where the game is to be played.
- Ticket and crowd situation: Will extra seats be erected? Will there be a television blackout for local fans? Pay-per-view? Is scalping tickets legal or "semi-legal?" Is scalping simply ignored by law enforcement officials? If tickets can be scalped, what are the going prices?
- Statements by coaches.
- Who is favored: Odds, if available. (pp. 38–39)

It is sometimes, although not always, possible to get quotations from players. Some college and university coaches demand that their players refrain from speaking to the press, especially before a major game. Others don't have such a rule. If it is possible to get good quotations from the players, don't hesitate to do so. If the college or university coach has a rule prohibiting his players from speaking to the press, make sure the coach is interviewed, but beware of pat answers.

Gelfand and Heath (1969) also suggested that there are several types of advance articles:

- The standard advance, published the morning or evening before the game.
- The roundup advance.
- The feature advance, which may be a *poll advance*, in which players, coaches, sports writers, and sometimes even fans give their opinions as to the probable outcome. It may also be the *comparison advance*, regularly written over the space of a week before a major contest. In it, World Series teams are compared, infield with infield, defense against defense; or bowl football teams are analyzed, tackles against tackles, halfbacks against halfbacks, and so on. It may also be the *season's outlook advance*, in which a well-informed and observant reporter covers the prospects for an important area team shortly before the season's opening. (p. 39)

The reporter's principal asset, Gelfand and Heath (1969) believed, is the "ability to analyze. The reader wants to know if the event is worthy of his presence. Also, he wants an indication of who will win and why." (p. 38)

That sentence is as true today as when it was originally written, but much has changed since the Gelfand and Heath textbook. We now have ESPN; a wide variety of sports channels; CNN News, which carries sports shows; a fourth network, Fox, that outbid CBS for the rights to NFL football; and other venues for sports programming.

To keep your own readers from defecting, these are possibilities to consider:

• Graphics. *USA Today* has been the point publication in the last few years in the use of graphics and color pages. *The Dallas Morning News* has won a Pulitzer Prize for graphics-oriented special coverage displays. Given that most major newspapers now employ graphic artists and designers, you may wish to coordinate your advance stories with the graphics department.

• Highlight an advance every day with a special blurb in a "skybox" above the logo or flag on the front page.

• Use a computer-designed box on the front page, as *USA Today* does, to statistically highlight the similarities or differences between two teams.

• Use color (if possible) with the advances to attract reader interest.

• Ask coaches not connected with the upcoming game to discuss the coaches who are involved.

• Use graphics-designed page layouts to highlight the competition between teams; for example, "When We Have the Ball" diagram the offense and the opponent's defense. "When They Have the Ball" diagram their offense and "our" defense.

How can a major newspaper use advances?

The Dallas Cowboys went to the Super Bowl twice in 2 years (Super Bowls XXVII and XXVIII, 1993 and 1994).

In the last six issues before the 1994 Super Bowl, *The Dallas Morning News* covered the upcoming game this way:

On Tuesday, there were two stories on page 1 under a head "Set for Success." One story was about Atlanta, the site of the game, under the head "Dallas looks to Atlanta as a model." The second article on page one was "Just the ticket" with a subhead "Air fare, Super Bowl seats available, but getting back could be tricky." Both articles were jumped to page A14. On that page the *Dallas Morning News* also ran a two-column by 9½-inch graphic, statistically comparing Dallas and Atlanta in terms of population, race, age, sex, crime rate, weather, airport size, real estate, transportation, and other factors.

That day *The Dallas Morning News* began a special Super Bowl section, titled "Super Bowl XXVIII." It contained eight pages (pp. B17–B24) all devoted to the Cowboys.

The articles on page B17 were headlined "Aikman recalls little of NFC title game" (he received a concussion), "Wizard of Odds" (what Las Vegas says), "Proving the line wrong," and "Jerry Jones' deep-pocket moves corrected early chaos."

Page B18 contained "Fan's View," "No matter who's playing people watch Super Bowl," "Fewer tickets in 1995," "Formula deserves 2nd shot," "Cowboys dominate area ratings" (in a box), and "Q & A with Chris Berman" (ESPN's commentator).

A full-page article, "Can't Kick the Habit," about kicker Ed Murray appeared on page B19.

"It's another Super Bowl rout for mighty Cowboys vs. Bills," "Bills enter Atlanta prepared for questions about futility," and "No bye week leaves less time for hype," all appeared on page B20.

Miscellaneous stats and two photos were on the next page. "Failure to win back-to-back titles haunts former Cowboys" was on page B21, and some jump material from the first section page on page B22.

Page B23 included "Atlanta's top tables are taken," "Air service plentiful to Atlanta," and "Cowboys were an easy pick" (in a box), plus the point spreads for all past Super Bowl games.

The last page contained match-ups: The Cowboys' center versus the Buffalo center, and the Cowboys' Emmitt Smith versus the Bills' Thurman Thomas, plus color photos. There were a total of 21 major stories in the special section on Tuesday.

On Wednesday, *The Dallas Morning News* ran one article on the front page, "Cowboys lineman just wants to be Lett alone" (about Leon Lett). The special section was again eight pages.

Page B13 included four articles: "Cowboy cornerback talks the talk," "Head coach Jimmy Johnson gets the picture," "Photo Day is mostly flash," and "Sans prediction headache, Aikman's mind at ease."

"Fan's view," "Atlanta hotel manager compares city to Dallas," "Magic required to get into this party" (by a *Morning News* society writer), "Long says his Raiders match Dallas well" about L.A. Raider Howie Long, and "When members of the media gather, can inane questions be far behind?" were on page B14.

"Oddsmakers expect 100 million wagers," a box headlined "Do You Have a Gambling Problem?," and (Martin Luther) "King home anchors large historic district" appeared on page B15.

Two major articles appeared on page B16: "Johnson's confidence is reflection of his coaching," and "Family ties can put you in a bind at Super Bowl," plus two jumps from the first section page.

Page B17 was more than 75% advertising, but two small articles were run on that page: "Smith shines only because Newton doesn't play defense," and "Cowboys try to get acclimated."

Pages B18 and B19 were the inside pages of the section, which means *The Dallas Morning News* could design through the inside gutters. There was a Q & A column with coach Jimmy Johnson, an analysis article with owner Jerry Jones, "Inside the Locker Room," "Stopping Thomas means stopping Bills," and a complete stats box from the entire season for the Cowboys and Bills.

Page B20 was full of miscellaneous quotations and two photos, plus profiles of Cowboys players Scott Galbreith and John Jett, and Bills players Russell Copeland and Jim Kelley.

Page B21 contained three articles: "In case of emergency . . ." (about backup players), "Haley limited but won't back off" about Cowboys' defensive end Charles Haley, and "Johnson's comments don't affect Bills."

The end page of the section carried three articles: "Corner's sentence: Stop end zone exclamations" about Alvin Harper versus Mickey Washington, one article about the Cowboys' Tony Tolbert and the Bills' Bruce Smith. There were 24 major stories in the special section on Wednesday.

The Thursday issue carried two front page articles—" '93 parade causes upset authorities" about violence in the Dallas parade after the 1993 Super Bowl win, and "Jerry Jones buys Collin tract for luxury-home development"—and color photos of the Atlanta stadium crew readying the stadium.

The front page of the "Texas and Southwest" section carried an article about Cowboys' fans having cowboys cut into their hair and females who were having Dallas Cowboys insets in their fingernails.

The special section first page carried four major stories: one article about the regular season game between the Cowboys and the Bills, which Buffalo won 13–10; a second article about the prior Super Bowl, which Dallas won 52–17; a third article headlined "Peach of an idea," about sports business in Atlanta, and "Under (assistant coach Butch) Davis, Cowboys defense 'gets after people.' "

The second page of the Thursday section contained articles about former Atlanta coach Jerry Glanville; one headlined "Hey, maybe opposites do attract" about one couple, she for the Cowboys, he for the Bills; "Mouthy ex-coach getting paid to talk" about an ex-Bills coach; and "In event of Super blowout, Enberg, Trumpy ready to fill in the blanks."

The next page contained two major articles: "Message pad," about seat cushions with the GTE emblem on them; and "NFL cities compete in good taste."

The next page (page B22) contained a column by Frank Luksa; an opinion piece by NFL quarterback Babe Laufenberg; short quotations from Edwin Pope of the *Miami Herald*, Vic Ziegel of the *New York Daily News*, Art Thiel of the *Seattle Post-Intelligencer*, and Ron Rapoport of the *Los Angeles Daily News*; and one article, "Bills don't qualify as lovable losers."

Page B23 was more than 75% advertisements, but did contain one article, "Jimmy Johnson's staff a laboratory for future NFL head coaches."

Page B24 contained four articles: "Apple spot at core of Super ads," "Taking it all in stride" (about Emmitt Smith), "Navigating city without car," and "Cowboys star in Atlanta's late show." (Page B25 was an advertising page.)

Page B26 contained three articles—"Life on the dark side of the boom" (about players who didn't perform well in the last Super Bowl), "Thomas' temperature rises under media glare," and "Dallas' chance to land Super Bowl remains slim"—plus two stories jumped from the first page of the special section.

Page B27 was a page of miscellaneous quotations, briefs, and photos. Page B28 also matched the last page of the previous day's sections: match-ups between Darren Woodson and Pete Metzelaars and Kevin Williams versus Russell Copeland. There were 24 major articles in the special section on Thursday.

On Friday, the front page of *The Dallas Morning News* carried one article, "Scalpers' heaven."

The first page of the special section (Section 14) carried only one article—"Dynasty in the Making"—under a color photo of a Cowboys kickoff, but the section itself was 16 pages.

Page H2 carried the Fan's Views column, and two society-related stories, "Ice sculptures hot items for Super parties," and "Fear not: Security chief Rathburn is a seer." There was also "Coke's new formula: Cable programming instead of commercials," plus one article about Atlanta, "Atlanta develops habit of drawing big events." (H3 was an advertising page.)

Page H4 contained columns by Blackie Sherrod and Frank Luksa, plus "Nate's World," a diary by Cowboy player Nate Newton.

Page H5 was almost all ads, except for one article "Handyman finally will get Sunday Cowboy fix," about a Tim Allen–type TV handyman.

Page H6 was a Q & A with Atlanta native Billy Payne, credited with bringing the Olympics to Atlanta. Page H7 was a full-page electronics chain ad.

Page H8 contained opinion pieces by NFL coaches Dave Wannstedt and Wade Phillips, plus ads. Page H9 was a lumberyard chain ad.

Page H10 contained brief profiles of Cowboy players Daryl Johnston and John Gesek, Bills players Henry Jones and Steve Christie, plus briefs and ads.

Page H11 and H12 were full-page advertisements.

The top third of page H13 was about the halftime entertainment scheduled for the Super Bowl, and page 14 was the jump-page from page 1. Pages H14 and H15 contained 75% ads. Page H15 held one story ("Cowboys have ingredients to be among NFL's all-time best") and Page H16 was a full-page ad. There were a total of 17 major stories in the special section on Friday.

Saturday's front page contained two Super Bowl-related stories: "Buffalo's a city with a complex," and "Mexican fans are traveling to game, planning parties."

The special section (section B) was 12 pages; page B1 contained three stories plus a box. The three stories were "Aikman keeps fortunes in perspective" (he had signed a contract with Dallas for 8 years for $50 million), "Jones is confident Cowboys can prosper under salary cap," and "Bills still Buffaloed by Super Circus: Bet Cowboys" by columnist Randy Galloway. The box on the page was a list of Cowboy players who were "keepers" for the next season.

Page B2 contained the Fan's View feature, two society-type articles and a miscellaneous column about people in the NFL and their plans for the Super Bowl, and one column about players in (or not in) the NFL Hall of Fame.

Page B3 contained two articles—work still to be done at the Super Bowl site and a "think" article: "Some media may protest flying of Confederate flag" (in Georgia).

Page B4 contained three major articles on who would officiate at the Super Bowl (plus a box showing where the officials are on the field), the sounds of music in Atlanta bars and lounges, and the commercials expected to be shown during the Super Bowl.

Page B5 contained two articles, one about NFL commissioner Paul Tagliabue and another about whether Cowboy Bill Bates would retire (no), plus a three-quarter-page sporting goods store chain ad.

Page B6 contained three major articles: "Cowboys tackle on guard for weight challenge," about the Cowboys defense, and profiles of Thomas Everett and Henry Jones.

Page B7 contained two articles, one about Super Bowl parties and one about Dallas-area Bills fans.

Page B8 contained two major articles, "Fans gaining appreciation for underdog Bills, players say" and "Aikman to skip Pro Bowl," plus jumps from page 1 of the section.

Page B9 contained briefs and statistics, plus about one-third page of ads. Page B10 was all statistics.

Page B11 contained three major stories: "Boom towns" about how the Dallas and Buffalo economies rise when the teams get to the Super Bowl; "On the surface, Georgia Dome field not a major factor" with a graphic of the Georgia Dome, and "Player security at a premium after recent attacks on athletes."

Page B12 contained columns by Frank Luksa, Babe Laufenberg, and Edwin Pope of *The Miami Herald*, plus a color cartoon of Jimmy Johnson. On Saturday, there were 28 major articles in the special section.

On Sunday, Super Bowl day, *The Dallas Morning News* carried two major stories on page 1, plus a color photo at the fold. The articles were headlined "Super Bowl carries lore of the rings" and "Profit-driven Jones builds fiscal champs." The rings reference was to Super Bowl rings given to the winning team.

The special section (section B) was 16 pages, with three stories on the first page: "Date with Destiny: Cowboys look to join elite group of repeat champs," "Three-piece outfit" (about Aikman, Irvin, and Smith), and "All things considered, Cowboys will beat Bills."

Page B2 contained the Fan's Views column, two society-type articles, and two Super Bowl media articles.

Page B3 contained one article that occupied the top third of the page: "Artificial turf gives groundskeepers a new set of worries."

Page B4 contained opinion articles by Jerry Sullivan from Buffalo ("History likely will judge Levy too much too harshly"), Dave Wannstedt, and Wade Phillips; one piece by Edwin Pope of *The Miami Herald*, and the jump of one page 1 story.

Page B5 was 75% ads, but it did contain one article ("Nate Newton's Diary") and a short piece indicating that coach Jimmy Johnson might consider offers from other NFL clubs.

Page B6 was all statistics. Page B7 was the jump page for the "Cowboys can join elite by beating Bills" story. It also had a graphic on the top third of the page: "When the Cowboys have the Ball" and "When the Bills have the ball."

Page B8 was the jump page for the "Trio" story, and also contained two major articles: "Official business," about NFL referees and "Cowboys' confidence not a sign of arrogance."

Page B9 contained 75% ads and one article ("Potent mixture") about offensive coach Norv Turner.

Page B10 contained three articles: "One goal for Buffalo linebackers: Catch 22" (meaning catch number 22—Emmitt Smith), and two articles under one head ("Stand and Deliver"), profiles of quarterbacks Troy Aikman and Jim Kelley.

Page B11 contained ads and one small article "Sanders gives charities 'Prime Time' week," about Deion Sanders.

Page B12 was statistics and predictions by celebrities.

Page B13 contained ads and one article: "Frito-Lay entertains clients at Super Bowl" (Frito-Lay is headquartered in the Dallas area).

Page B14 had one article ("To Levy's credit, Bills come to coach's defense") plus three quarters of a page of statistics.

Page B15 was a "house ad" by *The Dallas Morning News*, with a guest cartoon by Tom Toles of *The Buffalo News*. Readers of *The Buffalo News* saw a cartoon by *Dallas Morning News* cartoonist Bill DeOre.

Page B16 contained a color photo feature: "How the Cowboys move 6,000 pounds of equipment to the Super Bowl."

There were 26 major articles in the special section for Sunday, and a total of 140 from Tuesday through Sunday. 140 articles!

The reason why *The Dallas Morning News* published those special sections day after day is obvious: *The Dallas Morning News* is not only the "home paper" for the Cowboys, the event is broadcast worldwide and if *The Dallas Morning News* didn't make the effort to cover the Cowboys with such special sections, readers (and advertisers) would turn elsewhere. *The Dallas Morning News* could not afford the loss of readers or the loss of advertisers, and especially could not afford the loss of prestige if it failed to cover the Cowboys adequately.

PS: The Cowboys beat the Bills for the second straight year. The score was 30–13.

Chapter Eleven

Developing a Sports Feature
From a Sports News Event

A good writer can often develop a good feature from a news event. Many good features can be developed from these areas, including trends in sports, or other topics in sports. An example of a trend in sports might be the latest in exercise techniques. A topic story might be baseball card trading.

Equally important is the significance of human events. How can this be applied?

On October 30, 1993, Wisconsin defeated Michigan 13–10 at Madison. At game's end, hundreds of Badger fans rushed the field; many were crushed against chain link fences. By the thinnest margin, no one was killed. Dozens were rushed to area hospitals.

Here is Pete Dougherty's story, filed on the Gannett News wire. This is how the news story appeared the next day, in *The Houston Post.*

75 injured in Badger stampede

By Pete Dougherty
Gannett News Service

MADISON, Wis.—Jo Ellen Amato was lucky enough to hop the fence just before things got really bad.

The 18-year-old was at the front of a mob of students trying to rush onto the field Saturday to celebrate after Wisconsin had defeated Michigan 13–10 at Camp Randall Stadium.

Hundreds of Wisconsin students were about to get wedged into the fence and railings designed to keep fans from the football players.

She barely escaped onto the field before the mass squeezed against the chain-link fence. The fence bent and swayed and part eventually broke, but not until nearly squeezing the life out of several young people, their faces becoming blue, or even worse, ashen.

"I sat and watched people get crushed and there was nothing I could do," Amato said.

University of Wisconsin security chief Susan Riseling said about 75 people were injured when approximately 12,000 spectators scrambled out of five student sections. Reports from the city's three hospitals about three hours later showed 64 people were examined or treated. Seven victims were considered in critical condition.

The inclined tunnel that leads the players in and out of Camp Randall has metal railings in cement that don't move. The 10-foot wide track between the the stands and the field was temporarily blocked; the swinging gates, meant to keep the fans from the players, were fastened back so the teams could leave.

But that's right where the Wisconsin students sit, and they wanted on the field to celebrate the Badgers' big victory.

The ones who made it were fine, and there were hundreds of them, hugging players and each other, reveling in the win.

The ones who didn't, the couple hundred tucked in the corners around the tunnel, were in trouble. They got wedged between the fence, the railings, and the thousands of people pushing toward the field.

"I said, 'Open the gate, let them out—they're going to die,' " Amato said. "(The guard) said, 'I can't, there's football players coming.' I said, 'Would you rather have people die?' "

By the time the gate was opened, a couple minutes later, it was too late for many. Many in the first five or 10 rows were too wedged and tangled to move.

"They were trampled on top of each other and bent over the stands," said lineman Joe Panos, who helped clear the pile. "I thought they were gone."

"One girl just about died in his arms," teammate Yusef Burgess said. "A lot of people were seeing things they've never seen before. Seeing people's faces turn blue, that's not a sight you want to remember." (pp. B1, B7)

How can a feature story be developed from this news story? *By understanding the significance of human events.*

By November 2, Ed Sherman of the *Chicago Tribune* completed a follow-up story on that disaster. He focused on Michael Brin, a sophomore walk-on quarterback player for the Badgers. Brin was so far down the Wisconsin depth chart "he didn't even have his own number."

Sherman's story was published in the *Houston Chronicle* under the headline:

No. 3 in the program and No. 1 in her heart

By Ed Sherman
Chicago Tribune

MADISON, Wis.—Michael Brin was the unlikeliest of heroes Saturday.

Brin, a wide receiver from Highland Park, Ill., is so far down on Wisconsin's depth chart that last week's program listed him as a quarterback. A sophomore walk-on, Brin doesn't even have his own number.

Most Badgers fans know No. 3 as starting cornerback Kenny Gales. Brin, though, also wears No. 3, and that was the only number that mattered to Aimee Jansen.

Jansen found herself pinned up against a fence Saturday in the terrifying aftermath of Wisconsin's game with Michigan. She was caught in the crush of fans who tried to storm the field, and it got to the point where she couldn't breathe.

Then she saw "a No. 3" in a Badgers uniform who pulled her by the pant leg and hoisted her over the fence to safety.

Monday, Jansen had to find No. 3.

"I just wanted to say thank you, thank you very much," said Jansen, a sophomore from Antigo, Wis. "He saved my life."

Brin didn't get into one play Saturday in Wisconsin's 13–10 victory over Michigan, but no Badger shined more. Brin's quick actions also are being credited with helping revive two other students who stopped breathing, one of whom he gave mouth-to-mouth resuscitation.

On Monday Brin suddenly finding himself in the spotlight, being called a hero.

"The only reason why they're saying I'm a hero is because I was wearing pads. I don't feel like a hero," Brin said. "I feel like a guy who did the normal thing and reacted when he saw trouble."

Authorities are crediting the actions of Brin and others with helping to avert a full-blown tragedy. An estimated 69 people were injured when 12,000 Wisconsin students cascaded from the stands toward the field.

Seven people initially were listed in critical condition, but as of Monday evening, eight people remained hospitalized, five in good condition and three in fair.

Those figures are remarkable considering what the scene looked like Monday. The northeast corner of Camp Randall Stadium was strewn with twisted pieces of fence and railings. The weight of the people was enough to lift 6-inch bolts out of the concrete.

Witnesses described students being buried as much as 10 people deep. The injuries included broken limbs and extreme loss of oxygen.

"We're lucky, because it could have been much worse," Wisconsin Chancellor David Ward said. "We're fortunate we had so many people step up and help out."

Brin said he normally is one of the first players in the locker room, but he lingered on the field. As he walked toward the tunnel, he noticed a huge surge.

"That's when I saw the girl," Brin said. "She was folded over a fence."

Brin pulled out Jansen, and then he noticed a couple of girls weren't breathing. He quickly went over to one of them and started to apply mouth-to-mouth. He did it only briefly, "but it got her breathing."

Brin, a premed student, isn't certified in cardiopulmonary resuscitation, but he applied the lessons he learned in a high school health class. As for the other girl, he helped move her over to a bench and assisted in stabilizing her.

"It was a shock," Brin said. "Nobody expected it. You just acted on instinct."

One of the women who stopped breathing also tried to get in touch with Brin Monday. Brin wasn't sure of her name, but the memory of her face on Saturday hadn't left him. He desperately wanted to see the woman again.

"When I saw her, she was blue in the face," Brin said. "I have to see her cheeks all rosy red. I have to see it for myself."

Brin said he spent a depressing Saturday night, but his spirits brightened Sunday when he learned all the injured people were improving.

"It's a great feeling knowing a girl might be breathing because of me," he said.

He isn't likely to get close to the field for Saturday's game against Ohio State. He has been in only one play all season.

However, Brin's football skills didn't matter Saturday. He always will be remembered for what he did after the game.

"I haven't changed," Brin said. "I'm not a hero. I'm just Mike Brin." (p. B10)

Chapter Twelve
Writing the Investigative Sports Article

There are only a dozen or so major newspapers throughout the United States that have reporters working on special projects in sports.

Some of the papers that have special projects people are *The Los Angeles Times*; *The Des Moines Register*; the Newhouse newspapers in Syracuse, NY, which have been tracking problems in the athletic programs at Syracuse University; the *Houston Chronicle*; and papers in Pittsburgh and Phoenix.

Doug Bedell of *The Dallas Morning News* is such a reporter. Bedell is a native of Houston, Texas. He attended Northwestern University, in Evanston, Illinois, for $4\frac{1}{2}$ years as a pre-med major, then decided to "do anything different." He transferred to Baylor University, in Waco, Texas and graduated in journalism.

He was then hired by *The Beaumont*, Texas *Enterprise* as Assistant State Editor, then moved into bureau work in Lake Charles, Louisiana, then Port Arthur and Orange, Texas. In the mid-1970s, he moved to *The Dallas Times Herald* as a general assignments reporter. From 1980 to 1984, he worked for *The Louisville Courier Journal* as a court system reporter.

He returned to Texas in 1984 as a general assignments reporter for *The Dallas Morning News*. In 1986, he was assigned special projects in sports, where he does nontraditional sports stories, which have included steroid use, rules infractions, and other similar stories.

His assignments came directly from the recent status of the Southwest Conference (SWC), which was then Texas, Texas A & M, Texas Tech, Baylor, Arkansas, Rice Houston, Southern Methodist, and Texas Christian University. The SWC is now defunct: Texas, Texas A & M, Texas Tech, and Baylor have joined the Big Eight; TCU, SMU, and Rice have joined the Western Athletic Conference. As this is written the University of Houston has not yet affiliated with any other league.

Because of major football violations, Southern Methodist University received the NCAA "death penalty" (no football for 2 years) and almost all of the other SWC conference schools received NCAA warnings or probation in the recent past for sports rules violations.

Because *The Dallas Morning News* circulates into Oklahoma, it has also covered violations of the athletic programs at the University of Oklahoma.

During 1994, *The Dallas Morning News* published a series of articles about excesses in the athletic programs at Texas A & M University, in College Station, Texas. Reporter Olive Talley and others at *The Dallas Morning News* also contributed to this series.

"These stories encompassed, in part, how Texas A & M behaved when they had a 'windfall' of money from football victories.

"We ended up with documents a foot high—literally several thousands of pages," Bedell said (personal communication, June 1, 1994).

"We received them from several avenues: we got purchase records, vouchers and travel documents from the university; some (records) we received through Open Records Acts (requests). We also sued Texas A & M University and finally obtained an out-of-court settlement. Their response regarding documents has improved, although there has been some foot-dragging.

"We at least have an 'improved dialogue' with them about records."

Bedell worked at least 2 weeks on a story about how Texas A & M University squandered thousands and thousands of dollars for gifts, liquor, and other items given to players and university officials going to four recent postseason football bowls. The amount? Over $440,000 in 4 years.

In Bedell's lead, he writes, "Expenditures on these items are roughly enough to cover the annual scholarships for all 163 students in the women's athletic program, which consistently operates at a loss" (Bedell, 1994, p. 1).

"We compared their figures with figures from other schools. We put these (the A & M figures) into a database and used a (computer) spreadsheet program to see what we had.

"It's not uncommon for a university to behave like this. Universities use athletic championships as justification to reward those in all dimensions of the programs—athletes and staff alike.

"The public doesn't understand—and I didn't understand—the allowances given to athletes. The (automobile) mileage—the very generous mileage—given to each athlete as if they were individually driving to a bowl game. It gives you the impression it's just a hemorrhage of greenbacks at that time.

"Most sports departments are reticent to run these stories. But these times make it necessary to understand the finances of such programs. The financial changes going on are baffling unless you know what's behind the numbers.

"Many members of the public don't want to hear such things about sports programs. But it's mandatory that we tell our public what we understand about (sports) economic issues."

Later Texas A & M University president William Mobley called *The Dallas Morning News* to complain about (or correct) a small item about alcohol policy; that other funds—from Texas A & M alumni and others—were used for liquor purchases. But Bedell said that documents obtained from Texas A & M University did not reveal that and the documents they supplied were "all we had to work on" (personal communication, June 1, 1994).

Here then, is Doug Bedell's article, begun on *The Dallas Morning News* front page on Sunday, May 1, 1994. Note: Ross Margraves, Jr., cited toward the end of Bedell's article, resigned as a member of the Texas A & M Board of Regents.

A&M bowl funds go to purchase gifts
Athletic director says policy reflects traditional reward for success

By Doug Bedell
Staff Writer of The Dallas Morning News

COLLEGE STATION—Texas A&M University, whose football success has led it to five bowl appearances since 1990, has spent more than $440,000 during that period on complimentary tickets, souvenirs and merchandise for regents, administrators and prominent boosters.

The university's administration spent $161,955 on complimentary tickets and more than $260,000 on extra watches and other items given away, according to the school's financial records. For the 1993 Cotton Bowl, A&M hosted a banquet that cost $44,453, records show.

While bowl sponsors provide football players with complimentary watches, warm-ups and other memorabilia, the university routinely has purchased the same items for its dignitaries.

Expenditures on those items are roughly enough to cover the annual scholarships for all 163 students in the women's athletic program, which consistently operates at a loss.

A&M's financial records show that the bowl appearances grossed the university more than $10.7 million. Of that amount, the school netted about $1 million after deducting travel and hotel expenses, paying shares to Southwest Conference teams and covering other incidental expenses, including the merchandise and complimentary tickets and hotel expenses for VIPs.

Athletic director Wally Groff said bowl appearances are considered rewards for successful seasons, not for-profit enterprises.

"Absolutely," Mr. Groff said. "We view it that way, and that's why our policies are prepared the way they are."

Texas A&M athletics, meanwhile, are facing NCAA sanctions that will lop off an estimated $2 million in bowl and television revenue.

Similar practices of university-paid souvenirs for boosters, administrators and regents have sparked criticism at schools from the University of Texas to the University of Nebraska and University of Virginia.

Beyond the bowl expenditures, A&M athletic department documents also reveal several areas that have drawn the attention of the Texas Rangers and FBI in their ongoing inquiry into the conduct of A&M officials:

- Improper athletic department purchases of alcohol may have been illegally disguised on vouchers as food, ice and soft drinks. Internal university auditors identified the practice as a major athletic trouble spot.
- The athletic department has spent more than $21,000 to send board of regents chairmen and their wives to attend football banquets in New York City.

Source of controversy

Traditionally, bowl receipts have been liberally lavished on collegiate athletic entourages.

After the University of Texas last attended a Cotton Bowl in 1991, it wound up netting about $162,000 out of its initial receipt of $3 million. More than $80,000 was spent on purchases of jewelry and other items distributed among administrators and boosters, said Ed Goble, UT's assistant athletic director for business affairs.

"Texas, I think, has a philosophy regarding the Cotton Bowl," said Mr. Goble. "It is regarded not so much as a money-making proposition, but as a reward."

Criticism of bowl spending practices has cropped up throughout the country. More than 70 percent of major college athletic departments now record deficit budgets. And athletic departments have come under increasing pressure to spend more for women's sports scholarships and development.

At the 1992 Orange Bowl, for example, University of Nebraska administrators outspent their $1 million allotment by more than $100,000.

The next year, the administration cut back the size of the school's entourage, scaled down the length of hotel stays paid for by the university and banned the practice of giving nonathletic administrators souvenir rings, watches or other gifts.

After the 1990 season, University of Virginia officials were criticized over their decision to spend more than one-third of the school's nearly $2 million Sugar Bowl allotment on an entourage of 457 officials and guests.

Player 'awards'

Texas A&M's spending practices for players appear to adhere to a strict $300 NCAA cap on the value of bowl "awards." At the 1993 Cotton Bowl, players received $293 in merchandise—a $109 watch, $40 plaque, $45 camera and $99 warm-up suit.

Under the school's interpretation of regulations, players also received a minimum of $93 in gas mileage money—figured as if each player had driven to the Cotton Bowl from College Station or his hometown—even if he were from Dallas.

More cash ($100) was handed out for "unitemized expenses." A total of $416 went to each player as a food allowance.

Gifts for the 95 scholarship athletes are often given to the school by bowl sponsors. A&M regulations, however, permit the athletic director to purchase additional items from bowl receipts.

At the 1990 Holiday Bowl in San Diego, for example, A&M officials ordered 155 watches for $15,190, 207 sweat suits for $11,832, 220 shaving kits for $3,827 and 166 plaques for $5,740—all beyond the complimentary gifts given to players.

At the 1992 Cotton Bowl, the Aggies brought 170 extra men's watches for $21,250 and 45 extra women's watches for $5,625.

At this year's Cotton Bowl, awards for football players and VIPs totaled $85,813, including extra golf shirts, Sony Walkman units, plaques, ladies and men's watches and warm-ups.

Traditional spending

Mr. Groff, A&M's athletic director, said such spending is traditional. The gifts go to university administrators, some booster club officials and staff, and selected vendors.

A list of recipients is drawn up by the athletic director, head coach and the associate athletic director for business, Mr. Groff said.

"It's a difficult decision to know where you draw the line," said Mr. Groff, who was associate athletic director for business until his appointment to head the department. "It's pretty much ultimately the athletic director's decision."

Those honored with awards are "university-oriented," including members of the faculty athletic council, regents, top university administrators, the president and staff members of the 12th Man Foundation and, up until this year, car dealers who donated autos for athletic department use.

"It's people that basically work with the football program and travel to the football games," Mr. Groff said.

For the 1990 Holiday Bowl, 1992 Disneyland Pigskin Classic and the school's past three Cotton Bowls, the A&M athletic department spent $172,833 on complimentary tickets that were distributed among faculty, administration officials, regents and prominent boosters.

Mr. Groff said those tickets were handed out just like the awards. And, he added, so were free admission gifts to entertainment events held in conjunction with bowl appearances.

Party expenses are also deducted from the bottom line. This year A&M spent $37,400 for more than 600 extra admission tickets for entertainment events held from Dec. 26 through New Year's Day.

At the 1990 Holiday Bowl, A&M spent $4,261 on a hosted bar at the instructions of then-President William Mobley. The school also paid a total of $225 in hotel-room bars for A&M vice president Robert Smith, and regents Wayne Showers, Raul Fernandez, Doug DeCluitt, Ross Margraves Jr., John Mobley and Royce Wisenbaker.

A year later, the 72nd Legislature expressly banned alcohol purchases with public money.

Accountants in an internal audit for the period from Sept. 1, 1991, through March 31, 1992, included a "major finding" that alcohol purchases are not permitted under administrative policies and prohibited by state law when using athletic department funds.

Alcohol purchases

Mr. Groff said that within the past three weeks, FBI agents and Texas Rangers investigators have questioned him concerning athletic department purchases of alcohol.

In February, a Brazos County grand jury indicted two A&M regents' staffers on felony charges of altering expense records to cover up purchases of alcohol for the board of regents. A prosecutor has said more indictments are likely.

Current university policy allows open purchase of alcohol with gift money only.

More than 33 departments and the board of regents' office spent more than $47,000 over the past six years to purchase items from a College Station liquor store owned by J.J. Ruffino, according to the A&M controller's office.

Athletic department records show a similar pattern.

Invoices and vouchers obtained by *The News* show $808 worth of merchandise was purchased from Ruffino Catering from 1990 to 1993.

About $500 worth of invoices were paid after internal university auditors cited the athletic department for improperly using athletic funds for alcohol.

Mr. Groff said some of the vouchers were for single bottles of wine used by the athletic dormitory chef. Others, he said, were alcoholic beverages for parties and other social functions.

"The only way you got anything paid for was to do it that way," Mr. Groff said.

Asked how athletic accountants learned to submit the misleading vouchers, Mr. Groff replied, "Just like everybody else, I guess. We probably had it sent back. I don't remember exactly. It's been so long ago."

Mr. Groff said the federal and state investigators interviewed him concerning about $450 worth of bills from Mr. Ruffino paid over the past two years.

Since 1990, the athletic department has also spent more than $21,000 to send former board chairman William McKenzie and Ross Margraves Jr. and their wives to attend the National Football Foundation Hall of Fame banquets each December at the Waldorf Astoria in New York City.

Mr. McKenzie's trips in 1990 and 1991 totaled $6,496, while Mr. Margraves' trips from 1990 through 1993 cost $14,794.

Travel expense reports justified attendance by the wives "to promote public relations and represent Texas A&M University."

"I think these types of events are important to our university and in this particular instance, important to the success of or athletic program," Mr. Margraves wrote in a letter thanking athletic director Groff for the trip.

"I was pleased to see the strong A&M contingent that was in attendance. I know it did not go by you unnoticed that all of the other major universities in America had delegations in attendance, including the University of Texas and Rice from our own conference."

The Margraves' expenses for this past year's five-night trip included a $605 dinner at the Tribeca Grill for six couples, including Mr. Groff, head football coach R.C. Slocum and Arno Krebs, a Houston lawyer who has represented the school in internal investigations of possible sports rules infractions.

Trips' purpose

"The purpose of them going is to represent Texas A&M at the program," Mr. Groff said. "You have parties with ABC and ESPN. It's a public relations deal primarily, plus you meet the other schools. All of the big schools are represented."

Tips and charges to hotel bars were included in expense reports submitted by both Mr. Margraves and Mr. McKenzie, although auditors have pointed out that neither category is reimbursable under state regulations.

During the football season, regents, politicians and other dignitaries are invited to attend each Aggie football game. And, along with the president and chancellor's staff, the board members are given 16 seats on air charter for out-of-town games that require flying, Mr. Groff said.

During the 1992 Cotton Bowl, the athletic department picked up several days' room charges for regents Dough DeCluitt, Alison Brisco, Billy Clayton, Ross Margraves, Wayne Showers, Royce Wisenbaker, board administrator Vickie Running and their spouses.

Seven regents, Ms. Running and their spouses also attended the Disneyland Pigskin Classic in Anaheim, Calif., in August 1992 at a cost of more than $2,688 in hotel accommodations and chartered air fare at a cost of $400 apiece.

At the 1990 Holiday Bowl, records show, regents' rooms were stocked with liquor and costs were paid by the athletic department. (pp. 1, 34A)

AGGIE BOWL GAMES: PERKS SINCE DECEMBER 1990

Since December 1990, Texas A&M University has appeared in five bowl games: the Holiday Bowl in San Diego on Dec. 29, 1990; the 1991–92 Cotton Bowl; the Disneyland Pigskin Classic in August 1992; the 1992–93 Cotton Bowl; and the 1993–94 Cotton Bowl. According to A&M financial records, the team received guarantees from the five bowls of $10,775,000 million in gross income. Much of the revenue was spent on team transportation, hotels, food and paying predetermined shares to other members of the Southwest Conference. Other bowl revenue, meanwhile, went to pay for complimentary tickets, alcohol, parties, souvenirs and plaques for Aggies regents, administrators and influential boosters. The following expenses, based on A&M financial records, itemize expenses that were unrelated to the football team:

1. Holiday Bowl, San Diego, Dec. 29, 1990:
Guaranteed gate: $1,200,000
Discretionary spending of Bowl income:

$ 4,261.26	Bar hosted by A&M president William Mobley
$ 225.23	Bars in hotel rooms of Robert Smith, Wayne Showers, Raul Fernandez, Doug DeCluitt, Ross Margraves Jr., John Mobley and Royce Wisenbaker
$ 37.54	Liquor for press room
$ 3,080.00	77 extra jackets at $40 each (95 provided complimentary to team members)
$15,190.00	155 extra watches at $98 each (95 complimentary)
$ 775.00	155 extra hats at $5 each (95 complimentary)
$ 625.00	25 extra charms at $25 each (25 complimentary)
$ 1,125.00	45 extra tickets to Sea World at $25 each (125 complimentary)
$ 525.00	35 extra lunches at $15 each (125 complimentary)
$ 4,500.00	200 extra kickoff lunches at $22.50 each (125 complimentary)
$11,832.38	207 bowl sweat suits at 56.75 each*
$ 3,827.82	220 shaving kits at $16 each*
$ 450.00	250 Wilson bags at $3.50 each*
$ 3,097.00	207 Sahara shirts at $14.50 each*
$ 5,740.00	166 plaques at $33.00 each*
$55,291.23	**TOTAL**

2. Cotton Bowl, Dallas, Jan. 1, 1992
Guaranteed gate: $3,025,000
Discretionary spending of Bowl income:

$ 322.50	Two movies per day for 58 rooms on Spectravision
$ 975.00	Rental for four video games and one pinball machine
$21,250.00	170 extra men's watches (95 complimentary)
$ 5,625.00	45 extra women's watches at $125 each
$ 2,880.00	48 extra plaques at $60 each (95 complimentary)
$ 1,200.00	30 extra cameras at $40 each (120 complimentary)
$32,252.50	**TOTAL**

3. Disneyland Pigskin Classic III, Anaheim, Aug. 23, 1992
Guaranteed gate: $550,0000
Discretionary spending of Bowl income:

$ 2,500.00	50 tickets to Pigskin Classic Fashion Show
$10,176.00	extra watches and shirts
$ 900.00	extra "tailgate party" tickets
$ 1,875.00	extra luncheon tickets
$ 2,500.00	stadium suite
$17,951.00	**TOTAL**

4. Cotton Bowl, Dallas, Jan. 1, 1993
Guaranteed gate: $3,000,000
Discretionary spending of Bowl income:

$18,530.00	170 extra watches at $109 each (95 complimentary)
$ 4,905.00	45 women's watches at $109
$ 1,800.00	45 extra plaques at $40 each (95 complimentary)
$ 675.00	15 extra cameras at $45 each (120 complimentary)
$ 7,128.00	72 extra warm-ups at $99 each (95 complimentary)
$ 3,900.00	Reunion ranch party
$44,453.00	Cotton Bowl Party (Mr. Mobley paid $17,194 of total)
$ 3,800.00	152 Cowboys-Bears tickets at $25 each
$85,191.00	**TOTAL**

5. Cotton Bowl, Dallas, Jan. 1, 1994
Guaranteed gate: $3,000,000
Discretionary spending of Bowl income:

$14,175.00	135 extra watches at $105 each (95 complimentary)
$ 4,025.00	115 extra plaques at $35 each (95 complimentary)
$ 3,150.00	30 women's watches at $105 each
$ 8,613.00	87 extra warm-ups at $99 each (95 complimentary)
$ 1,575.00	45 extra Sony Walkman units at $35 each (95 complimentary)
$ 2,175.00	87 golf shirts at $25 each
$37,400.00	extra event tickets for administrators and boosters
$71,113.00	**TOTAL**

$261,798.73	**TOTAL NONFOOTBALL TEAM RELATED EXPENSES, 1990–94**

*Total does not include surcharges for logos, printing, other incidental expenses.
SOURCE: Texas A&M University financial records

Chapter Thirteen

Writing Editorials, Opinion Articles, and Columns

In the daily newspaper or monthly magazine, a sports writer or editor has the opportunity to express himself or herself on sports personalities and issues in the news. Usually the editorial, opinion piece, or column is limited only in length (the length of the newspaper column or the magazine page); the writer can usually write about whatever subjects he or she thinks appropriate. Along with the right to use the newspaper or magazine space, the writer has the responsibility to use the space wisely.

Editorials and opinion pieces on sports subjects are usually indicated with a subhead labeled "Editorial" or "Commentary."

Novice writers attempting to write a sports editorial or opinion piece may find the three-part format helpful. If the writer plans the article with these three key parts, the article may well be successful:

- *Premise.* What is the idea behind the article? If you can state the idea in one simple declarative sentence, the topic is workable (e.g., "University athletes should be paid like professional players because they bring in millions of dollars of revenue to a major university").
- *Evidence.* Prove your argument with facts, statistics, quotations, and other material.
- *Conclusion.* Wrap up your argument for your reader so there is no mistaking your conclusion.

In a column format, however, the writer has several choices of methods for presenting his or her material. How many types or styles of columns are there? In general, there are at least six types of columns:

146

- The editorial column, in which an opinion is presented with the weight of the newspaper or magazine behind the idea, in the same style as the editorial page of an average major metropolitan newspaper.

- The "my say" column, perhaps the most popular type of column and perhaps the hardest to write on a regular basis. This type of column is usually given to the staffer with the most seniority, so he or she may draw on previous experience for the material in the column. But even the most senior writer may find himself or herself eventually running out of material and ideas for the space. This is the personal opinion of the writer on a variety of sports issues often used with a mug shot of the writer.

- "Ask the expert." Some newspapers run interpretations of game rules and regulations, often prompted by questions from readers. This may well require the writer to possess a library of sports information books, major league rule books, sports almanacs, and the like.

- The sports trivia column. This may also require a personal library of reference books.

- Readers write–editors respond. This is a dialogue column in which readers write in comments, opinions, thoughts, biases, and complaints and the editors respond. This is the newspaper or magazine equivalent of the radio sports call-in show. *Car & Driver* magazine, for instance, carries on this spirited dialogue with sports car enthusiasts who write in to the magazine.

- The "Irish stew" column. This is a little of everything—some opinion, some second guessing, some name dropping, some editorial material, some guest commentary and quotations, some trivia, some response to readers, some humor, and perhaps even a sports obituary on occasion. To keep a column fresh every issue, the columnist may develop an Irish stew or potpourri approach.

The following are editorial and commentary articles that are exceptional examples of this type of sports writing.

Roy S. Johnson, senior editor of *Sports Illustrated*, writing in *Sports Illustrated* for April 20, 1992, discusses the Arthur Ashe case, in the end-of-the-magazine column titled "Point After." Johnson's commentary carried the headline and subhead:

None of Our Business

Arthur Ashe is a public figure,
but the media had no right
to make his illness a public matter

The first telephone call came to my office in early September. Another call came two months later, just days after Magic Johnson had stood at a podium in Los Angeles and delivered the shocking news that he was infected with the AIDS virus. Both callers were credible members of the tennis community, and both had the same message:

"You know about Arthur Ashe. He's got AIDS." Maybe I should have reacted to this disturbing information strictly as a journalist. After all, I'll wave the First Amendment flag until my arm falls off. And I'll defend until my last breath the public's right to know practically everything about anyone who falls into the category of "public figure."

But now my journalistic instincts were overcome by compassion and concern. I had been well acquainted with Ashe personally and professionally for more than a decade. Long before that, I had admired his athletic skill—and, more important, his dignity. My admiration for him had grown even stronger in recent years as I watched him fight racism, apartheid, and inequities in college athletics, and as he shared with me some of the insights and convictions that made him a respected champion of human rights throughout the world.

So that's why I said nothing. Not to the managing editor of this magazine. Not to my friends. Not even to Arthur. I could have picked up the telephone and asked him. But I didn't. I could have broached the subject during one of the many conversations we had since I received the first tip about him. But I didn't. In November, soon after Magic's announcement, Arthur and I spoke on the phone about AIDS and the backlash that Magic would surely face because of his promiscuous life-style. The questions were on the tip of my tongue: Were my sources right? And, if so, did Arthur feel any compulsion to join Magic as a spokesman in the fight against AIDS? But I didn't ask. I couldn't.

Last month Ashe was my guest at the United Negro College Fund's annual dinner in New York. Magic was one of the honorees. At one point the discussion at our table turned to Johnson's efforts to promote AIDS education and awareness, but by then I had just about put the calls about Arthur out of my mind. I had decided that if he wanted me to know about his condition, he would tell me. Otherwise, it wasn't my business. I had placed his privacy ahead of any desire to break the story in SI—and it wasn't a tough decision.

Last week the editors at *USA Today* weighed the same options and decided differently. They pursued a tip similar to the one I had received, and *USA Today* tennis writer Doug Smith confronted Ashe. Though Ashe neither confirmed nor denied having AIDS, he concluded he could no longer keep his condition secret. The next day, he reluctantly went public.

Right away the role played by *USA Today* ignited a debate. (Why couldn't all this energy have been channeled toward *fighting* the disease?) While the editors of many other papers said that they, too, would have pursued—and, if they could have confirmed it, published—the story, a rising tide of voices expressed outrage that Ashe's privacy had been violated.

"It's like the press has given up a touch of humanity," said Chris Evert. "It just kills his spirit."

"If the man dies one day earlier because of [stress caused by] this story . . . then [it] is not worth it," said Mike Clark, reader advocate of *The Florida Times-Union*.

Terming Ashe's illness "a significant news story," *USA Today* managing editor for sports Gene Policinski noted that the newspaper pursued the story as it would have had Ashe had cancer or some other life-threatening ailment. "We don't have a special zone for AIDS," he said.

Well, it's time we created one.

Overwhelming public ignorance remains one of the disease's greatest allies. People with the AIDS virus often are stigmatized by those who either stubbornly refuse to accept that the disease cannot be transmitted through casual contact, or who believe that people afflicted with AIDS somehow deserve their fate. Until these misconceptions are overcome, the media should offer most AIDS sufferers the same consideration it gives rape victims, who are ordinarily not identified in news stories.

Admittedly, the line that separates the news value of a public figure's medical condition from his right to privacy isn't always clearly defined. Should the public be alerted that a high-ranking government official has contracted AIDS? By all means. Do we need to know that a health-care worker has been infected? Yes. An athlete who's still active? Probably, because the state of his health is relevant to his profession. The CEO of a publicly held corporation? I guess so; his illness could have an impact on employees and shareholders.

And what if the person isn't as well respected as Ashe? Or doesn't have as good a relationship with the media? Nowadays rumors about the private lives of public figures surface almost daily, forcing reporters and editors to make all sorts of judgments about what is newsworthy. There are no hard rules, no easy answers.

Undoubtedly there are thousands of AIDS sufferers who might be considered public figures but who should be allowed to combat the incurable disease without enduring the added stress of public scrutiny and, all too often, condemnation.

Arthur Ashe was one of them. (p. 82)

Sam Smith of the *Chicago Tribune* wrote a commentary about Michael Jordan and the death of his father. This piece appeared in August 1993.

Reality intrudes on Jordan's charmed world

Commentary
By Sam Smith
Chicago Tribune

Everyone finds it out eventually. Michael Jordan did last week. The climate's not always perfect in Camelot.

For Jordan, the discovery of the tragic death of his father, James Jordan, last week in South Carolina allowed life to intrude, as it inevitably does, on all royal families.

And the Jordans, indeed, were our version of royalty: rich, successful, beautiful. We celebrated their triumphs and peered through the keyholes at their excesses and embarrassments. But we always cheered.

One might suggest the Jordans, especially Michael, have endured more than their share of long, cloudy winters.

There was the supposed Olympic snub of Isiah Thomas, Jordan's failure to attend the White House celebration with his teammates, the publishing of *The Jordan Rules*, the licensing dispute with the NBA that kept Jordan's likeness off All-Star Game T-shirts and then the reprimand from NBA commissioner David Stern for gambling with convicted drug dealer Slim Bouler.

And then there was the reluctant trip to the Olympics, where Jordan draped himself in an American flag so he wouldn't be seen wearing a rival sponsor's logo at the gold-medal ceremony. He opened the season with a court appearance at the Bouler trial during which he admitted he had been lying for a year that his payments to Bouler were a loan—not gambling payments.

Then there were accusations in a book that he had lost more than $1 million gambling and refused to pay his debt, more gambling questions when he went to Atlantic City to gamble before a key playoff game and a self-imposed boycott of the media for two weeks during the playoffs.

But the truth is little had changed in the life of Michael Jordan. For it was still Camelot, with perhaps the July and August of his life merely becoming a little too hot.

Jordan's fame grew only greater, as did his bank account. The Bulls won an almost unprecedented third straight NBA title, and if Jordan's smile didn't radiate as brightly as always, his star certainly did.

The life of Michael Jordan certainly was a pretty picture. But one doesn't make a picture without a negative.

The unexpected death of a parent is difficult for anyone, so it is that much harder when, as in Jordan's case, his father's death was from a gunshot, the body found floating in a stream, violence marking every bit of the end.

President John F. Kennedy's administration was known as Camelot in the early 1960s, perhaps our nation's last era of innocence. Someone wrote after Kennedy's assassination that we will laugh again, but we'll never be young again.

Michael Jordan will laugh again, but he'll never be the same.

That's because James Jordan was more than a father. He had the rarest of relationships with his son, Michael: He was a friend.

Like many boys, Jordan admired his dad, and credited him for his famous trademark, the hanging tongue, which Michael said he developed from watching his father work on the family car.

Jordan was quick to credit James, as in the 1992 playoffs against the Knicks, when Michael said he went not to a teammate or a coach for advice before the pivotal Game 7, but to his father. How should he approach the game? Aggressive, dad replied. Jordan was.

James was there, speaking for Michael this year when Michael's gambling came into question and Michael wasn't talking to the media. James, instead, convened a few of his press briefings to defend his beleaguered son.

The questions, beside what happened and how, and perhaps why, figure to be answered someday. But the inevitable answers will only come after some shocks.

Undoubtedly, Jordan will consider the wisdom passed onto him from his father. It was once said that the only cure for grief is action. When Michael was most troubled in recent years, James told him to play basketball, to bury his rage and doubt in his childhood and the kids' game that he rode to adulthood.

For so many years, Michael Jordan was sheltered from the real world by his talent, his money, his fame and his position. He mistook annoyance for adversity.

But Michael Jordan finally plunged down that magical stalk into the real world, where pain really does hurt, and where loss leaves a well of emptiness. He'll eventually climb out, but he'll never be a boy again.

Mitch Albom of the *Detroit Free Press* discusses the quarterback merry-go-round in Detroit in an opinion piece published in September 1993.

Fontes losing hearts of QBs
Lions' coach alienates all three

Opinion
By Mitch Albom
Detroit Free Press

PONTIAC, Mich.—They don't resent each other, and they don't resent the media. They resent the coach. Let's get that straight. Andre Ware, Rodney Peete and Erik Kramer, the three quarterbacks on this odd little merry-go-round in silver and blue stretch uniforms. Point the finger at one man: Wayne Fontes.

In this way, they are no different than most American workers. They blame the boss.

And, like most workers, they have to bite their tongue and keep it to themselves.

Andre Ware played all day Sunday in the win over Phoenix at the Silverdome. He was not bad, but not great.

He missed a lot of reads for a starting NFL quarterback, and he got away with some truly dangerous passes. And you wish he would hit more receivers in stride instead of making them jump. But he did throw a nice touchdown pass—two if you count the one that was called back—and in a couple of critical situations he looked off the first receiver, found the second and drilled it. On third down late in the game, he took a crushing hit from linebacker David Braxton—who nearly separated Ware's upper and lower intestines—and still delivered a first-down strike to Herman Moore. You mature on plays like that.

But when the game was over and the Lions had won, Fontes deliberately hedged on next week's starter, saying, "Talk to me Wednesday," then joked, "It'll give you guys something to write about."

And when Ware came in and heard that, he snarled, "What are you gonna do, have a quarterback tryout every week?"

Apparently, yes. That's the way Fontes wants it. Ware would, at times, like to bite Fontes' head off, and so would Rodney Peete, the former starter, who dressed quickly in the locker room Sunday after being demoted to "third quarterback" status, which means you only play if the Serbs and the Croats shake hands.

"Are you healthy?" Peete was asked.

"I'm fine. I could have played," he said.

"What do you think will happen next?"

He rolled his eyes. "Around here? I have no idea. I have absolutely no idea."

So that's two angry quarterbacks. The third, Erik Kramer, is still trying to get over the mistaken message left on his answering machine last week by William Clay Ford, the Lions' owner. Ford thought he was calling Ware when he left these words: "Andre, give me a call, I've got good news."

What was that all about? Kramer, by the way, is the voice on his own machine, and believe me, he sounds nothing like Ware. Which only goes to show you how out in left field the owner is when it comes to personnel on his team.

"He thought he was dialing 1-800-QUARTERBACK," Kramer said.

That's kind of how it works, isn't it? This week-by-week thing might be Fontes' idea of what's best—I have stopped trying to figure out Wayne, who is a wonderfully nice man, but has this boomerang way of coaching; if you stand still long enough he'll come back to the same idea all over again—and yet, he's losing his quarterbacks.

They gripe about him. They roll their eyes. All in private, of course. But the result is little confidence between the two most critical positions in the franchise, coach and quarterback.

Paul Daugherty of *The Cincinnati Post*, uses the "I" form lead to begin a column about Lenny Dykstra. This piece was published early in October 1993.

Dykstra harks back to tougher era

By Paul Daugherty
Cincinnati Post

ATLANTA—I like a ballplayer whose chaw slosh stains his uniform top. This is the plain truth.

There is a certain something about a man who stuffs a hamster-sized chunk of chewing tobacco into his left cheek before a game. Lenny Dykstra does this. He plays enter field for the Philadelphia Phillies. On the whole, he plays it with the sort of maniacal verve reserved for the foolish, the desperate and the guys who were major-leaguers 30 years ago.

This summer, Dykstra led the National League in runs, hits and walks, while playing in 161 games. The only game Dykstra missed was No. 158. It was the game after the Phillies clinched the National League East. Dykstra was temporarily incapacitated, due to, um, extreme celebration. This is how we like our ballplayers.

We have seen quite enough of players with multiple agents and players who play hard when the mood hits. We're dizzy with players carrying briefcases. Nothing good can come from a game played by men carrying briefcases.

The Phillies are not yet this way.

"We are," brags relief pitcher Larry Andersen, "a bunch of degenerates."

The Phillies are baseball's version of "Boys Night Out." At a time when ballplayers are as touchable as Alpha Centauri, the Phillies are our Everymen. Or at least as close as we're going to get.

Put it this way: The Phils are millionaires. But they belch just like you do.

And Dykstra, as much as anyone, is the Phillies.

"We're very interesting," he says.

It is 5 p.m. on Thursday. Dykstra has emerged from the Phillies' dugout for batting practice. He is in a "Not now, dude" mode with the media. But you know Dykstra is around.

He marks his territory with chunks of used cud. The telling brown flotsam leads straight to his feet.

"We give everybody their money's worth," he says.

Well, yes. The Phillies won the NL East by playing the kind of ball we remembered watching as kids. And stripped to its bones, baseball used to look a lot like Lenny Dykstra. Full-bore full of itself. A working man who was a little loose around the edges.

Tug McGraw, the ex-Phillies reliever-turned TV guy, says of Dykstra: "Somehow, Lenny wound up with Pete Rose DNA in his genes."

What's the word here? Ferocity? Dykstra plays that way. It's the sort of calculated recklessness that allows him to lead the league in walks and face-first slams into the center-field padding.

He won't win the Most Valuable Player Award in the National League this year, or any year. But he'll finish top five in the voting. And if the Phillies are to end the Atlanta Braves' two-year run as the league's best, they'll do it hanging on to Dykstra's vapor trail.

"Keeping Lenny Dykstra off base is a much bigger key for the Braves than keeping (Otis) Nixon off is for the Phillies," CBS analyst Tim McCarver says. "If Lenny has a big series, the Phillies can win."

It's pretty simple with Dykstra. When Dykstra plays, his teams win. He was a catalyst in 1986, when the Mets won 108 games and a World Series. When the Mets traded him to Philadelphia, in June 1989, they started a slow decline. Over the past three seasons, the Phillies are 38 games over .500 with Dykstra, and 33 under without him.

They list him as 5-10, but Dykstra is a few inches short of that. At 185 pounds, he looks compacted. He has no neck. At some previous point in time, he was 6-2 and 170.

Norman Braman, owner of the Philadelphia Eagles, was standing at the batting cage before Thursday's game, checking out Dykstra. The self-described "Dude" looks like a refrigerator with a head. Braman wondered aloud if Dykstra could play defensive back.

As you might expect, Dykstra's record is as spotty as his jersey. We don't ask our throwbacks to be perfect; we only ask them to be throwbacks. Dykstra has had his share of rough and tumble.

He was involved in a serious auto accident in May 1991, in which he broke ribs, collarbone and a cheek. He pleaded guilty to an alcohol-related driving charge from that mishap. That same year, major-league baseball handed him a one-year probation for admitting to illegal, high-stakes gambling.

"The public gets this impression that I'm a wild kind of person," Dykstra says. "That's not true. I think I'm a very mental player. I always have a plan."

Dykstra rolls the tobacco in his mouth, side to side like a tennis ball in a paint can. Frequently, he lets go with a stream of brown goo. Snuff remains popular with baseball players; loaded cheeks of extra-strength Red Man are just about obsolete. Then again, so is Dykstra's way of playing the game.

"Walks are an underrated statistic," he says. "You not only get on base, but you might make the pitcher throw eight to 10 pitches before you get on. It's a very important stat. By the way, who led the league in walks this year?"

Dykstra spits and walks away.

"OK, dude?" he says. At our feet is a mound of used-up cud.

Shannon Tompkins published this evocative piece about duck hunting in the *Houston Chronicle* on November 25, 1993. The title and subtitles were:

Of dawn, ducks and memories

"I could go back and pull the diaries and calendars that begin in 1968 and count the hunts, but there's really no reason. They all flood back, every hunt, in one way or another."

In his transcendental novel, *The River Why?*, author David James Duncan's lead character is a young adult man consumed by fishing and trying to come to grips with it.

The character, Gus, comes to understand that some people don't share his commitment, but can live happy lives nonetheless. But Gus also understands that *his* life is and almost certainly always will be defined by fishing, both in the physical and metaphysical sense.

That epiphany hits him when he realizes he can remember every one of the hundreds of fishing experiences he's had. And that, he sees, is not so much a sign of his cognitive ability as it is a manifestation of fishing's hold on his soul.

"It's not an ability to remember," Gus says to himself. "It's an inability to forget."

A couple of hours before dawn Saturday morning, with the stars of Orion the Hunter hanging in the cold sky overhead, I stood in the coastal marsh I've hunted for almost 25 years and felt a lot like Gus.

How many duck hunts? Three hundred? Four hundred? At least. There were those years in the '70s when I hunted 40 or 50 times in a 65-day season. Even last year, with a 39-day season, I made half the open days.

I could go back and pull the diaries and calendars that begin in 1968 and count the hunts, but there's really no reason.

They all flood back, every hunt, in one way or another. Maybe not every detail of every day afield, but pieces of all of them flash in my mind from time to time.

In the darkness ahead of Opening Morning, with the decoys on the pond and nothing left to do but wait and watch and feel, memories came in a torrent.

"Listen!" brother Les said, breaking the spell.

The sky, slowly turning deep pink and purple in the east, was alive with the sound of wings and whistles, quacks and honks. There were splashes in the shallow pond—unseen ducks alighting.

"This is the best time of the morning," Les said, his face pointed at the stars as he squatted next to the clump of cord grass he'd use as a blind.

He's right. Those are magic moments, those several minutes before legal shooting time, when birds begin flying, the sky pinks and you're flushed with adrenaline and anticipation. All things are possible. This could be the best day of your life.

Duck hunting, to me, is a lot like life. You're stupid if you spend it with people whose company you don't enjoy. And success depends on your ability, skills, and determination. Luck—chance—plays a role, too.

There are some things you can't control—the abundance of ducks, the weather, your own physical limitations. So you roll the bones, hoping for the best. And right before shooting time, when the dice are bouncing on the table, there's always the chance they'll come up "seven."

My idea of a rolling a "seven" has changed over the past couple of decades. It's had too. I've watched fewer ducks come to this marsh over the years.

Where 20 years ago, the sky was constantly dotted with skeins and clumps of ducks, now most days produce maybe half the ducks we'd see in, say, 1973. The decline of duck populations gets driven home when you've watched it from the same spot for 20 years or more.

Same goes for the number of duck hunters. When limits and season lengths were cut during the drought-plagued 1980s, a lot of people abandoned the marshes. A *lot.*

The number of waterfowl hunters in Texas dropped from 110,500 in 1980 to barely 55,000 in 1992. That 50 percent decline is, to me, embarrassing evidence of how many so-called hunters were interested not in the duck hunting experience but in the number of times they could pull the trigger. Maybe the marsh is better off without them.

If enough ducks are in the air for me to take a limit of three "big" ducks, then I'm tickled. Most times, that happens. But some mornings, even in this prime marsh, it's a struggle to get the opportunity to take a three-duck bag of gadwall, wigeon, pintail, mallard or mottled duck.

If you don't shoot teal, shovelers, ringnecks or scaup, you just might not shoot much.

Some recent opening days have been tough, so there was no guarantee that Les and I would see a lot of ducks. But the number of birds in the air ahead of shooting time Saturday certainly was encouraging.

When it was show time, we scrunched down in thick mottes of cordgrass, a gusty north-northeast wind at our backs. And the ducks came.

They came in waves. Clumps of gadwall. Pairs and trios of mottled ducks. Big squadrons of green-winged teal.

They swept downwind of the decoys, turned into the blustery wind and aimed for the opening we left for them among the decoys. It was almost like the old days.

We watched, giggling to ourselves, for maybe 20 minutes without shooting. Then Les got down to business. One shot, and a drake gadwall splashed, webs up, into the pond.

My turn.

The ducks just kept coming. I made a decision to pass everything and wait for the really big ducks—pintails, mallards, mottled ducks—and let everything else slide.

It took maybe five minutes of being bombarded by teal and spoonbills and gadwall before we heard that distinctive thin, reedy, drawn-out "quuuuuack."

I hit the call with three quick notes, and saw the bird swing around the east side of the pond, wings locked and silhouetted against the burnished sky. It called again. No doubt about what it was.

When the bird was right over the decoys, I struggled to my feet, lifted the gun and fired the first shot of a new season. The drake mallard dropped nearly at my feet. A gift from the gods.

It just got better. Ducks kept coming, swinging over the pond in the stiff wind and coming right to where we wanted them. We could have taken our limits no more than 20 minutes into the season, but we wanted this to last.

Les and I agreed to trade opportunities, vowing to shoot only at prime big ducks that were right over the decoys. The only time that vow was broken was when a drake bufflehead, a rare bird in this marsh, came out of nowhere. Les took the gorgeous little "spirit duck" for a place of honor on his wall.

We ended up with a beautiful string of ducks: two greenheads, the drake gadwall and bufflehead, a drake mottled duck and a drake pintail.

We shucked the duck loads from our pumps, replacing them with "T" shot in case some geese wandered too close, and sat back to enjoy the show.

For the next hour or so, we watched and photographed dozens of ducks piling into the pond, everything from a flock of Mexican squealers (fulvous whistling ducks) to a single wood duck. It was a beautiful thing, just sitting there, watching and talking.

Ducks were still hovering over the pond even after we'd collected the decoys and were preparing to leave. Gadwalls and shovelers, ringnecks and greenwings. Mallards and pintails.

"We're gonna remember this day for a long time," Les smiled and said as another bunch of gadwalls pitched over the empty marsh pothole.

Yeah. At least for the rest of our lives. We don't have a choice.

In this ingenious column, Dave Anderson of *The New York Times* speculates what might happen if Kenesaw Mountain Landis was alive today and applying for the job as baseball commissioner. This was published February 20, 1994.

Keney M. Applies for Commissioner

By Dave Anderson
New York Times

"Please sit down. On behalf of the baseball search committee interviewing candidates for commissioner, we're delighted you're here. You certainly have the look we're looking for. Your name again?"

"Keney M."

"Keney M. what?"

"Keney M."

"That's certainly a different name."

"Hey, it's the '90s."

"That's your real name?"

"No, in my first life my real name was Kenesaw Mountain Landis, but nobody has a name like that anymore. So in my reincarnation I decided to go by Keney M."

"In your first life you were Kenesaw Mountain Landis, baseball's first commissioner?"

"The very same. And when I heard people saying, 'If only Kenesaw Mountain Landis were alive today,' I thought I'd apply for the job."

"But you don't understand."

"What don't I understand?"

"The job has changed. Your flowing white mane and your firm chin project the image we want but we don't want a commissioner to have the power that you had when you were named baseball's first commissioner in 1920 after the Black Sox scandal. We don't even want a commissioner to have the power that Fay Vincent had when he resigned in 1992."

"You mean when Fay, for all practical purposes, was fired by the club owners because he believed in 'the best interests of baseball.' "

"Please, we don't use that phrase in baseball anymore. We prefer to think that a commissioner should be more of an office boy . . . I mean, more of an officer. . . . Yes, more of an officer and a gentleman."

Owners' interests all that matter

"But what's a commissioner without the power of the 'best interests of baseball' clause?"

"To use your words, Keney M., hey, it's the '90s. You'll have authority. If there's another strike by the players, you'll have the authority to negotiate the daily meal money."

"Meal money? The players are making millions and they still get meal money? No wonder so many clubs are losing money."

"We're not really losing money. That's just creative accounting. If we were losing money, we wouldn't be paying Bud Selig $1 million a year as the interim commissioner even though Bud really doesn't want the job."

"I don't understand. Bud doesn't want the job, but as long as nobody else gets the job, Bud keeps making $1 million a year."

"Your job, Keney M., is not to understand. Your job is to sit in an office on Park Avenue and wait for a phone call from some of the owners to tell you what to say and do."

"Suppose there's another Black Sox scandal? What's my authority if that happens?"

"You must remember that the Chicago club known as the White Sox is owned by Jerry Reinsdorf now, not Charles Comiskey as it was in your first life. Fay Vincent would be the first to tell you that Jerry certainly wouldn't appreciate eight of his players being banned from baseball. Now that I think of it, Jerry wouldn't even appreciate Michael Jordan being banned from spring training."

"Suppose there's another George Steinbrenner-Howard Spira scandal? Could I suspend George like Fay Vincent did?"

"I don't see why not. George might even like the idea. If he were suspended, he wouldn't be able to go to Yankee Stadium, and a game there without George would be a game with one less spectator. With all of George's complaints about Yankee Stadium, one less spectator is important. Yes, you probably could suspend George—as long as he agreed."

Just smile and do what you're told

"Is there any authority I would have?"

"Well, since the commissioner is in charge of the umpires during the World Series, you would have the authority to settle any dispute about the interpretation of the infield-fly rule if a controversy were to develop during a World Series game."

"What about removing a player from a World Series game? I did that in 1934 when the Detroit fans threw all those tomatoes at Joe Medwick of the Cardinals."

"If another Medwick scene developed, you must remember that in our new television venture with the NBC and ABC networks, we're hoping to land a big tomato-soup commercial. We wouldn't want to do anything that might antagonize a sponsor."

"But what's a commissioner without authority?"

"He's a commissioner we can tell what to do."

"In my first life, I told the owners what to do."

"Kenny M., you still don't seem to understand that it's the '90s, that baseball wants a commissioner who would put the mustard on the hot dogs for the club owners whenever he attends a game, who would choose the honorary batboys and batgirls for the All-Star Game, who would be the ticket-taker at the Hall of Fame induction ceremonies at Cooperstown."

"That's it?"

"If you do a good job at those tasks, maybe we'll let you throw out the first ball at the World Series some day."

"For the first game?"

"No, only if there's an eighth game."

On January 1, 1994, the *Anchorage Daily News* republished an "I" form column by Bill Conlin, sports columnist of the *Philadelphia Daily News*:

How it would be in one man's perfect world

By Bill Conlin
Philadelphia Daily News

PHILADELPHIA—When I'm King of the World . . .

There will be a baseball salary cap. Also a baseball thinking cap. What are the new San Francisco Giants owners smoking, ground-up $1,000 bills? The five-year contract that will pay third baseman Matt Williams $30.75 million means the small-market ballclub now has committed $92.5 million to just four players—Barry Bonds, Robby Thompson, Mark Portugal and Williams—over the next five years.

No wonder senior general partner Walter Shorenstein, the No. 2 guy in the limited partnership that saved the Giants a year ago, has thrown in his hand. Shorenstein, whose wealth has been estimated at $400 million, resigned before the Williams signing, saying he disagreed with the direction the club was heading. Safeway supermarket mogul Peter Magowan better reread those headlines. That was the NFL, not major league baseball, that just signed new TV contracts worth more than $4 billion with Fox, NBC, ESPN and TNT.

The way it works now, Walt, your guys signed a scaled-down contract with ESPN this year and entered into a risky, profit-sharing deal with NBC and ABC whereby everybody's profits will depend on how much advertising you can sell. With one of the smaller local TV and radio incomes and attendance traditionally wired to club success, it would appear the Giants are terribly overextended through the end of the century . . .

When I'm King of the World . . .

Minor league prospects will be able to refuse instructional league assignments only for medical reasons. . . . The Yankees signed high school lefthander Brien Taylor for $1.55 million in 1991. The signing shattered the existing amateur bonus structure after acrimonious negotiations that didn't end until after the kid had squandered his first season of professional ball. For an extra $500,000, Taylor lost a year at the *end* of his career, a time when he could have been earning $6 million or more. I wonder if agent Scott Boras flew that concept by the kid. Which is another reason why owners would rather suck the heads off a bottle of tapeworms than do business with Boras.

The agent completed a hat trick of sorts Tuesday when Taylor had his pitching shoulder rebuilt by Dr. Frank Jobe. Taylor will not pitch again before the 1995 season, if ever, after suffering a torn capsule and labrum in a bar fight near his Beaufort, S.C., home. Boras informed the Yankees, "It's nothing serious." You might remember Taylor's mother, Bettie, going on "60 Minutes" in '91, proud she had not permitted the Yankees to insult her boy with a mere $1 million offer.

Taylor had a decent 1993 season in Double A, but he's sushi-raw. The Yankees asked him to go to the instructional league to work on his pickoff move, his deficient fielding and maybe develop another pitch. Taylor refused. Now, he's got what's left of the $1.55 million. He's got police charges to deal with in the wake of a fight in which he says he was defending his brother. Best of all, Brien Taylor still has Scott Boras. And, somehow, I have a feeling they deserve each other.

I had been meaning to update "Mondo Cane," the dog crisis that has shattered the security-monitored calm of Indian Creek, the 44-resident neighborhood near North Miami Beach where Eagles owner Norman Braman hangs his overnight bag and Eagles Stadium blueprints. In case you missed the saga of rich man's inhumanity to rich man's dog, the Indian Creek council has arbitrarily outlawed six feisty breeds—American Staffordshire terriers, Staffordshire bull terriers, German shepherds, Doberman pinschers, Rottweilers and American pit bull terriers. Why such an eclectic mix? It turns out the ban was aimed at the noisy, foliage-soiling Rottweilers of our old friend Prince Turki bin Abdul Aziz, Norman's next-door neighbor. Aziz is a Saudi who showed up during the Persian Gulf War and spends about as much time on the island as Braman spends in Philly.

Among the projected canine casualties of war was Natacha, an 8-year-old Rottweiler belonging to filthy-rich auto dealer Gus Machado. But Natacha was grandfathered into the ordinance, which was a slap in Aziz's fez. Just between you and me, all this rich-people bluster sounds unconstitutional as hell. I mean, how do we implement this law, Norm, a house-to-house search? . . .

When I'm King of the World . . .

If you're taller than 7-foot, you've got to position yourself inside the foul line, or it's an illegal-offense violation, then a technical. . . . I've got my early assessment of Shawn Bradley down to six words: Wilt Was Better—In Eighth Grade. No doubt in my mind that the Mormon mission the Sixers center served in Australia was good for the inner man. And if he had chosen a life in the pulpit—I know, I know, every Mormon adult male is a minister—prayer in Perth would have been perfect. But you watch his court demeanor and realize that, in the absence of growing up tough in some urban hellhole, Marine boot camp would have been better.

Nor am I convinced that two more seasons in the Western Athletic Conference would have done much more to prepare a young man with minimal basketball instincts for the NBA. Right now, two monolithic, related, obstacles stand between Bradley and anything close to stardom: 1. He is unable to prevent all but the most marginal NBA centers from posting him up. 2. He is just as unable to post up enemy centers. Until he can master those elemental facets, you'll see his height and enormous wingspan wasted 18 feet from the basket, doing stuff the stiffs of the NBA world can do $4 million a year cheaper. (p. B7)

Ray Buck, columnist of *The Houston Post*, remembers "Jimmy V," Jim Valvano, in his column of February 28, 1994:

Valvano's words remain truthful

It doesn't seem like a year has passed since Jim Valvano made us laugh and think and cry during one of the most moving 10 minutes in sports television history.

Racked by cancer, the former North Carolina State coach and ESPN analyst slowly and painfully climbed the seven steps leading to a podium at the inaugural ESPYs to accept the Arthur Ashe Courage Award.

It would be Jimmy V's last public appearance. Two months later, he was dead at 47.

"Three things we all should do every day," he told us. "No. 1 is laugh. You should laugh every day. No. 2 is think. You should spend some time in thought. And No. 3, you should have your emotions moved to tears . . . could be (tears of) happiness.

"Think about it. If you laugh and you think and you cry, that's a full day."

Well, I saved those 10 minutes of videotape—and I'm glad I did. Watching them again Sunday gave me a full day.

'Don't ever give up'

I listened again to what Valvano had to say about dreams and hugs and family and goals and enthusiasm and his now-famous motto: "Don't give up, don't ever give up."

I saw again the part where he broke off in mid-sentence less than seven minutes into his speech: "The screen is flashing *30 seconds*. Like I care about that screen right now, huh? I got tumors all over my body. I'm worried about some guy in back going *30 seconds*?"

I heard him again say how the funding for AIDS research is "10 times" greater than the funding for cancer research—"and the amount of money pouring into AIDS is not enough," he clarified.

I cringed again at his grim statistics: Half a million people will die of cancer this year. One in every four of us will be afflicted with this dreaded disease.

Since Valvano's death on April 28, golf's Heather Farr has died of cancer and Paul Azinger has been diagnosed with lymphoma in his right shoulder blade. Mario Lemieux amazingly still plays hockey for Pittsburgh despite his ongoing bout with Hodgkin's disease, a form of cancer.

Sports, real world alike

The sports world is not unlike the real world, so we're reminded every now and then.

Tonight at 8, ESPN will air the second annual ESPYs—a.k.a., American Sports Awards. Keep a box of Kleenex handy, just in case.

Honored for his courage this time will be former American League umpire Steve Palermo, who was shot and paralyzed while trying to break up a robbery attempt outside a Dallas restaurant in July 1991.

Palermo had just worked a Texas Rangers game. He was enjoying dinner when came a cry of help that two waitresses were being robbed and assaulted by three thugs in the parking lot.

Palermo immediately joined several others from the restaurant in chasing down—on foot—one of the three suspects.

The other two fled in a car, only to circle back and carry out their cowardly attack by firing a .32-caliber pistol into the small group of captors.

Palermo carries on

Three shots hit former Southern Methodist football player Terence Mann, who since has recovered from his wounds. One shot hit Palermo, who was not so lucky. "I felt like somebody was pouring hot water on my legs," he later described.

The bullet grazed his spinal column—but it could've been worse. He isn't bound to a wheelchair; he didn't bleed to death.

An umpire normally isn't a sympathetic figure. Or a hero. But this one's story is about to touch us all.

I wanted so much for Jimmy V to be able to keep his promise and be there tonight to present the Arthur Ashe Courage Award.

On second thought, he is. (p. 1C)

Almost a month later—March 18, 1994—Buck devoted a column to Bobby Knight.

Knight no help to sports' image

Seeing Bob Knight featured on ESPN and NBC this week only proves that if you're a big enough jerk in this country, the networks will fight to get you on.

Knight routinely stiffs reporters after Indiana U. basketball games. He is vulgar, insensitive and boorish.

But because he's bigger than the game he coaches, he has his own set of rules. Temple's John Chaney loses it and gets suspended one game. Knight loses it—nothing.

Everybody is afraid of Bob Knight, that's the way he wants it. He's a control freak. When approached by ESPN and NBC, Knight chose Beano Cook and Bob Costas (must be an initials thing) to do the honors.

Costas' interview had some teeth, although I still want to know who dresses Knight in those red sweaters two sizes too small. It examined the complexity of a man whose record, community service and ideals are distorted only by his madness.

Read between the lines

He is a man with two sides.

• **Bob Knight says:** "The absolute essence of coaching is to teach."

His Eminence really means: "The absolute essence of coaching is to browbeat 19- and 20-year-olds."

• **Bob Knight says:** "I don't think I'm a horse's ass. I think I'm a pretty good guy."

His Eminence really means: "Moe Iba was a pretty good guy."

• **Bob Knight says** (on head-butting freshman Sherron Wilkerson): "We apparently collided heads. I didn't notice anything more about it at the time than two guys, in close quarters, one of 'em bending over, one of 'em leaning forward . . ."

His Eminence really means: "I went too far—but I can't say that. I'm Bob Knight."

• **Bob Knight says** (on the chair-throwing incident earlier in his career): "Am I the only coach in history who's ever thrown a chair? A coat? A clipboard? A water cooler? I may be the most infamous chair-thrower—but certainly not the only one."

His Eminence really means: "I can do better than that. I bet I can toss Damon Bailey above the backboard. Wanna see?"

Wait 'til Father's Day

• **Bob Knight says** (on kicking his player-son Patrick earlier this season): "Patrick knows there's no one on the face of the earth that I love more than him. He understands that."

His Eminence really means: "Patrick understands he made a really careless, bad, blind pass out on top." Oops, he did say that.

- **Bob Knight says:** "We don't get there with milk and cookies. These (three national championship) banners would not be hanging above my head if that's the way I coached."

His Eminence really means: "Help! Maybe I'm losin' it. I haven't won a national championship since Woody Hayes died in 1987. Is that how *my* career is going to end? Like Woody's? Am I going to punch some kid from the other team and get myself fired? (Pause) Wait a minute, what am I thinking? They can't fire me at Indiana. I *own* Indiana."

A loose cannon

I asked UH's Alvin Brooks of and Rice's Willis Wilson—members of the "new breed" of that grew up with March Madness and the media explosion—what they thought of Knight.

They pretty much agreed: Great coach, loose cannon.

"He sends a signal that reinforces a lot of negative notions that people have about college coaches," Wilson said. "That's a little bit troubling."

Said Brooks: "He wins, fills his building and graduates most of his kids . . . he just doesn't always conduct himself in a manner conducive to leading young men."

Imagine if Knight—whose team plays Ohio U. late tonight in the first round of the NCAA tournament—could do all of those things?

"Then," said Brooks, "you'd have Dean Smith."

Touché. (p. 1B)

After the tawdry Tonya Harding–Nancy Kerrigan affair, Associated Press sports writer Jim Litke wrote a column about Harding. This appeared in the *Huntsville*, Texas, *Item* on March 18, 1994.

Tonya got what she deserved

By Jim Litke
AP Sports Writer

For everyone who thought this day would never come, Tonya Harding finally ran out of shoelaces to break. She finally ran out of costumes that would come undone, out of doctor's notes and court orders, out of flip answers and tearful excuses. And she finally ran into a judge who said no more do-overs.

Some people still argue that fining her heavily and forcing her out of competitive skating is just a slap on the wrist. But justice in this instance was served and not, like so many other times in the past 10 weeks, swerved around.

No, she is not going to jail. But she is not going to Disney World, either. At least not until she gets permission from her probation officer first, cashes in the frequent-flyer miles from the Norway trip and ponies up the admission fee. Even then, Mickey Mouse will not be greeting her at the gate as he did Nancy Kerrigan, with a smile on his face and fistfuls of money overflowing his mitts.

Under the plea-bargain agreement, she had to surrender the one thing that defined her, the oasis where she could hide and forget all the other harsh, hurtful places in her life. She kept holding out for one more chance to make everything right, and now even Harding must realize that is gone for good.

For the foreseeable future, her life will consist of suffering through a series of small humiliations and cutting costly deals so they don't become large ones.

The only character, real or imagined, who is willing to pay her Mickey Mouse dollars right now is a Japanese wrestling promoter. And while Harding could probably use the $2 million, and while she has worn sillier costumers of her own choosing, the opportunity sounds too grubby—even for her.

A stint with the ice shows, or selling the rights for a made-for-TV movie are options that could keep her solvent for some time, at least. But as with the offer to wrestle, the only way Harding gets paid now is by playing the tough, clumsy villain.

And frankly, it's hard to think of a sentence more fitting than that. Because what probably made Harding fall in love with skating as a young girl, what kept her there and made her fight so long and so hard to stay there, was the chance to play a role different than the one life kept pushing her into.

For those who still feel that the punishment didn't fit the crime—whatever Harding's real involvement was—there will be more.

While the controversy roiled, Harding made the people from the U.S. Figure Skating Association and the U.S. Olympic Committee appear timid and inept. But now that the skate is on the other foot, they are eager to been seen as neither. They have lawyers, too, and more money to boot. And all the time it seemed she and her legal team were skating circles around them, these people were only sharpening their blades.

With her admission of guilt, the USFSA can now initiate proceedings to strip Harding of the national championship she won last December in Detroit.

Maybe this whole affair was best summed up by what Harding's replacement, 16-year-old Nicole Bobek, told reporters of how she was informed that she was going to the world championships in Japan:

"I was told she was sick and would not be able to compete."

Harding is sick, all right, heart sick.

She should be. (p. 7A)

Dan Barreiro, of the *Minneapolis–St. Paul Star Tribune* wrote a commentary piece about rough play in the NBA. This article was published the first week in May 1994.

Rough play in NBA not new or outrageous

Commentary
By Dan Barreiro
Minneapolis Star Tribune

After a bloody week in the NBA playoffs, the awful bleating has begun from the tea-and-crumpet set. Call the cops, the pacifists say. They're killing the game. They're turning the NBA into the National Brawling Association.

Did you see the full-court riot that broke out in Atlanta? All the other spats that have turned physical? And when are they going to do something about all those utterly dreadful 87–83 games?

Here's a little advice to the pacifists: Relax. Lighten up. Read a Fabio romance novel. Take up shuffleboard.

You say you loved the Suns' wide-open, free-wheeling 140–133 victory over the Warriors on the West Coast on Wednesday night. Defense was optional. I say I loved the Knicks' scratch-and-claw, nothing-comes-easy 90–81 victory over the Nets on the East Coast on Sunday. Offense was optional.

You say you loved Charles Barkley scoring 56 points and doing a tap dance on a big kid named Chris Webber. I say I loved the way the Knicks refused to wither and played suffocating defense with Patrick Ewing thrown out of the game in the second quarter.

You'll take Dan Majerle bombing in another 3-pointer. I'll take Charles Oakley hurtling himself out of bounds to get an offensive rebound.

You say the Phoenix–Golden State game is what pro basketball should be all about. I say an occasional effort to play defense is helpful.

But there is room in pro basketball for both styles, and the contrast between the two makes the NBA all the more compelling, especially when those styles meet on the court.

Which they have been doing for a long, long time.

Do people really have memories this short? Do they really believe this debate is new?

More than 10 years ago, the Celtics and Lakers met in the NBA Finals in two straight playoffs. Do the tea-and-crumpeters forget some of those battles, some of those brawls? The Celtics, remember, were the physical team whose game was to play defense and wear down an opponent. The Lakers were the elegant team that wanted to frolic in the open court and play a game called Showtime.

Pat Riley complained the Celtics were thugs. The Celtics complained the Lakers were prima donnas. The matchups were historic.

And if you think there have been some hard takedowns in this year's playoffs, what about Kevin McHale's infamous mauling of Kurt Rambis under the basket on a breakaway? You think the Celtics won two titles in three years by being sweet and polite?

The past two years, the Bulls and Knicks provided the contrast. The Bulls were an outstanding defensive team, but with Michael Jordan, were about grace and athleticism. The Knicks were about heavy lifting. Phil Jackson complained the Knicks were thugs. Riley, in a new role, complained the Bulls were prima donnas. The matchups were semi-epic.

No NBA playoff would be authentic without a little spilled blood. The fact is, there is no one team today as singularly bent on the destruction of its opponents as the Pistons were when they won their back-to-back titles. And even the Pistons actually were less offensive by the time they won their second title.

Certainly, there are individuals who must be muzzled, and not surprisingly, Public Enemy No. 1 is a former Piston, Dennis Rodman. When Rodman sticks to running and jumping and rebounding and defending, he remains one of the most intriguing players in the league.

When he resorts to the indefensible tactics he tried on the Jazz last weekend, Rodman is an on-court hoodlum who must be punished. And the league did, taking him out of the pivotal Game 3 of the Spurs' series with Utah. The frightening thing now is that Rodman sees himself as a martyr, and martyrs have been known to do desperate things. This guy needs a good doctor.

Nobody would defend the disgraceful acts of cowardice that took place during Game 2 of the Hawks–Heat series. On the street, Keith Askins gets jail time for the sucker punch he threw at Doug Edwards.

The pacifists say those incidents have helped create a climate in which it is impossible for offenses to flourish. Nonsense. Those incidents have nothing to do with taking offense out of the game.

Offense is hurting in the NBA for two reasons. The first is that few players want to do anything but dunk anymore because the dunkers make all the highlight reels and shoe commercials. What should worry the purists is that too many players refuse to develop and refine other offensive skills.

The other is that more teams are paying some attention to playing defense. There is great irony in all the praise for the Phoenix–Golden State point-o-rama, in which both teams were entertaining, but nobody guarded anyone.

Once upon a time, many games were ending with 137–134 scores, and do you know what people were saying about the league? They were whining that teams met so little resistance on the offensive end that all the scoring lost its meaning. Now, there are a number of teams—the Knicks, Bulls, Hawks, Sonics and Rockets among them—that are actually attempting to play more than token defense. Pacers coach Larry Brown even has Reggie Miller taking charges.

There is one thoroughly alarming NBA trend that is well worth hammering. It is simply this: A young player now makes three good plays in a row and he wants the action stopped and a monument erected in his honor.

Latrell Sprewell nails a slam dunk and then gets in the face of Charles Barkley. Isaiah Rider nails a slam and then gets in the face of Hakeem Olajuwon. Sprewell and Rider are talented young players, but what have they really done in this league?

There is far too much yapping going on from players who don't have the credentials to do it.

"It's changed a lot," Magic Johnson says of younger players in general. "Everybody cares about me. Where's my minutes? Where's my shots? What's wrong with my game? It's a lot of that now, and I don't like that side of it."

It's an obnoxious side to the game, and the league should find a way to deal with it. And nobody's suggesting that the pro game be turned into roller derby. Brawls like the one in Atlanta should be dealt with severely. As for all the ranting and raving that pro basketball is being ruined by those 87–85 games, key down. Pro basketball? To steal a slogan that McHale would endorse, it ain't croquet, baby.

TIPS ON WRITING EDITORIALS, OPINION ARTICLES, AND COLUMNS

1. If you can state the idea to yourself in a short, declarative sentence, it's probably a workable idea. If you cannot state the idea in a clear, concise way, you have not yet clarified the idea into a workable form.

2. Your material may be easily written if you remember three topics: premise, evidence, and conclusion. State the idea, provide evidence to prove and buttress your case, and conclude the editorial or column.

Note that if you do not use the "I" form early in the editorial or column, don't use the "I" of the author abruptly toward the end of the material. Perceptive readers may wonder why you have changed the style and tone of the material needlessly.

Chapter Fourteen

Seven Common Stylistic Errors Sports Writers Should Avoid

Sports writing is often the best and worst writing in a newspaper—and often these best and worst examples can be found on the same sports page.

Errors of style can be corrected on an editor's screen, but the best solution to sports writing style errors is not to let them appear on the reporter's screen in the first place.

The following are seven common stylistic errors that should be avoided in the reporter's original copy.

THE ONE-SENTENCE PARAGRAPH

If your writing becomes predictable, no matter what the subject, a perceptive reader may simply turn the story off because of observed sameness of style.

One-sentence paragraphs are important and dramatic. One of the most dramatic passages in the Bible is: "Jesus wept."

Quoted material is often one-sentence replies because people often speak in one-sentence replies.

Veteran reporters hear their own words and sentences as they create articles; they listen for cadence and rhythm and style. They want a story to sing.

Novice reporters often simply hammer out words on a computer screen and save the story when they are finished, without listening to the sound of their words and sentences on their screen.

Here is a key: If you read your story to yourself and the story has awkward gaps, misplaced emphases, and illogical sentences, it must be rewritten. If, on the other hand, you can read the story with style and grace, if the pauses appear where they should appear, if the sentences and paragraphs have a flow and a meter and a cadence to them, then you have written your story well.

Good writing includes not only one-sentence paragraphs, but multisentence paragraphs as well.

THE EXCESSIVE EXAMPLE

In *Sports in America*, his thorough analysis of sports and our society, James Michener (1976) wrote:

> My affection for John Kieran and Red Smith is considerable; they have added luster to the sports page. Many of my friends believe Jim Murray of the *Los Angeles Times* to be their inheritor, and he has been named sports writer of the year numerous times by a restricted group of experts who always choose Chris Schenkel as the television pundit.
>
> Murray is one of the funniest men alive, and a short, quick collection of his best lines would rate high: "This club has a chance to go all the way. So did the *Titanic*."
>
> But Murray has a bad habit which his young imitators work into the ground. He takes one subject, usually worthy of comment, then beats it to death, with crack after crack, belaboring the idea long after the dullest reader must have tired. Of Luis Rodriguez, the Cuban welterweight, he says: "This face is old, yet young. The eyes are merry, yet sad. It is not a fighter's face. It is a clown's face. Fernandel in burnt cork. Grimaldi without bells. Durante in boxing shorts." This habit of excessive citation can be seen at its most flamboyant in his introduction to his book about football. (p. 329)

In short, descriptive phrases do not have to be used in triplicate to be effective.

THE BLIND ATTRIBUTION

A story about golf champion Arnold Palmer might read like this:

> Palmer was noted for "Arnie's Army," his devoted followers who watched him play every hole in every major tournament.
>
> The native of Latrobe, Pa., often said, "_____."

Was Palmer a native of Latrobe, Pennsylvania? He was, but don't make your story a sports trivia challenge. Perhaps the reference to Latrobe had never been cited in the article prior to that reference. If it was not, you lead your reader through a guessing game.

Again:

Nolan Ryan was one of the most durable pitchers in modern baseball.
The native of Alvin, Texas, once said, of his fame, "_____."

Was Ryan a native of Alvin, Texas? Again, yes, but these two references could most easily be phrased this way:

Palmer was noted for "Arnie's Army," his devoted followers who watched him play every hole of every tournament.
Palmer, a native of Latrobe, Pa., often said "_____."

And:

Nolan Ryan was one of the most durable pitchers in modern baseball.
Ryan, a native of Alvin, Texas, once said, of his fame, "_____."

Writers must, however, scroll up through their copy to make sure there aren't too many paragraphs beginning:

Palmer _____.
Palmer _____.
Palmer _____.

Or:

Ryan _____.
Ryan _____.
Ryan _____.

Equally vexing is the sports writer who refers to an athlete, let's say a football player: "Joe Jock says he will _____." A paragraph later or, worse, several paragraphs later, the writer uses this phrase: "This six foot, three inch fullback _____." Does he still mean Joe Jock? We assume so, but may not know.

Don't needlessly confuse your readers. Don't play guessing games with your readers and don't make them mentally sort through the most obscure of sports trivia to identify subjects in your articles.

EXCESSIVE ADJECTIVE AND ADVERB USAGE

If a major league baseball player has a .185 average, avoid temptation to write "a meager .185 average" or an "anemic .185 average." If a football player runs a 40-year dash in record time, avoid the temptation to write "a blistering 40-yard time."

Just as the continual use of the one-sentence paragraph robs the reader of any real involvement in the article, so excessive use of adjectives and adverbs also robs the readers of any decision-making thought processes in reading the article.

Was the .185 average "meager" or "anemic?" Let the reader decide. Was the time "blistering?" Perhaps, but let the reader make the judgment. Offer factual evidence to support your claim that the time was fast, but let the reader mentally add that sort of qualification.

If the time was the fastest ever in the 40-yard dash, let the reader mentally add *"Holy Smoke!"* or whatever else he or she wants to think about the achievement.

If you make all the decisions for the reader in the article, if you qualify all the achievements and times, then you leave the reader very little room to be involved in the article. You leave the reader very little reason to care about your article. Ultimately, you leave the reader very little reason to continue reading your piece.

THE Q & A FORMAT

Unless you are requested to do so, avoid the pure question-and-answer format, as used in the *Playboy* "Interview of the Month" and in other magazines.

The format is simply this:

> Question: "Don't you think that . . . ?"
> Jock: "Yep, you bet . . . I think that. . . ."
> Question: "On subject B, do you believe . . . ?"
> Jock: "Nope, I think. . . ."

Playboy interviewers and editors spend week after week during the interviewing stages of a *Playboy* interview, then week after week cutting, trimming, and rearranging the interview questions and answers to make the interview seem as spontaneous as possible. Yet even the best interviews may leave readers glassy-eyed with fatigue and disinterest.

Try to read more than one lengthy *Playboy* interview—say two at one time—and then decide how fresh this format is.

The Q & A story, at its best, leaves little involvement for the reader. The Qs and As march down the page; There is little change of pace, except for the length of the answers, there is no literary style, and little to delight or enchant the reader. It's stenographic journalism, and no one ever won a Pulitzer Prize for stenography.

CLICHÉS

No one past the fifth grade would use a phrase like "quiet as a mouse," yet sports writers use sports clichés in articles frequently:

- "We play 'em one game at a time . . ."
- "It's a physical game . . ."
- "Blazing speed . . ."
- "Grid classic . . ."
- "Archrival . . ."
- "He went to the well once too often . . ."
- "That win is the icing on the cake . . ."
- "He gave 110 percent . . ."

And a hideous new phrase, which I believe came from Monday Night Football, "His athleticism . . ."

Avoid every cliché. Every one. To use any cliché (except in a direct quotation) is to signal to your readers that you are sloppy, mediocre, and unimaginative. Strive for fresh phrases, new images, and bright writing. In his book, *On Writing Well: An Informal Guide to Writing Nonfiction*, William Zinsser (1985) stated: "What keeps the average writer from writing good is, first, the misapprehension that he shouldn't be trying to. He has been reared on so much jargon, so many cliches, that he thinks they are the required tools of the trade" (p. 137).

UNFATHOMABLE NUMBERS

Sports fans are traditionally numbers fans. Some are statistics junkies. Sports writers are often tempted to chain statistics together, assuming the chain must mean something; assuming that it is important to pile numbers, averages, and statistics together. Statistics may be more important to a ballplayer's career than they logically would be in any article. Zinsser (1985) also wrote:

> True, every sports addict lives with a head full of statistics, cross-filed for ready access, and many a baseball fan who once flunked simple arithmetic can perform prodigies of instant calculation in the ball park on a summer afternoon. Still, some statistics are more important than others. If a pitcher wins his twentieth game, if a golfer shoots a 61, if a runner runs the mile in 3:48, please mention it. But don't get carried away. (p. 138)

Chapter Fifteen

Endnote:
"Football minus frills–
and drills"

In the Introduction to this book, we wrote "sports writing isn't just *scores* and *standings*. These days, sports is more *ethics* and *anguish*, more front page than back section."

Do you ever wish that sports could be pure and simple and clean again (if it ever was)? Did you ever wish you could cover a coach and a program that was nearly perfect?

Consider football coach John Gagliardi; he coaches at Minnesota's St. John's University, in Collegeville. If you ever wished to cover a perfect coach and a perfect program, John Gagliardi is such a coach and he runs that kind of program. So, for an upbeat end to this book, here is Richard Vega's article, "Football minus frills—and drills." It appeared in *USA Weekend* magazine (published by *USA Today*), for October 29–31, 1992.

The article carries the subhead: "A Minnesota college coach's winning strategy: no slogans, no whistles, no problems."

After a tentative knock on the door, a 215-pound defensive end pops his head into the coach's office. He's flustered; he needs to get something off his chest. The coach invites him in warmly. The player's problem? Well, gosh, he was wondering if he could captain the St. John's football team in the upcoming game against Gustavus Adolphus College. Turns out his best friend is their captain. No problem, the coach says. He whips out a folder and pens in the senior player as captain. The deal is done.

That's pretty much how coach John Gagliardi, 66, conducts business at St. John's University in tiny Collegeville, Minn. Real loosey-goosey. The team's captains rotate weekly. There are no film sessions or playbooks, no blocking sleds or wind sprints. No player gets cut; everyone plays. (*See box at right.*) Gagliardi doesn't even carry a whistle. Somehow, though, this relaxed regimen has led to three national championships, including

Gagliardi's rule book

OVERALL PROGRAM
No athletic scholarships
No big staff
No captains; seniors rotate
No freshman or JV program
No discipline problems
No players cut

SEASON
No staff or player meetings
No film sessions after Monday
No special diet
No special dormitories
No slogans
No superstitions
No playbooks

PRACTICES
No practice pants; shorts or sweats worn
    all season
No agility drills
No lengthy calisthenics
No blocking sleds
No dummies
No tackling
No laps
No wind sprints
No use of words like "hit" and "kill"
No clipboards
No practice on Sundays
No practice in rain or extreme cold,
    heat, wind

No long practices (limit of 30–90 minutes)
No practice under lights to prepare for
    night games
No water or rest denied
No hazing of freshmen

GAMES
No big scenes when we score; we expect
    to score
No field phones
No player unplayed in a rout
No spearing allowed
No foul play tolerated
No grading game films
No counting tackles
No "big" games we point to
No special pre-game meals
No special post-game meals
No computer analysis
No cheerleaders

RESULTS
No player has not graduated
No discipline problems
No player has been lost through ineligibility
No graduating class has not had players
    go on to graduate schools
No wider point margin in national playoff
    history
No team has had fewer injuries
No small-college coach has won as
    many games

the 1976 NCAA Division III title, and 18 conference championships. (The current season ends Nov. 13.)

"I'm always amazed how well it works," says Gagliardi, who insists on being called "John," not "Coach." He is soft-spoken; his eyes are in a perpetual Mr. Magoo-like squint—hardly the kind of drill sergeant qualities associated with football. He expects his players to keep fit on their own time without baby-sitting.

Ken Roering, 51, a former All-American player for Gagliardi, calls him "a marvelous teacher" who keeps plays simple at first, then adds them till the team has memorized a playbook. "He gives students small doses they can absorb."

Gagliardi began his career at 16 at a Catholic high school in Colorado. When the football coach left to fight in World War II, Gagliardi took over, making revolutionary changes: no calisthenics, no scrimmages and, most unbelievable, thirsty players actually could drink water. "We were near the coal mines, and we'd see mules coming out," Gagliardi says. "First thing they gave them was a drink." He figured what was good enough for mules was good enough for his team.

At season's end, the team won the league championship. The coach likens that team to kids home alone goofing off. Fifty years later, the same can be said of the 1993 Johnnies.

At 4:15 during a recent afternoon practice, it's calisthenics time . . . sort of. The seven captains (seniors rotate) face the team. "Three jumping jacks!" one captain barks. The players perform dutifully, then pat themselves on the back with loud cheers. "Nice Day Drill!" another captain shouts. The players flop onto their backs like sea lions, joyfully yelling: "What a nice day!," "The football gods are out!" and *"Seinfeld's* on tonight!"

"You're relearning the game," says Ryan Murray, a senior. "It turns from physical to mental."

By game day, the Johnnies have transformed the mental aspect of the game into old-fashioned, hard-hitting football. They stuff running backs, sack the opposing QBs and make spectacular touchdown passes.

The players are Gagliardi's extended family. (His wife and their four kids all are football buffs, too.) After one practice, Gagliardi treats his seniors and starters to dinner at an all-you-can-eat establishment in nearby St. Cloud. There they load up on biscuits and country gravy, chicken wings and frozen yogurt. The mashed potatoes disappear in seconds. As the players stroll out, laughing, jostling, full to the point of bursting, they shake hands with their coach. "Thanks, John," they say. Gagliardi gets a little kick asking each if they had enough to eat. His face beams; his eyes squint.

What a nice day! (p. 8)

Glossary of Newspaper and Magazine Terms

Advance: A sports story about an event, written prior to the event.

Angle: The point-of-view, focus or emphasis in an article.

Annual: Yearly special or extra issue devoted to seasonal subject, such as a Christmas annual (issue).

Art: Illustrations, drawings, diagrams, or other nonprint material that accompanies an article; common name for all nontextual material.

Assignment: Any specific task given to an individual; for example, a commissioned article assignment to a freelancer by a magazine.

ATT: The *As Told To* story. An athlete's autobiography that is prepared for publication by a writer; the writer shares the byline credit, such as, "My Life in Football" by Joe Jock, As Told To Writer Charley Someone.

Author's Alterations (AAs): Changes or corrections made by the writer in textual material (usually in galley proof form) before the material is printed.

Back Issue: Any issue of a magaize or newspaper printed prior to the current-date (newsstand) issue.

Back-of-the-Book: Secondary articles, columns, and other material literally or figuratively printed behind the primary articles.

Back Shop: Composing room area of a newspaper.

Bingo Card: Postage-paid insert in a magazine, that readers can complete and return to begin a magazine subscription. So called because they are often the size of bingo playing cards.

Bleed: To run an illustration past the margins to the edges of a page.

Blue-Pencil: Slang for editing corrections. So-named because blue pencil or ink can't be photographed by photo-offset cameras.

Blurb: Short description of an article or subject.

Body (of the article): The core of an article; that is, material following the lead segment.

Book: Industry slang for *magazine.* So named (perhaps) because some monthly dummies are the sizes of books.

Byline: A line of type printed before or after an article, identifying the author.

Camera-Ready: Material that has been corrected and is ready to be photographed for photo-offset printing.

Caption: Material that explains the contents of a photograph or illustration. Sometimes called *art lines* or *cut lines.*

Center Spread: The two facing pages at the exact center of a magazine.

Circulation: The number of copies of a magazine or newspaper printed, distributed, or sold during a specific period.

Clean Copy: Pristine text, unmarred by many editing symbols. Opposite of *dirty copy*.

Close (Closing date): The deadline for all material for a newspaper or magazine to be on the press.

Cold Type: Material prepared for printing without old-fashioned hot metal; that is, without Linotype machines.

Commission: Same as *to assign an article*.

Contents Page: Page usually near the front of a magazine that lists the contents of the issue.

Copy: All written material in manuscript form that will eventually be considered for publication.

Copyeditor: Person who reads and corrects all copy prior to publication.

Copyright: The legal ownership of a manuscript.

Cover (noun): The outside front page, inside front page, inside rear page, and outside rear page of a magazine or *to cover* (verb): To gather all the facts necessary for an article.

Crop: To mark unwanted sections of a photograph or illustration.

Cut (noun): A metal engraving of an illustration. Or *to cut* (verb): To edit material.

Cutlines: Same as *caption* or *art lines*.

Dateline: Line on an article, giving the location and date that the article originated; such as, Washington, Feb. 23.

Dead: Material that has been *killed*; that is, material that will not be printed.

Deadline: Time when all material to be published must be written, copyedited, and ready for the press.

Department: Specific section of a magazine or newspaper, involving special features or area of interest.

Dirty copy: Material that has been heavily copyedited, such that it is illegible. Opposite of *clean copy*.

Double-Spread: Two facing pages treated as one unit.

Dummy: Planning or proof pages for an issue that has not yet been printed; a checking copy to make sure changes and corrections have been made to a particular issue.

Edition: Same as *issue*.

Editor: Person who reads, changes, or verifies all material and makes it ready for publication, in a newspaper or magazine.

Editorial Content: All nonadvertising material in a newspaper or magazine; the literary contents of a publication.

Editorialize: To express a position or opinion on behalf of the publication, as in an editorial or publisher's or editor's column.

Editor's Note: Material that helps explain an article or author or a position that a publication has taken on an issue.

Engraving: Same as *cut*.

Feature (noun): A human-interest article, or *to feature* (verb): To emphasize or give permanence to.

Filler: Incidental (usually short) material that is used to complete columns or pages.

Flag: The name of a newspaper or magazine recognizable not only by name, but also by design; for example, the Gothic flag of *The New York Times*.

Format: The size, design, and appearance of a magazine.

Four-Color: Pages that are printed in the colors of red, yellow, blue, and black inks.

Free Lance: Person who contributes articles, photographs, or any other material without the security of a staff salary.

Front-of-the-Book: Articles of primary importance literally or figuratively printed at the front of the magazine.

Galley Proof: Vertical column of material typeset for checking purposes.

Gatefold: A page in a magazine, that is larger than the normal page and that must be folded to fit inside the magazine; for example, the *Playboy* Playmate-of-the-Month pages.

General Magazine: Any magazine edited and published for a wide reading audience, all ages, interests, religions, and so on. *Life* and *The Saturday Evening Post* are examples. Opposite of special-interest magazine.

Ghost Writer: Person who writes material that will eventually be published under the name of another person.

Graf (or *Graph*): Short for *paragraph*.

Gutter: The inside margins of pages.

Handout: Publicity release.

Head: Headline.

Horizontal Magazine: Same as *general magazine*.

Hot Type: Material prepared with hot metal; that is, Linotype machines. Opposite of *cold type* or photo-offset composition.

House Ad: Advertisement that promotes the same newspaper or magazine that published it.

House Organ: Publication issued by a commercial firm to promote interest in the firm by employees, stockholders, or the public.

HTK: *Head to Come*; headline not yet ready.

Human Interest: Feature article with emotional appeal to the reader; different than straight news, which is presumably toneless in content.

Insert: Material that has to be added to the inside of a previously completed article, or a specially prepared advertising supplement to a newspaper or magazine.

Inventory: Material on hand in a magazine or newspaper office, that may be used at any time.

Issue: Same as *edition*.

Italic: Script type that slants to the right, like handwriting. Italic type is often used to emphasize or highlight material.

Jump: To continue a story from one page to another or from one section to another.

Jump Head: Headline over the second or continued part of a story.

Keep Standing: Material that is held in a newspaper or magazine's inventory. Opposite of *kill*.

Kill: To delete material set for publication.

Kill Fee (*Kill Rate*): Payment made to a writer after an article is assigned, completed, then killed by a magazine. The kill rate or kill fee is usually a percentage of the fee paid for a published article. The writer usually retains legal rights to material killed by a publication.

Layout: The design of a page including textual material, or art that will later be published.

Lead: Beginning segment of an article.

Libel: A defamatory statement or representation published without just cause, expressed in print or by pictures, that exposes the subject to public hatred, contempt, or ridicule.

Linotype: Trade name for a keyboard-operated typesetting machine that produces a line of type in the form of a metal slug.

Little Magazine: Small circulation magazines, often less than 8½" × 11", that contain poetry, fiction, or avant garde material. Because of lack of advertising or subscription base, little magazines often die quickly. They are the publishing equivalent of the Mayfly.

Localize: To stress the local angle of a story.

Logo: Same as flag or masthead.

Magazine: Regularly issued publication that contains fiction, nonfiction, and art, and that is aimed at a specific reading public. Carries the original definition of powder magazine, that is, storehouse.

Makeup: The consistent design of a total publication.

Mark up: To edit copy and make corrections on galley proofs.

Market: The audience for a magazine or publication.

Masthead: Material usually printed toward the front of a magazine, that lists title, editors and staff members, address, and subscription rates.

More: Used at the bottom of a page, often in parentheses, to indicate that there are additional pages to the article.

Morgue: Newspaper or magazine library or files.

Ms.: Manuscript.

Must: Material so marked has a high priority and should be printed.

Nameplate: Same as *flag* or *logo*.

Nonfiction: Material based on facts; not fiction.

Obit: Obituary; biography of recently deceased person.

Offset: Printing process in which an inked impression is made on a rubber ''blanket'' and then transferred or ''offset'' to paper.

OK for Press: Notation meaning "Can now be printed."

Op-Ed Page: The right-hand page opposite, or facing, the editorial page. Many metropolitan newspapers use the Op-Ed page as a continuation of editorials, essays, letters-to-the-editor, and other allied material.

On-Sale Date: Date on which a particular issue is available for sale throughout the publication's circulation area.

One-Shot Book: Magazine that has only one planned issue. One-shot books are often published after the death of a president, the Pope, or other famous or notorious people. There were a variety of one-shot books published after the death of Elvis Presley.

On Spec (On speculation): Any material written and submitted for publication without prior financial agreements with a magazine.

Outline: Topic-by-topic skeleton of an article.

Overset: Material that has been set in type but not used by a newspaper or magazine.

Over-the-Transom: Unsolicited material that is submitted to a magazine, that must be sorted, read, bought, or returned. (Some magazines will not read over-the-transom material because of the costs of staff member's time to read and reply to it.) Over-the-transom material becomes part of the magazine's *slush pile*.

Pack Journalism: The tendency of journalists to deliberately or accidentally write like each other. The press that covers Washington, DC has been accused of pack journalism, as have many sports writers.

Pad: To lengthen with additional materials.

Periodical: Publication issued at regular intervals longer than one day; that is, for example, magazines, not newspapers.

Personality Piece: Biography on a person in magazine form.

Pics or *Pix*: Pictures.

Piece: Slang for *article*.

Play up: To emphasize.

Policy: Official viewpoint of a magazine as stated in editorial columns or other features; such as "The Playboy Philosophy," a series in *Playboy* written by publisher Hugh Hefner.

Profile: Personality article.

Promotion: Active campaign to enhance the acceptance and sale of a newspaper or magazine.

Proof: Copy of material used for checking and correction purposes.

Proofread: To check such material prior to publication.

Pulp: Magazines printed on cheap newsprint; often carries the connotation of sensational material.

Put to Bed: To put on press; to close an issue.

Query Letter: Letter from a freelance writer outlining an article idea and asking for an acceptance from a publication on the idea.

Quote: Quotation.

Readability: The ease with which a story can be read; visually, pertains to legibility and design of article or layout.

Readership: Surveyed or estimated audience of a magazine; not the same as circulation.

Regional Advertisements: Advertisements that appear in issues of a magazine for a particular region.

Rejection Slip: Small letter sent to freelancers with articles that a publication has decided not to buy.

Reprint: Article printed separately and sent to readers or advertisers after the article has first appeared in print. Scholarly magazines often sell reprints to authors for their own distribution. Or, an article that had appeared previously in another publication.

Researcher: Editorial staff member who supplies facts necessary for an article or who verifies facts in an article. Slang term for researcher is *checker*, in news magazines.

Résumé: Summary of education and experience, sent by individual to prospective employers.

Rewrite: To write manuscript again.

Rim: Edge of copy desk, where editors check material.

Rough: Full-size sketch of layout.

Roundup: Article that is largely summary in nature.

Running Head: Headline that gives magazine title, date, volume, and page, printed at the top of magazine pages.

Running Story: Story that is continuing and that may demand follow-up articles on a day-to-day or week-to-week basis.

SASE: *Self-addressed stamped envelope*. Many magazines require a writer to enclose a SASE to receive an answer to a query. The writer pays the return postage.

Scoop (noun): Exclusive material, or *to scoop* (verb): To beat the competition.

Seasonal Story: An article emphasizing a season, holiday, or celebration. Must be prepared well in advance, sometimes as much as a half-year in advance for monthly magazines.

Shelter Books: Magazines related to the home.

SID: Sports Information Director. The promotion-and-publicity arm of a college or university's athletic department.

Sidebar: A short feature that accompanies a longer article. The sidebar usually focuses on one aspect of the larger article; an aspect that the larger article may have only touched on.

Sister Publications: Magazines that are published by the same firm: *Time*, *Life*, *Fortune*, *Money*, *People*, and *Sports Illustrated* are all sister publications, published by Time, Inc.

Slant: To emphasize a particular aspect of a story.

Slick: A magazine printed on high-gloss heavy paper. Common industry term for mass circulation consumer magazines.

Slug: Abbreviated headline used to identify each story. In hot metal composition, a line of type.

Slush Pile: Unsolicited manuscripts that arrive at magazine editorial offices and that must be sorted, read, and accepted or returned.

Solicit: To commission an article, photographs, or other material from contributors.

Special-Interest Books: Magazines that are edited for a special subsection of the population; those interested in a hobby, craft, or other particular subject.

Split Run: A press run that is stopped to change an advertisement.

Staffer: Magazine staff member, writer, researcher, editor, and so on.

Style: A writer's individual expression through the special use of grammar, spelling, punctuation, and point of view.

Summary Lead: A lead that generally covers most of the "5 W's and the H": Who, What, When, Where, Why, and How.

Syndicate: Organization that sells photographs or textual material to a variety of publications. A journalism wholesaler.

Taboo: Words, phrases, or subjects that cannot be published for moral or legal reasons.

Take: One page of copy. As more and more publications are written and edited on computers, *take* is likely to fade from writers' vocabularies. Originated (perhaps) in earlier years when a fast-breaking story was *taken* page by page from the writer to the backshop.

Tear Sheet: Articles or advertisements torn from a published newspaper or magazine and sent to writers or advertisers to verify that the material (article, ad) was published.

Teaser: Headline or blurb printed on the front cover of a magazine to interest readers in the magazine's content.

Think Piece: Interpretative article or essay slanted to make a reader think about the subject. Sometimes condescending term referring to such issues as oil production, taxes, and other hard-to-explain subjects.

Thirty (30): Used on the last page of an article to indicate *the end*.

Tight: Issue that has little room for any additional material.

Title: Same as headline.

TK: Indicates material *to come*; not yet ready.

Typo: Typesetting mistake.

VDT: *Video Display Terminal.* Typewriter keyboard and television-type screen that allows a writer to compose his story on the keyboard, view it on the screen, edit it, and enter it into a computer for storage and retrieval. Electronic storage and publication is said to constitute the third stage of communications, from mechanical to electric to electronic.

Vertical Magazine: Same as *special interest magazine*; not necessarily a magazine that is vertically designed.

White Space: Blank spaces on a page, left blank for design purposes.

Work-For-Hire: Writing that is assumed by a magazine to be done as staff work. Freelancers who sell material on a "work-for-hire" basis generally lose all other further legal rights to the work.

XXX: Used in copy to indicate *facts to come* (or needed); "There are XXX automobiles in Russia this year." Newsmagazine usage.

Glossary of Sports Terms

ARCHERY

American Round: 30 arrows from 60 yards, 50 yards, and 40 yards each.

Anchor Point: Point on the archer's face to which the bowstring or arrow nock is brought for each shot.

Archery Golf: Game similar to golf in which archers shoot for the target—that is, a small ball—and count the number of arrows required.

Arm Guard: Protective cover made of leather or other material that protects the forearm from the bowstring as the arrow is released.

Arrow Plate: Material set in a small ledge in the bow to protect the bow as the arrow slides across it.

Arrow Rest: The ledge on the bow that the arrow sits on prior to release. The arrow slides across it upon release.

Back: Side of the bow away from the string.

Backed Bow: Bow in which the back and belly are made of different material.

Belly: Side of the bow nearest the string.

Brace: To string the bow.

Broadhead: Arrow with large, flat point used in hunting.

Butt: Target backing, usually made of a bale of straw.

Cast: The distance a bow can shoot.

Cock Feather: Feather of a different color than the rest, which is set at right angles to the arrow head.

Columbia Round: For women: 24 arrows shot at 50, 40, and 30 yards each.

Composite Bow: Bow that has pulleys at the top and bottom ends, which *lessen* the pull as the string is drawn back. State-of-the-art in archery.

Creeping: Letting the hand slowly inch forward momentarily before the arrow is shot. Will likely ruin the accuracy of the shot.

Double Round: Round shot twice.

Drift: Inaccurate shot because of crosswinds between the archer and the target.

Fletching Jig: Small mechanical machine to attach feathers to arrow.

Fletchings: Feathers attached to arrow to help it "fly" smoothly and accurately through the air.

Flight Arrow: Used for long-distance accuracy shooting; has small feathers.

Flight Shooting: Competition to shoot flight arrows the farthest.

Follow: Tendency of some bows to "warp" to their strung shape.

Form: The archer's stance and technique.

Full Draw: A bow is said to be at full draw when the archer pulls the arrow back completely, just before releasing.

Handle: Midsection of the bow, which the archer grips.

Hen Feathers: Feathers other than the cock feather.

Holding: Keeping the arrow at full bowdraw momentarily before shooting.

Limbs: Upper and lower parts of the bow, with the handle in between.

Loose: To release tension on the bow; to shoot the arrow.

National Round: For women: 48 arrows shot at 60 yards, 24 at 50 yards.

Nock: Groove in the end of the arrow opposite the point; the bow string is inserted in the nock.

Nocking Point: Point on the bow string where the nock is placed. Usually marked by archer.

Overbowed: Using a bow that has a pull too strong for the archer.

Point Blank: Target distance so short that there is no allowance for trajectory of the arrow.

Quiver: Receptacle for holding arrows, usually leather, often decorated.

Range Finder: Mechanical device used to determine distance to target.

Reflex Box: Bow whose tips curve toward bow back when unstrung.

Round: Shooting a determined number of arrows at a target at a specific distance.

Shaft: Main part of the arrow.

Shooting Glove: Glove that protects the two fingers that hold the arrow nock on the bowstring.

Spine: The relative stiffness of an arrow.

Tackle: Archery equipment. Similar in usage to fishing tackle.

Target Face: Front of a target.

Trajectory: Path of an arrow in flight toward the target.

Underbowed: When a bow is too weak for the archer.

Vane: The feather of an arrow.

Weight: The pull of a bow in pounds or the weight of an arrow in grams.

Wide: Arrow that misses the target on either side.

Windage: Effect of wind on the arrow in flight.

BADMINTON

Backhand: Stroke made with the back of the hand toward the opponent's end of the court. Usually cross-body stroke.

Bird: See shuttlecock.

Clear: High shot that falls near the back line.

Cross-Body Stroke: A shot, in which the player's arm crosses in front of the torso.

Cross-Court Shot: Any shot that crosses the net on a diagonal path.

Drive: Hard shot that crosses the net horizontally.

Driven Clear: Any drive that goes to the back court, but not high enough for the opponent to kill.

Drop: A shot that falls close to the net.

Fault: A violation of the rules that involves the loss of a point or the loss of a serve.

Forehand: A shot made with the palm of the hand facing the opponent; a shot that is not a cross-body shot.

Hand-Out: The loss of a serve.

Let: A shot that hits the top of the net, but falls on the opponent's side of the court.

Over-Head Stroke: Shot made over the player's head.

Rally: To return the shuttlecock several times without scoring a point.

Receiver: Player who receives a serve.

Server: Player who puts the shuttlecock in play.

Setting the Game: Deciding how many further points will win the game, when it is tied.

Short Serve: Serve that barely clears the net, but lands in the opponent's court.

Shuttlecock: Feathered object—now usually plastic—that is batted back and forth across a net in the game.

Smash: Powerful overhead stroke that sends the shuttlecock over the net and in a downward arc.

Toss Serve: To throw the shuttlecock into the air so it comes down to be served across the net. Similar to a tennis serve.

BALLOONING

Aeronaut: Person who pilots or acts as crewmember in an aerostat.

Aerostat: A flying machine using a container filled with hot air or gas that is supported by its bouyancy relative to the air surrounding it.

Airspeed: Speed in flight relative to the air surrounding the vehicle. Airplanes and powered dirigibles have air speed. Hot air balloons, which drift with the wind, have only ground speed.

Airway: An air corridor designated by the Federal Aviation Administration (FAA), controlled by Air Traffic Control (ATC) and marked by radio navigation beacons.

Airworthy: The state of being ready to fly.

Altimeter: A barometer that measures height above sea level.

Altitude: Generally cited as height above sea level, but may be given as height above ground level, abbreviated A.G.L.

Annual: Inspection that must be conducted every 12 months to certify airworthiness. Also applies to airplanes.

Apex: The top of a balloon.

Approach: The act of losing altitude to come to rest on the ground. Also applies to airplanes.

ATC: *Air Traffic Control*. The federal-government-sponsored agency that regulates air traffic, especially in and around large airports.

Attitude: A position relative to the horizon.

Ballast: Weights used to maintain a flight altitude. Now seldom found in hot air balloons.

Balloon: Lighter-than-air vehicle that obtains its "lift" from hot air or a gas such as hydrogen, helium, or methane. Also refers to the envelope itself, which contains the air or gas.

Barograph: A barometer that shows variations in air pressure as altitude or height above a specific point, on a paper graph.

Basket: Same as *gondola*.

Blast Off: Quick ascent.

Blast Valve: A valve control that sends full pressure through the balloon's burner system, to provide maximum hot air for lift.

Blimp: A nonrigid or semirigid airship.

Burner: Heating device that mixes air and butane or propane to produce a hot flame as a heat source for lifting hot air balloons.

Burner Mount: Frame that supports the burner unit in the gondola.

Ceiling: The height above ground level of a cloud base.

Champagne: Sometimes carried in a gondola to celebrate a first flight, or a solo flight, or sometimes given to a farmer to placate him for a forced landing in a farm field.

Checklist: A list of safety items to check before ascent, to make sure the balloon is airworthy. Also applies to airplane safety.

Cross-Country Flight: Flight between two points.

Crown: Same as *apex*.

Dirigible: An aerostat that can be steered.

Downwind: Flying in the same direction as the wind is blowing.

Drag Line: Line formerly used with dirigibles and blimps. The line was held by crew members on the ground to prevent premature ascent.

Drift: A flight away from a specific target designation, caused by crosswinds along the flight path.

Envelope: The fabric part of the balloon, that holds the hot air or gas.

Federal Aviation Administration (FAA): The federal government agency that regulates air traffic.

Forced Landing: Landing accomplished in an emergency situation.

Gondola: The lightweight basket that contains the crew and instruments for a flight. Formerly wicker, now usually aluminum.

Ground Speed: The speed of a craft in flight, as measured in relation to miles-per-hour on the ground.

Inflator: Gas or electric blower that forces hot air into the balloon envelope on the ground, to inflate the envelope.

Loft: A balloon repair shop.

Lofting: The act of landing in which the gondola hits the ground, bounces into the air, then hits the ground again.

Logbook: A pilot's book of all flights taken. Also applies to flying, sky diving, and boating.

North Pole: Same as *apex*.

Preflight: Inspection before ascent to check that all parts of the envelope and gondola are airworthy. Also applies to airplanes.

Pyrometer: Device that measures the temperature of air or gas inside the top of the envelope. The pyrometer will warn if the inside temperature is getting too high—above 250° to 300° (Fahrenheit). Excessive heat will damage the envelope fabric.

Red Line: Warning line on a pyrometer that shows when the inside temperatures of the envelope are too hot.

Regulator Valve: Adjustable valve that controls the fuel flow through the burner system.

Rip Cord: A cord that is attached to the balloon envelope, that allows a slit to open to vent hot air or gas, to allow the balloon to deflate.

Skirt: Fabric around the bottom edge of the balloon.

Solo: Single flight; flight without passengers.
Suspension Lines: Lines that connect the balloon envelope to the gondola.
Temperature Differential: Difference between temperature inside the envelope and outside.
Tether: Line used to hold a balloon near the ground.
Touch-and-Go: Series of landings and takeoffs without a complete stop on the ground.
Variometer: Device that measures that rate of rise and descent of a ballon.
Weigh Off: Slow ascent of a balloon.

BASEBALL

Aboard: On base when the side is retired.
Advance: To move to the next base.
All-Pro: Player elected to a team of exceptional players. (Also appropriate in basketball, football, and other sports.)
All-Star: Same as *All-Pro*.
All-Time: The best who ever played a game at that particular position. (Appropriate for almost all team sports.)
Alley: Imaginary line or lane between outfielders playing in their normal positions.
American League: One of two major professional major leagues, now split into two divisions. In the Eastern Division are: Baltimore, Boston, Cleveland, Detroit, Milwaukee, New York, and Toronto. In the Western Division are: California, Chicago, Kansas City, Minnesota, Oakland, Seattle, and Texas. Abbreviated AL.
Artificial Turf: Synthetic grass substitute, sold under a variety of brand names. Also called *carpet*.
Assist: Credited to a player who throws to a base to aid in an out.
Babe Ruth Baseball: Non profit organization that sponsors summer baseball for youth aged 9–18.
Backstop: A screen that protects spectators behind the plate from pitches that might get away from the catcher.
Bad Hop: Awkward bounce that allows a ball to get away from a fielder.
Balk: Illegal act by the pitcher that allows all runners on base to advance one base. A balk is technically a pause during the normal pitching motion.

Baseball Annie: Woman attracted to baseball players.
Basket Catch: Catch made with the glove held at waist level with the palm up.
Battery: The pitcher and catcher as a team.
Battery-Mates: Same as *battery*.
Batting Average: Number of hits divided by the number of times at bat.
Batting helmet: Protective hatlike helmet now required of all professional teams, to prevent injury to the head by a pitched ball. Protective helmets were first used in 1941 by the Brooklyn Dodgers.
Bean Ball: Ball thrown to deliberately hit (or just barely miss) a batter's head. In 1920, a ball thrown by Carl Mayes of the Yankees hit and killed Ray Chapman, of the Cleveland Indians, which has been baseball's only fatality. Also called *brushback* and *knockdown pitch*.
Bench Jockey: A player who seldom plays. He "rides the bench."
Big League: Either or both professional leagues.
Bleachers: Seats in the outfield area, usually cheap seats, in an area of a stadium without a roof.
Bottom of an Inning: The last half of an inning.
Box Score: A condensed report of a game that shows the lineups for both teams, runs batted in, score, and so on. The baseball equivalent of shorthand reporting.
Breaking Ball: A ball that curves in or out as it crosses the plate area.
Bronx Cheer: A "razzberry" sound made by a spectator. Usually made in contempt.
Bullpen: Area behind the outer fences of a baseball field where relief pitchers warm up and wait for their possible entry into the game.
Bunt: A ball that is not swung at. The batter holds the bat horizontally and taps the ball into the infield.
Bush League: Minor leagues. Carries the connotation of amateurish, unprofessional, not yet top-flight.
Cactus League: Spring training league that plays in the Southwest.
Cellar: The lowest team statistically in a league's standings is said to be "in the cellar."
Charley Horse: A slight muscle pull or strain, usually in the leg muscles. Also appropriate in football, track and field, and other sports.

(To) Choke Up: To be unable to play to the best of a player's ability because of fear or tension. *To choke up on a bat*: To hold it higher than the normal grip position.

Clean-Up: The fourth position in the batting order.

Clothesline: Baseball hit in such a straight line that clothes could be hung on the level.

Contact Hitter: A player known for an ability to hit the ball regularly for base hits, although probably unspectacular ones.

Count: The number of balls and strikes a player has when he is batting.

Cup of Coffee: A brief visit to the major leagues by a minor league player. He is said to have visited the majors just "long enough for a cup of coffee."

Curve: A ball thrown in such a way that it curves in flight toward the batter's box.

Cy Young Award: An award made annually to the pitcher who has made an outstanding record that year. Voted by the Baseball Writer's Association.

Designated Hitter: A player who comes to bat for a team, but who does not field. Allowed in the American league, but not in the National League. Allowed once every other year in the World Series. Abbreviated DH.

Diamond: The infield part of a baseball field.

Disabled List: A player who is injured and can not play is placed on the disabled list. Also appropriate in football.

Doctor: To secretly treat a baseball to gain an advantage.

Doctored Bat: To treat a bat so it is not of regulation weight, for an advantage to the batter. A doctored bat is usually made lighter by drilling a hole in the bat and covering the hole so the doctored area cannot be seen.

Double-Dip: Two games played in one day, a doubleheader.

Double Play: Two consecutive outs during the same play.

Downtown: A home-run ball that clears the outfield fences and flies into the seats is said to have gone downtown.

Dugout: An area where team benches are located, usually slightly lower than the spectator's seats so as not to block the view of the field. One is located on the first base side of the field, the other on the third base side.

Earned Run: Run that scores as a result of base hits, stolen bases, sacrifice hits, walks, hit batter, wild pitches, or balks and before fielders have had a chance to retire the side.

Error: Is charged against a player when a misplay (ball that is dropped, etc.) causes the play to continue, when without the error, the play would have been over.

Extra Innings: A game that goes beyond the normal nine innings to break a tie.

Fair Ball: A hit ball that remains inside the playing area of the field.

Farm Team: A minor league team associated with a major league team is said to be a farm team because that's where major league players are "grown" or developed.

Fast Ball: A baseball thrown at 100 mph or more.

Fielder's Choice: When a defensive player chooses to retire a base runner previously on base, rather than the batter who hit the ball.

Fielding Average: Put-outs, assists, and errors, divided into put-outs and assists.

Fireman: A relief pitcher who wins games in the late innings by putting out the opposition's "fire."

Flake: A psychologically unreliable ball player.

Foul Ball: Ball that rolls off the field of play before reaching first base or third base, or lands off the field of play past first or third base.

Foul Tip: A batted ball that fields directly into the catcher's mit and is caught by the catcher. This is a fair ball.

Frame: An inning.

Free Agent: A player not under contract to any club and who can negotiate a contract with any club in the league.

Fungo Bat: Lightweight bat used for batting practice.

Gamer: A player who plays with an injury.

Goat: Nickname for a player who loses a crucial game.

Go Down Looking: To take a called third strike for an out without swinging.

Go Down Swinging: To swing and miss at a third strike and be called out.

Golden Glove Award: An award made every year to the fielders with the best performance at each position.

Grand Slam: A home run hit with the bases loaded, thus scoring four runs.

Grapefruit League: Spring training league, played largely in Florida.

Hit: Ball hit in such a way that the batter may reach base safely or preceding base runners may reach an additional base or bases safely.

Hook Slide: To slide into second or third base or home plate while avoiding a player's tag, but while keeping one foot pointed toward the base.

Hot Corner: Third base.

Iceman: A relief pitcher who can "ice" an opponent's "hot streak." Same as *fireman*.

Iron Mike: Pitching machine that is used during batting practice.

Infield Fly: Fly ball with runners on first and second, or on first, second, and third, that is hit into the infield and that can be handled by the infielders for an out.

In the Hole: Unfavorable position for the batter. If the batter has two strikes against him and no balls called, he is said to be in the hole.

Junk Pitch: An unorthodox pitch or slower than normal pitch.

Junk Man: Pitcher who relies on junk pitches for effectiveness.

Knockdown Pitch: A pitch deliberately thrown at the batter's head or thrown so close to the batter that he must fall to the ground to avoid being hit by the pitch. Same as *bean ball*.

K: Indicates a strikeout in a baseball box score. A backward K indicates a swinging strikeout.

Lead: A few steps away from a base taken by a runner toward the next base.

Line Drive: A ball hit in a straight line.

Lineup Card: Card given by the manager to the umpire that lists all the players to be used during a game by their position in the batting order.

Little League: A minor league for youngsters that plays on a field that is one third smaller than normal. Now headquartered in Williamsport, PA, the Little League plays a World Series every year.

Load the Bases: To have runners on first, second, and third base at the same time.

Long Reliever: Relief pitcher who can pitch five innings or more.

Magic Number: The number of games that a particular team must win to win a divisional race and thus qualify for playoffs leading to the World Series.

Major League: Refers to either or both the National League or the American League.

Minor League: Any league other than the two major leagues.

MVP: Most Valuable Player. Award given to the outstanding player in each league each year. Awarded by the Baseball Writers Association.

National League: One of two professional major leagues, now divided into two divisions. In the Eastern Division are: St. Louis, Montreal, Philadelphia, Pittsburgh, New York, Florida, and Chicago. In the Western Division are: Los Angeles, Cincinnati, Atlanta, San Francisco, Colorado, Houston, and San Diego. Abbreviated NL.

Nightcap: Second game of a doubleheader, often played at night.

No-hitter: A game in which a pitcher does not allow any base hits by the opposing team.

Off-Speed Pitch: Slower than normal pitch.

On Deck: Player waiting to bat next.

Outfield: That part of a baseball field beyond the base paths that connect first, second, and third bases.

Out In Front Of: To swing too early at a pitch.

Passed Ball: Is charged against the catcher when he drops the ball or loses possession of it and that loss causes a runner to advance a base or bases. Called an error if the catcher drops a called third strike; the player is allowed to advance to first base.

Pennant: A league divisional champion team. So called because the team is allowed to fly the league flag or pennant during the next season.

Perfect Game: A game in which a pitcher allows no opposing players to safely reach base.

Pick Off: To throw a runner out with a quick throw to a fielder who tags the runner out, off base.

Pinch Hit: To hit in place of another player; to substitute for.

Pinch Run: To run in place of another player.

Pitcher of Record: The pitcher who is officially charged with winning or losing a game.

Pitcher's Duel: A close game in which opposing pitchers have both performed well.

Pitcher's Mound: A slightly elevated part of a playing field that the pitcher throws from. Generally elevated 10 inches higher than normal ground level.

Pitch Out: A pitch that is thrown wide of the plate so a catcher can throw to put out a runner who is off base.

Play-by-Play: A running account of a game in progress.

Playoff: Games conducted at the end of a season to determine a league championship.

Pop Fly: A high fly ball.

Portsider: Same as *southpaw*.

Put-Out: Credited to fielder who handles a ball in a play that results in an out for a baserunner.

Rabbit Ball: A ball that bounces or hops in a lively manner.

Rain Check: A ticket stub that can be used again if a game is rained out and replayed later.

Rain Out: To rain hard enough to cause a game to be postponed.

Ribbie: Abbreviation for *Runs Batted In*. Important offensive statistic for ball players.

Relief Pitcher: A pitcher who does not start a game, but who comes in to relieve the starting pitcher in late innings.

Retire the Side: To put out three batters to end an opposing team's turn at bat.

Rhubarb: A noisy argument.

Rookie: An inexperienced player, a novice.

Rookie of the Year: An award made by the Baseball Writers of America to the outstanding first-year players in the American and National Leagues.

Rosin Bag: A bag that contains powdered rosin. This is handled by the pitcher between pitches to allow him to keep a firm grip on the ball.

Rotation: The regular order in which pitchers are used by a team.

Run Batted In: A run that scores because of a hit by another player.

Run Down: To chase a runner between bases and tag him for an out.

Running Squeeze: Runner on third base begins running toward home plate, as the ball is pitched, hoping that the batter will bunt safely and allow him to score.

Sack: The first, second, and third bases.

Sacrifice Bunt: Batter bunts the ball to advance a baserunner and is called out while the baserunner advances safely.

Sacrifice Fly: Ball hit to the outfield that results in an out for the batter, but a successful advance for a runner on base.

Safety Squeeze: Runner on third heads for home plate when the ball is bunted. Slightly different than *running squeeze*.

Sandlot Ball: School yard baseball, or any other informally organized game.

Save: When a relief pitcher wins a game begun by a starting pitcher, he is said to have saved the game.

Set Down: Same as *retire the side*.

Seventh-Inning Stretch: Spectators' tradition of standing and stretching before the home team comes to bat in the seventh inning. Spectators usually go to the restrooms, get a beer, or otherwise take a break.

Shake Off a Sign: Occurs when a pitcher refuses to pitch a specific type of ball that the catcher signals him to pitch.

Shoestring Catch: Catch of a ball made at the shoe level. Also appropriate in football.

Short Reliever: Relief pitcher used for only a few innings, or a relief pitcher who is effective for only a few innings.

Shut Out: To prevent an opposing team from scoring through an entire game.

Sign: Signal shown to the pitcher by the catchers to indicate what kind of ball to throw next. First base and third base coaches may also signal to runners and batters, and the manager may signal to his team from the dugout.

Sinker: Pitch that drops vertically as it crosses the plate.

Slugger: Hitter known for many hits and runs.

Southpaw: Left-handed player. Usually refers to left-handed pitcher.

Speed Gun: Portable radar unit used to determine the speed of a pitched ball.

Spitball: Illegal pitch caused by the pitcher adding some foreign material, such as spit or vaseline, to the ball.

Spring Training: Time before the start of major league season in which players regain playing abilities lost during the off season. Major leagues also test minor league players during this time. Generally starts in March and ends just prior to the season.

Stand-Up Double: A hit that allows the runner to reach second base without sliding.

Stand-Up Triple: A hit that allows the runner to reach third base without sliding.

Stolen base: Runner advances successfully without the aid of a base hit, put-out, walk, force-out, fielder's choice, passed ball, wild pitch, or balk.

Strike Zone: The area that the pitcher must throw in to successfully throw strikes. Generally from the hitter's armpits to his knees, when he is in a normal batting position.

Stuff: A pitcher's effectiveness; either he has good stuff or not.

Switch Hitter: Player who bats both right- and left-handed.

Tape-Measure Homer: Long home run that might be measured for a record.

Texas Leaguer: Fly ball hit just over the head of the shortstop or second baseman, just barely into the outfield.

Three and One: Three balls and one strike on the batter.

Tools of Ignorance: Mask, glove, and pads used by a catcher.

Top of the Inning: The first half of an inning.

Top of the Order: The first batter in the batting order.

Triple: A hit that allows the batter to reach third base successfully.

Triple Play: A play in which three baserunners are put out.

Twin Bill: Same as *doubleheader*.

Twilight Doubleheader: A doubleheader with the first game scheduled about twilight.

Unearned Run: Any run that scores on the basis of an error by an opposing player.

Walk: To be awarded first base because of four balls pitched by the pitcher.

Wild Pitch: Pitch thrown so that the catcher cannot control it.

Wind-Up: The motion of a pitcher prior to releasing the ball.

Winter Ball: Organized baseball played during the off season.

World Series: A best-of-seven game series played by the champion teams of the American and National Leagues.

BASKETBALL

Air Ball: Shot that misses the basket and the backboard and hits "only air."

All-Court Press: To closely guard the offense all over the court.

Alley-Oop Shot: Shot made by one player to another player on the same team who is waiting under the basket to instantly tip the ball in for a score.

Assist: A quick pass from one player to another, which results in a quick score.

Backboard: Flat 4- × 6-foot surface, suspended above and perpendicular to the floor, to which the basket rim is attached. In some cases, the backboard may be fan shaped and approximately 35 × 54 inches, with a 29-inch radius. Players may bank the ball off the backboard to score.

Back Court: The half of the court that a team defends.

Ball Control: The ability to maintain possession of the ball through dribbling or passing.

Bank Shot: A shot that bounces off the backboard into the basket.

Basket: An 18-inch metal ring with a suspended cord net. Players attempt to shoot the ball through the ring to score.

Blocking: To impede an opponent. (Blocking is a foul.)

Boxing Out: The position of a defensive player under the basket that does not allow an offensive player a favorable position for a shot or rebound.

Buzzer Shot: Shot that is made as the buzzer goes off, signaling the end of the first half or the end of the game.

Center: The player responsible for the center jump and for playing the "pivot position" near the basket. Usually the tallest player on the team.

Charging: Contact against an opponent by a player with the ball. (Charging is a foul.)

Charity Line: Free-throw line.

Charity Shot: Free throw.

Clutch Player: Player who can be depended on to score in a crucial moment.

Cold: A player or team temporarily unable to score.

Collapse: When two defensive players converge on an offensive player the moment he receives the ball.

Conversion: A successful free throw.

Corner Men: Forwards who are key rebounding players.

Defensive Boards: The backboard of a defending team's basket.

Double Dribble: A dribble that is resumed after having once been stopped; this is a rules violation. The ball goes to the opposite team.

Double Figures: To score 10 points or more during a game.

Double Foul: When two players on opposite teams foul each other at the same time.

Double Team: To guard one offensive player with two defensive players at the same time.

Down Court: The end of the court that a team is defending.

Draw a Foul: To behave so as to deliberately be fouled by an opponent.

Dribble: To control the ball by bouncing it repeatedly on the floor.

Drive: Powerful effort toward the basket.

Dunk: To jump up and push the ball through the basket from above.

Fade-Away Shot: To shoot while moving away from the basket.

Fast Break: To drive toward the basket before the defensive team has a chance to set up in position to block the drive or the shot.

Follow-in: To follow the progress of the ball to be position for a rebound.

Forward: Player who operates to the side of the offensive back and who is usually a good rebounder.

Foul: Violation of a rule, which results in a free throw by the opposing team. Fouls generally include: blocking, charging, pushing, holding, tripping, illegal substitution, and delaying the game.

Free Throw: Opportunity to score one point unhindered from the foul line as a result of a foul by the opposing team.

Freeze: An attempt to keep possession of the ball by one team, to maintain a lead in the score, or to dribble to kill time on the clock.

Front Court: The half of the court that contains the team's own basket. Opposite of *back court*.

Full-Court Press: Same as *all-court press*.

Garbage Shot: Any easy or uncontested shot.

Give and Go: To pass to a teammate and drive to the basket to await a return pass, which would set up a scoring opportunity.

Goaltending: Any interference with the ball when it is in its downward arc above the rim of the basket, or trapping the ball against the backboard.

Guard: Usually a small player who brings the ball into the forecourt and passes to the forwards or the center for a shot.

Gunner: Player who shoots obsessively at the basket.

Hardship Case: A college basketball player who enters the professional basketball draft before his college eligibility is used up, pleading that family poverty necessitates an early entry into professional basketball. Also called *poverty case*.

Held Ball: When two opposing players each hold the ball and neither can gain complete possession.

Holding: To prevent an opponent from moving freely. Usually a foul, if caught by the officials.

Hook Shot: High arcing shot made by swinging the arm from behind the back, up over the shoulder.

Hot Hand: Player who temporarily has a high shooting average.

Inside Man: The center of the team, usually the tallest player, who plays with his back to the basket, then jumps for a rebound.

In Your Face: Player who is guarding his opponent in a close and intimidating manner. Often refers to schoolyard tactics.

Inside Game: Refers to maneuvers close to the basket.

Jump Ball: To put the ball in play by tossing it in the air between two opposing players; the one who can jump up highest for it takes possession.

Lay-Up Shot: A shot made close to the basket that bounces off the backboard into the basket.

Loose Ball: A ball that is in play but not in possession of either team.

Man-to-Man: Defensive play in which each defensive man has a special offensive player to guard.

Multiple Foul: Two or more fouls committed at the same time.

NBA: National Basketball Association.

Net: The mesh sleeve that is attached to the basket rim.

Offensive Boards: The backboard rebounding area of a team's offensive basket.

One-and-One: A rule in college basketball in which a player receives the right to a second foul shot if the first foul shot is successful. This rule is also used in women's and high school basketball.

One-on-One: A situation in which a specific offensive player is guarded by a specific defensive player, or when a specific offensive player challenges a specific defensive player.

Open: A player who is not guarded by an opponent or who has an unguarded path to the basket.

Outlet Pass: Player who grabs a rebound and passes to a teammate to establish a fast break.

Outside Shooter: A player who has the ability to make long shots.

Overhead Shot: A two-handed shot in which the ball is released over the player's head.

Overtime: A 5-minute period of play to decide a game that is tied at the end of regulation time. Abbreviated OT.

Pass: To move to the ball to a player on the same team by throwing it across the court.

Personal Foul: Rules violation when a player contacts an opponent when the ball is in play.

Pivot: To take one or more than one step with one foot, while in possession of the ball. The other foot must remain stationary.

Play for One: To possess the ball and to shoot when there is time for only one shot.

Post: Same as *post man*.

Post Man: Player who stands in a particular position on the court. The high post is near the free-throw line; the low post is close to the basket. He coordinates offensive plays from that position. Also called *pivot man*, because his play is crucial to the play.

Pressing Defense: Defense that attempts to break an offensive drive by closely guarding the ball.

Rebound: To attempt to gain possession of the ball when it has bounced off the basket or the backboard without going through the net.

Rim: Metal hoop, 18 inches wide, through which the ball must fall to score. The net is attached to the rim.

Run-and-Gun: Aggressive type of play in which a team frequently runs the length of the court for a fast break. Also called *run-and-shoot*.

Screen: To protect a teammate in the act of shooting by standing between him and an opponent.

Set Play: A play in which offensive positions are deliberately taken; opposite of run-and-gun play.

Shave Points: To illegally limit the number of points scored, to affect a bet on a basketball game.

Shot Clock: Clock that indicates that the team with the ball has a time limit to take a shot.

Sky Hook: High hook shot that is impossible to block.

Slam Dunk: Hard dunk shot.

Stall: To keep possession of the ball to maintain a lead or to keep the opposing team from gaining control of the ball. Usually occurs when a team is trying to run out the clock.

Technical Foul: Foul committed by a player not in possession of the ball, or a foul committed by a coach, or an unsportsmanlike call while the ball is dead. Often abbreviated T.

Thirty Second Clock: Same as *shot clock*.

Three Point Play: Foul committed during the act of successfully scoring; the player then gets one foul shot after the basket.

Throw In: Act of beginning play by throwing the ball into the court from an out-of-bounds position.

Tip-Off: The jump ball used to begin play.

Toss-Up: A jump ball.

Tower: See *tree*.

Traveling: To take more than the maximum steps allowed while in possession of the ball at the end of a dribble.

Tree: A center who is so tall and powerful that he cannot be moved or outrebounded.

Trailer: Player who follows behind a player with the ball.

Turnover: To lose the ball to the opposition because of a mistake, a foul, or a stolen ball.

Two Against One: Two offensive players playing against one defensive player, or vice versa.

Two-Time: Same as *double dribble*.

Upcourt: The end of the court that one team is attacking.

Zone: Particular area of the court.

Zone Defense: Type of play in which each player is responsible for a particular part of the court and responsible for the play when the action enters that zone.

Zone Press: Type of play in which a player is responsible for close man-to-man coverage when the action is in his zone.

BOATING & FISHING

Aft: Towards, near, or at the stern of a boat.

Back Cast: Drawing the rod back, the first movement in the cast.

Backlash: Line that becomes tangled by rolling over itself in the reel during the cast, because there is too much play in the reel. (Note: Some modern reels have an anti-backlash mechanism built in.)

Bait: Natural or artificial lures to attract fish.

Bait-Casting: Placing a natural or artificial lure in the area of fish by using a rod and reel.

Ballast: Weight, usually metal, placed low in the boat, or externally, on the keel, to provide stability.

Batten: A light wooden or plastic strip inserted into a pocket in a sail to help shape it.

Beam: The width of a boat at its widest.

Berth: A bunk or sleeping place in the cabin of a boat.

Boom: A spar that is used to extend the foot of a sail.

Bow: The foward part of a boat.

Bucktail: A fly used in bass fishing.

Clew: The lower aft corner of a fore-and-aft sail or either corner of a spinnaker.

Cork Arbor: The part of the reel to which the line is attached.

Cowling: A cover over the engine of a boat.

Dry Fly Fishing: Casting a fly so it resembles an insect on the water.

Ferrules: Metal connections between sections of a take-apart rod.

Flies: Artificial lures that resemble insects.

Fly-Casting: Placing a fly in the area of fish by using a rod and reel.

Fore: Toward or at the bow of a boat.

Fore-and-Aft: In line from bow to stern; on, or parallel to, the centerline.

Forward Cast: Forward movement of a rod that places the lure into the water. Final step in back cast–forward cast movement.

Furl: To roll a sail and secure it to its yard or boom.

Gaff: Small hook used to bring fish on board a boat.

Genoa: A larger jib used in light breezes.

Gimbal: A device consisting of a pair of rings pivoted on axes at right angles to each other so that one is free to swing within the other: A ship's compass will keep a horizontal position when suspended in gimbals.

Guides: Small loops on the rod. The line runs through these guides.

Halyard: A rope, wire, or chain by which a sail, flag, or yard is hoisted.

Head: Toilet on board a ship.

Helm: The steering apparatus.

Hooking the Fish: Setting the hook in the fish after it takes the bait or lure.

Hull: The frame or body of a ship, excluding the spars, sails, and rigging.

Inboard: Motor mounted inside the boat or ship.

Jib: A fore-and-aft triangular sail, set forward of the mast.

Keel: The fixed underwater part of a sailing boat used to prevent sideways drift and to provide stability.

Knot: A measure of speed: one nautical mile (6060.2 feet) per hour.

Lanyard: A short line or rope used to attach one object or item to another.

Leader: Material that connects the lure or hook to the line.

Leech: The aftermost edge of a fore-and-aft sail; both side edges of a square sail.

Lures: Artificial or natural bait used to attract fish.

Mast: A pole or system of attached poles, placed vertically on a vessel, used to support the sails.

Net: Mesh device on a metal frame to pull fish out of the water.

Outboard: Motor attached to the stern of a vessel.

Plane: To gain hydrodynamic lift as the boat lifts up on its bow wave.

Port: Left side of a ship when looking forward.

Reel: Mechanical device that winds or unwinds line for fishing.

Reel Set: Part of the rod handle to which the reel is attached.

Rig: The form in which a vessel's mast, spars, and sails are arranged.

Rudder: Movable underwater part of a vessel used for steering and to prevent side-slipping.

Sheet: The line attached to the clew of a sail, used to trim it. When the sheets are brought in and made fast they are said to be sheeted together.

Ship: Vessel large enough to carry its own lifeboat or lifeboats.

Shrouds: Wires that support the mast on either side; part of the standing or permanent rigging.

Spar: Long wooden beam, generally rounded and used for supporting or extending the sails of a ship.

Spinnaker: A lightweight three-cornered sail, set flying from the masthead and controlled by sheets from each clew.

Spinner: Artificial lure that spins as it is drawn through the water.

Spoons: Artificial bait that generally resemble kitchen spoons.

Starboard: The right side of a vessel when looking forward.

Stern: The aftermost part of a vessel.

Still Fishing: Fishing with bait held motionless in the water.

Strike: When a fish grabs the bait or hook.

Tack (noun): The forward lower corner of a fore-and-aft sail. Or *to tack* (verb): To turn the bow of a boat through the wind so that it blows across the opposite side.

Tackle: Fishing gear—rod and reel.

Tip: Smallest end of the rod.

Torque: A force that produces a twisting, rotating, or spinning motion.

Trapeze: A support used by the crew of a racing boat to enable them to move their weight outboard.

Trim: The adjustment of the sails of a vessel.

Trolling: To fish with a moving line.

Winch: A crank with a handle.

Windlass: A device used for hauling or hoisting, usually for sails.

Yacht: Vessel used for private cruising, racing, or other noncommercial purposes.

BOWLING

Alley: Same as *lane*.

Anchor: Last bowler on a team.

Approach: The act of taking 3, 4, or 5 steps, swinging the arm and releasing the ball toward the pins.

Beer Frame: Frame during a bowling game in which the player with the lowest score buys beer for the team.

Box: See *frame*.

Brooklyn: Ball that crosses the lane and hits the 1-2 pins first, instead of the 1-3 pins.

Creeper: A ball that rolls slower than normal.

Double: Two strikes in succession.

Foul: To go beyond the foul line during the approach.

Foul Line: Line that marks the end of the approach and the beginning of the lane. To step over the line during the approach results in a foul.

Frame: Box in which the scores are marked: 10 frames make a game.

Gutter: Channel on each side of a bowling lane in which balls can drop and roll into the pit without touching any pins.

Gutter Ball: Ball that drops into side gutter without hitting any pins.

Handicap: Bonus score or adjustment to an individual's score or team score, based on averages.

Head Pin: #1 pin.

Hook: Ball that breaks to the left for a right-handed bowler.

Kegler: German for bowler.

Lane: Bowling alley: 41 inches wide and 60 feet long from the foul line to the head pin, usually made of wood. An additional 16 feet, consisting of the bowler's approach to the foul line and from the head pin to the end of the lane, is made of maple, the lane of pine. Formerly called *alley*.

Line: Complete game scored on a scoring sheet.

Loft: To loft a ball means the bowler releases it too late; the ball arcs into the air and hits the lane heavily, instead of sliding onto the lane from the bowler's grip.

Mark: A strike or spare in a particular frame.

Pit: Area behind the lane where all pins are scooped for resetting.

Open Frame: Frame in which the bowler has made no strike or spare.

Pocket: Space between the 1 pin and the 2-3 pins.

Sleeper: A standing pin hidden from the bowler's view.

Spare: All pins knocked down on two balls.

Spot: Aiming point on the alley.

Strike: All pins knocked down on the first ball.

Three Hundred (300): Perfect game.

BOXING

Ali Shuffle: Rapid series of front-and-back foot movements made famous by Muhammad Ali. The advantage was said to be tactical—to show his opponent he was in control of the fight and could still move quickly.

Answer the Bell: To get up from a corner to begin fighting when the bell sounds. If a fighter fails to answer the bell, he is declared the loser in that round.

Apron: The floor outside the boxing ring. It is approximately 2 feet wide.

Arm Puncher: A boxer whose strength is only in his arms; lacks the power of his body behind his punches.

Arm Weary: Tired of throwing punches.

Backpedal: To retreat across the ring.

Bang: To punch hard, without finesse.

Beat the Count: To get up before the count is over.

Bell: A bell that is rung to indicate the beginning and the end of a round.

Below the Belt: A punch that lands below the top of the hipbones, generally in the crotch. If a *low blow* is deliberate, a fighter may be disqualified.

Bleeder: A fighter who cuts easily.

Bob and Weave: To move side to side and up and down to evade an opponent.

Body Punch: Blow delivered to the body of an opponent; that is, the abdomen or ribs.

Bolo Punch: Punch that begins in a wide arc from below the hips swinging upward. Popularized in the early 1940s by middleweight champion Ceferino Garcia, who described the punch as comparable to the swing of a bolo knife cutting through the jungles. Now thought of as any wildly exaggerated punch that begins low.

Break: To withdraw from a clinch when ordered to do so by the referee.

Bum: Unskilled fighter, often thought of as being *punch-drunk*.

Can't Lay a Glove On: A boxer so clever defensively that his opponent can't hit him.

Canvas: The floor of a boxing ring.

Carry (To Carry a Fight): To hold back from ending a fight to make a weak opponent look better than he is.

Cauliflower Ear: A deformed ear; caused by too many blows to the ear.

Challenger: A fighter who fights a reigning champion.

Class: Same as *division*.

Clean Break: To separate from a clinch.

Clinch: To hold an opponent with both arms so neither fighter can score cleanly.

Club Fighter: A small-time boxer with medi-ocre skills; a fighter who fights mainly in local clubs.

Coldcock: To knock out an opponent with one blow.

Combination: Two or more punches in rapid succession.

Contender: A fighter good enough to be a challenger. Popularized in a speech by Marlon Brando in the film *On The Waterfront*, "I cudda been a contenda . . . "

Corner: Any of the four corners of a boxing ring, or, the particular corner assigned to each fighter.

Cornerman: One of the assistants allowed to be in a fighter's corner between rounds.

Count: Counting 10 seconds after a fighter has been knocked down. If a fighter does not arise after the 10 count, the opponent wins the fight by a knockout.

Counter: To respond to an opponent's punch by returning a punch.

Counterpuncher: A boxer who prefers to wait for an opponent's punch to deliver a punch.

Cover Up: To protect the body and head from an opponent's punches, with the arms.

Cross: A punch delivered over and above an opponent's lead, such as a right cross.

Cut Man: Assistant in a fighter's corner who is responsible for stopping cuts or bleeding.

Cut Off The Ring: To move sideways across the ring to reduce the room an opponent can maneuver in.

Dance: To use rapid footwork.

Decision: To win a fight based on the number of points scored by judges witnessing a fight, in which there is no *knockdown* or *technical knockdown*.

Distance: The maximum number of rounds in a fight. (*To go the distance*, to fight 12 rounds in a 12-round fight.)

Division: A category of fighters based on weight. In general, these are the professional divisions:

Flyweight	112 lbs.
Bantamweight	118 lbs.
Featherweight	126 lbs.
Junior Lightweight	130 lbs.
Lightweight	135 lbs.
Junior Welterweight	140 lbs.
Welterweight	147 lbs.

Junior Middleweight	154 lbs.
Middleweight	160 lbs.
Light Heavyweight	175 lbs.
Heavyweight	Unlimited

Down and Out: To be knocked down and be unable to rise.

Down for the Count: Same as *down and out*.

Draw: Same as tie.

Drop a Guard: To lower the gloves; to leave face or body unprotected.

Elimination Bout: One of a series of matches to determine an eventual champion.

Fight Card: Series of bouts on the same program.

Five-Point Must System: A method of scoring in which the winner of a round is given five points, the loser, less than five. In the case of a tie round, both fighters are given five points.

Five-Point System: A method of scoring in which the winner of a round is given one to five points and the loser is given fewer, usually less than one point difference. In the case of a tie, neither fighter is awarded any points for the round.

Footwork: The movement of the feet during a fight.

Foul: Any illegal action or blow during a prizefight, usually a blow to the back of the head or neck, a blow below the belt, wrestling or head butting, or punching after the bell.

Go Into the Tank: To intentionally lose a fight.

Golden Gloves: A program of locally sponsored amateur fights that lead to the National Golden Gloves Tournament.

(To) Guard: To hold the gloves close to the face or body to protect from an opponent's punches.

Gym Fighter: A fighter who looks good in the gym, but bad during a bout.

Handler: Someone who helps train a fighter or acts as a cornerman during a fight.

Haymaker: A knockout punch.

Headgear: Padded headpiece that is used during training to protect the head.

Heavy Bag: Large stuffed canvas bag, approximately 1–1½ feet in diameter and at least 3 feet long, hung from the ceiling of a gym, that a fighter punches to help strength, power and technique.

(To) Hit on the Break: To punch during the break period, as required by a referee.

Hungry: A fighter who financially or professionally desperately needs a win.

Infighter (Infighting): Fighting close to an opponent.

In the Bag: Fight that has been decided before it has begun.

In the Tank: Fighter who deliberately loses a fight.

Jab: Direct punch used to bother an opponent or keep him off balance. Usually not a knockout punch.

Kayo: To Knock Out.

Knockdown: To punch an opponent and cause him to fall onto the canvas. Once a fighter has been knocked down, the referee begins the 10-count.

Lead: The first in a series of punches.

Left: A punch thrown with the left hand.

Long Count: Any count that takes longer than a strict 10 seconds. Usually is a controversial count.

Low Blow: A blow below the hip-line, usually to the crotch and usually a foul.

Main Event: The most important and the last bout during a boxing program.

Majority Decision: A decision made by two of three boxing judges.

Make the Weight: To gain or lose pounds to enter a specific weight class, for a fight in that class.

Mandatory Eight Count: A rule that indicated that when a fighter has been knocked down, the referee must count to eight before the fight can proceed, to protect the downed fighter.

Measure: To hold a gloved hand against a stunned fighter to guide a knockout blow.

Mouse: A swelling around the eye.

Mouthpiece: Protective rubber guard worn inside the mouth to protect the teeth and lips of a fighter.

Neutral Corner: Either of the two corners of a ring *not assigned* to a particular fighter and his cornermen.

No Contest: An act of ending a fight by a referee because of problems not directly connected to the two fighters, such as a power blackout.

No Knockdown: A rule by a referee during a fight that a fighter who was on the canvas was not there because of a knockdown, but rather a slip or a push.

On the Ropes: Leaning helplessly on the ring ropes; usually means the fighter cannot defend himself.

Out: Knocked out.

(To) *Outpoint*: To win a fight with the highest number of points awarded by the judges.

Palooka: An unskilled fighter.

Preliminary Bout: One bout on a boxing program before the main event.

Pugilism: The art of boxing, from the Latin *pugunus*, fist, and *pugil*, boxer.

(To) *Pull a Punch*: To land a punch without full force.

Punch-Drunk: To suffer the effects of taking too many punches to the head. A punch-drunk fighter is said to slur his speech and generally give the impression of being drunk on alcohol.

Punched Out: Tired from throwing too many punches.

(To) *Put Away*: To knock out an opponent.

Quick Count: A count that takes *less* than 10 seconds.

Rabbit Punch: An illegal punch to the back of the opponent's head.

Reach: A measure of arm length. Generally speaking, a boxer with a longer reach than his opponent will have an advantage in the ring.

Referee: The official in the ring who controls the action during a fight, watches for fouls, and separates fighters in a clinch. Sometimes called *the third man*.

Rematch: A bout in which two fighters who have fought each other previously fight again.

Ring: An elevated 18- to 20-foot square area surrounded by three ropes attached to vertical posts at each corner. Sometimes called *the squared circle*.

Ring Savvy: Knowledge of the tricks and techniques of boxing.

Roadwork: Running that is part of a boxer's training and conditioning.

Rope: Ropes that are strung at 2-foot, 3-foot, and 4-foot heights around a boxing ring.

Round: Any 3-minute period during a boxing match.

Saved By the Bell: A boxer who is about to be counted out is said to be saved by the bell when the bell to signal the end of a round is rung before the count is up. No fighter can be saved by the bell during the final round of a bout.

Scorecard: A card on which an official keeps score of rounds won or lost by each fighter.

Second: One man who is allowed in a boxer's corner between rounds to advise him.

Slip: To dodge a punch.

Slug: To punch hard.

Slugger: A fighter with little finesse.

Spar: To box in practice.

Sparring Partner: An opponent during a sparring match.

Speed Bag: Lightweight punching bag used for coordination.

Split Decision: Decision of the judges in which two judges vote for one fighter, and the third judge votes for the opponent.

Standing Eight Count: A count of eight given by the referee when a boxer has been hurt. In professional boxing, this is a knockdown.

Step Back: To separate from a clinch.

Stop a Fight: The act of a referee to end a bout, when one fighter cannot continue.

Straight-Up Fighter: A boxer who does not bob or weave.

The Sweet Science: A famous book on boxing by the late boxing critic A. J. Liebling.

(To) *Take a Dive*: To deliberately lose a fight.

Take the Count: When a boxer allows himself to be counted out.

Tale of the Tape: A boxer's measurements: reach, chest, weight, and so on.

Technical Draw: Termination of a bout because of an accidental injury to one fighter.

Technical Knockout: The end of the fight as ruled by the referee when one fighter is unable to continue. Abbreviated on fight cards as *TKO*.

Ten Point Must System: A method of scoring a bout in which the winner of a round is given 10 points and the loser of the round about 2 points less. In the case of a tie, both fighters receive 10 points.

Three Knockdown Rule: If a fighter is knocked down three times in one round, the fight is over and he loses. Not a universal rule.

(To) *Throw in the Towel*: A fighter's cornermen concede defeat by throwing a towel into the center of the ring from the corner.

Timekeeper: Official at ringside who keeps track of the time of the rounds and the time between rounds.

Title: Highest level of any weight class.

Twenty Point Must System: A method of scoring in which the winner of each round is awarded 20 points and the loser a lesser number. In the case of a tie, both fighters are awarded 20 points.

Unanimous Decision: A decision in which all judges vote for one boxer.

Undercard: Any bout on a program prior to the main event.

Warning: A statement by the referee that a boxer has fouled his opponent and points will be subtracted from his score.

WBA: World Boxing Association.

WBC: World Boxing Council.

Weigh-in: Ceremony before a bout to ensure that boxers' weight is within the class designations.

Weight Division: See *division*.

White Hope: A White boxer who is a contender for a title held by a Black boxer.

Win on Points: To win by a decision.

FENCING

Advance: To move toward the opponent.

Attack: To attempt to hit the opponent by moving the body or the weapon foward.

Attack of Second Intention: An attack that is meant to be defended, so the attacked may score on a counterattack.

Balestra: See *jump advance*.

Benefit of the Doubt: If two side judges disagree and if the meet director has no opinion, no point is scored.

Blade: Strong: near the guard.
      Middle: center section.
      Weak: tip end.

Bout: Contest between two fencers.

Button: Small pad on the tip of a weapon to prevent injury to an opponent.

Competition: Contest with one type of weapon.

Epee (Dueling sword): Weapon generally similar to the foil, but with a heavier handle and heavier guard.

Fleche: Running attack. Illegal in college fencing, women's fencing, and public school fencing.

Foil (French Foil): Weapon approximately 35 inches long, with a flexible four-sided blade, and cup guard for the hand, weighing about

17.5 ounces. The tip has a small guard or button to prevent injury to the opponent during a bout.

Guard: The standing position when two fencers face each other momentarily prior to the bout.

Invitation: To invite an attack by moving toward an opponent.

Jump Advance: A lunge in which both feet leave the ground at the same time and meet the floor at the same time.

Jury: Usually four judges and a meet director.

Lunge: Key offensive movement in fencing; a long reach with one leg, preceeded by a thrust with the foil. In a successful lunge, the fencer's whole body follows the arm and leg thrust instantly.

Mask: Mesh protector for the competitor's face.

Match: Contests between two teams with one type of weapon.

Meet: Contests between two or more teams in which more than one type of weapon is used.

Pass: A touch that would not inflict a puncture or wound.

Phase: Continuous action during a bout. Similar to a tennis volley.

Pool: Fencers or teams in a round-robin tournament.

Redoubled Attack: A lunge, followed by a second lunge.

Remise: A delayed riposte.

Retreat: To move away from an opponent.

Return (Riposte): To advance after a successful defense.

Sabre: Weapon similar to the foil in size and weight, but with a two-sided blade, instead of the four-sided blade of the foil.

Touch: A hit on the opponent that would inflict a puncture or wound if the tip of the blade was not padded.

Tournament: Series of competitions with one or more types of weapons, organized on an individual or team basis.

FIELD HOCKEY

Advancing: Foul committed when the ball rebounds from a player's body.

Backing Up: Defensive play behind or outside the bully.

Bully: Action to start or restart a game. Two opposing players alternately strike the ground and each other's stick three times before touching the ball.

Circular Tackle: An attempt to take the ball from an opponent on the player's right side.

Covering: To guard the goal—usually refers to a player away from the action on the field.

Defensive Hit: A free hit toward the goal from 15 yards away.

Dodge: To elude an opponent while controlling the ball.

Dribble: Series of strokes used to control the ball while moving it down the field.

Drive: Hard stroke with a backswing to propel the ball downfield.

Fielding: To control an approaching ball before passing it or moving it downfield.

Flick: Stroke with no backswing.

Foul: Violation of the rules.

Free Hit: A play following a violation of the rules. Taken by the team that was fouled.

Goal: Score made when the ball crosses the goal line after being touched by a player inside the striking circle.

Holding the Whistle: When a play continues after a whistle by an official, when, in the opinion of the official, it is better to allow the play to continue than to stop it and award a penalty.

Lunge: Play used to take the ball from an opponent on the opponent's left.

Marking: Defensive position close to an opponent. Similar to guarding in basketball.

Obstruction: To interfere with an opponent by placing any part of the body between the opponent and the ball. A foul results.

Offside: A foul when a player receives the ball while in an illegal position.

Push-Pass: Quick pass without any backswing on the stroke.

Roll-In: Method of putting the ball in play after it has gone out of bounds.

Scoop: Short pass in which the ball is lifted with the front end, or toe, of the stick.

Stick Side: The player's right side.

Sticks: Foul committed when the player raises the stick shoulder high or higher at the beginning or end of a stroke.

Striking Circle: Inside the curved line that is the goal-shooting area.

FOOTBALL

Activate: To move a player from a reserve or injured list to a list of eligible players.

All the Way: To score a touchdown.

Audible: When a quarterback changes the play by the use of a code, at the line of scrimmage, just before the ball is snapped. By calling an audible, the quarterback hopes to fool the defense, which may be ready for a different play.

Backfield (Defense): Consists of four players, two defensive cornerbacks and two safeties or three defensive backs and one safety.

Backfield (Offense): Usually consists of a quarterback, a fullback, a halfback, and a flanker back.

Backfield in Motion: On the offensive team, one player is allowed to run parallel to the line of scrimmage or back away from the line of scrimmage before the ball is snapped. If the back runs toward the line of scrimmage, it is a penalty for backfield in motion or illegal procedure.

Balanced Line: Offensive line in which there are an equal number of linemen on each side of the center.

Ball Control: To keep possession of the ball by gaining yards until a score is made. To keep gaining yards (and first downs) prevents the opposing team from gaining possession.

Blitz: When a defensive back moves toward the quarterback before the ball is snapped, he is said to be *blitzing*.

Block: Offensive maneuver in which a player uses his body to keep a defensive player from the ball carrier.

Blue-Chip: Quality college player to be selected by a professional team.

Bomb: Long arcing pass that may be caught for a touchdown. Also sometimes called a *rainbow*.

Bootleg: A running play in which the quarterback hides the ball from the defense by holding it against his thigh, away from the defensive line. He may or may not run in the direction of the rest of his backfield.

Bowls: These are the postseason bowl games, their dates (for the end of the 1994 season), and locations:

Date	Bowl/Site
Dec. 15	LAS VEGAS/Las Vegas, NV
Dec. 25	ALOHA/Honolulu, HI
Dec. 27	FREEDOM/Anaheim, CA

Dec. 28	INDEPENDENCE/Shreveport, LA
Dec. 29	COPPER/Tucson, AZ
Dec. 30	SUN/El Paso, TX
Dec. 30	GATOR/Jacksonville, FL
Dec. 30	HOLIDAY/San Diego, CA
Dec. 31	LIBERTY/Memphis, TN
Dec. 31	ALAMO/San Antonio, TX
Jan. 1	ORANGE/Miami, FL
Jan. 1	PEACH/Atlanta, GA
Jan. 2	HALL OF FAME/Tampa, FL
Jan. 2	COTTON/Dallas, TX
Jan. 2	CITRUS/Orlando, FL
Jan. 2	CARQUEST/Miama, FL
Jan. 2	FIESTA/Tempe, AZ
Jan. 2	ROSE/Pasadena, CA
Jan. 2	SUGAR/New Orleans, LA

On a year-to-year basis, the dates may change slightly. Note: Some skeptics have observed that the bowls that carry the most prestige are those named after *countable (or measurable) items*: roses, gators, cotton, peaches, sugar, oranges, rather than those named after a *concept or ideal*: liberty, freedom. That seems to hold true.

Breakaway Back: Offensive backfield player with enough speed and agility to elude the defense.

Bring in the Chains: To call time out to allow the sideline crew to bring in the 10-yard chain to determine if the team on offense has made 10 yards and thus a first down.

Broken-Field Runner: Runner with the ability to dodge defense players in the open.

Broken Play: Play that was not executed. The defense may have guessed the play, the offense may have not heard the quarterback's count, the offense backfield players may have run into each other—any number of reasons (excuses) may account for a broken play.

Bump and Run: Occurs when an offense player bumps a defensive player to slow him down, then runs past him.

Buttonhook: A pass play in which the receiver runs downfield 10 or 15 yards, then turns back in a semicircle toward the quarterback, to catch a pass. Because many football fans don't know what a buttonhook looks like, this play also resembles a fishhook (without the barb).

Cadence: The rhythm that a quarterback has when he shouts the codes for the play and the ball snap.

Chalk Talk: Teaching session, usually at halftime, in the locker room, by a coach, often illustrating what the team is doing wrong, by the use of X's and 0's on a chalkboard or blackboard. Sometimes an assistant coach will briefly conduct a chalk talk on the sidelines for a small group of players, the defensive line, for instance, when the offense has the ball.

Chain Crew: Team of officials who stand along one sideline and measure whether a team has gained 10 yards in four plays, from the first down. The chain crew will move onto the field to measure, if they are not certain from the sidelines that a team has gained 10 yards. A time out is called during the measure.

Circus Catch: A catch made by a receiver that shows great ability and dexterity—usually made one-handed.

Cleats: Small knobs or stubs on the bottoms of the players shoes to help them gain traction. Sometimes a cleat will catch in the turf and a player may break or sprain an ankle.

Clipping: To illegally block an opponent by hitting the backs of the legs and knees. Very risky and potentially injurious.

Clothesline Tackle: To tackle an opponent by thrusting a stiff arm out to catch the opponent by the neck.

Coach: The equivalent of a teacher or professor, the coach teaches the team fundamentals, his methods and playing philosophy. It is said that a football coach "has to be smart enough to teach the game, but dumb enough to think that it's important."

Coffin Corner(s): To kick into either corner of the defensive end of the field so the ball goes out of bounds and leaves the defense to begin an offensive series of plays within their own 10-yard line.

Color Man (Color Commentator): TV announcer who adds feature material to the commentary of a game.

Conversion: The opportunity that a team has, after scoring a touchdown, of gaining additional points by running or passing the ball over the goal line again, or by kicking it over the goalposts.

Cornerback: Defensive backfield player who

has the responsibility of stopping an offensive play once the ball-carrier reaches the "corners" (sides) of the defensive backfield.

Crackback Block: Run by an offensive player that ends with a block at the back by a defensive player. Like a clip, it too, is potentially very dangerous to the defensive player, who may not be watching or know the offensive player is about to block.

Crawling: To gain added yardage when the play is over by crawling with the ball at the bottom of a pile of tacklers.

Cut Back: Offensive play by a receiver who runs down the side of the field and cuts back toward the center of the field.

Cup: Same as *in the pocket*.

Dead Ball: After a play is over and when the referee blows his whistle to indicate that the play is over. Any foul after that is a *dead ball foul*.

Delay: To hold a position at the line of scrimmage momentarily to confuse an opposing lineman.

Delay of Game: The offensive team has 30 seconds to begin a play. If the play has not begun in 30 seconds, the referee may call a delay of game penalty.

Depth Chart: A coaching chart showing the #1 player at each position, then #2, then #3, and perhaps even #4 at some positions.

Diamond Defense: Defensive formation with seven men on the line, then one back (fullback) then two backs behind him (halfbacks), then one back (safety) behind them. Called a diamond because from above, the backfield formation would have the shape of a diamond.

Dime Defense: Six defensive players (one more than the *nickel*, or five-man defense).

Dive Play: Offensive play in which the ball carrier literally dives over the line of scrimmage.

Double Team: Occurs when two offensive players block one defensive player.

Down and In: An offensive play in which a receiver runs down the field and in toward the center of the field.

Down and Out: An offensive play in which a receiver runs down the field then out, toward the sideline.

Downing the Ball: On a kickoff, a player on the receiving team may catch the ball in the end zone. He may elect not to run the ball out of the end zone. In that case, he downs the ball, by touching one knee to the ground. The next play begins on the offensive team's 20-yard line.

Draft: The act of choosing eligible college players, on a team-by-team basis. The worst team in the professional league has the first chance at eligible college players, to (in theory) equalize the teams in terms of player-by-player ability.

Draw Play: An offensive play in which the quarterback drops back from the line of scrimmage as if he is going to pass, then hands the ball to a runner, who may gain substantial yardage through the defense, which was expecting a pass.

Drop Back: Occurs when a quarterback receives the ball from the center and moves away from the line of scrimmage to pass, or to hand the ball to a runner.

Dump Pass: To quickly throw the ball to the closest eligible player to avoid a loss in yardage (or an embarrassingly inept play).

(To) Eat the Ball: To down the ball with a loss of yardage, to prevent a more substantial loss of yardage. Usually involves embarrassment to the ball carrier.

End Around: Offensive play in which an end runs in an arc through his own backfield, receives the ball and carries it into the defense at the other end of the field. The end must have superior speed to make much yardage on an end around play.

End Zone: Teams score points by running, passing, or kicking the ball into the end zone. It is 10 yards deep; there is one at each end of the playing field.

Extra Points: Awarded after a touchdown; on a play from scrimmage, two points are awarded if the ball is run or passed successfully over the goal line; one point if the ball is kicked between the goal posts.

Face Mask: Metal cage that prevents injury to the player's face. May be grabbed by an opponent and still cause injury to the player's neck. A penalty results if an official catches a player grabbing or holding another player's face mask.

Fade Back: Occurs when the quarterback takes the ball from the center and retreats from the line of scrimmage to pass the ball or hand it off to another back.

Fake: Any movement or motion intended to fool the opposing team.

Fair Catch: A player may make a fair catch on a kickoff, return kick, or kick from scrimmage by raising his hand clearly above his head. If he is tackled after a fair catch signal, a penalty results. He may not take more than two steps after catching the ball. The ball is put in play at the point of the catch. If the player drops or fumbles the catch, it is a fair ball and may be recovered by the defense.

Field Goal: A kick over the crossbar and between the goal posts that results in three points for the kicking team.

Films: Films of an opponent's previous games are studied by a coaching staff to prepare a team for an upcoming game.

Fire Out: To move from the line of scrimmage offensively when the ball is snapped.

First Down: An offensive team has four tries to gain 10 yards. If they gain 10 yards within the four tries, they have a first down and are then eligible to gain 10 more yards in another four tries.

Flag: Penalty marker used by officials.

Flag Football: A nontackle form of football in which players wear (usually) two streamers of cloth. The play is stopped when a defensive player grabs one or both flags from an offensive player's waist.

Flak Jacket: Padded protective vest worn under their uniforms by quarterbacks (and occasionally by others) to prevent rib, abdomen, or kidney injury. Named after the similar jackets worn by World War II airmen to prevent injury by anti-aircraft fire.

Flanker: A backfield player who is positioned away from the rest of the linemen.

Flat Pass: A pass thrown parallel to the line of scrimmage and with a flat trajectory.

Flea Flicker Play: An offensive play in which the quarterback fakes a pass, then laterals to an offensive back, who then passes to a third offensive player; a risky play because the ball may be fumbled or the pass intercepted.

Flex Defense: In this defense, as the ball is snapped, the ends drop away from the line and become additional linebackers.

Fly Pattern or *Fly Pass*: Play in which an end runs ("flies") past the defense and hopes to score by simply outrunning the defense and catching a pass for a touchdown.

Foul: Any violation of the rules.

"Four Yards and a Cloud of Dust": Famous Ohio State techniques, used by coach Woody Hayes, of using a fullback down after down to gain "four yards" (and a cloud of dust) into the line, without passing each down.

Franchise Player: A single player so valuable to a team he is said to be able to "save a franchise," financially, by himself.

Free Ball: A ball that is not in possession of either team.

Free Safety: Defensive backfield player who plays in the deep defensive and has no specific man-to-man responsibilities.

Front Four: The two tackles and two guards on the offensive line.

Fullback: Offensive player who lines up behind the quarterback and who usually has the job of gaining short yardage in tough situations.

Fumble: To lose control or possession of the ball.

Fundamentals: Basic skills that any football player should know. Also applies in other sports.

Game Plan: Strategy devised by the coaches to cover general offensive plans and general defensive plans.

Gang Tackle: To tackle the ball carrier by two or more players at the same time.

Gap: Real or imaginary hole between two players in correct position.

Giveaways/Takeaways: The relationship between fumbles lost by Team A and recovered by Team B to fumbles lost by Team B and recovered by Team A; a relatively new NFL statistic.

Goal-Line Defense: Special defense when the offensive is within the 10-yard line and is close to a touchdown. Generally, defensive players will be closer together, as they have less field to cover.

Go Against the Grain: To run away from the traffic flow; for example, if all the offensive backfield is running to the right, the ball carrier runs to the left.

Gridiron: Common name for the football field.

Grind it Out: To make yardage in short gains, as in Woody Hayes' "Four Yards and a Cloud of Dust" system.

Grounding the Ball: If a passer cannot find an eligible receiver, he may throw the ball over the heads of all receivers. This is called *grounding the ball* or *intentional grounding*. The passing equivalent of *eating the ball*.

Gut Check: A crucial situation; team members pause to check their courage. Do they have enough to win the game? Variations: *gutting it up*, and so on.

Halftime: A 30-minute pause between the second and third quarters of a football game. Allows teams to rest and regroup and allows TV networks a chance for commercials.

"Hail Mary" Pass: Long bomb, usually thrown in a desperate situation. When the pass is in the air, the quarterback (and coach) pray that some offensive player will be under it and catch it for a touchdown. Doug Flutie of Boston College threw a Hail Mary and defeated The University of Miami 47–45 in the last second of the game during the 1984 collegiate season.

Hand-off: An offensive play in which one player (usually the quarterback) hands the ball to a second player.

Hang Time: The seconds of time a kick stays in the air. A longer hang time will allow the kicking team a chance to get downfield and stop the receiving team from advancing the caught ball.

Head Hunter: Player who willfully looks for an opportunity to injure an opponent.

(To) Hear Footsteps: To hear (but not see) an opponent moments before a tackle.

Heisman Trophy: Award given annually to the best collegiate player in the country.

Holding: To illegally impede an opponent by grabbing the uniform, arm, leg, or any other available part of the opponent.

Honey Shot: Shot of cheerleader or other pretty girl during a televised game.

Hot Dog: Player who deliberately shows off for the opposition, audience or TV cameras.

Huddle: Brief meeting before a play. The quarterback announces the play and the count to the rest of the team.

I Formation: Offensive backfield formation in which the halfback is behind the quarterback and the fullback is behind the halfback. So called because the backfield formation looks like the letter I.

Impact Player: A player whose presence can make a significant difference to a team's win-

loss record. Similar to *franchise player*.

Ineligible Receiver: Player (usually a lineman) who may not catch the ball.

Interception: Occurs when a defensive player catches a ball intended for an offensive player.

In the Trenches: Offensive and defensive linemen at work doing their jobs at the line of scrimmage when the ball is snapped.

Intentional Grounding: When the quarterback passes the ball during an offensive play, the officials may call intentional grounding if they decide that there was not a receiver near the play and that the quarterback simply threw the ball away to avoid a loss. A penalty results.

Interception: Pass caught by a defensive player, that was intended for an offensive player.

Interference: Penalty for illegally blocking the action of a player or a play.

Jammed: A running play that is stopped at the line of scrimmage is said to have been jammed.

Keys: Movements by certain players, or team formations that signal how a play will develop. Coaches watch previous game films in order to discover keys.

Kicking Tee: Small plastic device that holds the ball in correct position for a kick.

Kicking Unit: Special team used in kicking situations.

Line of Scrimmage: An imaginary line or vertical plane passing through the ball and parallel to the goal lines, marked by the nearest yard number (line of scrimmage, 35-yard line). There is a line of scrimmage for each team and the area between the two is the *neutral zone*. Any player who enters the neutral zone before the ball is snapped is guilty of being offside.

Look In: A pass play in which a receiver runs diagonally down the field and "looks in" (looks back toward the quarterback) for the pass.

Man-to-Man: Defense in which each player is responsible for one specific offensive player.

Messenger: Player who enters the game with a specific play from a coach.

Mid-Field: The 50-yard line.

Misdirection: Play in which the "flow" of the backfield misdirects the defense away from the path of the actual ball carrier.

Momentum: Enthusiasm working for a particular team. Momentum can "flow" from one team to another depending on the game, score, or players.

Mousetrap: Offensive play in which a defensive player is allowed past the line of scrimmage after the ball is snapped, then blocked (mousetrapped) so he may not reach the ball carrier.

Multiple Set: Offensive plays that can't be predicted. A variety of possible plays.

NFL: National Football League.

Nickel Defense: A pass defense in which the coaches insert an extra defensive backfield player—the fifth back; thus the name.

Nose Tackle: Defensive player whose position is in the center—the nose—of the line.

Numbering System: In football, numbers from 1–89 are assigned to particular positions, in this system:

1–19:	Quarterbacks
20–29 & 40–49:	Halfbacks
30–39:	Fullbacks
50–59:	Centers and linebackers
60–69:	Guards
70–79:	Tackles
80–89:	Ends and flankers

Nutcrackers: Drills or exercises during training camp in which coaches hope to find the toughest players.

Offside: A penalty when one player—offensive or defensive—moves across the line of scrimmage before the ball is snapped.

Off the Ball: How quickly a lineman can react when the ball is snapped.

On the Same Page: Everyone knowing what to do and going out on the field and doing it; being in sync with the playbook.

One-Back Offense: Formations that involve only one offensive backfield player, other than the quarterback. This back, usually the biggest and the most powerful, is used in running situations.

On-Side Kick: A kick that is deliberately short—10–15 yards, so that the kicking team can recover it immediately if the receiving team fumbles it.

Option: A play in which the quarterback has the choice, depending on the offense and the defense, of keeping the ball or passing it.

(To) Pay the Price: To play while injured as a condition of keeping the job; to receive an injury while playing; a masochistic macho image of

a football player who will play while hurt without complaining or without leaving the game. Considered a complimentary term by most players. Also applied to other contact sports.

Penalty: A loss of yards as a result of a foul.

Penetration: Moving into the opponent's part of the field, either defensively or offensively.

Period: A 15-minute segment of a 60-minute football game.

Piling On: Jumping on or tackling the ball carrier after the play is officially ruled ended.

Pit: Offensive and defensive linemen "in the trenches," at or near the line of scrimmage, are said to be "in the pit."

Pitchout: An underhanded toss of the ball from the quarterback to another player.

Place Kick: To kick a football when it is held motionless by a player or when it rests on a kicking tee.

Playbook: A team book of possible plays, offensive and defensive, that team members usually memorize during summer camp. Highly guarded by team coaches, even though most plays are no longer secret.

Plug a Hole: To fill a gap in the line, during a play.

Pocket: Protective screen of players around a quarterback, who is getting ready to pass. A quarterback who is "out of the pocket" has inadvertently outrun or been chased away from his protective cover of players.

Pooch Kick: Short- or medium-range kick, usually soft and high. Similar to an approach shot to the green in golf. A finesse kick. The pooch kicker may not be the same as a field goal kicker or a kick-off specialist.

Post Pattern: A pass pattern in which the receiver runs toward the goalpost.

Power Back (power runner): Offensive back who can gain yardage because of his superior size or speed.

Power Sweep: An offensive play in which the ball carrier runs around the end of the line of scrimmage and has at least two players ahead of him blocking.

Prevent Defense: Defense that will give up small yardage but that will not give up extensive yardage. Often, if time is running out, the defense will go into a prevent defense, willingly giving up small gains by the offense, but not yielding a touchdown.

Pulling Guard: An offensive guard who "pulls" away from the line of scrimmage when the ball is snapped, to help protect the quarterback or ball carrier.

Punt: A kick on fourth down by the offensive team when it cannot get a first down on the next play.

Quarter: Same as *period*.

Quarterback: Offensive team leader who calls the plays in the huddle, then takes the ball from the center to begin the play. He either runs with it, passes it, or hands it off to another.

Quarterback Sneak: Short yardage play in which the quarterback takes the ball from the center and follows the forward motion of the center, into the line of scrimmage.

Racehorse: Pass receiver with exceptional speed through the defensive backfield.

Read The Defense: To know what defensive men will do in a play because of their positions (or keys) at the line of scrimmage.

Read The Offense: To know what offensive men will do in a play because of their positions (or keys) at the line of scrimmage.

Red Dog: Same as *blitz*.

Red Shirt: To hold a player out for a season, usually to allow an injury to heal.

Referee: Senior official during a football game. He stands behind the offensive backfield before each play.

Reverse: A running play in which the ball carrier hands the ball to another back, running in the opposite direction.

Retire a Number: To honor a player by holding a ceremony and officially declaring that the number he wore during his playing days will never again be used by the team.

Rookie: Novice member of a football team. A player recently out of college on a professional team.

Roughing the Quarterback (Roughing the Catcher, Roughing the Kicker, etc.): Hitting the player unnecessarily hard, or after the play is over, perhaps with an intent to injure. Calls for a penalty if the officials see the incident.

Run to Daylight: Run to an open part of the field.

Running Back: Offensive ball carrier other than the quarterback.

Rushing: To gain yardage by running with the ball.

Sack: To tackle the quarterback for a loss.

Safety: Is scored when a ball carrier is tackled behind his own goal. A safety scores two points for the defense.

Sarah: Coaching code for a strongside formation or play.

Screen Pass: A pass that is thrown parallel to the line of scrimmage or a pass that is completed behind the line of scrimmage. Or, a pass that is thrown to a receiver who is screened (blocked) from the defensive by another offensive player.

Scrimmage: The line on which a play takes place.

Secondary: Defensive positions behind the line of scrimmage.

Shank a Kick: To miskick a ball so that it travels only a few yards (football equivalent of hooking a golf ball).

Shoestring Catch: To catch a football at the ankle (shoestring) level.

Shoestring Tackle: To tackle a ball carrier below the knees.

Shotgun: Offensive formation in which the quarterback stands to receive the snap a few (5–10) yards behind the center. This gives the quarterback slightly more time to find his receivers for a pass.

Shovel Pass: Pass that is thrown underhanded to a receiver.

Skirt the End: To run offensively around the defensive end.

Smurf: In the NFL, a "midget," that is, a player under 6 feet tall and under 180 pounds.

Snap: To start a play, the center throws the ball upwards between his legs to the waiting hands of the quarterback.

Soccer Kicker: To kick the ball with the instep of the foot, instead of with the point of the toe. Soccer kickers are said to have more accuracy than regular kickers. Soccer kickers are often Europeans who learned their technique by playing soccer first, then football.

Spear: To hit an opponent using the top of the helmet as a weapon. It is illegal and calls for a penalty when caught by the officials.

Special Teams: Players assigned to a kickoff team, for instance, or a prevent defense team or a nickel back team.

Spike: To energetically throw the ball down after a touchdown. Many players make a real show of spiking the ball. Too much spiking (or dancing) in the end zone after a touchdown is now a penalty.

Split the Uprights: To accurately kick an extra point or field goal straight through the goalposts.

Squib Kick: A kick that is hard to catch because it is wobbly or bouncing.

Straightarm: A defensive play in which the player uses a locked arm to thrust an opponent away from a tackle.

Strongside: The side of an offensive line having more players than the opposite side of the same line.

Student Body Right or (Student Body Left): A running play in which the entire team, plus coaches, cheerleaders, and trainers seem to be running in the same direction to protect the ball carrier. Established at the University of Southern California.

Stuffed: Same as *jammed*.

Stunting: Defensive formation in which players are out of their usual place, to fool the offense.

Submarine: To hit a ball carrier low.

Substitute: A player who is not a starter, sent in to play because another player has to leave the game. Also appropriate in other team sports.

Sudden Death: A period after the normal four quarters of play. If the game is tied at the end of regulation play, the game goes into sudden death and the first team to score wins. There is no additional play after a score in sudden death.

Suicide Squads: Kickoff and kickoff return teams in which individual players are assumed to sacrifice themselves for the team. Usually a thankless job, but a position in which a rookie can prove himself worthy of a permanent job on the team.

Super Bowl: The championship game of the National Football League. Played at various locations at the end of the regular season.

Sweep: Running play in which the offensive line swings toward a sideline and the ball carrier follows that protective wall.

Swing Pass: Short pass thrown by the quarterback toward the sideline.

Tackle: To stop a ball carrier and throw him to the ground.

Tailback: Running back in the offensive backfield farthest from the line of scrimmage.

Taxi Squad: Players good enough to keep on the team but not exceptional enough to use regularly. So named because an early professional team owner used them to man his fleet of taxi cabs to give them work and also keep them available for the team. Now used for any group of nonregular players.

T Formation: Offensive formation in which members of the offensive backfield are lined up parallel to the line of scrimmage and behind the quarterback. So called because the backfield formation looks like the letter T.

Three-Point Stance: Stance that the linemen assume before the ball is snapped. They have both feet on the ground, are crouched low to the ground, and have one hand touching the ground. ground.

Throw Into a Crowd: To throw toward more than one receiver. Usually a Hail Mary pass will be thrown toward a crowd.

Throw It Away: When a quarterback deliberately throws a pass over or past a receiver so that he will not risk having the pass intercepted.

Time Out: To stop the clock that marks the 60 minutes of the game.

Touchback: Occurs when a ball is dead off the field behind the goal line in possession of the offense, when the ball was downed or the ball carrier was downed by the defense. Different than a safety: A safety occurs on the field of play behind the goal lines; a touchback occurs *off* the field of play behind the goal line. The ball is put into play at the nearest 20-yard line.

Touchdown: Scores 6 points for the offensive team when the ball is carried or passed over the goal line.

Touch Football: Informal game in which the play is stopped when the ball carrier is touched with two hands of an opponent.

Trap: To allow a defensive player to cross the offensive line, then block him from the ball carrier once he has crossed into offensive territory.

Triple-Threat Player: Player who has the ability to run, pass, and kick the ball well. Because college and professional football is so complex, there are few triple-threat players. Most are happy to specialize in just one aspect of the game.

Turk: Nickname for assistant coach or other member of the coaching staff who has the job of telling players in training camp that they have been cut from the team. So named because of the image of a Turkish fighter with a broad sword.

Turn In: Pass pattern in which the receiver runs downfield then turns toward the middle of the field to catch a pass.

Two-Minute Drill: Special exercises to take advantage of the last 2 minutes before the end of the first half or before the end of the game.

Two-Minute Warning: Special warning given to each coach by the officials that there is 2 minutes left before the end of the first half or before the end of the game.

Two-Way Player: Player who can play offense and defense. Because of the specialization of football, there are as few two-way players as there are triple-threat players.

Umpire: Another key official during a football game.

Unbalanced Line: Offensive line that has an unequal number of players on one side of the center than on the other side.

Uprights: Vertical poles on the goal posts. Place kickers must kick extra points and field goals between the uprights to score.

Veer Offense: Complicated offense in which the quarterback can either: (a) run with the ball; (b) give it to the fullback; (c) run toward the sidelines and pitch to a running back; or (d) pass. The veer takes advantage of the fact that the defense may react quickly to one of these options, thus allowing the quarterback to quickly execute another of these four options. How to prevent the success of the veer? Down the quarterback behind the line of scrimmage before he gets a chance to execute the veer.

Wanda: Coaching code for a weakside formation or play.

Weakside: Opposite of strongside. The side of the offensive line with the fewest players from the center.

Wide Receiver: Formerly known as the split end, a lineman eligible to catch passes, whose position on the line of scrimmage separates him from the rest of the line.

Wild Card: Team eligible for playoffs in the National Football League that did not outright win its division race toward the Super Bowl.

Wishbone: Offensive formation in which the quarterback lines up behind the center and the three other backs are behind him; seen from

well behind the line and from above, the formation looks like a Y or like a chicken wishbone. The quarterback may keep the ball with two of the backs blocking ahead for him, or he may pitch out to one of them; similar in general respects to the option-style play of the veer offense.

X's and 0's: Chalkboard symbols for offensive and defensive players and strategy. It's a compliment to a coach if it is said, "He really knows his X's and 0's."

Zebras: Because of their black-and-white striped jackets, officials are sometimes called zebras (also true in basketball).

FRISBEE

Acceleration: Any technique used to add spin to a disc.

Aid: Any device such as a stick or thimble used to add spin to a disc.

Air Bounce: A throwing style in which the disc bounces off a cushion of air that builds up underneath it.

Backhand: A cross-body throw of the disc with the thumb on top of the disc and the fingers underneath.

Belly: The underside of a disc.

Blind: Any throw or catch performed while looking away from the disc or target.

Bobble: To mishandle or juggle a catch.

Body Roll: Any technique in which any part of the body is used for the disc to skip or bounce off of.

Bottom: Same as *belly*.

Break Tip: Any contact made with a disc in flight to alter its flight pattern or speed.

Brush: To accelerate the spinning action of a disc by slapping it on the side edge.

BTB: Behind the back.

BTH: Behind the head.

BTL: Between the legs.

Burbled Air: Turbulent, unpredictable air.

Catapult: To throw a disc with the fingers.

Cheek: Inside rim of a disc.

Co-oping: Two or more players sharing the same disc; usage similar to team play in other sports.

Cross-Body Throw: Any throw on the left for a right-handed player and vice versa.

Crown: Top of the disc.

Delivery: A player's complete throwing motion.

Dip: Any sudden drop in the flight of a disc.

Discwork: Any movement or motion to control a disc.

Drop: A missed disc catch that hits the ground.

Edge: Bottom surface of the disc rim.

Facing Stance: Any stance taken to the disc in which the thrower faces the target.

Flamingo: Any catch a player makes close to the ground, on one leg.

Floater: A throw that hovers in the air.

Frisbee: Trade name for a specific plastic flying saucer, now a generic term for all plastic flying saucers.

Frisbee Golf: A game played with discs similar to golf. In frisbee golf, players aim toward a large basket, instead of a small golf hole.

Gyre: A wobbling motion in a disc in flight caused by a bad throw, turbulent air, or a warped disc.

Hover: A throw in which the disc drops to the ground slowly, with little or no forward glide.

Lead: To throw ahead of another player who is running so that that player can catch the throw without breaking stride.

Lip: Outside rim of a disc.

Move: Any motion used to throw or catch a disc.

Nose: The leading edge of a disc in flight.

Siamese Catch: Any catch made by two (or more) players at the same time.

Slider: A throw that makes the disc skid across the ground.

Stability: The "flying properties" of a plastic disc.

Stall: Occurs during the flight of a disc when forward motion dies.

Tacking: When a disc holds its course without deviations across a wind.

Terminations: Any movement on the part of a player that stops the flight of a disc.

Tipping: To control the disc by repeatedly touching the underside of the disc.

Top: The upper side of a disc.

Trail: Any movement to catch a disc by grabbing the back edge as it passes the player.

Trap: To catch a disc with two parts of the body: both hands, hand and a leg, and so on.

Tricking: Performing disc routines.

Z's: The spin that a disc has in flight.

GOLF

Ace: Hole in one.

Action: To put spin on the ball.

Address: Correct body position before hitting the ball.

Approach: To hit a short- or medium-length shot to the green, with an iron.

Apron: Area immediately surrounding the green.

Away: Refers to the ball that is furthest from the cup, when more than one golfer is playing a particular hole.

Best Ball Tournament: Tournament in which the better score between members of a two-person team on each hole is used as the team score.

Birdie: One under par on a particular hole.

Bogey: One over par on a hole.

Bunker: Common name for a sand trap.

Caddy: Person who carries the golfer's clubs.

Can: To sink a putt.

Casual Water: Water on a course after a rainstorm; not part of a permanent hazard such as a pond or lake.

Course Rating: The difficulty of a particular course.

Divot: Ground cut up by the clubhead during a swing.

Dog-Leg: Hole that has a sharp bend to the left or the right from tee to green.

Double Eagle: Three strokes under par for any particular hole.

Driver: No. 1 wood, usually only off the tee.

Eagle: Two under par for a particular hole.

Fairway: Ground between the tee area and the putting green, excluding any hazards.

Flag: Banner on top of a metal pole inserted in the cup, to indicate the hole, to golfers at a distance from the green.

Fore: Signal shouted to indicate to those on the course that a golfer is about to take a stroke.

Foresome: Match in which two players play against two other players, or all four play against each other.

Green: Manicured grass area where each hole is located.

Hazard: In golf, any bunker, water (except casual water), trees, brush, or other natural obstacles.

Head: The part of the club that strikes the ball.

Hole: In golf, the hole is 4¼ inches deep and 4 inches in diameter. The hole may be anywhere on any particular green, and may be moved from time to time.

Hole High: An approach shot that is on the green as far as the hole, but to the right or the left.

Hole in One: A drive shot from the tee that hits the hole.

Hole Out: To sink a putt.

Home: The green.

Honor: The first person or the first team to drive from the tee is said to have the honor. Generally, those who have the honor are those who won the previous hole.

Hook: A shot that curves in flight from the right to the left, for a right-handed golfer.

Iron: A golf club with a metal lead, used for medium shots toward the green.

Leader Board: A billboard-size chart, generally located near the clubhouse, that shows the leader of a tournament. Lowest scores (below par) are at the top of the board, followed by par, then above par.

Lie: The position of the ball on the fairway or green.

Match Play: Competition in which the winner is decided by the total number of strokes taken for each *hole*. A team may win a *hole*, lose a *hole*, or halve a *hole* (take the same number as the opposition).

Medal Play: Competition in which the total number of strokes by a player is used in determining the winner.

Nassau: Another alternate method of scoring: one point for the first 9 holes, one point for the second 9, and one point for the entire 18 holes.

Open: A tournament that allows both amateurs and professional golfers to play.

Par: Average shot for a particular hole.

Penalty Stroke: One stroke added to the total for a violation of the rules.

Pigeon: Easy mark. Victim.

Provisional Ball: Ball played when a previous ball was hit out of bounds or lost.

Pulled Shot: A shot that is straight, but to the right of the green (or hole) for a right-handed golfer.

Push-Shot: A shot that is straight, but to the left of the green (or hole) for a right-handed golfer.

Putt: A delicate stroke on the green to roll the ball toward the hole.

Rough: Weeds or other natural hazards at either side of the fairway.

Shank: To hit the ball with the heel of the club.

Slice: A shot that curves from left to right for a right-handed golfer.

Storke Play: Same as *medal play*.

Summer Rules: Playing the ball as it lies anywhere on the course.

Tee: Small wooden peg that a ball is placed on before being driven.

Topping: To hit the top of the ball, thus causing it to roll along the ground without any loft.

Trap: A bunker, a sand trap.

Waggle: To wiggle the body, arms, or legs, when the golfer addresses the ball.

Wedge: Heavy club used for hitting out of sand.

Whiff: To miss the ball completely during a swing.

Winter Rules: To drop the ball for an advantage if it is in the rough during play.

Wood: A golf club with a wood head, used to hit distance shots from the tee.

GYMNASTICS

All-Around: Competition in which the gymnast must perform in the floor exercise, side horse, long horse, horizontal bar, parallel bars, still rings, and long horse.

Approach: To walk to the equipment, prior to the gymnastic routine. Similar to the approach in golf.

Balance: To maintain equilibrium during a routine.

Break: To stop to dampen the bounce of a trampoline.

Check: To slow or stop body revolutions during a trampoline routine.

Gainer: A backflip in which the performer lands ahead of the take-off spot.

Perfect Ten: Redundant phrase. Ten is the top score that any gymnast can receive.

Pommels: The curved iron handles of a side horse.

Spotter: Guard who stands beside a trampoline to catch the gymnast if he or she bounces or falls off the trampoline bed.

Vault: A leap or jump aided by the gymnast's hands.

HANDBALL & RACKETBALL

Ace: Serve that is untouched by an opponent; scores a point. Same usage in table tennis, tennis, badminton, and other sports.

Anticipation: The ability that a player has to guess where the opponent's shot will rebound so the player can be in a position to return it.

Avoidable Hinder: Intentional interference of one player by another. Penalty is the loss of a score or the addition of a score by the player who was hindered.

Back Court: The area behind the short line to the rear wall.

Backswing: Beginning motion to hit the ball. Similar usage as in a golf backswing.

Back-Wall Shot: A ball that is hit after it rebounds from the back wall.

Ball: In handball, the ball is 1 7/8 inches in diameter and weighs between 2/10 and 3/10 of an ounce.

Blocking: To hinder an opponent's shot by placing all or part of the body between the opponent and the ball.

Bolo Shot: A shot hit with the fist, underhanded (handball).

Bone Bruise: Deep bruise of the palm of the hand (handball).

Bottom Board: Lowest part of the front wall.

Bye: Tournament in which some favored players are allowed to progress without playing the first rounds.

Ceiling Serve: A serve that strikes the ceiling after it bounces off the front wall.

Ceiling Shot: A shot that is hit directly to the ceiling, then the front wall, then the floor, and then rebounds to the back wall.

Center Court Position: The middle of the court about 3 to 5 feet in front of the short line. Ideal position for offensive and defensive play.

Change of Pace Shot: Any shot that changes the tempo of the game, either faster than normal or slower than normal.

Consolation: Round of a tournament in which first-time losers face each other.

Control: The ability to hit a ball to any specific spot.

Court: A standard handball court is 40' by 20' by 20'.

Crosscourt Shot: A shot that is hit diagonally across the court.

Crotch: Any place where two surfaces meet: wall–wall, wall–ceiling, or wall–floor.

Crowding: Playing too close to the opponent.

Cutthroat: A game for three players in which two play against the server.

Dead Ball: Ball that is not in play.

Die: A ball that hits the front wall without much bounce.

Dig: To return a low shot before it reaches the floor.

Doubles: A game in which two players oppose two other players.

Error: The inability to return a playable ball.

Fault: Illegally served ball. Generally similar usage as in tennis.

Floater: A ball that travels so slowly that the opponent has time to set up a return shot.

Fly Shot: A shot that is returned before it hits the floor.

Forehand: Shot made from the same side of the body as the playing hand.

Front-and-Back: Doubles play in which one partner covers the front court and the other partner covers the back court.

Game: When 21 points are scored by one player or team.

Game Point: Point that will win the game for a player or team, if it is won.

Half-and-Half: Same as *side-by-side* play.

Hinder: To accidentally interfere with an opponent.

Hop: To put spin on the ball by snapping the wrist (handball).

IRA: International Racketball Association.

Inning: One complete round of play in which each player or each team has the opportunity to gain or lose the serve.

Kill Shot: A shot that strikes the front wall so low that it is unreturnable.

Lob: Ball that hits the front wall high then rebounds in a high arc toward the back wall.

Masters: In singles competition, players must be over 40 years of age; in doubles, one must be at least 40 and the partner at least 45 (racketball).

Match: Two out of three games.

Off-Hand: The left hand if the player is right-handed, and vice versa.

Pass Shot: A shot that is hit out of reach of the opponent.

Place: To hit the ball accurately to a particular part of the court.

Power Serve: A ball that is hit low off the front

wall and bounces toward a rear corner (hand-ball).

Ready Position: The stance taken by a player to receive a serve.

Receiving Line: A line 5 feet in back of the short line. Players waiting for the serve must stand behind this line until the ball is served.

Roadrunner: Player whose specialty is retrieving (racketball).

Run-Around Shot: A shot that hits one side wall, the back wall, and a second side wall.

Screen: Ball that passes too close to a player's body for it to be seen clearly by the opponent.

Seamless 558: Ball used for racketball. Ball is 2½ inches in diameter and weighs approximately 1.4 ounces.

(To) Serve: To put the ball in play.

Service Box: 18"-wide boxes at each end of the serving line. Nonserving partners must stand in one of these boxes while the other partner serves the ball.

Service Court: Area in which the ball must land after hitting the front wall.

Service Line: Line 5 feet in front of and parallel to the short line.

Service Zone: Where the server must stand when serving the ball.

Sharp Angle Serve: A shot that hits the front wall close to the floor and bounces at an angle to the right side wall and back toward the server.

Shooters: Players who rely on kill shots (racket-ball).

Short Line: Line in the middle of the floor from side to side halfway between the front and back walls. The serve must carry over this line from the front wall.

Side-by-Side: Doubles play in which partners stand side-by-side, as opposed to front-and-back.

Straddle Ball: Ball that moves between the legs of a player.

Straight Kill Shot: Ball that hits the front wall and returns on the same line.

Volley: Same as *fly shot.*

Wallpaper Ball: Ball that hugs the wall so closely that it is hard or impossible to return (racketball).

Winners: Kill shots (racketball).

HANG GLIDING

Aileron: Hinged panel at the rear of a wing that can be adjusted to tip up or down to control maneuvers in flight.

Airfoil: Wing or other surface shaped to obtain lift from the air through which it moves.

Airframe: The structural skeleton of a hang glider or aircraft.

Airspeed: Speed measured in miles per hour of a hang glider relative to the air that surrounds it.

Altitude: Height above mean sea level or above ground level, abbreviated as A.G.L.

Angle of Attack: The angle at which the air meets the forward tip of a wing.

Axis: Line of a plane. May be *longitudinal* (nose-to-tail); *lateral* (wingtip-to-wingtip); or *vertical* (bottom-to-top) of the aircraft.

Bank: To tip to one side.

Biplane: Aircraft with two wings.

Center of Gravity: Center point of the weight of a hang glider.

Chord: Length of a wing, measured from tip to back, or trailing edge.

Crab: To move through the air sideways to the wind.

Control Bar: The bottom end of a metal triangle suspended beneath the wing of a hand glider. The pilot holds this bottom end and uses it to control the flight of the flighter.

Dive: To descend steeply through the air.

Drag: Resistance through the air created by the hang glider.

Drift: To move sideways through the air.

Elevator: Hinged, horizontal tail surface of a hang glider that will force the nose up or down.

Empennage: All tail parts of a hang glider or airplane.

Fin: Vertical section of tail assembly.

Foot Launch: Take off accomplished by the pilot without mechanical aids.

Fuselage: Body of a hang glider.

G Force: The total force on the surface of a hang glider, measured in terms of the force of gravity.

Glide: To coast along the wind, in flight.

Glider: Motorless aircraft that depends on gravity and winds for flight.

Glide Ratio: Ratio of glide distance to height lost because of weight.

Ground Effect: A cushion of air under the wing when the glider is in flight close to the ground.

Ground Loop: To roll a hang glider end-over-end on the ground.

Ground Speed: The speed of a glider rated in miles per hour.

Hang Glider: An unpowered single- or dual-seated vehicle whose take off and landing capability is dependent on the pilot and whose flight characteristics are generated by air currents only.

Landing Speed: The rate in miles per hour of the landing.

Leading Edge: The front edge of a wing.

Lift: The upward or "carrying" capability of wing surface.

Mushy: Inadequate hang glider response to pilot control.

Logbook: Record of all flights.

Pancake: To fall to the earth flatly is "to pancake in."

Pitch: Nose-up or nose-down flying characteristics.

Porposing: A series of nose-up and nose-down maneuvers, resembling a swimming porpoise.

Prone Harness: Harness used to enable the pilot to lie flat in a hang glider.

Rogallo Wing: Triangular or V-shaped wing developed by Francis Rogallo.

Rudder: Hinged panel attached to the rear edge of the tail fin. Controls yaw in flight.

Soar: To fly without power and without loss of altitude.

Sink: To lose altitude in the air.

Sink Rate: The rate of descent.

Sock: Wind indicator used to indicate direction of winds on the ground.

Span: Length of wing, tip-to-tip.

Spin: Downward corkscrewing action.

Stability: Ability of an airworthy hang glider to fly in a controlled position if the pilot lets controls loose.

Stabilizer: Fixed horizontal tail panel.

Stall: Loss of air flow caused by an excessive angle of attack (excessive wing up or wing down).

Strut: Wing brace.

Stick: Control bar used to move ailerons and elevator.

Swing Seat: Suspension system that allows the pilot to sit upright to pilot a hang glider.

Tactile Flight: Flight control through the use of the senses. Opposite of instrument control in aircraft flight.

Trailing Edge: Rear edge of a wing.

Trim: The balance of a hang glider in flight.

Turbulence: Unpredictable and "bumpy" air currents.

Updrafts: Air currents moving up.

U.S.H.G.A.: United States Hang Gliding Association, official representative of the sport of hang gliding.

Wind Sheer: A sudden and dangerous "waterfall of wind" that often accompanies thunderstorms and that can knock small or large aircraft from the sky.

Wing Loading: The total weight of the hang glider and pilot divided by the total wing footage.

Yaw: To turn flatly on the vertical axis.

HORSE RACING

Allowance: A race in which horses are matched by age, sex, or money won and in which poorer horses are allowed to carry less weight.

Bug Boy: An apprentice jockey, one who has not won 40 races.

Chalk: The odds-on favorite to win—as in "the chalk horse."

Claiming: A race requiring owners to state their horses' values before the race. The horses then can be bought, or "claimed," for that price before the race.

Colors: Also called "silks" these are the distinguishing jackets and caps worn by jockeys.

Daily Double: A wager in which the player attempts to pick the winners of two races on the day's card.

Exacta (also called Perfecta): A wager in which the player attempts to pick the winner and second-place finisher in order.

Field Horses: Two or more horses grouped together for betting purposes. A bet for one field horse is a bet for all in that group.

Furlong: Either 220 yards or 1/8 mile.

Futurity Race: A race for 2-year-olds scheduled far in advance, sometimes before the horse is born.

Handicap: Weight added to superior horses to make a race more even.

Handicapper: The person who assigns the amount of weight to be added to a horse. More commonly, the term refers to someone who rates horses and their chances of winning.

In the Money: Gamblers can win on three positions: win, place, and show. The horse owners, however, take a portion of the purse for running fourth, or "in the money."

Irons: The stirrups. A jockey is said to be "in the irons" when he races.

Inquiry: A review of a race by track officials, who look for violations of racing rules.

Maiden: A horse that has not won a race.

Morning Line: Odds set by a handicapper on the morning of race day before bets are taken. Generally not considered a good basis on which to place a bet, because ratings are based on past performance only.

Objection: A complaint filed by a jockey as soon as a race ends; leads to an inquiry.

Player: Anyone who bets on horses.

Paddock: The enclosure where horses are saddled immediately prior to a race.

Pari-Mutuel: A system of odds-making determined by the bettors, based on the amount of money wagered on each horse. Means "between ourselves" in French.

Photo Finish: A race so close at the finish that a final decision is withheld until a photograph taken at the wire can be developed.

Post time: All horses are in the gates and ready to race. Signals the end of betting.

Purse: The prize money awarded in a race.

Quinella: Similar to the Exacta, but bettor wins no matter which of his two chosen horses finishes first and second.

Rail: The fence around the infield. A horse running the shortest route is said to be "on the rail."

Slow Track: Refers to a wet track, which slows down the horses.

Scratch: A horse that has been withdrawn from a race.

Sprint: A short race designed for fast horses with less endurance.

Stakes Race: A race for superior horses that have owners who must nominate them far in advance and must pay an assortment of high fees, assuring a big purse.

Steward: A race official, ususally on horseback, who monitors the race, horses, jockeys, and trainers for any improprieties.

Super Six: A wagering opportunity in which the player is asked to pick the winners of six consecutive races.

Tarmac: The paved outdoor viewing area near the finish line.

Thoroughbred: A specific breed of horse developed in England from the Arab, Turkish, and other breeds.

Tip Sheet: Any number of supposedly authoritative printed sheets bearing the names of horses given the best chances of winning.

Totalizator (or Tote Board): Big computer board that "totes" the odds on each horse and figures payoffs.

Trifecta: Wagering requiring player to pick first-, second-, and third-place finishers.

Win, Place, and Show: First, second, and third placers.

Wire: The finish line.

Wire-to-Wire: Refers to a horse that leads a race from start to finish.

Reprinted by permission of *The Dallas Times Herald*

ICE HOCKEY

Advance: To move the puck toward the goal.

Attacking Zone: Area of the opponent's goal.

Back Diagonal Pass: To pass to a teammate across the ice on a diagonal line and behind the passing player.

Blind Pass: To pass to a teammate without looking at that player.

Blue Line: Line that shows each team's defensive zone. Similar to the 25-yard line to the end zone in football.

Bodycheck: To use a player's body to stop an opponent. Generally the same usage as "block" in football.

Breakaway: To skate toward the opponent's goal with only the goalkeeper to beat for a score.

Center Zone: Area between offensive and defensive zones.

Check Back: To skate toward the player's goal to help the goalkeeper.

Clearing the Puck: Moving the puck away from the team's own goal.

Cover Up: To guard an opponent near a team's own goal to prevent a score or attempted score.

Defensive Zone: Area of the team's own goal.

Dig: To fight for the puck; to take it away from an opponent.

Drop Pass: To stop the puck and allow a teammate to pick it up.

Face off: When the puck is dropped between two opposing players to start or restart play.

Feeding: To pass the puck to a teammate.

Forechecking: To check an opponent in his zone of the ice.

Goal: In hockey, the goal is 4 feet high and 6 feet wide and made of net. When the puck enters the net, one point is scored.

Hat Trick: Three goals in one game by the same player.

Major Penalty: Five minutes (or more) in the penalty box.

Minor Penalty: Two minutes in the penalty box.

Neutral Zone: Center area of the ice from one blue line across the red line to the other blue line. Roughly similar to the area from the 25-yard line across the 50-yard line to the opposite 25-yard line in football.

Offside Lines: Same as blue lines.

Penalty Box: Seat off the ice that a player must sit in to serve time for a foul.

Penalty Time: Specified time that a player must spend in the penalty box.

Poke Check: To stab at the puck with the stick.

Red Line: Line that separates the ice into two halves. Similar to the 50-yard line in football.

Save: Defensive play by the goalie that prevents a score.

Uncovered: Offensive player left in front of opponent's goal without a defensive player blocking the goal.

Zamboni: Machine that rebuilds and smoothes the ice. To suggest that a player skates "like a Zamboni" would hardly be a compliment.

MOTOR SPORTS

Altered: Automobile or motorcycle that has been modified after it leaves the factory.

Apex: The point during a turn in which the car comes closest to inside edge of the corner. A tight apex usually means a good turn.

Back Off: To reduce speed.

Banking, Banked Turn: Turn that has a raised outer side to help driving control during the turn.

BHP (Brake Horse Power): Net power available at the output end of the engine. Brake refers to a dynamometer, a measuring mechanism, not the brakes of the car.

Bite: Tire traction on the road.

Block: Cylinder-containing unit of the engine.

Blower: Supercharged engine.

Blown: Two meanings: a blown engine may mean (a) an engine equipped with a supercharger, or (b) an engine that has a massive failure during a race.

Brick Yard: Common name for the Indianapolis 500.

Bucket Seat: Single seat contoured to body shape.

CC: Cubic centimeters. Engine displacement is usually referred to in CCs.

Camber: The angle at which the tires sit on the road.

Can-Am: The Canadian–American Championship for race car drivers.

Charger: Aggressive driver.

Chassis: Underside part of the car, usually consisting of frame and axles, brakes, wheels, engine, transmission, driveline, and exhaust components.

Chicane: Barriers added to an existing road to make the turns tighter or to add a turn or series of turns to an existing straight road.

Christmas Tree: Series of vertical lights that act as a "countdown" to the start of a drag race. There is a green "Go" light; a yellow "Warning" light, and a red "Foul" light, which means the driver jumped the start. The Christmas tress is positioned so that the driver can see it at the start of a drage race.

Circuit: Course used for racing in which drivers repeat the same route.

Closed Event: Race in which spectators or unauthorized drivers are not admitted.

Club Race: Race for members of a particular sports car club; usually refers to an amateur race.

Cool-Off Lap: Extra lap after a course that is driven at a slower speed than the race, to ensure that the engine parts cool slowly.

Cut-Off Point: A location before a turn at which point the driver takes his foot off the throttle and brakes the car for the turn.

Detroit Iron: Uncomplimentary term used by sports car elitists to describe most Detroit-made vehicles.

DNF: Did Not Finish. Started the race, but did not complete it.

DNS: Did Not Start. Entered the race, but did not start.

DOHC: Double Over-Head Camshaft cylinder head.

Dial In: To make adjustments to an engine. To "fine tune" it.

Differential: Gear-drive mechanism that transfers power from drive shaft to wheel. Differential refers to different speed of each wheel in a turn.

Displacement: Volume in cubic measure of a cylinder or engine.

Drafting: Same as *slipstreaming*.

Drift: Controlled slide, using engine power to keep the car on the road.

Driver's School: Special school for race drivers, using a closed race course to teach time trials, racing, and so on.

Esses: Winding curves on a race course.

ET: Elapsed Time. Drag racing term for a timed ¼-mile straight run.

Fire Suit: Protective fire-resistant suit worn by drivers.

Flags: Flags used in motor racing carry the following meanings:

- Black: Return to pits.
- Blue (motionless): Another car is following you closely.
- Blue (waved): Another driver is trying to pass you—make room.
- Checkered (black and white): Driver has completed the race.
- Green: Starts the race.
- Red: Stop—clear the course.
- White: Emergency vehicle on the course.
- Yellow (motionless): No passing, caution.
- Yellow with red stripes: Caution—oil on the course.

Flagman: Official responsible for displaying various flags to drivers.

Flat Four: Horizontally opposed four-cylinder engine (old VWs had flat four engines).

Flat Out: Racing at maximum speed.

Flat Six: Horizontally opposed six-cylinder engine (the Corvair had a flat six engine).

Flip: To turn over or to roll over.

Flying Start: A "running start," passing the starting line at race speed, or nearly race speed.

FoMoCo: Parts made by Ford Motor Company.

Formula: Regulations governing a race car that involve engine displacement, length and width, weight, size of fuel tank, and type of fuel used. In general, these are common formulas for race cars:

- Formula I: Race car powered by a non-supercharged V-8 or V-12 engine from 1,600 to 3,000 cc (up to 450 horsepower). Generally has a wedge shape, wide treadless tires, and 13-inch wheels. Has a self-starter and a transmission with four or five forward gears, plus reverse.
- Formula II: Slightly smaller version of Formula I car; has supercharged four-cylinder production engine of 1,300 to 1,600 cc. Generally more popular in Europe.
- Formula III: Racing car powered with a production engine up to 1,600 cc. Has specific limitations on air intake to the engine.
- Formula A: Similar to Formula 5000.
- Formula Atlantic: British car similar to American Formula B.
- Formula B: Formula car powered by a nonsupercharged production engine of 1,100 to 1,600 cc, powered by gasoline. Formula B is smaller and lighter than Formula 5000.
- Formula C: Formula car powered by an engine up to 1,100 cc.
- Formula F (Formula Ford): Formula car powered by a nonsupercharged 1,600 cc English Ford or Ford Pinto engine.
- Formula 5000: Formula car powered by an engine of 1,600 to 3,000 cc or a production V-8 engine of up to 5000 cc. No supercharging allowed. Must run on gasoline. Generally similar to the Formula I automobile.
- Formula V: Formula car that is powered by a Volkswagon 1,200 cc engine, gearbox, transmission, and wheels.

- Formula Super V: Formula car that is powered by a Volkswagon 1,600 cc engine and gearbox, and runs on gasoline.

Four Wheel Drive: Mechanism that allows power to be distributed to all four wheels.

Fuel Cell: Special rubber-like container for gasoline, built so that it will not be split open during a crash. Might be called a "safety gas tank."

Full Bore: Driving at maximum throttle.

Funny Car: Drag race car that has had unorthodox modifications. Generally, a funny car has a one-piece body, is powered by a supercharged engine and has a driver's compartment behind the engine. The engine is completely exposed, rear wheels are wide, and front wheels are bicycle-type. Often contains a parachute-stopping device.

FWD: Four Wheel Drive.

Getting a Tow: Same as *slipstreaming*.

Grid: Position for cars at beginning of race. Also refers to markings on a track.

Gymkhana: Competition for best time on a Chicane-type course.

Hairpin: Ultratight turn on a race course.

Hairy: Frightening occurrence.

Hemi: Car with hemispherical combustion chambers.

Hill Climb: Race for the best clock time up a prescribed hill course.

History: Same as *totalled*.

IFS: Independent Front Suspension.

IRS: Independent Rear Suspension.

Impound Area: Area where cars may be required to be taken after a race so that officials can inspect them to make sure they have satisfied entrance requirements.

Jet Dragster: Drag racer powered by a jet engine.

Lap: One complete circuit of a race course.

La Mans Start: A start in which drivers run from a starting line, get into their cars and drive away.

Line: The best path through a race course.

MPG: Miles per gallon.

Mags: Wheel rims made of magnesium; used because magnesium is very light.

MoPar: Parts made by Chrysler Corporation.

Mule: Unattractive prototype automobile, made for testing or demonstration purposes only, usually without finishing touches, such as chrome.

NASCAR: National Association for Stock Car Racing.

OHV: Over Head Valve.

Oval: Oval-shaped track.

Pace Car: Vehicle used to pace racers at the start of a race.

Paddock: Area near the track where cars are worked on. Usually similar to *pits*.

Pit: An off-the-track area where a driver can get gas, minor repairs during the race, tire changes, and advice from crew members.

Pit Lane: Lane that drivers use to enter and exit the pit area to and from a race course.

Pit Stop: Stop made during race for fuel, minor repairs, and so on.

Prototype: Test model of a new car.

Pump Fuel: Fuel that is "consumer quality," that is, that can be obtained at any gas station.

Qualifying Times: Trials used to determine race position based on best time during trials.

Rally: Race organized to test navigational skills of driver and navigator. Contestants are given a route map and must check in at various predetermined points to obtain their time from point to point. Best time wins.

Roll Bar: Safety bar that protects the driver in the case of a roll-over accident. Sometimes called *headache bar* for obvious reasons.

SCCA: Sports Car Club of America.

SOHC: Single Over Head Cam engine.

Shut the Gate: To block a driver's path during a race.

Slipstreaming: To drive slightly behind another driver during a race to take advantage of reduced air resistance.

Slingshotting: To drive around the lead car after slipstreaming.

Sports Car: Racing automobile with high performance characteristics.

Sporty Car: Car that is promoted as a sports car but because of mediocre characteristics, is really not a sports car.

Stand On It: To hold the throttle pedal completely on the floor.

Standing Start: Race start with all cars motionless, with drivers ready and engines idling.

Starter: Official who controls the start of a race.

Stock: Automobile that has not been modified since being delivered from the factory.

Street Legal: Automobile that has been modified for race use, but has to be remodified for safety (street) purposes.

Supercharger: Engine that has been modified by a mechanism that blows exhaust air back into engine at a higher rate than air entering the engine from the outside. Gives a power boost to the engine.

Tach (Tachometer): Meter that measures engine speed in revolutions per minute.

Time Trials: Laps on a specific course for the fastest speed.

Totalled: Completely wrecked.

Torsion Bar: Rod in a suspension system attached to prevent side slipping of the automobile.

Transaxle: Transmission and rear axle mounted as a single unit.

POCKET BILLIARDS
(Pool)

Action: Betting on games. *Fast action* is heavy betting.

A "G": One thousand dollars.

Angled: When the lip of a pocket prevents a straight shot from the cue to an object ball.

Army: Betting money: "I've got my Army with me."

Backer: Banker for a gambler. A nonplayer usually, who supplies betting money. The backer will usually cover all losses, but will take a percentage of the hustler's winnings.

Bank Shot: A shot against a cushion and then into a pocket.

Billiards (or three-cushion billiards): A game played on a table without pockets. Billiards is played with three balls, two white and one red. Each player (only two can play at one time) uses a white ball as a cue, and shoots to strike the other two. The cue ball must touch the cushions at least three times before striking the second of the two object balls. Billiards is a very difficult game that demands a thorough knowledge of table angles and English. Billiards is played for money much less frequently than pocket pool.

Break: The shot that opens the rack; the first shot of a game.

Bridge: The act of holding the table end of the cue stick between the index finger and the thumb. There are two kinds of bridges: the closed bridge, with the index finger circling the cue, or the open bridge, with the cue sliding down the fleshy part of the hand, between the thumb and index finger. The closed bridge is more accurate and preferred. Bridge also refers to the mechanical bridge, a device used to aid the player in making shots he couldn't normally make.

"C" Note: One hundred dollar bill.

Call Shot: A shot that requires the player to tell others which ball he or she intends to shoot into that pocket.

Carom: A rebounding shot of one or more balls.

Chalk: Dry lubricant for the cue tip. Without frequent chalking, scratches (missed shots) are likely.

Combination Shot: A shot in which the cue ball strikes one or more balls. The object ball finally is hit by one of the other balls. A "chain reaction" type of shot.

Con: The art of making a bet, that is, "to con." From the criminal's lexicon—"the con game."

Cue Ball: The plain white ball that is hit into the numbered balls.

Cue Stick: The instrument of the game. Sticks usually weigh between 15 and 21 ounces and average 55 inches long. Pros and hustlers prefer a heavier cue, usually 20–21 ounces.

Cue Tip: The leather end-piece of the stick that is chalked.

Cushion: The cloth-edge of the table rails.

Cut: To hit an object ball so that it will angle.

Draw or Reverse English: Stroking the cue ball below its center will cause it to "draw" (spin) back toward the player.

Dumping: A game that a hustler deliberately loses to fool spectators who have bets on the match. Not a common practice. No hustler wants a reputation as a "dumper."

English: The art of adding spin to the cue ball to make it swing to the left or right after hitting the object ball. An essential part of a position game.

Eight-Ball: Mostly an amateur's game. Players pocket either the low balls (numbered 1–7) or the high balls (numbered 9–15), then call the shot on the eight ball to win.

Follow Shot: Stroking the ball above its center will cause it to follow the object ball. Follow shots are also used in position games.

Fun Players: Lambs. Tournament winners. Amateurs.

Heart: Courage. "That player has real heart."

High Run: The number of balls consecutively pocketed before missing, in one game or tournament.

Hugging the Rail: Stroking action that will cause the cue ball or the object ball to roll down the rail along the edge of the table.

Hustler: A lion. A money player. Not an amateur.

Jaw: When the object ball hits the sides of the pocket and bounces back and forth without dropping, it is said to have "jawed."

Knife and Fork: Hustlers' eating and sleeping money. That is, "I have to remember my knife and fork" (remember not to bet it on a game and thereby risk going broke without money to eat with).

Kiss: See Carom.

Lamb: An innocent; an amateur.

Lemoning: Winning in an amateurish fashion or deliberately losing a game.

Lion: A hustler.

Lock-Up: A game that can't be lost, because of inferior opponents. A cinch.

Locksmiths: Hustlers who specialize in playing lock-up games.

Making a Game: Setting up some action or betting.

Massé: Extreme English on the cue ball. Perhaps the most difficult shot in the game. The cue stick must be held almost straight up and down.

Miscue: The scratch or miss shot, caused by inaccurately stroking the cue ball.

Natural: A simple shot; a lock-up shot.

Nine-Ball: A hustler's game, because it is fast and because bets can be made on individual balls, usually the five ball and the nine ball. Only the first nine balls are racked. They are pocketed in rotation (1–9) and the game is won by pocketing the nine. The nine can be pocketed on a good break shot or by shooting it from another ball, such as, cue ball to three ball to nine ball to pocket.

One-Pocket: Another hustler's game. Each player shoots into one corner pocket of the table.

O.P.M.: Other People's Money, which hustlers prefer to play with.

Position: The arrangement of the balls on the table. A good player can keep all balls on one-half of the table, thereby enabling him or her to shoot short shots and stay alive in the game.

Rack: The triangular arrangement of balls on the table before the game begins. Also refers to the wooden triangle used to form the balls into this shape prior to the game.

Rotation: Shooting the balls according to numerical sequence.

Run: Consecutively pocketing as many balls as possible (see *high run*).

Safe: To shoot so as not to leave your opponent room to shoot. "Playing it safe."

Scratch: A playing error in which the cue ball falls into a pocket. Some hustlers scratch deliberately to fake incompetence.

Setup: An easy shot. Same as "natural."

Shortstop: A player who can be beaten only by the top players.

Snookered: A bad position, that is, one in which the player can not shoot a straight shot.

Speed or True Speed: The player's ability.

Spot: To give away points or balls to one's opponent; that is, to handicap.

Stalling: Occasionally losing a game to keep an opponent betting.

Stroke: The act of hitting the cue ball. "To find my stroke," is to develop a good swing. The stroke is as important as the golfer's swing.

Sucker: The object of the hustler's attention; a loser.

Takedown: The amount of money won on the tables.

Weight: Points of ability. To "give away weight," is to give away points in a handicap game. "A heavyweight," is a top-flight player.

RUGBY

Advantage: Play may be allowed to continue after a rules violation if the fouled team gains territory or a technical advantage.

Cross-Kick: An attacking kick across the field of play.

Dead Ball: Play is dead when the referee blows the whistle.

Defending Team: Team on defense in its own half of the field.

Drawing Your Man: To make an opponent commit himself to attack the ball carrier, rather than to attack a player about to receive a pass.

Dribbling: To control the ball with short kicks, often with the shins or with the instep of the foot.

Drop Kick: The ball is dropped to the ground and kicked on the rebound. Similar to old usage in American football.

Drop-Out: Method of starting play from behind the 25-yard line, when an attacking team kicks, passes, or knocks the ball into the in-goal without a score. A drop kick is also used to begin play again from the center of the field after an unsuccessful conversion attempt.

Dummy: To pretend to pass the ball.

Falling on the Ball: A player may fall on the ball usually by turning his back to the opposing team. The player may not hinder the play by doing so and may not handle the ball in falling on it.

Field: A rugby field is 110 yards long from in-goal line to in-goal line; 75 yards wide.

Five-Yard Scrum: If a defending player kicks, passes, or knocks the ball out of the field of play or over his own goal line, the referee may call a scrum on the 5 yard line on the opposite side of the field from where the ball went into the in-goal area. The ball is given to the attacking team.

Fly Kick: A wild kick.

Foot-Up: Any member of the front row of either team in a scrum who advances either foot before the ball goes into play. A penalty results.

Foul: A foul results in rugby when a player strikes an opponent, tackles early or late, kicks or trips another player, or holds or pushes an opponent without the ball.

Free Kick: A kick for a score that may be made after a fair catch.

Game: Consists of two halves of 35 minutes each (40 minutes in an international game). There is a 5-minute period at halftime, but no player is allowed off the field.

Goal: A successful kick that results in 3 points.

Grounding the Ball: A player grounds the ball by falling on it or holding it on the ground to score a *try*, which is somewhat similar to a touchdown in American football.

Grubber Kick: A kick that bounces along the ground.

Hacking: To fly kick the ball.

Halfway Line: Similar to the 50-yard line in American football.

In-Goal Area: Equivalent to the area behind the goal line in American football.

Knock-On: This occurs when a player propels the ball toward the opponents dead-ball line. (Beyond the end zone in American football).

Line-out: A line formed by two teams parallel to the touch line waiting for the ball to be thrown in between them.

Locks: The second line of players in a scrum.

Lying Deep: In attack, the backs adopt a deep formation to allow themselves running room. Somewhat similar to the backfield formation in a kick return in American football.

Lying on the Ball: There is a penalty for stopping play by lying on the ball.

Lying Shallow: In defense, the backs adapt a formation closer to their opponents.

Mark: A fair catch from a kick or an intentional throw forward. The player must shout "mark." Similar to a fair catch in American football.

Maul: Action surrounding a player with the ball.

No-Side: The end of the game.

Number of Players: There are 15 on each side in amateur rugby, 13 in professional play.

Numbering System: There is no set numbering system for players as there is in American football.

Offside: This occurs when a player is ahead of the ball, when it was last touched by a member of his team. No penalty except if the player obstructs an opponent, plays the ball himself, or is within 10 yards of an opponent who is waiting to play the ball.

Penalty Kick: This is awarded to a team after a rules violation by the opposing team.

Penalty Try: If a try would have scored (in the opinion of the referee) without a foul, a team that has been fouled may attempt a try.

Place Kick: A kick made from a ball on the ground.

Player Ordered Off: Player has been thrown out of the rest of the game for a rules violation.

Punt: A kick made before it touches the ground. Similar usage to American football.

This is a tactical movement in rugby, but does not score.

Push Over Try: When the ball is in a scrum and the defending team is pushed into its own in-goal area, a push over try is scored when a member of the attacking team falls on the ball.

Referee: Sole rules judge on the field during play.

Ruck: A loose scrum.

Scrummage: A scrum is formed by players from each team prior to the begin of play. The front row of each team in a scrum is composed of three players. The ball is thrown into the scrum and the players fight to control the ball with their feet. When one team controls the ball, the scrum is wheeled and opened and field play begins.

Substitutions: Players may not be substituted in rugby except when they are injured so badly that they are unable to continue. In special matches or international matches, now more than two players may be substituted for medical reasons and the injured player may not return to the game.

Tackle: A player holding the ball may be tackled so the ball is on the ground or so that he is not free to continue play.

The Pack: The forwards.

Touch-Lines: Similar to sidelines in American football.

Touch-Down: Not a score. This occurs when a player downs the ball in his own in-goal area.

Try: A score in the goal area. Counts 4 points.

Up and Under: A kick within the field of play timed so that the kicking team is under the ball when it comes down.

Wheel: When the ball is in a scrum, the scrum turns and breaks open and the team possessing the ball advances.

SCUBA DIVING & SKIN DIVING

Air Embolism: Illness caused when a diver holds his or her breath during an ascent to the surface.

Anoxia: Insufficient supply of oxygen.

Aqualung: Trade name now synonymous with scuba.

Atmospheric pressure: Air pressure at sea level.

Ballast: Weights used to allow the diver to sink or maintain a specific depth.

Bends (Caisson Disease): Excess nitrogen in the body, that expands as the body ascends.

Buddy Line: Safety technique in scuba diving in which two divers are linked by a safety line.

Buoyancy: The upward force exerted by water or other fluids on a submerged or floating body.

Compressor: Machine that is used to fill air tanks for scuba diving.

Cousteau: Jacques Cousteau, famous explorer, co-inventor (with Emile Gagnan) of the Aqualung, in 1942.

Cylinder: Same as *tank*.

Decompression: To lessen the pressure underwater; to ascend to the surface.

Dry Suit: Waterproof rubber suit worn by scuba divers.

Embolism: Presence of air bubbles in the diver's circulation system.

Face Mask: Mask used by scuba divers and skin divers that allows a clear view under water.

Fathom: Approximately 6 feet.

Fins: Rubber froglike "feet" that aid in scuba diving and skin diving.

Flotation Gear: Life vests and other bouyant material that allow the diver or swimmer to float.

Frogmen: Scuba divers trained for underwater demolition, exploration, and so on.

Hyperoxia: Excess oxygen in body tissues.

Hyperventilation: Breathing rate higher than normal.

Mae West: Life jacket for use on the surface of the water.

Narcosis (Nitrogen narcosis): Illness that results when the diver dives too deep and nitrogen in the diver's air supply has a narcotic effect. Divers have been known to spit out their scuba mouthpiece and drown.

One Atmosphere: Air pressure at sea level; 14.7 pounds per square inch.

Recompression: Treatment for decompression illness by the use of a compression chamber that reduces compression levels at a safe rate.

Regulator: Mechanical device that governs the flow of air from the scuba tanks to the scuba diver.

Scuba: Stands for Self-Contained Underwater Breathing Apparatus.

Skin Diving: Diving, generally on the surface

of the water without scuba tanks, and usually with a snorkel.

Snorkel: J-shaped breathing tube that allows the skin diver to view under water (face down) while breathing surface air, without inhaling water.

Spear Guns: Pressure power guns used underwater to stun or kill marine life.

Tanks: Metal containers used to contain the scuba diver's air supply.

Tidal Volume: The volume of air that enters and leaves the lungs during normal breathing.

Toxic: Poisonous.

SHUFFLEBOARD

Court: A shuffleboard court is 6 feet wide and 52 feet long, with a concrete or terrazo surface.

Cue: A stick no longer than 6 feet, 3 inches, used to propel discs toward the target.

Dead Disc: Disc that remains on (or returns to) the court after striking an object other than a live disc.

Disc: Shuffleboard discs are made of wood and are 6 inches in diameter and ¾ to 1 inch thick. Four are red and four are black.

Foot of Court: The end opposite the Head.

Game: Based on 50, 75, or 100 points. Match play is best 2 out of 3 games.

Head of Court: The end where play begins to start a match.

Heistation Shot: A shot in which the player pauses momentarily during the shot. Illegal.

Round: Playing all discs from one end of the court is a round.

Scoring: One 10-point area, two 8-point areas, two 7-point areas and one 10-off area.

SKY DIVING
(Parachuting)

"A" License: Beginning license issued by the U.S. Parachute Association.

A.O.D.: Automatic Opening Device. A barometric- and speed-oriented mechanism that will automatically open the jumper's main parachute after a predetermined number of seconds (CAP-3) or will automatically open the jumper's reserve parachute at a minimum safe altitude (Sentinel). Basic Safety Rules (BSRs)

suggest outfitting all novice jumpers with Sentinels on their reserves.

A.S.O.: Area Safety Officer, in charge of safety requirements and minimum safety standards for several area drop zones or clubs.

Accuracy: The art of free-fall jumping in which competitors aim for a target disc. Expert accuracy jumpers can hit the disc time after time; misses are usually measured in cents in competition. *Style* and *accuracy* are slowly fading in popularity in favor of *RW* and *Sequential RW*.

Altimeter: Mechanical device that automatically gives the jumper a readout of actual height above ground. Altimeters are getting smaller and smaller. They are now sold to fit on the wrist, strapped to the chest strap of most parachute harnesses, or worn on the top of a chest-mount reserve. Altimeters measure in thousands of feet or in meters.

Apex: The top of a parachute.

Arch and Count: Basic student learning technique and position. The arch prepares the student for free-fall and the count prepares him for a delay before opening his parachute.

Assist Pocket: A pocket built into the top of a *sleeve* that catches air during deployment and aids in proper deployment of the sleeve.

"B" License: Second license issued by the U.S.P.A.

B.S.R.s.: Basic Safety Rules (Regulations). Rules, laws, and guidelines issued by the F.A.A., U.S.P.A., and local officials governing jumping.

B 4, B 12: Surplus parachutes, modified for sport use.

Backloop: Back flip done in free-fall. Completion of backloops, front loops, and barrelrolls are requirement for the U.S.P.A. "C" license and are highly recommended for good RW jumping.

Backpack: The main parachute, worn on the back and the reserve on the chest, as opposed to the *piggyback* or *pigrig*, a tandem combination of the main and reserve, both worn on the back.

Bag Deployment: Deployment of the main parachute from a bag, similar in size and shape to a knapsack, as opposed to a sleeve deployment. A bag will usually, although not always, allow a parachute to be packed smaller and tighter than a sleeve.

Barrelroll: Side roll, to the left or right, done in free-fall. Also a requirement for the class "C" license and good RW techniques.

Base: The "anchor" position in any relative work formation. The base is caught in free-fall (*pinned*) by the second, or pin jumper. A good base-and-pin combination is necessary to good fast stars. Without a stable base-and-pin the rest of the formation may be sacrificed.

Base Jumping: Skydiving from an altitude high enough to be reasonably safe, but without an airplane or helicopter (*without any aircraft*). The sky diver may jump from a skyscraper (*Building*), TV *A*ntenna, a bridge (*Span*), or a natural height such as a cliff (*Earth*). Not for the inexperienced. Jumpers usually face arrest if they jump from office buildings or other such "non-jumpable" facilities. Has nothing to do with "base-and-pin" RW jumping.

Baton Pass: In the earliest days of RW jumping, a baton pass between two jumpers in free-fall was considered the ultimate achivement. Now no one bothers with this; everyone goes to four- or eight-man or larger stars.

Batwings: Rigid or semirigid extensions on the jumpsuit arms and legs. Because rigid batwings made it impossible for the jumper to bend his or her arm and pull the ripcord, batwings were judged suicidal and outlawed years ago. Not to be confused with underarm additions to the jumpsuit that are cloth and flexible.

Beech: Twin Beech aircraft. Beeches and other aircraft capable of carrying 8, 10, or 12 jumpers (or more, in the case of aircraft like the SkyVan and the DC-3) made RW jumping possible.

Beer Run: In many parachute clubs, the achievement of some individual goal—first free-fall, first two-man, SCR jump, first ride under a high performance canopy, or other achievement—means that the participant buys beer for everyone; sometimes beer to drink, sometimes beer to be showered over the jumper in question. Requirements vary with each parachute club. It's a rare jumper who hasn't had to buy beer for everyone sooner or later.

Bells: Jumpsuits with bell-bottomed sleeves and legs. The bells flare out in free-fall like the skin of a flying squirrel and allow the jumper greater capability for falling faster or slower and approaching a star with greater accuracy.

Blown Star: Free-fall star formation broken by a jumper who approaches the star too fast or too hard.

"Bomb Out": Unpoised exit out the door of a jump plane. Mass exits during RW jumps are usually bomb outs.

Breakaway: See *cutaway*.

Break-Off Altitude: The altitude at which jumpers abandon RW jumping and get clear of each other for opening. With large stars (say 40 or 50 jumpers), break-off for some may well be as high as 5,000 feet.

Bungee: Heavy elastic bands that surround the container. When the sky diver pulls his or her ripcord, the pins and cones separate, the bungees pull the sides of the container apart, and the pilot chute emerges to begin the deployment sequence. Spring-loaded pilot chutes would probably emerge without the aid of bungees, but most old-style backpacks employ two or three bungees to ensure that the pilot chute emerges.

Butterfly Snap: Wide, butterfly-shaped flange used to connect the chest reserve parachute to the main harness.

Butt Strike: A classic fall in which the jumper hits the ground tailbone first rather than feet first. May cause temporary injury to tailbone, but is usually not serious. Jumpers who land with a butt strike in front of *whuffos* usually injure their pride most of all.

"C" License: Third license issued by the U.S.P.A.

C.S.O.: Club Safety Officer, who ensures safe jumping at a particular sport parachute club or drop zone.

Calendering: A process of treating fabric so that threads in the fabric are compressed and thus, less air gets through the fabric. A tighter weave results.

Canopy: The fabric. The umbrella. The parachute. Does not usually include lines, risers, or capewells.

Canopy Assembly: The parachute, sleeve, pilot chute, lines, sleeve retainer line, and sleeve. Everything ready to be packed into a container and harness.

Canopy RW: Relative work in which parachutists "fly" two or more canopies. The upper parachute of a two-man *canopy stack* may fly with his feet entwined in the top of the canopy below him. Usually, although not always, attempted with square parachutes.

Canopy Release: Mechanism that will release a main parachute so that a parachutist may deploy a reserve. Formerly all metallic, although modern state-of-the-art releases may be velcroed fabric.

Capewell: Canopy release made by the Capewell Manufacturing Company. Generic term for all canopy releases is "capewell."

Caterpillar Club: Club for all pilots who had to make a parachute jump to save their own lives in early aircraft. Charles Lindbergh was a member. Presumably named because of the lowly caterpillar that produced the silk used for early (pre-World War II) parachutes.

Center: A commercial parachute business that rents gear, sells supplies, offers the first jump course, and offers aircraft for RW jumps. Comparable to a ski center.

Center Pull: Reserve parachute harness with the ripcord centered, neither on the jumper's left nor right.

"Cents": Centimeters away from dead center, a nearly perfect score in accuracy jumping, as in "I had a three-cent jump last time."

Cessna: Principal aircraft for jumping. Cessna aircraft make up 85% of the jump aircraft used for beginning and novice parachutists.

Chuting Up: The act of putting on and checking one's parachute gear prior to boarding the aircraft.

Clear-and-Pull: Five second (or less) free-fall delayed opening. Same as *hop-and-pop*.

Clock: Before general use of the altimeter, parachutists used a stopwatch to gauge time and height in free-fall. A jump from 12,500 feet to an opening point of 2,500 feet was a *60-second-jump*. Because of the clocklike face, altimeters are now often called *clocks*. Sky divers who formerly used both an altimeter and a stopwatch now generally use only the altimeter. timeter.

Cloverleaf: Ripcord handle with general shape of three-leaf clover.

Cone: Cone-shaped piece of hardware, pierced to allow a pin to be inserted. The *pin-and-cone* lock the parachute pack closed. When the ripcord is pulled, the pins pull out of the cones, allowing the container to open and the sleeve or bag to emerge, thus beginning the development sequence.

Conference: Multistate subdivision of the United States for administrative purposes, by the U.S. Parachute Association.

Conical: One type of reserve parachute, usually 26 feet in diameter.

Connector Links: Metal hardware that connects the risers and the suspension lines.

Container: The part of the parachute pack that holds the parachute. The container is joined to the *harness*, which is fitted to the parachutist.

Controlled Air Space: The sky above Air Force bases, cities, and other areas where parachuting is generally not allowed.

Control Lines: Same as *steering lines*.

Conventional Rig: Parachute system with an old-style, chest-mounted rig is considered conventional. New rigs are pigrigs.

Crabbing: Steering a parachute sideways to the wind for accuracy in landing. If the wind is north-to-south, the parachutist will crab by facing east or west.

Cross Connector Links: A set of lines connecting the risers on some reserve parachutes.

Cross Pull: A ripcord that is across the body from the hand and arm used to pull; that is a cross pull for a right-handed parachutist would be a ripcord on his left side.

Crown Lines: Lines across the apex of the ParaCommander or other similar parachute. Used to create tension during packing and help straighten the apex.

Cutaway: The act of activating the capewells to jettison a malfunctioning main parachute so a reserve may be deployed without opening into the main. The parachutists' first cutaway is usually an awesome and memorable occasion.

"D" License: An advanced parachuting license.

D Rings: Metal rings, shaped like the letter "D" to which the chest-mounted reserve is attached.

DC-3: The Douglas workhorse of World War II, still in operation on some drop zones.

DL-7: Specific modification in which the steering modifications look like the letter "L" (there are two) and are seven panels apart.

D.O. Jump: Delayed Opening. Free-fall of 10 seconds or more.

DZ: Drop Zone. Where parachuting and skydiving is permitted.

Data Card: Card carried inside the reserve container providing the name of the owner, type of canopy, and particularly, when the reserve was last packed and by which rigger.

Dead in the Air: A jumper without horizontal speed; one who is simply moving down. Can be compared to a stalled ship that is "dead in the water."

Delay: Any free-fall skydive in which the jumper opens his own parachute after leaving the jump plane. Delays are usually 10 seconds, 20 seconds, 30 seconds, 45 seconds, 60 seconds, and over 60 seconds.

Delta: A free-fall body position in which the jumper's head and torso are lower than the legs. This allows the jumper to move diagonally downward and forward through the sky. RW jumpers who wish to become expert in their sport must master the *Delta* and *Track*.

Demo Jump: Any jump made off the usual drop zone, for spectators; usually at a county fair, circus, or other similar event. Only qualified jumpers can make Demo jumpers because of the added hazard of roads, power lines, buildings, spectators, and other obstacles.

Deployment: The act of the canopy opening after the jumper pulls his or her ripcord.

Deployment Bag: An alternative to the sleeve.

Dirt Dive: Rehearsal by all jumpers of a planned RW jump on the ground at the DZ.

Disc: Target for accuracy jumpers.

Dive: A head-down position used to catch a star or other formation. Also refers to the *jump*.

Docking: The art of approaching a star and entering by breaking the grip of two jumpers previously in the star, and thus widening the circle, or completing the formation, if not a round star.

Door Exit: Exiting the aircraft at the door, rather than on the strut.

Dope Rope: See *static line*. Uncomplimentary term.

Downwind Landing: Landing the parachute in the same direction as the wind is blowing increases the parachutist's landing speed. Not usually recommended.

Dummy Ripcord: Handle with a colored "flag" attached. Novice jumpers must make several good, precise dummy ripcord pulls before they can graduate to free-fall jumping. The dummy ripcord pull occurs when the parachutist is still on the static line.

Dump: To pull the ripcord and begin the development sequence, as in "I forgot where I was and dumped at 5,000 feet."

Exhibition Jump: Same as *demo jump*.

Exit: To leave the aircraft; may be either a *poised exit* or *bomb out*.

Expert: Sky diver with a "C" or "D" license.

F.A.I.: *Federal Aeronautique Internationale*; international governing body that controls international sky diving, hang gliding, soaring, and other sky sports. The U. S. Parachute Association licenses sky divers in this country on behalf of the F.A.I.

F.P.S.: Feet-per-second.

Field Packing: Immediate rolling or stowing the canopy in the pack for the trip back to the DZ, in the case of a missed spot or for packing later, if the parachutist wishes to repack at home.

Flake(verb): To *flake a parachute* is to fold the panels for packing into the container, prior to jumping. A *flake* (noun) is a psychologically unreliable person to jump with. Most every DZ has its own local flakes.

Flare/Flarepoint: Point at which the jumper ends a dive and raises his head to approach the formation.

Flat Circular: Particular type of reserve canopy.

Flat Spin: An uncontrolled spin, caused by inadequate body position and worsened by centrifugal force. Usually encountered by novice free-fall jumpers. If not stopped in time, can lead to blackouts and possible death.

Flat Turn: Controlled turn. Jumpers in free-fall can turn left or right by using their shoulders, arms, and legs like rudders.

Flight Line: Where the jump planes and other aircraft are fueled. No place to pack or dirt dive.

Floater: An RW jumper who, because of weight or jumping ability, exits *before* the base and pin (often by hanging on the edge or outside of the aircraft door) and *floats* (waits) for the base and pin to establish the beginning of the formation.

Flotation Gear: Used when a DZ is dangerously close to a body of water deep enough to drown in. Flotation gear comes in a variety of sizes and shapes, but is usually kidney-shaped or basketball-size inflatable balloons. Some jumpers believe that water gear that size is un-reliable in keeping an adult afloat for any length of time.

Flyer: RW jumper who exits the aircraft last (or nearly last) and has to dive considerable distances to reach the base and pin, substantially lower than he was on exit.

Frappe: To *go in*, a fatality.

Frappe Hat: Lightweight leather hat worn by RW jumpers. Nonrigid. Officially not recommended for novice jumpers.

Free-Fall Jump: A delay of 10 seconds or less. More than 10 seconds is a *delayed opening* jump.

Frog: Basic body position in free-fall. The body is relaxed and this is modified stable position. The frog is an accepted position for jumpers past the novice class. The head is slightly raised, chest slightly raised, arms bent at 45 degree angles. May be tightened into more compact position for greater vertical descent. So called because the basic position looks slightly like a frog at rest.

Front Loop: Front flip in free-fall. Must be mastered for a class "C" license.

Funneled Star: Star that breaks apart and falls into its own center.

Glide Angle: The angle in which the parachute moves forward or the angle in which the parachutist approaches the target in accuracy jumping.

Golden Knights: Nickname for the U.S. Army parachute exhibition team, headquartered at Fort Bragg, NC.

Grip: Hold that the jumper has on another jumper to cement a formation. A *double grip* is a tandem grip by two jumpers on each others' arms, legs, or torsos.

Hand Track: A method of moving forward in the air by vectoring air with the arms and hands. Usually an ineffective way to build or sustain horizontal speed toward the objective.

Hard Pull: Ripcord pull that takes more than normal effort (more than about 22 lbs. pressure). Packing problems usually account for hard pulls. A claim of a hard pull by a novice free-fall jumper is often attributable to unfamiliarity with the gear.

Harness: The part of the parachute system that the jumper tightens to form a cradle for his body. Usually the harness attaches at the chest,

legs, and lower belly. The F.A.A. issues regulations regarding the strength of webbing used in the harness. A tight but comfortable harness lessens opening shock; a loose harness distorts opening shock and may cause injury to the jumper, especially in the groin.

Hazards: Anything that can cause injury or death to the jumper. Notably, large and deep bodies of water, electrical wires and power lines, buildings and other obstructions, man-made and natural.

Helmet: Required by all jumpers. Many RW jumpers are using hockey helmets and frappe hats instead of the usual rigid motorcycle helmet. Old cliché and rule of thumb: "If you have a $5 brain, use a $5 helmet."

Hesitation: Deployment sequence slower than the usual 1½ to 3 seconds. Hesitations are usually caused by the failure of the pilot chute to clear the jumper's back quickly enough.

High Performance: Usually defined as a ram-air or wing-type parachute. Rates of forward speed for the three basic chute types are: rag chute or cheapo, up to 7 miles per hour forward; ParaCommander or PC-type, up to 17 mph; wing-type chute, 23 mph and faster.

Hockey Helmet: Used by RW jumpers, who think they get a better "feel of the air" with a lightweight helmet. Officially not recommended for novice jumpers.

Holding: Facing the wind, under canopy. If the prevailing wind is coming from the north at 10 mph and if the jumper is using a canopy with a "built-in" forward speed of 10 mph, facing into the wind will give him a speed of zero, thus he is holding. Turning with the wind or *running*, would, in this case, give him a forward speed of 20 mph (wind speed plus built-in speed of the parachute).

Hop-and-Pop: Same as *clear-and-pull*. An exit and free-fall of less than 10 seconds. Usually 5 seconds or under. The jumper *hops* off the step or door of the aircraft and *pops* open his parachute.

Hypoxia: Lightheadedness, giddiness, lack of motor control and reasoning ability caused by lack of oxygen to the brain. Jumpers above 12,000 feet (mean sea level) should be aware of the problems and potential dangers of hypoxia. The F.A.A. has set guidelines regarding use of oxygen at high altitudes.

Inboard Pull: Ripcord handle that is inside the left or right shoulder, rather than on the outside of the harness.

Instructor: Person who has passed all qualifying tests offered by the U. S. Parachute Association and is thus qualified to teach the first jump course and to instruct novice jumpers.

Intermediate Canopy: Paracommander or PC-type parachute.

I/E: Instructor/Examiner. Qualified by the U.S.P.A. to certify instructors.

Jumper: Informal slang for all sky divers.

Jumpmaster: Qualified leader in an aircraft full of static line or novice parachutists. The jump-master will decide the jump run, coordinate it with the pilot, decide on the exit point and generally take command of the aircraft, subject to the flying decisions of the pilot. A *jumpleader* acts as leader in an aircraft full of expert jumpers.

Jump Run: Straight and level flight at the correct altitude toward the exit point. The jump-master may, during the jump run, offer course corrections to the pilot.

Keel Turn: A turn in free-fall using a leg as a fulcrum.

Kicker Plate: An inexpensive aluminum "pie dish" that is used to seat the reserve pilot chute. The kicker plate is jettisoned when the reserve is opened. Some jumpers with quick reflexes and even quicker presence of mind are said to be able to catch the kicker plate in mid-air as the reserve opens.

L/D (Lift to Drag) Ratio: The relationship between the lifting characteristics of the parachute as opposed to the resistance by air on the forward speed of the canopy and the drag of gravity. Applied in generally the same way to airplanes.

Legal Age: Usually 18 to parachute, but may vary by locality. Check with your local DZ.

Lift: An airplane load of parachutists. As in, "I've signed up for the next Beech lift."

Line-Over: A malfunction in which one (or more) suspension lines has looped over the canopy.

Load: Generally same as *lift*.

Lobster Tail: Color combination seen on many ParaCommanders and other similar canopies. Front and side panels are one color, back panels a contrasting color, thus making the canopy appear like a lobster tail.

Logbook: Record book kept by all serious jumpers. The log will usually list all jumps in sequence, and has space for date of jump, location of the jump, aircraft type, jump type (static line, free-fall, or delayed opening), altitude, delay in seconds, total free-fall time, distance from target, wind speed, parachute type, reserve type, maneuvers during jump (four-man RW, eight-man RW, etc.), comments, and a space for a signature by a licensed parachutist, a jumpmaster, or instructor who witnessed the jump, or the jump pilot. New RW logbooks have space to diagram each jump. Logbooks must be kept for licenses, qualification of 12- and 24-hour free-fall awards, 1,000 jump awards, and other qualified and earned ratings.

Loft: Rigger's shop, where parachute repairs and sales are made. Lofts must maintain certain standards as required by the F.A.A.

MA-1: A 36" spring-loaded pilot chute. Used on ParaCommander and other similar parachutes and on many standard backpacks. The new "throw-away pilot chutes" are rapidly replacing the spring-loaded pilot chute.

Mae West: Malfunction caused by a suspension line over the canopy. So called because the parachute looks like a large bra, instead of like a round canopy.

Main: Principal canopy, as opposed to the reserve.

Malfunction: Any problem with the main canopy that may require a cutaway and deployment of the reserve. Malfunctions come in two types: A *total* malfunction occurs when the main parachute does not come off the jumper's back. Often called a *pack closure*. A *partial* malfunction may be either a *streamer*, which occurs when the sleeve deploys but the parachute does not emerge from the sleeve, or a *Mae West*. If the jumper has a total, he activates his reserve; if he has a partial, he does a cutaway, using his capewells and then activates his reserve. Failure to cutaway may mean that the reserve tangles with the partially open main above him, thus offering the jumper a nearly zero chance of safe recovery and descent.

Manifest: To sign up a complete load or lift of jumpers. Many jump centers require a complete manifest and tickets before jumpers can board the aircraft.

Mass Exit: In large-star RW, a nearly simultaneous exit, in which all the jumpers fall out the door like a line of dominos. Mass exits are an art; the best stars are put together when the mass exit is tight.

Modification: Any change in the basic characteristics of a parachute made by the factory or by a qualified rigger. Modifications may be a removal or change in a parachute panel, or change in the suspension or steering lines. Only qualified riggers and parachute factories are allowed to make major modifications. The F.A.A. has issued guidelines about which types of modifications may or may not be made outside the factory.

NB-6, NB-8: Surplus parachutes, Navy issue.

Night Jump: Officially described as a parachute jump made from at least 5,500 feet, 1 hour after official dark until 1 hour before official dawn.

Novice Jumper: One who has made one or more parachute jumps but not yet qualified by a class "A" license.

O.D.: Olive drab. The color of most surplus parachutes (no one in his or her right mind would buy a new parachute in olive drab).

"On the Step": Novice static line or novice free-fall student poised on the step of a Cessna or other similar jump plane, ready for the "Go" from his jumpmaster.

"On the Wrists": In a star and flying with other "skygods."

Opening Altitude: Altitude when the jumper should have a good canopy over his head. Usually this is 2,500 to 2,800 feet above ground level. Could be higher for mass jumps—large star attempts.

Open Modifications: Modification not covered by mesh. Open modifications are potentially hazardous because a pilot chute may entangle through the modification and cause a partial malfunction.

Opening Shock: The quick stop that the jumper comes to when the parachute deploys fully. The velocity goes from 120 mph at terminal to 10 mph within 2 or 3 seconds as the parachute opens. Opening shock used to be a major problem in military jumping, but since the advent of new generations of gear since the late 1940s and early 1950s, opening shock is no longer a real problem, although some jumpers are prone to complain about it. Faulty body po-

sition (head down) may lead to a hard opening shock when the harness flips the jumper into an upright position.

Outboard Pull: The ripcord handle under the left or right shoulder blade, but outside the edges of the webbing, rather than inside, over the jumper's chest.

Out-of-Date: Reserve that needs to be repacked because it is past the deadline for legal use. U.S. Parachute Association members now need to repack every 120 days.

Oxygen: Needed for high altitude jumps. Consult your A.S.O. or drop zone operator for specifics in your locality. The F.A.A. sets guidelines for oxygen use by high altitude sky divers.

PC: ParaCommander. Since 1964, when it was first introduced, the ParaCommander has been the most popular and generally best received parachute in sport parachuting.

P.L.F.: Parachute Landing Fall. The best way to encounter the ground. The P.L.F. is taken with the legs together, knees bent, arms and hands in. The jumper is prepared to roll sideways (never straight forward onto his face or straight back, which may cause a whiplash). The jumper takes the ground shock on the side of his legs, side, shoulders, and does a complete roll, if necessary. The P.L.F. is elementary and necessary; the *stand-up* is a landing in which the jumper takes all the ground shock in his legs. It sometimes feels as if the jumper's knees are going through his spine and skull. The P.L.F. and stand-up are generally approved methods, the alternative is a *crash-and-burn*, in which the jumper encounters the ground with other parts of his or her anatomy, not at all gracefully and often painfully.

P.O.D.: Pack Opening Device. Similar to a *bag* system of packing and deployment.

Pack (Noun): *The pack* is the jumper's complete parachute system; *to pack* (verb) is to flake and stow the parachute to make ready for jumping.

Packing: The act of flaking the parachute, stowing the lines and closing the container, to make the equipment jump-ready.

Packing Card: See *data card*.

Packing Mat: Protective canvas, plastic, or other material used to protect the parachute from dirt, oil, or anything else while packing on the ground.

Packing Table: Protective table used when conditions are not suitable for packing on the ground. Some DZ's make packing tables from old diving boards, which are the right width; Several dovetailed together will make a packing table the right length.

Panel: One portion of a parachute. Parachutes have different shaped panels for different portions of the parachute.

Pap: Short for Papillon, a Fench-designed parachute similar to the ParaCommander.

Parachute: From the French words *para* (to guard against) and *chute* (to fall): Thus parachute means literally "to guard against a fall."

Parachutist: A jumper who has achieved a Class "A" license. A free-fall jumper. In the eyes of the public, *parachutist* and *daredevil* are still synonymous.

Pass: Straight and level flight at the right altitude toward the exit point. One aircraft may have multiple passes at various altitudes: "Give me one pass at 2,500, one at 4,500, and one at 7,500 on this lift," the jumpmaster may say to the pilot.

"Peas": Target for accuracy jumpers usually made of *pea gravel*, plastic fiber, sawdust, or other similar material.

"Pencil-Packing": To repack a reserve parachute illegally by simply changing or adding a new "date of repack" to the data card.

Pigrig: Tandem main-reserve parachutes worn on the jumper's back. The Wonderhog and other similar systems are the latest "state-of-the-art" in pigrigs. The front reserve is quickly becoming passé in sport parachuting because of increased bulk and inferior flying characteristics.

Pilot Chute: Small parachute that leaves the parachutist's container first. The jumper's weight pulling against the fully deployed pilot chute pulls the rest of the assembly out of the container and off the jumper's back. In England, the pilot chute is sometimes called the *Extractor* chute.

Pilot Error: In aviation, any crash, injury, or fatality caused by mental lapses or mistakes on the part of the pilot. Many jumping injuries or fatalities are similarly caused by "pilot error" on the part of the jumper.

Pin (noun): *The pin* is a metallic prong that slips into the *cone*, to lock the parachute container closed until the parachutist pulls the ripcord. *To pin* (verb) is the act of catching the *base* jumper in free-fall to establish the *base–pin* section of a free-fall formation.

Pin-Check: A last-minute safety check performed before the parachutist boards the aircraft. Another jumper, a jumpmaster, or instructor checks the complete main and reserve to see that the pins and cones are set properly; that the reserve is *in date*; that all latches are properly snapped and; in general, that the main and reserve parachutes are properly set for the jump. A pin-check also includes calibrating a Sentinel, if the parachutist wears one.

Poised Exit: An exit from the aircraft step or door in which the parachutist is ready seconds or minutes prior to the actual exit. Poised exits are required of novice jumpers, to learn correct positions and reactions. Later they graduate to *bomb outs* (unpoised exits).

POPS: Organization for "senior citizen" parachutists. Stands for *Parachutists Over Phorty*. Its insignia shows a worried Father Time, jumping in a rocking chair, pulling his ripcord with a walking cane, his fingers crossed for good luck. Membership is open to parachutists over phorty—or, forty.

Porosity: How much air can get through what kinds of material. Parachute fabric is classified either low porosity or high porosity. *LoPo* parachutes generally drop slower and let the jumper down softer.

Prop Blast: Turbulence caused by the aircraft propellor. Jumpers often become unstable on exit when they hit the prop blast, or, as it is sometimes called, *prop wash*.

R2's, R3's: Generic name for any surplus round parachute. Same as *cheapo*.

Railroad: To strike a free-fall jumper hard enough to cause possible injury, to destroy a formation, or to knock a sky diver out of position. At the least, to railroad a fellow jumper is discourteous; it can cause a possible fatality if the jumper is knocked out and does not wear an automatic opener, such as a Sentinel.

Ram-Air: New square type parachute. So called because the air flows into the front of the parachute cells and out the back; similar in concept to the intake and exhaust of a jet engine. Ram-air parachutes have the advantage of increased forward speed in the air (25–30 mph), but are also more difficult to handle and are generally regarded as the "sports cars" of the parachute world. Common ram-air parachutes are the StratoStar, StratoCloud, Cobra 10, ParaFoil, and others.

Relative Wind: An aviation concept, introduced to the world of sky diving by Pat Works in his book *The Art of Freefall RW*. Relative wind is the wind that always comes at the jumper from the direction toward which he is moving.

Relative Work: See *RW*.

Repack Cycle: The dates on which the reserve parachute must be opened, checked and re-packed. Repacking now is due every 120 days for U.S P.A. members. For years, the repack cycle was 60 days.

Reserve: The parachutist's second parachute.

Rig: The parachutist's complete outfit, ready to jump. Same as *gear*.

Rigger: F.A.A. licensed parachute repairman and repacker (in the case of reserves). Only riggers may repack reserves, and the rigger must sign the data card, giving his name, F.A.A. license number, and the dates. *Junkyard riggers* are those who make repairs, or equipment with spare parts or cheap equipment. A good rigger is your best friend when you need to use a reserve in the air. Many jumpers have been known to give their rigger a bottle of his or her favorite liquor when the reserve opens promptly as needed during a malfunction or cutaway. Needless to say, an inept rigger is no-body's friend.

Ripcord Housing: Steel conduit that protects the ripcord.

Ripstop: Nylon that resists tearing. Ripstop nylon is also used for sailboat sails, as well as parachute fabric.

Risers: Webbing that begins at the capewells and extends over the jumper's head, where *suspension lines* are connected to the risers with *connector links*. Risers and most webbing on the parachute harness should withstand 5,000 pounds of pressure before splitting or breaking.

Running: The act of facing a parachute in the same direction the wind is blowing, for maximum advantage and speed. To run is to add the wind speed and the built-in forward speed of the parachute for maximum velocity. Opposite of *holding*.

RW: Relative work. To make a free-fall sky dive with others; to jump relative to someone else. The act of completing (or attempting) a multiperson formation using hand-holding or other physical connections to establish a forma-tion in free-fall. Most jumpers believe that RW is the best part of sky diving. RW techniques have changed the face of sport parachuting. Only a few years ago, a baton pass between two jumpers in free-fall was considered expert jumping. Now RW techniques involve 50 (or more) jumpers connected in various "megafor-mations." See Pat Works' *The Art of Freefall RW*.

S.C.R.: Star Crest Recipient. The most respect-ed and generally most sought-after earned award in sky diving. The S.C.R. is awarded to any member of an eight-man (or larger) free-fall formation held together for five seconds or 1,000 feet. Formerly awarded by the Bob Bu-quor Memorial Star Crest Association.

S.C.S.: Like the S.C.R., but awarded to the eighth, or following jumpers in a free-fall for-mation. Stands for Star Crest Soloist.

Saddle: The portion of the harness on which the parachutist sits. A split-saddle harness is one with separate leg straps individually con-nected.

Sentinel: Automatic barometric- and speed-computer that will fire the parachutist's reserve open if the parachutist falls through the last 1,000 feet without having a good canopy over his head. The most popular automatic opening device in sport parachuting. Manufactured by S.S.E. Inc., Pennsauken, NJ.

Sequential RW: Relative work jump in which several different free-fall formations are com-pleted. A four-man RW team might go from a Skirmish line to a four-man star to a Murphy star during one jump, for instance.

Short-lining: In static line jumping, a jump-master will *short-line* a static-line jumper by pulling in the static line to prevent the jumper from being entangled in the line or to begin the deployment sequence faster than normal. To *short-line a canopy* is to trim (shorten) the sus-pension lines to alter the flying characteristics of the parachute.

Shot Bag: Weighted pouch used to hold down a parachute during packing.

Silk: What parachutes were made of before rip-stop nylon, pre-World War II. The phrase still remains, "Hit the silk," a reference to early military paratroop jumping. Modern jumpers have never even seen a silk parachute, much less jumped with one.

Sitting Up: The jumper sits up in free-fall to stop. He literally raises his torso, arms, and head.

Skirt: The bottom edge of a parachute canopy.

Skygod: Expert free-fall jumper, usually with an SCR, SCS, or other RW experience and achievements. The skygod is sometimes a less-than-complimentary term, meaning a jumper who demands an ideal position on the load, or first lift, to the exclusion of others. An inconsiderate RW jumper, obsessed with his or her own perceived importance and abilities.

Sleeve: Long cloth protection for the canopy; the sleeve holds the canopy in the container and acts to slow the deployment sequence during opening. The sleeve also has room on the outside for stowing bands—rubber bands used to keep the suspension lines. In some containers and some systems, the sleeve has been replaced by the bag or P.O.D. (Pack Opening Device). The sleeve is one of the new innovations that make sport parachuting comfortable at opening shock time.

SL Jump: Static Line jump, in which the parachutist's canopy is pulled open by a static line, an unbreakable line that runs from the backpack to an anchor in the airframe of the aircraft. The novice graduates from an automatic static line to a self-actuated free-fall parachute rig.

Slots: Positions in an RW formation. *Near-side slots* are positions on the side of the formation nearest the aircraft; *far-side slots* are on the side of the formation opposite the aircraft. Far-side slots presume more *flying* ability on the part of RW jumpers to reach the other side.

Smoke (noun): Smoke, in the sense of a smoke grenade, worn on the boot, helps spectators locate a sky diver during a free-fall exhibition, such as a county fair. A smoke grenade will also be dropped on the peas by a competition director to indicate to an aircraft approaching jumprun that winds on the ground have become too hazardous for safe landings. Jumpers will also watch for smoke from "natural" situations such as chimneys and fires, to gauge wind direction during canopy control toward the DZ. "*To smoke* it in" (verb) means to drop in free-fall be-

low the generally accepted altitudes of 2,500 to 2,000 feet. *Smoking it in* during competition such as a conference meet or a turkey meet may be cause for grounding.

meet may be cause for grounding.

Split Saddle: Harness with separate leg straps.

Spot: The art of determining the opening point, to get parachutists back to the general area of the DZ. Inept spotters often receive a chilly reception when the load of jumpers ends up "in the boondocks"—acres or miles away from the DZ, especially on a hot day. Spotters who jump square parachutes are also occasionally received badly because their parachutes can get them back to the DZ when round jumpers may be stuck off where the weeds are high and uncut. Spotters who take separate passes are stuck with their own spot, of course.

Stability: The art of achieveing a poised position in free-fall, usually face-to-earth. A stable position is a necessary achievement for all free-fall formations.

Stabilizer Panel: Panels at the bottom of the sides of parachutes such as the ParaCommander and at the bottom edge of squares.

Stalling: Pulling down steering lines or risers to alter the forward drive of the parachute.

Stand-Up Landing: A landing done skillfully, with the shock taken by the knees; as opposed to a P.L.F.

Star: Formation achieved by linked free-fall jumpers. Because later formations have involved diamonds, triangles, lines, and other geometric symbols, the star is now sometimes called a *round*.

Static Line: Unbreakable line that opens the parachutist's container automatically. Static lines are usually 15 feet long—long enough to clear the tail of the aircraft. Military paratroop jumps are almost always static line jumps; most novice jumpers learn on the static line and most of their gear is military surplus.

Steering Lines: Lines that end in *toggles* on the jumper's risers. The parachute can be steered to the left or right by pulling down on the left or right toggle, which alters the flying configuration of the parachute. *Sawing*, or rapid alternate pulling of the toggles, usually does little good and only scares the novice when not much happens to the parachute.

Stick: Military slang. A partial or complete

load of static-line paratroops dropped on the same DZ.

Stiffener: Metallic plate at the top of the rip-cord housing used to prevent a pack closure by a stuck ripcord. Used on old-style containers. Containers that employ the throw-away pilot chute have no need for a stiffener because the ripcord (the bridle line for the pilot chute) is velcroed to the harness.

Stirrup: Elastic band holding the leg of the jumpsuit tight to the foot of the jumper.

Stowing Band: Rubber band used to tuck away the suspension lines neatly and to aid in a neat, clean deployment of the lines during the open-ing sequence.

Streamer: Malfunction in which the sleeve elongates, or the bag clears the jumper, but the parachute does not emerge (or emerge fast enough). Usually means a cutaway.

Strut: Diagonal brace between the wing of a Cessna or other similar aircraft and the bottom of the fuselage. Novice jumpers are told to hold the strut until the jumpmaster gives the com-mand "Go!" All jumpmasters have stories about novice jumpers who fail to let go of the strut on command and are either pushed or thrown off the step.

Student Jumper: Person who has gone through the ground school but hasn't yet made his or her first jump.

Style: The art of acrobatics (front loop, back loop, barrelroll) in free-fall done as quickly and as smoothly as possible in competition. Slowly falling out of favor; most jumpers with ex-perience are working toward RW competition.

Style Tuck: Compressed position roughly simi-lar to a "cannonball" position in diving, with the face down. The style tuck allows the sky diver to complete the *style series* in minimum time.

Surplus: Army, Navy, or Air Force equipment used largely for novice jumping.

Suspension Line: The lines connecting the *canopy* to the *harness*, at the *risers*, with *con-nector links*.

T.S.O.: Technical Standard Order. Government authorized gear. Equipment must be T.S.O.'d for use in national competition.

T-10: A surplus main parachute. Originally non-steerable.

Target: Center disc used in competition. Gener-

ally 3–15/16 inches (10 centimeters) in diameter. ameter.

Temporary Locking Pins: Used during the packing of a reserve; must be removed before use.

Terminal: The ultimate and faster drop rate in free-fall. A trade-off between the pull of gravity and the drag of the jumper's gear and body position. Usually around 120 mph. A reserve opening at terminal is an awesome experience because the reserve opens faster than a main (usually) and thus exposes the jumper to a harder opening shock. Most RW formations are attempted at terminal because of the momentum that the jumper can use to change positions, and to move across the sky. Nonterminal RW offers the sky diver little leverage with which to work.

Throw-Away Pilot Chute: Pilot chute designed without coil spring. Made to be folded up like a pocket handkerchief and stowed in a pocket along the harness. In free-fall, to deploy the main, the jumper pulls the throw-away air-stream; the pilot chute is attached to a *bridle cord*, which pulls the bag or pod out of the container. The advantages of the throw-away pilot chute are: (a) without a coil spring it packs smaller, and (b) because the sky diver throws the pilot chute to his side, it enters clear air beside him and thus offers little chance for a hesitation in the turbulent air over the jumper's back. New, state-of-the-art design (introduced about 1976–1977).

Tie-Down Straps: Straps that connect the reserve with the jumper's harness to prevent the reserve from bounding around in free-fall, which can be annoying, if not dangerous.

Toggles: Wooden pegs used to aid the jumper's hold on the steering lines.

Total: Pack closure. No parachute comes off the sky diver's back after a ripcord pull.

Track: Body position with the head and torso lower than the legs; allows the sky diver to pick up extensive distance. The sky diver makes his body into a wing and extends his "forward glide."

Tri-Conical: Type of reserve canopy design.

Two-Five: Common abbreviation for altitude (2,500 feet). Jumpers will abbreviate all altitudes; as in, "I'm booked for a 7,5 (7,500 feet) jump, then a 12,5 (12,500 feet) jump in the Beech."

U.S P.A.: United States Parachute Association, headquartered in Washington, D.C.; the governing body for all sport jumping in the United States. Offers liability insurance, a monthly magazine *Parachutist*, and other benefits to members.

Waiver: Legal release that most parachute clubs ask jumpers to sign relieving the club of responsibility in case of injury. Note: In many states, the waiver is of little good (to the club) except to warn the prospective parachutist that he or she may be engaging in a risky participatory sport. Some states do not allow anyone to sign away responsibility for injury or death.

Water Jump: Deliberate jump into a body of water (lake or river) for a demo jump or for U.S.P.A. license purposes.

Wave-Off: A safety measure, especially when other jumpers are in free-fall in the immediate area. Before pulling his or her ripcord, the sky diver waves his or her arms energetically horizontally across the chest to warn other sky divers that he or she will very soon pull the ripcord. A wave-off is done to avoid sky diver–canopy collisions.

Whuffo: Any spectator not acquainted with the pomp and glories of skydiving. So named after an apocryphal farmer who watched sky divers and then asked, "Wha' fo' you jump outta them airplanes, fo' '"?

Wind: Sometimes a hazard to jumpers.

U.S P.A.: United States Parachute Association, headquartered in Washington, DC; the governing body for all sports jumping in the United States. Offers liability insurance, a monthly magazine *Parachutist*, and other benefits to members.

rents in the air and thus make a determination of the *opening point* that will take the parachutist along a *wind line* to the *disc*. Note: The *exit point* and the *opening point* are seldom the same place in the sky.

Wind Line: A direct line from the opening point to the target. Because of their forward drive capabilities, square parachutists are seldom worried about the wind line.

Wing: Square or ram-air parachute, called a wing because of its appearance and flying capabilities.

Wonderhog: One type of tandem system sold under that name.

Wrist Mount: Velcro band used to attach an altimeter on the jumper's wrist where it is visible.

W.S.C.R.: Women's Star Crest Recipient.

W.S.C.S.: Women's Star Crest Soloist.

XX-rated: Jumper who has been in a 20-man formation.

Zapped Out: A jumper who became unstable out the door (or) who broke up a formation.

SNOW SKIING

Airplane Turn: A turn in midair, as when a skier is jumping a mogul.

Alpine Events: Skiing events that were said to develop in the Alpine countries of Europe. Alpine events are the downhill, slalom, and giant slalom. See *Nordic events*.

Camber (Bottom): The built-in arch of the ski as seen from the side. The camber is designed to distribute the skier's weight over the complete length of the ski.

Camber (Side): The built-in arch on the sides of the ski. The cut is designed to allow the ski to turn.

Christi: A ski turn in which both of the skis are parallel.

Corn Snow: Granular, rough snow, usually develops in the spring.

Edge Set: Steel edges of the ski that "bite" into the snow.

Fall Line: Shortest distance down a hill.

Flex: The bending properties of a ski.

Forebody: The part of the ski ahead of the bindings.

Groove: The indentation that runs along the bottom of the ski to improve stability. Similar in nature to the tread on a tire.

Herringbone: A method of climbing up a hill with skis.

Hip: The widest part of the rear end of the ski.

Inside Edge: The right side of a left ski and the left side of a right ski.

Inside Ski: The ski that is inside a turn. The right ski on a right turn; the left ski on a left turn.

Linked Turns: Series of turns in opposite directions; that is, left–right–left or right–left–right.

Mogul: Small mound of snow created by skiers turning in the same place on a hill.

Nordic Events: Ski jumping and cross-country skiing.

Outside Edge: The left side of a left ski and the right side of a right ski.

Outside Ski: The ski that is outside on a turn. The left ski on a right turn; the right ski on a left turn.

Rotation: To turn the skier's body in the direction of a turn.

Safety Binding: Locking device that releases the skis from the skier's boots in the case of a fall, to prevent injury to the skier's ankle or leg.

Schuss: To ski down the fall line, usually too fast to be in complete control.

Sideslip: To ski diagonally down a hill.

Sitzmark: A hole or mark left in the snow by a skier who has fallen.

Snowplow: To form the point of a V with the tips of the skis to slow down.

Spring Snow: Same as *corn snow*.

Sweep: A check of the complete skiing area of a mountain by members of the ski patrol to make sure all skiers are down the mountain for the night.

Tail: The rear end of the ski.

Tip: The front end of a ski.

Torsion: The amount that a ski can twist.

Track: A warning to a skier in front that a second skier may not avoid a collision.

Traverse: To ski across a hill.

SOCCER

Caution: Warning by the referee for unsportsmanlike conduct. Because of possible language differences between teams, the referee shows this caution by waving a yellow card.

Charging: Attempting to unbalance a player in possession of the ball.

Chip: A kick that rises above a player.

Clearance: Kicking or heading the ball away from the goal area. The goalkeeper may throw the ball to clear it.

Corner Kick: Kick made by the attacking team from a corner arc; this is awarded when the ball goes across the goal line without resulting in a score, and when the ball was last touched by a defensive player.

Direct Free Kick: Awarded after a severe personal foul. Similar to a free throw in basketball.

Dribbling: To control the ball with the player's feet.

Drop Ball: To put the ball in play by the referee by dropping it between two opponents. The ball is in play when it touches the ground.

Drop Kick: A ball that is put in play by being dropped on the ground; it is kicked on the bounce.

Goal: Is scored when the ball passes over the goal line, between the uprights and under the crossbar.

Goalkeeper: Player who guards the goal. In soccer, the goal keeper may carry the ball in the penalty area, or may throw it or kick it.

Goal Kick: Kick-in by a member of the defending team from the goal box. A goal kick results when the ball crosses the goal line without a score and when it was last touched by an offensive player.

Halfway Line: A line that runs across the field at mid-field. Similar to the 50-yard line in American football.

Hat Trick: Three goals in one game by one player. Same usage as ice hockey.

Heading: Method of directing the ball with the head. A skill that highly rated players have.

Indirect Free Kick: A free kick in which a score can result only after the ball has struck another player.

Instep Kick: Kick made with the instep or inside of the foot. Instep soccer kickers are now highly prized in American football because of their accuracy.

Kick-Off: A kick from the center circle at the beginning of each quarter and after each score.

Live Ball: A ball in play after a free kick or throw-in or after it has been touched by a player, or has touched the ground after a drop.

Match: A game.

Offside: Refers to the position of a player in relation to the opponents when a ball is put in play.

Off The Ball: Players who do not have possession of the ball.

Overhead Kick: A player who kicks the ball over his own head.

Penalty Kick: Direct free kick made from the penalty mark; this kick is awarded to the offensive team for a foul committed by the defense within its own penalty area.

Save: Play made by the goalkeeper to prevent a score.

Striker: An offensive player.

Tackling: An attempt to *kick* the ball away from an opponent. Players may not be held in tackling.

Touchlines: Side boundary lines in soccer.

Volley: To kick the ball while it is in the air.

SURFING

Angling: Riding across a wave.

Backing Out: Pulling out of a wave that could have been ridden.

Back Wash: Water from a wave that is returning to sea.

Bailing Out: Jumping off and getting safely away from the surfboard.

Barge: A huge, cumbersome surfboard.

Beach Break: A wave that breaks on the beach.

Belly Board: A small surfboard used for body surfing.

Blown Out: Choppy surf, poor for surfing.

Body Surfing: Surfing while lying prone on a belly board, or prone surfing without a board of any kind.

Break: When a wave crests and collapses.

Catching a Rail: When the tip of the surfboard cuts into the water.

Choppy: Rough water.

Crest: The top of a wave.

Crossover: When a surfer moves one leg ahead and in front of the other.

Dig: Paddle actively.

Ding: Blemish in a surfboard.

Double-Ended: Surf board that has similar shape on both ends.

Face of the Wave: The concave shape of a wave as it faces the shore.

Feather: Splashes of water from the top of a wave.

Fiberglass: Composition of most surfboards.

Fin: Keel of a surfboard.

Flat: Water with no waves for surfing.

Glassy: Smooth water.

Goofy Foot: Position on a surf board with the right foot forward.

Gremmies: Rude group of surfers.

Hairy: Big wave, difficult to surf successfully.

Hang Five: To dip five toes over the front edge of a surf board.

Hang Ten: To dip ten toes over the front edge of a surf board.

Head Dip: When a surfer dips his or her head into a wave.

Highway Surfer: Surfer who spends all his or her time out of the water, "talking big waves."

Hot Dogging: "Jus' showing off."

Hump: A large wave.

Inside: The side of a wave toward the shore.

Kick Out: To turn away from the shore to end a ride.

Log: A heavy surf board.

Nose: The front of a surf board.

Outside: The side of a wave toward the open sea.

Over the Falls: Over the top edge of a breaking wave.

(To) Pearl: To nose the board over, in the water.

Pick Up a Wave: To catch a wave for a ride toward shore.

Prone Out: To end a ride by lying down on the board.

Psyched Out: Afraid.

Pushing Out: Paddling out through the breaking waves to get in position to surf in toward the shore.

Rails: Side edges of a surf board.

Shoot the Tube: To ride under the crest of a wave.

Showboating: *Same as hot dogging.*

Soup: The foam a wave makes.

Stall: To slow down to attempt to stop.

Stoked: Excited.

Surfing Knots: Bumps and abrasions that a surfer receives during surfing. Usually on the knees, usually from repeated contact with the board.

Swell: A wave that has not yet crested or broken.

Trimming (or) *Trimming the Board*: Settling into the correct position so the board rides smoothly in the water.

Tube: The hollow or semihollow part of a wave.

Wax: Paraffin used to make the board less slippery.

Wet Suit: Like a scuba diver's suit, this suit protects the surfer from water that is too cold.

Wipe-out: To fall from the board.

SWIMMING & DIVING

Approach: The steps taken toward the end of the board (Diving).

Backstroke: To swim with alternate arm strokes while on the back.

Back Jackknife: Common name for the inward pike dive (diving).

Breaststroke: To swim by stroking under the water, with outward strokes beginning at the chest.

Butterfly Stroke: A stroke in which the arm motion begins with each arm stretched out sideways. The swimmer then brings both arms out of the water, swinging them together and into the water past the head; the arms are then brought sideways underwater.

Cast: Imperfect entry into the water (diving).

Crawl Stroke: Commonly known as *freestyle*. The swimmer's arms are brought forward one at a time over the shoulder and into the water; as one arm is pulling through the water, the other arm is entering the water, after being thrown over the swimmer's shoulder.

Cutaway: Common term for an inward dive.

Degree of Difficulty: Rate for a dive. Each dive has a rating from 1.2 to 2.9 depending on its difficulty.

Entry: How the diver enters the water.

Flutter Kick: Quick up-and-down kick of the feet, to accompany a swimming stroke.

Freestyle: Usually refers to the crawl stroke, but may be any stroke the swimmer wishes to use, during a freestyle (choice) event.

Groups: Categories for all various dives. Forward, backward, reverse, inward, twist, and arm stand groups.

High Board: The 3-meter board.

Hurdle: The jump at the end of the diver's approach to the end of the board.

Individual Medley: A four-course swimming competition in which a butterfly stroke is used in the first quarter; a backstroke used in the second quarter; a breaststroke in the third quarter; and freestyle in the last quarter.

Jackknife: Common name for the forward pike dive.

Kickboard: Board used to support a swimmer as he or she practices kicking style.

Lap: From one end of a swimming pool to the other end.

Layout: Diving position in which the body is extended without any flexing.

Low Board: The 1-meter board.

Medley: A swimming event in which the swimmer must use the butterfly, backstroke, breaststroke, and freestyle.

Pike: Diving position in which the body is bent at the hips and the legs are kept straight.

Pull: The part of a swimming stroke in which the arm motion is exerting the most power.

Push: The final part of a swimming stroke.

Reach: The lift of the arms and the legs during the take-off from the board.

Riding the Board: The act of riding the spring of the diving board for maximum upward thrust.

Scissors Kick: A kick used in swimming sidestroke. The cycle is begun with the legs together; one leg is then thrust forward and one backward, on a plane parallel with the surface of the water. The knees are bent during the return portion of the cycle. The scissors kick is somewhat like the opening and closing of a pair of scissors.

Six-Beat Crawl: A version of the crawl in which there are six beats of the legs in a flutter-style kick to one full arm cycle. Most common version of the crawl.

Stroke: The arm action during swimming.

Tuck: Position in which a diver is curled into a ball.

TABLE TENNIS

Note: Many of the terms in Table Tennis and Outdoor Tennis are similar.

Ace: A serve that is not returned by the opponent.

Ad: Abbreviation for Advantage.

Advantage: First score after deuce (tie at 20–all).

All: Same as tie, that is, 20–all.

Backhand: Stroke used with the back of the hand facing the opponent.

Backspin: Stroke in which the ball spins toward the server.

Ball: Made of celluloid, approximately 4¼ inches in diameter, hollow, and weighing 37–41 grams.

Chop: Stroke hit with a downward stroke of the paddle, giving the ball backspin.

Dead Ball: Called when the ball bounces twice on the table, or after a point.

Deuce: When the score is tied 20–all. Winner must score two consecutive points.

Drop Shot: Shot played so that it dies before the opponent can return it.

Finger Spin: Spin imparted by the server's fingers during the serve. Illegal technique.

Forehand: Opposite of backhand. Stroke with the palm of the hand facing the opponent.

Game: The winner in table tennis is the player who first scores 21 points, or two consecutive points after deuce.

Let: Means "play the point over" and occurs if the ball touches the top of the net and falls into the opponent's court after a serve.

Mixed Doubles: Male and female player as a team.

Net: Table tennis net is mesh. The top of the net is 6 inches above the table.

Push Shot: Ball is stuck with a pushing motion of the paddle so there is no spin on the ball.

Slice: Stroke with the paddle so that the ball spins away from the server.

Slice: A late stroke so the ball spins away from the paddle.

Volley: Illegal stroke of the ball while it is in the air, and before it has touched the table.

TENNIS

Ace: Serve that is not returned by the opponent. Scores a point.

Ad: Abbreviation for Advantage.

Advantage: The point scored immediately after deuce. If the same player scores the next point, that player wins. If the opponent scores the next point, the score returns to deuce.

Advantage Court: The left-hand service court.

Alley: The area between the singles and doubles sideline on each side of the court. The singles court is made 4½ feet wider for doubles play with the addition of the alley.

All-Court Game: Style of play that includes both net play and baseline play.

Approach Shot: Made when a player makes a shot and approaches the net.

Backcourt: The area of the court near the base lines, as opposed to the area near the net.

Backhand: Shot made with the back of the hand facing the net or opponent.

Backspin: A stroke that imparts spin on the ball in the direction of the server.

Baseline: End boundaries of the court, 39 feet from the net.

Break: To win a game served by the opponent.

Break Point: When the score is love–40, 15–40, or 30–40, the next point will win the game.

Bye: A term used to refer to a player who does not have to play in qualifying rounds of a tournament.

Center Mark: Mark in the center of the baseline, indicating the server's possible location. The server may stand to either side of the center mark.

Changeover: A pause in a match when the players change sides of the court after odd-numbered games. They also have a chance to rest, cool off, and have something to drink.

Choke: To hold the racket toward the face (strings); to shorten the grip.

Chop: A ground stroke that applies downspin to the ball.

Clay Court: Tennis court with a service of clay or that resembles clay.

Club Player: Tennis player who plays regularly at a tennis club, rather than a tournament professional.

Consolation: Rounds of a tournament in which first-time losers continue to play other losers.

Cross-Court: A shot made from one side of the court diagonally into the opposite court.

Cut Stroke: A shot in which the racket hits the ball at an angle to apply spin to the ball.

Deuce: When each player has won three points or when the score is tied after three points.

Dink: Soft shot that barely clears the net.

Double Elimination: Tournament in which no player is eliminated until he or she has lost twice.

Drop Shot: A shot that barely clears the net and that has more vertical bounce than bounce across the court.

Fault: An error, usually during the serve.

Fifteen: The first point won by a player.

Five: A scoring term used to indicate the number of games won or the number of the set. Used unofficially as an abbreviation for fifteen.

Flat Serve: A serve that has no spin.

Foot Fault: A serve declared illegal because of the placement of the feet during the serve.

Forecourt: Usually refers to the area of the court near the net.

Forty: The third point won by a player.

Game: A player has won a game in tennis when he or she has four points and is two points ahead of the opponent.

Groundstroke: A stroke that is made after the ball has bounced off the ground, as opposed to a volley, which is a stroke when the ball is in the air.

Gut: The stringing in a racket.

Handicap: A system of equalizing competition between players of unequal ability.

Kill: A powerful stroke, a ball hit so hard or placed so well that the opponent cannot possibly return it.

Let: Play in which the ball touches the top of the net and falls into the correct court. The point is replayed, as in table tennis.

Linesman: An official in tennis who observes the game and decides if the balls are in the court or not.

Lob: To hit a ball in a high arc.

Love: No score.

Love Game: Game in which a player or team fails to score a point.

Love Set: Set in which a player or team fails to score a point.

Match: Two out of three sets or three out of five.

Match Point: A point which, if won by the player, will make him or her the winner of the match.

Net Game: An individual's style of play near the net.

Out: A ball that lands out of bounds.

Overhead: Shot to return a lob, usually with an arm motion over the head. Also called "smash shot."

Poaching: To play in a partner's side of a doubles court.

Rally: Prolonged exchange of shots by both players or by members of a doubles play.

Ranking: Listing of players by their ability and records of past play.

Round Robin: Type of tournament in which all players play all other players.

Seeding: Placing top tournament players in a tournament in such a way that they will not compete against each other until the final rounds.

Service Line: The line drawn across the court 21 feet from the net and parallel to the net.

Set: The first player to win six games provided that the player is at least two games ahead of the opponent (6–3, 6–4, 7–5, etc).

Set Point: A point that, if won by the player, gives him or her the set.

Smash: A stroke used to return a lob, usually powerfully.

Slow Court: A court with a rough surface on which the ball bounces slowly or clumsily.

Stroke: The movement of hitting the ball with the racket.

Thirty: A scoring term; the second point scored by a player.

Topspin: To hit the ball to impart spin away from the server.

Unseeded: Player whose ability does not qualify him or her for special placement in a tournament.

Volley: To return a ball to the opponent by hitting it before it bounces on the ground.

Wightman Cup: Trophy awarded to the winner of the annual tournament between the top women's team from the U.S. and the top women's team from England. Held alternately in the U.S. and England.

Wimbledon: The All England Lawn Tennis Championship played annually in the summer at the All England Tennis and Croquet, Wimbledon, London. Begun in 1877, it became an open event in 1968. The tennis equivalent of the Super Bowl in professional football.

TRACK & FIELD

Anchor: Last runner in a relay team.

Baton: Metal, cardboard, wood, or plastic cylinder that is passed from runner to runner in a relay race.

Crossbar: Metal or wood bar about 16 feet long that serves as an obstacle that the high jumper or pole vaulter must cross without knocking down.

Dead Heat: Tie finish between two or more runners.

Exchange Zone: Area of race track approximately 20–22 yards long where a baton pass must be made.

Flight: One lane of hurdles.

Get Set: To hold the starting position in a running race; the command just before "Go."

Go: The command to begin a running race.

Heat: Preliminary set of races in which the winners qualify for semifinal or final races.

Hurdle: Wooden or metal obstacle that a runner must leap over in a steeplechase or hurdles competition.

Lane: Path marked on a track. A runner must stay in his own lane during a specified part of a race or a complete race.

L-type hurdle: Hurdle and base that resemble the letter L.

Mark: The spot where the broad jumper, discus, hammer, javelin, or shot lands.

On the Mark: Command to take a starting position behind the scratch line, prior to a running race.

Pace: A runner's speed, as in slow pace, fast pace.

Planting Box: Slot at the immediate front of the pole vaulting pit, where the vaulter places or plants the pole for a vault.

Pole: The inside lane of a running track; or the vaulting pole used in pole vaulting.

Preliminaries: Same as *heats*.

Qualify: To survive the heats and enter final races.

Rabbit: Runner who may lead the field during the early stages of a long race, but who may set a pace too fast to continue the lead to the finish.

Relay Leg: One runner's part of a relay race.

Scratch Line: A line that runners or jumpers must not cross before the race begins. Similar to the *line of scrimmage* in football.

Seeded: To place the fastest runners in separate heats so they do not meet until the final races.

Slipstreaming: To run slightly behind another runner so the second runner does not have to fight the wind. Also appropriate in motor sports, where one car will slipstream another.

Starting Blocks: Objects that a runner uses to keep correct foot position before a race begins.

Stride: One step in a running race.

Take-Off Board: Board that a broad jumper uses to begin his jump from.

Throwing Section: Area in which a thrown object (javelin, discus, etc.) must land.

Toeboard: Board that a shot-putter must not step on or across during the act of putting the shot.

Trail: One attempt in field events; one javelin throw, and so on.

Trial Heat: Same as *heat*.

VOLLEYBALL

Antenna: 2½- to 3-foot high vertical rod attached to each side of the net. If a ball hits the antenna, it is out of play.

Attack Block: An attempt to block the ball before it crosses the net.

Block: A defensive move to intercept the ball near the net.

Bump Pass: An underhand pass using the forearms to strike the ball.

Contacted Ball: A ball that has been touched by any part of a player's body.

Court: Playing court should be 59 feet by 29 feet, 6 inches, with a center line under the net.

Dig: Underhand pass made near the floor level.

Dive: A low attempt to block a ball from hitting the floor.

Double Block: A block at the net by two team members.

Floater Serve: A serve that travels erratically.

Foul: Illegal play.

Game: Volleyball games are won when a team first reaches 15 points with a 2-point advantage.

Net: Top of net should be 7 feet, 11¾ inches for men; 7 feet, 4½ inches for women.

Netting: Making contact with the net while the ball is in play. Offending team loses possession of the ball or the loss of one point.

Off-Speed Spike: A slow spike.

Out of Bounds: Ball is out of bounds if it strikes any object out of the court, or if it strikes the antenna.

Overhand Pass: Pass made with both hands held head-high.

Scoring: One point is awarded for each score. Only a serving team may score a point.

Serving: The act of putting the ball into play by propelling it over the net and into the opponent's court.

Set: An overhead pass designed to allow a teammate to spike the ball.

Spike: A ball hit hard into the opponent's court.

Spiker: Player who performs a spike.

Spin Serve: Serve that has spin imparted by wrist action.

Side Out: Exchange of serve after a previous serving team fails to score.
Thrown Ball: Judgment by an official that the ball was momentarily caught or came to rest. Penalty results.
Underhand Serve: Basic serve in which the ball is struck with the heel of the server's hand.

WATER SKIING

Aquameter: Device used to measure miles per hour in a speedboat. Now a generic term for all such gauges.
Banana Peel: Trick or slalom ski with rounded tips, which vaguely resembles a banana peel.
Barefoot: Skiing barefoot, which can be accomplished by kicking the skis off while skiing 34 mph or faster.
Barrel Roll: A tumble off a water ski ramp during a ramp jump.
Board: To climb into a boat.
Boarding Ladder: Small ladder to make boarding a boat easier.
Bobble: To lose balance but recover during skiing.
Buoy: Water marker.
Cat: Common abbreviation for catamaran, or twin-hulled boat.
Deep Water Start: A ski tow that begins in water too deep for the ski ends to touch bottom.
Dock Start: Ski tow that begins with the skiier sitting on the edge of a dock.
Double Handles: Twin handles on the end of a ski rope, so two skiiers can be towed behind one boat.
Doubles: Two skiers behind the same boat.
Gate: Entrance to a slalom course.
Heel Hold: To hold the ski tow bar with one heel.
Helicopter Spin: Complete 360° spin in the skis after jumping from a ski ramp. The skis resemble the blades of a helicopter in flight.
Hit It: Command from skier to boat to accelerate to begin a ski tow.
Hot Dog: Showing off. Similar to Surf usage.
In Gear: Command from skier to boat to shift from neutral just prior to ''Hit it'' command.
Kite: Wing-apparatus used to become airborne while being towed behind a boat.

Pass: Straight run over a ski course.
Plane: The action of skis riding on the surface of the water.
Ramp: Incline plane used for water ski jumping.
Run: Two passes over the same course in competition.
Single Handle: One towing handle at the end of a tow rope.
Slalom: Zig-zag course between obstacles, similar in nature to a slalom run on snow skis.
Three-Sixty: Complete 360° turn while being towed by a ski boat.
Toe Hold: Holding the tow line with a toe.
Tow Line: Line used to pull water skiers. Usually made of polyethylene or nylon.
Trick Riding: Any fancy maneuver that can be accomplished while water skiing.
Wake: Turbulance caused by the boat propellor.
Water Skis: Invented and patented October, 1925 in the U.S. by Fred Waller, motion picture inventor (who later invented "Cinerama").

WEIGHTLIFTING

Barbell: A steel bar approximately 5–6 feet long, with wheel-shaped or disc-shaped weights attached to each end for weightlifting.
Cheating: To lift weights by using muscle groups not appropriate to that event, or to use a body position not appropriate to that event.
Class: Group of contestants as determined by weight. In U.S. powerlifting, the classes are:

Bantam Weight	123½ lbs.
Featherweight	132¼ lbs.
Lightweight	148¾ lbs.
Middleweight	165¼ lbs.
Light Heavyweight	181¾ lbs.
Middle Heavyweight	198¼ lbs.
Heavyweight	220¼ lbs.
Light Super Heavyweight	242½ lbs.
Super Heavyweight	Unlimited

These divisions are the same for International Powerlifting, except that there is no Light Super Heavyweight division. These are also the same for Olympic weightlifting, except that there is no Light Super Heavyweight division.
Clean: First action in a Clean & Jerk competi-

tion. To lift the barbell to shoulder height before it is jerked overhead.

Disqualification: To void a lift or other action because of a rules violation.

Dumbbell: Short barbell, 10–20 inches long, used for hand and arm lifts.

Repetition: To repeat a lift or action.

Reverse Grip: A grip in which the knuckles of one hand are under the bar and the knuckles of the other hand are over the bar.

Set: A predetermined number of repetitions.

Steroids: Drugs used by some weightlifters, football players, and other athletes to build muscle bulk. The use of steroids is certainly controversial and potentially harmful.

Supine position: Lifting position lying down.

SPORTS GAMBLING TERMS

Action: The money wagered on a sporting event.

Bookie: A person who accepts wagers on sporting events.

Buck: $100 bet. Also known as a Dollar.

Dime: $1,000 bet.

Exotics: A bet other than a straight bet or parlay.

Hedge: To bet opposite original wager to reduce the action on a game.

Juice: A bookmaker's commission.

Laying off: When a bookie gets too much "action" or wagering, he will pass some of the action off to another bookie to reduce the financial risk.

Nickel: $500 bet.

Off the board: A game where no bets are being accepted.

Over/under: A figure representing the total points scored in a contest. The bettor can bet on the actual total being greater or less than the predicted total.

Parlay: The coupling of two or more bets as one larger bet. For example, a bettor would pick the winners of three games on a wager. He wins if all three teams win (often against the spread).

Pick (or Pick'em): A game where neither team is favored.

Player: Someone who places bets, legally or with a bookie.

Press: To bet a larger amount than usual, often when trying to make up for previous losses.

Points spread: The predicted difference in score between the favored team and opponent. Also called the Line or Spread.

Sports book: Wagering specifically on the outcome of sports games. Can be professional leagues or college teams. Sports books are illegal in most areas, but is the main source of betting for bookies.

Squares: Illegal but rarely enforced by the police, football squares allow participants to pick a square off a grid of 100 squares, each corresponding to a possible quarter, half or final score from a football game.

Tout service: A business that sells opinions on sporting events.

Selected Readings

Deford, F. (Ed.). (1993). *The best American sports writing: 1993*. Boston: Houghton Mifflin.

Euchner, C. (1994). *Playing the field: Why sports teams move and cities fight to keep them*. Baltimore: Johns Hopkins University Press.

Fensch, T. (1984). *The hardest parts: Techniques for effective nonfiction*. Austin, TX: Lander Moore Books.

Fensch, T. (1988). *Writing solutions: Beginnings, middles & endings*. Hillsdale, NJ: Lawrence Erlbaum Associates.

Goldstein, N. (Ed.). (1992). *The Associated Press stylebook and libel manual*. Reading, MA: Addison-Wesley.

Koppett, L. (1994). *Sports illusion, sports reality: A reporter's view of sports, journalism and society*. Champaign: University of Illinois Press.

Miracle, A. W., Jr., & Rees, R. C. (Eds.). (1994). *Lessons of the locker room: The myth of school sports*. Amherst, NY: Prometheus Books.

Rapoport, R. (Ed.). (1994). *A kind of grace: A treasury of sportswriting by women*. Berkeley, CA: Zenobia Press.

Wiebusch, J., & Silverman, B. (1994). *A game of passion: The NFL literary companion*. Atlanta, GA: Turner.

References

Aikman keeps fortunes in perspective. (1994, January 29). *The Dallas Morning News.*

Aikman recalls little of NFC title game. (1994, January 25). *The Dallas Morning News*, p. B17.

Aikman to skip Pro Bowl. (1994, January 29). *The Dallas Morning News.*

Air service plentiful to Atlanta. (1994, January 25). *The Dallas Morning News*, p. B23.

Albom, M. (1994). A tragedy too easy to ignore. In F. Deford (Ed.), *The best American sports writing, 1993* (pp. 409–415). Boston: Houghton Mifflin.

Albom, M. (1993, September). Fontes losing hearts of QBs. *The Detroit Free Press.*

All things considered, Cowboys will beat Bills. (1994, January 30). *The Dallas Morning News.*

Anderson, D. (1994, February 20). Keney M. applies for commissioner. *The New York Times.*

Apple spot at core of Super ads. (1994, January 27). *The Dallas Morning News*, p. 24B.

Artificial turf gives groundskeeper a new set of worries. (1994, January 30). *The Dallas Morning News.*

Aschburner, S. (1994, March). [Article about the San Antonio Spurs basketball team]. *Minneapolis Star and Tribune.*

Associated Press. (1993, December). [Article about Indiana University basketball coach Bobby Knight].

Associated Press. (1994, February). [Profile of Olympic ski star Picabo Street].

Atlanta develops habit of drawing big events. (1994, January 28). *The Dallas Morning News.*

Atlanta hotel manager compares city to Dallas. (1994, January 26). *The Dallas Morning News*, B14.

Atlanta's top tables are taken. (1994, January 25). *The Dallas Morning News*, p. B23.

Barreiro, D. (1994, May). Rough play in NBA not new or outrageous. *The Minneapolis–St. Paul Star Tribune.*

Barry, D. (1994). The old ball game. In F. Deford (Ed.), *The best American sports stories* (pp. 304–321). Boston: Houghton-Mifflin.

Bedard, P. (1994, April). Dodge Neon. *Car and Driver*, p. 57.

Bedell, D. (1994, May 1). A & M bowl funds go to purchase gifts. *The Dallas Morning News*, pp. 1, A34.

Best, N. (1993, November). [Article about runner Keith Brantly]. *Newsday.*

Bills don't qualify as lovable losers. (1994, January 27). *The Dallas Morning News*, p. 22B.

Bills enter Atlanta prepared for questions about futility. (1994, January 25). *The Dallas Morning News*, p. B20.

Bills still Buffaloed by Super Circus: Bet Cowboys. (1994, January 29). *The Dallas Morning News.*

Blackistone, K. (1994, March). Article about athlete Dwight Stewart. *The Dallas Morning News.*

Blakeslee, S. (1994, April 24). Kayaking in Splendor for Cardiac Fitness. *The New York Times*, pp. 60–63, 93.

Blinebury, F. (1993, November 22). Cowboys smart but get wiser. *Houston Chronicle*, p. C6.

Blount, Ray, Jr. (1994). Blunder road. In F. Deford (Ed.), *The best American sports writing, 1993* (pp. 21–30). Boston: Houghton-Mifflin.

Blount, T. (1993, November 22). Angry fans cutting Belichick no slack. *Houston Chronicle*, p. 8C.

Blount, T. (1993, December 5). Oilers recall Glanville era with mixed emotions. *Houston Chronicle.*

Bock, H. (1994, April 5). [Article about formal pro athletes who turn to coaching]. The Associated Press.

Boom towns. (1994, January 29). *The Dallas Morning News.*

Brady, J. (1976). *The craft of interviewing.* Cincinnati, OH: Writers Digest Books.

Brennan, C. (1994, February). [Article about British ice dancing team Torville and Dean]. *The Washington Post.*

Brooks, B., Kennedy, G., Moen, D. R., & Ranly, D. (1985). *News reporting and writing.* New York: St. Martin's Press.

Brown, C. (1993, November). [Article about the NFL "class of '83"]. *The Minneapolis–St. Paul Star and Tribune.*

Buck, R. (1993, December 5). Pardee's steadying hand pulls Oilers through. *The Houston Post*, p. B17.

Buck, R. (1994a, March 8). Knight no help to sports' image. *The Houston Post*, p. 1B.

Buck, R. (1994b, February 28). Valvano's words remain truthful. *The Houston Post*, p. 1C.

Buffalo's a city with a complex. (1994, January 29). *The Dallas Morning News*, p. 1.

Can't kick the habit. (1994, January 25). *The Dallas Morning News*, p. B19.

Carpenter, D. (1994, February 18). [Article about Olympic speed skater Dan Jansen's victory]. The Associated Press.

Clarey, C. (1993, September 24). When continents collide, in new blazers and all. *The New York Times.*

Clarke, L. (1994, January). [Article about black student athletes]. Knight-Ridder Tribune News Service.

Cochran, M. (1994, January 29). [Article about the Dallas Cowboys]. The Associated Press.

Coke's new formula: Cable programming instead of commercials. (1994, January 28). *The Dallas Morning News.*

Conklin, M. (1994, February 15). [Article about U.S. Olympic hockey team]. *The Chicago Tribune.*

Conlin, B. (1994, January 1). How it would be in one man's perfect world. *The Anchorage Daily News*, p. B7.

Corner's sentence: Stop end zone exclamations. (1994, January 26). *The Dallas Morning News*, p. 22B.

Cowboy cornerback talks the talk. (1994, January 26). *The Dallas Morning News*, p. B13.

Cowboys can join elite by beating Bills. (1994, January 30). *The Dallas Morning News.*

Cowboys' confidence not a sign of arrogance. (1994, January 30). *The Dallas Morning News.*

Cowboys dominate area ratings. (1994, January 25). *The Dallas Morning News*, p. B18.

Cowboys have ingredients to be among NFL's all-time best. (1994, January 28). *The Dallas Morning News.*

Cowboys lineman just wants to be Lett alone. (1994, January 26). *The Dallas Morning News*, p. 1.

Cowboys star in Atlanta's late show. (1994, January 27). *The Dallas Morning News*, p. 24B.

Cowboys tackle on guard for weight challenge. (1994, January 29). *The Dallas Morning News.*

Cowboys try to get acclimated. (1994, January 26). *The Dallas Morning News*, p. B17.

Cowboys were an easy pick. (1994, January 25). *The Dallas Morning News*, p. B23.

Cropper, C. M. (1994, September 18). When horses are worth more dead than alive. *The New York Times.*

Custred, J. (1993, December 26). Dance ends far too soon for big stars. *Houston Chronicle*, p. B19.

Dallas' chance to land Super Bowl remains slim. (1994, January 27). *The Dallas Morning News*, p. 26B.

Dallas looks to Atlanta as a model. (1994, January 25). *The Dallas Morning News*, p. 1.

Date with destiny: Cowboys look to join elite group of repeat champs. (1994, January 30). *The Dallas Morning News.*

Daugherty, P. (1993, October). Dykstra harks back to tougher era. *The Cincinnati Post.*

Davis, O. (1994, February 18). [Article about U.S. luge athlete in Winter Olympics]. *The Detroit Free Press.*

Deford, F. (Ed.). (1994). *The best American sports writing, 1993.* Boston: Houghton-Mifflin.

Dierker, L. (1993, August 23). [Article about Philadelphia Phillies]. *Houston Chronicle,* p. C5.

Dierker, L. (1994, March 21). [Article about baseball executive Len Colemen]. *Houston Chronicle,* p. C2.

Do you have a gambling problem? (1994, January 26). *The Dallas Morning News,* p. B15.

Dougherty, P. (1993, October 31). 75 injured in Badger stampede. *The Houston Post,* pp. B1, B7.

Dynasty in the making. (1994, January 28). *The Dallas Morning News.*

Estes, C. (1993, December). He is 'The Club' in human form. *The Birmingham Post-Herald.*

Estlinbaum, R. (1993, September 23). [Article about sport fishing in the Gulf of Mexico]. *The Houston Post,* p. C10.

Ettkin, B. (1994, March). [Article about NBA players Kevin Johnson and Mark Price]. Scripps Howard News Service.

Failure to win back-to-back titles haunts former Cowboys. (1994, January 25). *The Dallas Morning News,* p. B21.

Family ties can put you in a bind at Super Bowl. (1994, January 26). *The Dallas Morning News,* p. B16.

Fans gaining appreciation for underdog Bills, players say. (1994, January 29). *The Dallas Morning News.*

Fan's view. (1994, January 25). *The Dallas Morning News,* p. B18.

Farmer, N. (1993, September 28). [Article about the University of Texas–Rice University football game]. *Houston Chronicle,* p. B1.

Fear not: Security chief Rathburn is a seer. (1994, January 28). *The Dallas Morning News.*

Feldman, C. (1993, October 4). Hard hitter. *Houston Chronicle,* p. D1.

Fensch, T. (1984). *The hardest parts: Techniques for effective nonfiction.* Austin, TX: Lander Moore Books.

Fensch, T. (1988). *Writing solutions: Beginnings, middles & endings.* Hillsdale, NJ: Lawrence Erlbaum Associates.

Ferro, J. (1993, December). [Article about the Navy football team]. Gannett News Service.

Fewer tickets in 1995. (1994, January 25). *The Dallas Morning News,* p. B18.

Formula deserves 2nd shot. (1994, January 25). *The Dallas Morning News,* p. B18.

Fort Lauderdale Sun-Sentinel. (1993, December). [Article about Miami Dolphin linebacker Bryan Cox].

Fowler, E. (1993, September 24). [Article about the 1993 Ryder Cup matches]. *Houston Chronicle,* p. B1.

Freeman, D. (1993, October 16). [Article about upcoming Dallas Cowboys–San Francisco 49ers football game]. The Associated Press.

Freeman, D. (1994, January 27). [Article about athlete Michael Irvin]. The Associated Press.

Frito-Lay entertains clients at Super Bowl. (1994, January 30). *The Dallas Morning News.*

Gangelhoff, B. (1994a, September 14). I'm not just a jock. *The Houston Post,* pp. D1–D2.

Gangelhoff, B. (1994b, February 3). Magazine cheats women athletes. *The Houston Post,* p. D1.

Gelfand, L. I., & Heath, H., Jr. (1969). *Modern sportswriting.* Ames: Iowa State University Press.

Georgatos, D. (1993, October). [Article about the October 2 University of California–University of Oregon football game]. The Associated Press.

Gergen, J. (1994, March). [Article about basketball coaches John Wooden and Denny Crum]. *Newsday.*

Glauber, B. (1993, February). [Article about free-agency in the NFL]. *Newsday.*

Goldberg, D. (1993). [Article about NFL coach Don Shula]. The Associated Press.

Goodman, W. (1994, June 19). Television, meet life. Life, meet TV. *The New York Times,* Section 4, pp. 1, 6.

Grissom, K. (1993, December 9). Patience key in trophy hunting. *The Houston Post,* p. B12.

Grissom, K. (1994a, March 20). [Article about the Port Aransas, Tx., Gulf of Mexico fishing tournament]. *The Houston Post,* p. B20.

Grissom, K. (1994b, March 27). Snorkeling off the Keys opens eyes to new world. *The Houston Post,* p. B21.

Haley limited but won't back off. (1994, January 26). *The Dallas Morning News*, p. B21.

Hall, C. W. (1994, April 5). [Article about athlete Julie Croteau]. *The Washington Post*.

Handyman finally will get Sunday Cowboy fix. (1994, January 28). *The Dallas Morning News*.

Harasta, C. (1993, December 20). Hayes played large role in biggest game. *The Dallas Morning News*, p. 1B.

Harris, T. (1994, May 15). 15 varsity letters, but she still ranks No. 2 in her class. *The Kansas City Star*, p. C13.

Hartley, W. B. (1972, March). Building the magazine article. *The Writer*.

Hauser, M. (1994, February 15). King part of gala to combat AIDS. *The Houston Post*, p. C9.

Head coach Jimmy Johnson gets the picture. (1994, January 26). *The Dallas Morning News*, p. B13.

Hershey, S. (1994, April 10). [Article about the 1994 Masters golf tournament]. Gannett News Service.

Hey, maybe opposites do attract. (1994, January 27). *The Dallas Morning News*.

Hillyer, J. (1994, March 8). [Article about the Golden State Warriors and the Portland Trail Blazers]. *The San Francisco Examiner*.

Hirshey, G. (1988, September 22). Arc of a diver. *Rolling Stone*, pp. 87–91.

History likely will judge Levy much too harshly. (1994, January 30). *The Dallas Morning News*.

Hoffman, R. (1994, March). [Article about university athletes Grant Hill and Glenn Robinson]. *Philadelphia Daily News*.

Hofmann, R. (1994, May). [Article about the New York Knicks]. *Philadelphia Daily News*.

Hohlfeld, N. (1994). Help wanted. *Houston Chronicle*.

Howland, S. (1993, December 12). Patience pays off big time for hunter. *The Houston Post*, p. B12.

Ice sculptures hot item for Super parties. (1994, January 28). *The Dallas Morning News*.

In case of emergency.... (1994, January 26). *The Dallas Morning News*, p. B21.

In event of Super blowout, Enberg, Trumpy ready to fill in the blanks. (1994, January 27). *The Dallas Morning News*.

Inside the locker room. (1994, January 26). *The Dallas Morning News*, p. B18.

It's another Super Bowl rout for mighty Cowboys vs. Bills. (1994, January 25). *The Dallas Morning News*, p. B20.

Jackson, J. (1993, November 20). [Article about the Detroit Pistons]. Gannett News Service.

Jeansonne, J. (1994, February 15). [Article about Olympic pairs ice dancing]. *Newsday*.

Jerry Jones buys Collin tract for luxury-home development. (1994, January 27). *The Dallas Morning News*.

Jerry Jones' deep-pocket moves corrected early chaos. (1994, January 25). *The Dallas Morning News*, p. B17.

Jimmy Johnson's staff a laboratory for future NFL head coaches. (1994, January 27). *The Dallas Morning News*, p. 23B.

Johnson, R. S. (1992, April 20). None of our business. *Sports Illustrated*, p. 82.

Johnson's comments don't affect Bills. (1994, January 26). *The Dallas Morning News*, p. B21.

Johnson's confidence is a reflection of his coaching. (1994, January 26). *The Dallas Morning News*, p. B16.

Jones is confident Cowboys can prosper under salary cap. (1994, January 29). *The Dallas Morning News*.

Jordan, P. (1994). The wit and wisdom of the white rat. In F. Deford (Ed.), *The best American sports writing, 1993* (pp. 250–266). Boston: Houghton Mifflin.

Just the ticket. (1994, January 25). *The Dallas Morning News*, p. 1.

Kern, M. (1993, December 31). [Article about football coach Bobby Bowden]. *The Anchorage Daily News*, p. B7.

Kernan, K. (1993, October). [Article about athlete Lenny Dykstra]. Copley News Service.

King, F. (1993, November 18). Abundance of game makes hill country hunt a snap. *The Houston Post*.

King home anchors large historic district. (1994, January 26). *The Dallas Morning News*, p. B15.

Knight, B. (1994, January). [Article about hostility in the NBA]. *The Seattle Post-Intelligencer*.

Koppett, L. (1981). *Sports illusion, sports reality: A reporter's view of sports, journalism and society.* Boston: Houghton Mifflin.

Kravitz, B. (1993, November). [Article about athlete Mark Macon]. *Rocky Mountain News*.

Kuklick, B. (Ed.). (1989). *Thomas Paine: Political writings*. New York: Cambridge University Press.

Laird, C. (1994, March 5). Tough bucks. *Houston Chronicle*, pp. C1, C4.

Layden, T. (1993, December 10). [Article about athlete Charlie Ward]. *Newsday*.

Laye, L. (1994, March). [Article about coach Denny Crum]. *The Charlotte Observer*.

Leavell, L. (1993, October 13). [News article about a fire in Texas Stadium, Dallas]. The Associated Press.

Leland, E. (1993, August). [Article about Michael Jordan's father]. *The Charlotte Observer*.

Life on the dark side of the boom. (1994, January 27). *The Dallas Morning News*, p. 26B.

Litke, J. (1993, October 23). [Article about athlete Dave Stewart]. The Associated Press.

Litke, J. (1994, March 18). Tonya got what she deserved. *Huntsville Item*, p. 7A.

Long, G. (1994, February 11). [Article about the death of race driver Neil Bonnett]. *The Miami Herald*.

Long says his Raiders match Dallas well. (1994, January 26). *The Dallas Morning News*, p. B14.

Lopresti, M. (1993, December). [Article about University of Nebraska football program]. Gannett News Service.

Lopresti, M. (1994a, January). [Article about halfway point in 1993–1994 college basketball season]. Gannett News Service.

Lopresti, M. (1994b, March). [Article about NFL rule that will allow a two-point PAT]. Gannett News Service.

Lopresti, M. (1994c, September 15). Column about the baseball strike and the premature end of the 1994 baseball season. Gannett News Service.

Magic required to get into this party. (1994, January 26). *The Dallas Morning News*, p. B14.

Message pad. (1994, January 27). *The Dallas Morning News*.

Mexican fans are traveling to game, planning parties. (1994, January 29). *The Dallas Morning News*, p. 1.

Meyers, C. (1994, February 22). [Article about the Olympic 4×10 K men's race]. *The Denver Post*.

Michener, J. (1976). *Sport in America*. New York: Random House.

Monroe, M. (1993, October 5). Jordan to announce retirement. *The Denver Post*.

Moran, M. (1993, September 3). Don James finds that roses outnumber the thorns. *The New York Times*.

Mouthy ex-coach getting paid to talk. (1994, January 27). *The Dallas Morning News*.

Muck, P. (1994, February 21). From hiding, Herzeg denies he's deadbeat dad. *Houston Chronicle*, p. A17.

Murphy, M. (1994, May 11). What handicap? *Houston Chronicle*, p. 1C.

Nate Newton's diary. (1994, January 30). *The Dallas Morning News*.

Nate's world. (1994, January 28). *The Dallas Morning News*.

Navigating city without car. (1994, January 27). *The Dallas Morning News*, p. 24B.

Nelson, M. B. (1994, June 23). Bad sports. *The New York Times*, p. A11.

NFL cities compete in good taste. (1994, January 27). *The Dallas Morning News*.

'93 parade causes upset authorities. (1994, January 27). *The Dallas Morning News*.

No bye week leaves less time for hype. (1994, January 25). *The Dallas Morning News*, p. 20B.

No matter who's playing people watch Super Bowl. (1994, January 25). *The Dallas Morning News*, p. B18.

Oddsmakers expect 100 million wagers. (1994, January 26). *The Dallas Morning News*, p. B15.

Official business. (1994, January 30). *The Dallas Morning News*.

On the surface, Georgia Dome field not a major factor. (1994, January 29). *The Dallas Morning News*.

One goal for Buffalo linebackers: Catch 22. (1994, January 30). *The Dallas Morning News*.

Patton, R. (1993, October). [Article about the biggest players in pro basketball]. *The Fort Lauderdale Sun-Sentinel*.

Patton, R. (1994, January 2). [Article about 1994 Sugar Bowl]. *The Fort Lauderdale Sun-Sentinel*.

Paul, J. (1994, January). [Article about the Texas Christian University basketball program]. *The Fort Worth Star–Telegram*.

Peach of an idea. (1994, January 27). *The Dallas Morning News*.

Photo day is mostly flash. (1994, January 26). *The Dallas Morning News*, p. B13.

Pierce, C. P. (1994). The next superstar. In F. Deford (Ed.), *The best American sports stories, 1993* (pp. 322–336). Boston: Houghton Mifflin.

Player security at a premium after recent attacks on athletes. (1994, January 29). *The Dallas Morning News*.

Potent mixture. (1994, January 30). *The Dallas Morning News*.

Profit-driven Jones builds fiscal champs. (1994, January 30). *The Dallas Morning News*, p. 1.

Proving the line wrong. (1994, January 25). *The Dallas Morning News*, p. B17.

Purdy, M. (1993, September 7). Dear Joe: Steve gives thumbs up to week 1. *The San Jose Mercury News*, pp. 1B, 3B.

Putnam, P. (1985, September 9). KOed by his dreams. *Sports Illustrated*.

Q & A with Chris Berman. (1994, January 25). *The Dallas Morning News*, p. B18.

Ramsey, D. (1993, January 10). Mackey reaches again for basketball's glory. *The Syracuse Herald American*, p. D7.

Reddick, D. (1949). *Modern feature writing*. New York: Harper & Bros.

Reeves, J. (1994, March). [Article about athlete Jose Canseco]. *The Fort Worth Star–Telegram*.

Reilly, R. (1994). What is the Citadel? In F. Deford (Ed.), *The best American sports writing, 1993* (pp. 337–350). Boston: Houghton Mifflin.

Robertson, D. (1993, October 7). He's Michael to the bitter end. *Houston Chronicle*, p. B1.

Rodriquez, K. (1994, January). [Article about the 1994 Fiesta Bowl game]. *The Miami Herald*.

Roe, J. (1993, August). [Article about 1993 Walker Cup matches]. *The Minneapolis–St. Paul Star Tribune*.

Ryan, B. (1993, October). [Article about the October 2 Boston College–Syracuse University football game]. *The Boston Globe*.

Sanders gives charities "Prime Time" week. (1994, January 30). *The Dallas Morning News*.

Sans prediction headache, Aikman's mind at ease. (1994, January 26). *The Dallas Morning News*, p. B13.

Scalpers' heaven. (1994, January 28). *The Dallas Morning News*, p. 1.

Schaap, J. (1994, May 15). Now he tackles injustice. *Parade*, p. 12.

Schroeder, D. (1994, April). Lidar enters the radar wars. *Car and Driver*, p. 95.

Sheridan, C. (1994, May 1). [Article about an Atlanta Hawks–Miami Heat basketball game]. The Associated Press.

Sherman, E. (1993, November 2). No. 3 in the program and No. 1 in her heart. *Houston Chronicle*, p. B10.

Simpson is charged, chased, arrested. (1994, June 18). *The New York Times*, p. 1.

Smith, S. (1993, August). Reality intrudes on Jordan's charmed world. *The Chicago Tribune*.

Smith shines only because Newton doesn't play defense. (1994, January 26). *The Dallas Morning News*, p. B17.

Solomon, A. (1994, March 21). [Article about Michael Jordan]. *The Chicago Tribune*.

Some media may protest flying of Confederate flag. (1994, January 29). *The Dallas Morning News*.

Sparano, V. T. (1993, December). [Article about planning ahead for hunting/fishing trips]. The Gannett News Service.

Spencer, S. (1994). [Article about personalities in the NBA]. *The Seattle Post-Intelligencer*.

Stand and deliver. (1994, January 30). *The Dallas Morning News*.

Starevic, N. (1993, October 13). [News article about knife attack on tennis star Monica Seles]. The Associated Press.

Stoda, G. (1993, December). [Article about athletes Bobby Crawford and Dugan Fife]. *The Detroit Free Press*.

Stopping Thomas means stopping Bills. (1994, January 26). *The Dallas Morning News*, p. B18.

Sullivan, B. (1993, August 20). Cowboys try Roper experiment. *Houston Chronicle*, p. C2.

Super Bowl carries lore of the rings. (1994, January 30). *The Dallas Morning News*, p. 1.

Taking it all in stride. (1994, January 27). *The Dallas Morning News*, p. 24B.

Thomas, C. (1993, September 9). Woman of steel. *Houston Chronicle*, pp. C1, C5.

Thomas' temperature rises under media glare. (1994, January 27). *The Dallas Morning News*, p. 26B.

Three-piece outfit. (1994, January 30). *The Dallas Morning News*.

To Levy's credit, Bills come to coach's defense. (1994, January 30). *The Dallas Morning News*.

Tompkins, S. (1993a, August 1). [Article about the joys of fishing]. *Houston Chronicle*, p. B21.

Tompkins, S. (1993b, November 25). Of dawn, ducks and memories. *Houston Chronicle*, p. B16.

Truex, A. (1993, December 24). On top and nonstop. *Houston Chronicle*, p. 1C.

Under Davis, Cowboys defense "gets after people." (1994, January 27). *The Dallas Morning News*.

Vega, R. (1992, October 29–31). Football minus frills—and drills. *USA Today*, p. 8.

Webb, E., & Salancik, J. (1966). The interview or the only wheel in town. *Journalism Monographs, 2,* 21.

When members of the media gather, can inane questions be far behind? (1994, January 26). *The Dallas Morning News*, p. B14.

Whitt, R. (1993, September 19). [Article about athlete Steve Beuerlein]. *The Fort Worth Star–Telegram*.

Wieberg, T. (1994, April). [Article about football coach Barry Switzer]. *USA Today*.

Williams, D. (1993, October). [Article about NFL expansion plans]. *The Memphis Commercial Appeal*.

Wilstein, S. (1994, April 4). [Article about tattoos on university basketball players]. The Associated Press.

Wizard of odds. (1994, January 25). *The Dallas Morning News*, p. B17.

Woods, M. (1993, April 30). [Article about pro basketball all-stars]. Gannett News Service.

Wulf, S. (1994, April 4). [Article about new alignments in pro baseball]. *Sports Illustrated*, p. 93.

Zinsser, W. (1985). *On writing well: An informal guide to writing nonfiction* (3rd ed.). New York: Harper & Row.

Name/Title Index

247

Subject Index